Wheels of Fortune

Ohio History and Culture

Edited by Debbie Van Tassel
Pictures edited by Susan Kirkman

With a Foreword by Rita Dove

Wheels of Fortune

The Story of Rubber in Akron

Steve Love and David Giffels

The University of Akron Press   Akron, Ohio

LIBRARY OF CONGRESS CATALOGING-IN-PUBLICATION DATA

Love, Steve, 1946–

      Wheels of Fortune : the story of rubber in Akron / Steve Love and
David Giffels ; edited by Debbie Van Tassel ; photos edited by Susan
Kirkman; with a foreword by Rita Dove.

        p.   cm. — (Ohio history and culture)

     Includes bibliographical references and index.

     ISBN 1-884836-37-2 (cloth : alk. paper). — ISBN 1-884836-38-0
(pbk. : alk. paper)

     1. Rubber industry and trade—Ohio—Akron—History. 2. Tire
industry—Ohio—Akron—History. 3. Goodyear Tire and Rubber
Company—History. 4. B.F. Goodrich Company—History. 5. Firestone
Tire and Rubber Company—History. 6. General Tire & Rubber Co.—
History. I. Giffels, David. II. Van Tassel, Debbie. III. Title.
IV. Series.

HD9161.U53A385   1998

338.4'76782'0977136—dc21   98-36729

                               CIP

Contents

Series on Ohio History and Culture

Foreword

Two images stand out from my childhood. Studying local history in fourth grade with the help of a slim book titled *The Akron Story,* I am staring at the black-and-white photograph of a rubber plantation in India. India seemed impossibly far away, unimaginable; but there were those rubber trees—huge implacable trunks whose lashed sides streamed white latex. The second image unreels like a home movie: we are driving down Market Street, on the way to my grandmother's house on the east side of town, when suddenly the grain silos surge into view—a cluster of gigantic cylinders, brilliantly white. Those silos were magical not only because they housed the raw ingredients of my favorite breakfast, but also because they were the shape of the Quaker Oats carton on the kitchen table in the morning, where I sat daydreaming as I sleepily stirred milk and sugar and butter into my steaming bowl. For such a cozy, homey object to loom up before my very eyes, majestic and purposeful, seemed miraculous. It meant that my dreams were somehow connected to this larger picture, that the place where I lived was a vital connection to the world—just as those rubber trees, so stoic waiting to be drained, signaled the beginning of a process that nurtured my hometown's livelihood.

The Akron I grew up in was governed by two scents: the stench of the rubber factories and the smell of burning oats from the Quaker Oats silos—sensations that often overwhelmed visitors but were so prevalent that most Akronites no longer paid them any attention. Neither smell was pleasant, but both aroused the imagination of children. The rubber brought to mind huge truck tires rolling out of Akron to travel the globe, an oddly thrilling reminder that the wheels of commerce never stop turning: in the lingo of the times, it meant that this was a *happening* town. The chewy, bitter aroma of Quaker Oats, on the other hand, enveloped me in a feeling of security, bringing to mind the comfort of the kitchen and its warm oven—it was a delicious push-pull still very vivid in my storehouse of memories.

Then there were the blimps. How proud they made us! On the ground, they were majestic, even when moored in the huge gray hangar; in the air, they were sheer magic—silvery lozenges bobbing, rising. What a spectacular way for Akron to send her emissaries all over the map!

"The saving grace of America," Franklin D. Roosevelt once declared, "lies in the fact that the overwhelming majority of Americans are possessed of two great qualities—a sense of humor and a sense of proportion." The history of Akron points to an abundance of these two ingredients. Consider what attracted our forebears to this cluster of hillocks smothered with hickory and oak, with one incredibly crooked river (the Little Cuyahoga) coursing through some rather formidable gorges. Instead of turning back to the already-domesticated establishments of the East or continuing west to find flatter, more manageable acreage, these visionaries took a good look at the whole picture and said: "Water power! We can build a life here."

True to their ancestors, Akronites still approach daunting tasks with determination, energy, and a healthy dollop of creativity. Proof of the pudding lies in the fact that Akron is one of the few old manufacturing hubs which has survived the loss of labor-intensive factory production by turning itself into a corporate center, a feat requiring perseverance, faith in human resources, and—last but not least—imagination. (Speaking of imagination, allow me an aside to present a case in point: Akronites appear to be the only human beings who call that strip of grass between the sidewalk and the street the devil's strip. Elsewhere people use such boring terms as "tree-line" and "right-of-way"—but nothing as poetic as *devil's strip!*)*

The Akron I grew up in was a town where class systems were not so rigid that one couldn't make it by dint and savvy and heart; a place where it was possible to purchase your own home and even have a backyard and garden; a city where you could expect a decent education for your children. And, to a large extent, that Akron still exists.

The story you are about to enter is a narrative of daring and determination, greed and compassion, triumphs wrested from adversity, and generosity borne from injustices righted. In the course of this journey, you will see how Akron became what it undeniably still is today: a unique American city built with vision and grit and love, a monument to the resilience of the human spirit and its capacity to create, to explore, and to persevere. As *Wheels of Fortune* makes ebulliently clear, the Akron story is far from over.

—RITA DOVE

*Editor's note: As noted in the *Dictionary of American Regional English*, vol. 2, devil's strip, or devil strip, is a northern Ohio colloquialism peculiar to Akron, Barberton, and Youngstown, used to describe the strip of grass or trees between the sidewalk and the curb, known elsewhere as the tree lawn. The origin of this term is murky; one version has it that a judge was called on to determine whether a homeowner or the city was responsible for the upkeep of the strip of land. In frustration, the judge is supposed to have said, "If it's not the city's upkeep and not the owner's upkeep, it must belong to the devil"—hence devil's strip or devil strip.

To know one place well is to know all places better.

— EUDORA WELTY

Preface

In September 1993, Dale Allen, then editor of the *Akron Beacon Journal,* received a letter from Shirley Miller Albright, an Akron native living in Michigan. Albright, whose father, David Miller, had worked for General Tire and Rubber Company as a rubber chemist for forty-eight years, asked a simple question: "Has anyone bothered to do a history of any, or all, of the tire companies?"

Her letter proved to be the seed of an idea that grew into "Wheels of Fortune," a yearlong series of newspaper stories that tapped deeply into a rich, but fading, era of Akron's history. While histories had been written of some of the city's major rubber companies, no one since World War II had undertaken the task of telling the whole story of the Rubber City. And an awful lot had happened since then.

By the mid-1990s, the story had a beginning and an end. The tire manufacturing jobs were gone, and the flurry of activity that led to the foreign purchase and exodus of all but one of Akron's Big Four tire companies was complete.

It took several years for Shirley Albright's idea to approach reality. The paper was just wrapping up one yearlong project—the Pulitzer Prize-winning "A Question of Color" series on issues of race in Akron—and needed time to gear up another major effort. Reporting, writing, and illustrating the story of Akron's rubber history, with all its divergent and disparate elements, would require far greater planning and resources than most newspapers our size could muster easily.

And so, in the spring of 1996, the decision was made to spin this tale in weekly installments, every Sunday for a year. A team was formed, with Debbie Van Tassel, a *Beacon Journal* editor, at the helm; staff writers Steve Love and David Giffels as the primary writers and researchers; photo editor Susan Kirkman; and a rotating team of reporters assisting with research and interviews. Over the course of the project, interviews were conducted with nearly 350 people. Startling discoveries were made: an unpublished memoir by longtime Goodyear president Edwin J.

Thomas; an uncommonly strong but little-known job pipeline between Akron's rubber shops and the tiny town of Spencer, West Virginia; and the willingness of key players to usher us, for the first time, behind the scenes of some of the pivotal moments in the history of the Rubber Capital of the World.

"Wheels of Fortune" was an extraordinary undertaking for a newspaper, but it was also something that only a newspaper, with its resources and its grass-roots sense of a community, could have done. With the city of Akron apparently prepared to take great strides into the next millennium, we thought it important to take a final, complete look at a century of industry and industriousness, the way one pauses to reflect at the end of a long journey.

The *Beacon Journal* recognizes the importance of this undertaking to the Akron community, as well as its potential value to scholars, and has agreed to donate all original research to the University of Akron Archives. This volume represents an abridged version of the newspaper series—the sheer bulk of fifty-two newspaper sections was more than a single book could hold. But the story is here, the story of a people and a place and, we hope, lessons learned.

We are pleased that the University of Akron Press has chosen to publish this rich and informative history of our city, and we hope it will stand decades to come as the definitive account of the people and the events that shaped Akron's Wheels of Fortune.

—JOHN L. DOTSON JR., PUBLISHER
Akron Beacon Journal

Acknowledgments

This project could not have succeeded without the contributions of the following *Beacon Journal* staff members: former editor Dale Allen, associate editor David Cooper, and managing editor Glenn Guzzo for their support and advice; staff writer Glenn Gamboa, who provided research and interviews and wrote supporting articles over the course of the project; copy editor Joe Kiefer; and weekend news editor Val Pipps. The prototype for the weekly special section was designed by staff artist John Backderf, with additional design work by assistant managing editor for graphics and design Susan Mango Curtis.

The following staff writers provided invaluable research, interviews, oral histories, and supporting stories: David Adams, Katie Byard, Jim Carney, Bob Dyer, Mary Ethridge, Janet Frankston, Sheryl Harris, Ron Kirksey, Diane Lore, Maura McEnaney, Charlene Nevada, Bill O'Connor, Doug Oplinger, Jim Quinn, Marilyn Miller Roane, Thrity Umrigar, and Mary Vanac.

Staff photographers who contributed were Mike Cardew, Matt Detrich, Ken Love, Phil Masturzo, Robin Tinay Sallie, Karen Schiely, Lew Stamp, Ed Suba Jr., Paul Tople, Jocelyn Williams, and Robin Witek.

In addition, informational graphics were created by staff artists Brad Guigar and Rick Steinhauser; editing assistance came from enterprise editor Michelle LeComte, associate managing editor Stuart Warner, and picture editor Michael Chritton; photo research was aided by Sandy Bee Lynn and the rest of the library staff; and technical support was provided by four-color prepress coordinator Tracy Kane, graphics systems coordinator Phil White, technology manager Art Krummel, and assistant managing editor for technology Bruce Winges.

We are also indebted to a number of people and organizations who provided us with information, photographs, fact checking, and other help: Matt Contessa, Akron deputy mayor for labor relations and former president of URW local 5;

Trevor Hoskins, senior vice president for public affairs, Bridgestone/Firestone; Ben Kastein, historian of the Rubber Division of the American Chemical Society; George Knepper, distinguished professor of history emeritus at the University of Akron; Joan Long, Rubber Division, American Chemical Society librarian at the University of Akron; Daniel Mainzer, former staff photographer for Firestone Tire and Rubber and General Tire; John Miller, University of Akron archivist; Dan Nelson, University of Akron professor of history; John F. Seiberling, former Goodyear attorney and U.S. congressman; Bob Troyer, Firestone family spokesman and former public relations manager for Firestone and Bridgestone/ Firestone; Bridgestone/Firestone Corporation; Canal Place; Continental General Tire; and Goodyear Tire and Rubber Company.

And, of course, we thank the many, many people who opened their homes, shared their photo albums, told their family stories, and otherwise offered their assistance and support.

Introduction

There are places in this town where the wind blows clean through with nothing to stop it. Places where men and women once worked, where they drank, prospered, argued, and manufactured lives for themselves. Massive sections of this town are gone, yet we can still feel their presence, the way an amputee swears to God he can still feel his missing limb.

Akron, Ohio, once called the Rubber Capital of the World, is a place where science, money, and power created a dizzying upward spiral, but also a place rooted in simple things—families and churches and neighborhoods.

To look around now, you'd have a hard time putting together a picture of the past. Gone is Firestone Tire and Rubber Company's Plant 2, a tire factory so mammoth and so heavily constructed it took two years to tear down. Gone is the Crystal Bar on South Main Street, one of many where, at shift change, the bartenders set up a shot and a beer at every stool. Gone are the days and nights when regiments of workers streamed into Akron's thriving rubber plants to make tires, hoses, belts, blimps, tennis balls, and fighter planes.

Gone is the black snow. And gone is the time when Akron was recognized—more than anything else—for its smell, the ubiquitous tang of molten rubber. Max Long, a Barberton resident whose family migrated here from southern Ohio to cash in on the job boom, remembered it well: "My mother always said that for the first couple of weeks, she hunted everywhere for the dirty diaper and never found one. She finally realized that she was smelling the rubber plants."

Between 1910 and 1920, Akron was one of the fastest-growing cities in the country. Its population grew by 200 percent—from 69,067 to 208,435. Rubber created a gold rush in Akron, as people yanked up their roots and followed the smell. They came from far (Hungary, Russia, Italy, and Austria) and near (Pennsylvania, Kentucky, and Tennessee). And, of course, they came from West Virginia, so many that Akron became known as the Capital of West Virginia. The town grew like a teenager on steroids. Housing couldn't keep up, and workers rented beds in shifts. Families slept in chicken coops. Gin mills and rowdy saloons operated nonstop. Factories mushroomed with additions. By 1930, 40 percent of the nation's tires were built in Akron.

In the Depression era, when consumers could ill afford cars and, therefore, needed fewer tires, Akron lost 4 percent of its population. But during World War II, the rubber shops became war machines, and the city quickly rebounded with a new wave of immigration. This time, the influx came primarily from the rural South, where jobs were scarce. Each of the big rubber companies contributed to the war effort, but none with more impact than Goodyear Aircraft Corporation, which employed thirty-two thousand workers at the war's peak.

As things stabilized and the work force shrank back to postwar levels, the industry cruised along healthily for more than twenty years. Then, in the 1970s and 1980s, the wheels came off. Firestone was body-slammed by the recall of its 500 radial tire. Goodyear was sucker-punched by takeover artist Sir James Goldsmith. GenCorp was whacked with a takeover attempt. And the B. F. Goodrich Company was simply outrun. By 1983, there were virtually no tire-building jobs in Akron. Companies were taken over by foreign owners. Ironically, jobs and headquarters moved to the South; the region that once exported so many workers to Akron had become a magnet for industries seeking lower labor costs. Only Goodyear has kept its top brass here. Akron went from being an industrial capital to being a lower-case player in an international field.

If this town experienced growing pains in the early part of this century, it has endured even more stinging pain as the century—and the industrial prosperity—wanes. It is the pain of withdrawal. In the 1980s, for the first time in Akron's history, the number of housing units declined. Not only were new houses not being built, but old ones were disappearing. People were vanishing, too. From 1970 to 1990, Akron lost more than fifty thousand residents, more than a fifth of its population.

In the 1990s, an uncertain Akron struggled to redefine itself, possibly as a center for polymer research, possibly as a stronghold for the service sector. Downtown projects such as the Advanced Elastomer Systems building, Canal Park, the John S. Knight Convention Center, and Inventure Place show a town grasping for a new image. To be sure, the place we once knew as the Rubber City is all but gone. Present-day Akron is a book with more than a few pages torn out. Some of the holes are physical—empty places in the landscape where people used to work, places in the sky where smokestacks once stood.

And some of the holes are spiritual, right in the middle of people's lives.

Wheels of Fortune

1 Tire Town No More

THERE IS A SLIVER OF TIME every Akron winter when people begin to lose hope. Those who have lived here know it well. It creeps in sometime between the last of the beautiful snows and the first crocus. It is a time of cruel skies and steel-cold days, when every corner is filled with the sludge of winter's plows and the sun is an absentee landlord.

It was during this time that part of Akron's hope ended forever.

February 1982 went out like a scorpion, tail raised. Akron had suffered through a wicked winter, burdened by the hardest times since the Depression. To curb expenses, Mayor Roy Ray had cut six hundred city workers' jobs and eliminated two hundred vehicles from the motor pool. The city had to borrow $13 million to rescue the Recycle Energy System project from default. And the mayor was gearing up to ask voters to approve a charter amendment that would allow him to borrow more money. Jobs in Akron's rubber shops, once the surest thing in town, were fast becoming a memory. Young people were leaving the city in droves, some never to return. Old-timers were giving up dreams of a cozy retirement. Layoffs had accumulated like piles of snow left by the plow. General Tire was the only company still operating a full-scale tire plant in Akron, a truck tire factory that employed more than twelve hundred workers. The *Beacon Journal*'s lifestyle pages carried stories on coping with job relocation, and an editorial implored belea-guered Akron residents to quit clinging to the past and to look to the future. The question was, what future?

Rubber worker Nate Trachsel, a lifelong Akron resident, had the good fortune to spend those last days of February in Daytona Beach, Florida, where it was al-most possible to forget the cold and gray back home. Trachsel was pure Akron, the son of a tire builder, sturdy, soft-spoken, and thick-shouldered. He was in Florida not for vacation, but to represent Akron's Local 9 at a meeting of international leaders of the United Rubber Workers. As the president of the union at General Tire in Akron, Trachsel most likely had the future of the Rubber Capital of the World on his mind when he was called away to the telephone. By the time he had hung up, that future was gone.

The caller was M. G. "Jerry" O'Neil, son of General Tire's founder and now the chairman and president of the company. O'Neil, with his deep voice and Irish wit, was known for his bluntness. His message to Trachsel was swift and devastating: General's Plant 1, the last stronghold in a town that had soared to prosperity on the wheels of a single industry, was closing. Tire building was finished in Akron.

O'Neil and Trachsel had worked hard to save the plant, but the result was in-evitable. On the phone, they exchanged the kind of sorrow that men exchange, a reserved, keep-your-chin-up remorse. Soon other calls would be made, then more and more, as the chain reaction spread through the town and across the nation. The Rubber City had fallen.

Trachsel felt a sudden, horrible emptiness as he hung up the receiver. "I felt like a man who had been beat so bad that I didn't want to do anything anymore," Trachsel recalled. "It just kicked the guts out of me."

Back home, the 1,265 men and women who made tires in Plant 1 came and went like ants in a hill, oblivious to the coming news but burdened with an un-easiness that had plagued them for some time. Rumors that General would close Plant 1 had been circulating for months. And they weren't hard to believe. B. F. Goodrich had quit making passenger tires in Akron in 1975; Goodyear Tire and Rubber had closed its tire factory in 1978; Firestone Tire and Rubber had fol-lowed suit in 1981. Given the loss of more than sixty-one hundred production jobs since 1975, the out-of-work tire builder was a cliche in the town that had in-vented the profession.

On the cold morning of Monday, March 1, 1982, Ed Kalail, General's head of public relations, sat at his desk in the office complex at 1 General Street. On the desktop was a small stack of press releases bearing the ugly news. The statements had been prepared well in advance; for six months or more, the top people at Gen-eral had been planning this day's strategy. Kalail would handle the crush of media; the salespeople would tell the customers; purchasers would inform suppliers; and so on. A little after 8:00 AM, Kalail gathered up the press releases and headed out to his car. He would begin the rounds to the *Akron Beacon Journal* and local radio stations, then come back and wait for the phone to ring.

In the factory, where the news was suspected but not yet known, gallows hu-mor hung as heavy as the yellow smell of burning rubber. Kenneth Moorer, an electrician who had put in more than twenty years at General, was working on a tire press when he headed back toward the plant's electrical shop for a part. Like the rubber shops that had closed their doors in the past several years, General's Plant 1 was a relic. Built in 1915, it had worn wooden floors, chipped paint, and a multistory design. Modern tire making required one-story factories for raw materials to enter one end, a finished product to exit the other. As Moorer headed down the ramp toward the shop, he passed some workers going the other way. They laughed as they told him the latest rumor that the plant was closing. Moorer, a big man with an easy smile, chuckled in response. But the talk nagged at him, and he picked up the phone on the desk at the electrical shop.

"I called [Trachsel]. He says, 'Yes, it's the truth. They're going to close the plant,'" Moorer recalled. "I think everything went out of me then."

Soon everyone would know. Trachsel made a beeline back to Akron after his phone call from O'Neil. He arrived at the plant later that day and made the rounds, telling everyone who hadn't already heard. Eyes turned as dark as carbon black. Teeth clenched; muscles tightened. Some workers wanted to trash the machinery. Others cursed O'Neil. Trachsel implored them not to do anything rash. They had a stake in this, not just as people who would lose their jobs, but as people who had put their own money aside to help build a new plant in Akron.

Three years earlier, an unusual meeting had taken place. Even then, talk of a General plant closing clouded the air, and O'Neil had asked if he could address a gathering of Local 9, not to send one of his negotiators or to pass along a message through Trachsel, but to talk to them directly. In a town where labor-management hostility was a trademark, it was an extraordinary request. The workers agreed, and with a certain exuberance. Wanting the boss to arrive in style, a couple of the fellows with nice cars, Lincolns and Cadillacs, picked up O'Neil and chauffeured him to the Local 9 union hall on Massillon Road. The men packed into every corner of the hall, some spilling over into the kitchen. O'Neil stood to speak, and they fell silent.

"We've got a problem," O'Neil told the rank and file. "You don't have to be an expert in manufacturing. You don't have to be an efficiency expert. All you have to do is go out to that factory and know that it can't exist too much longer. It's inefficient. It's multistory. Normal, everyday manufacturing facilities are all on one floor. They're very efficient. This will never be efficient. So it has to be torn down. We have to replace it."

The proposal was that the workers would take a pay cut, and the money would be put into an escrow account to be used to build another factory. In return, O'Neil and his executive team would do all they could to keep production jobs in Akron. Trachsel and his men met with General managers to hammer out the deal. It was lauded nationally as a landmark in labor-management relations. Local 9 agreed to loosen some of the rules in its strict contract and to take a 36-cents-an-hour pay cut in return for the company's promise to try to build a new plant in the Akron area. If the plan didn't work, the money would be returned. The contract compromises broke with Akron tradition. In the old days, no one worked on Sunday. Under the new guidelines, there would be a seven-day workweek at the proposed plant. In the old days, laid-off workers with seniority could bump younger workers out of a job. The new rule: no bumping. Managers would have more control over who worked which job. The old ways, the ones that seemed unproductive, were cast aside.

(Foreground) Nate Trachsel, president of URW Local #9 at General Tire, listens as General Tire President M.G. (Jerry) O'Neil praises a revised company-union contract at a press conference in April 1979. The new contract called for a pay cut, with the money saved by the company to be accrued in an account to help pay for a new plant in Akron. (*Akron Beacon Journal*/Dennis Gordon)

In the past, there had been a knee-jerk belligerence: Whatever the company offered, the union asked for more. And management usually gave it. But these were different times. The tire industry had been on a rocky ride for more than a decade. Foreign competition was racing around the Akron companies, which had always had the fast lane to themselves. The Americans had been slow to respond to a growing consumer interest in a new kind of tire, the radial. Now that it had arrived from Europe, it was rolling roughshod over the once-dominant domestic makers, who were not equipped to reinvent the wheel. As the cost of doing business rose, jobs were being moved from Akron, with its high wage scale and strong union, to the South, where labor, often unorganized, came cheaper.

Maybe it was forward thinking that inspired General's rank and file to accept the deal, but more likely it was desperation. Whatever it was, it didn't work. In the end, O'Neil looked at the bottom line and concluded a new plant just wasn't feasible. He had considered building on land near Akron Municipal Airport or in Northfield, but decided instead to close the Akron plant. Roy Ray, then the mayor, said he never felt he was given a fair shot to try to encourage General to stay. And he was incensed he got no advance word from O'Neil that the plant was closing.

O'Neil said there was nothing the city could have done. As it was, General's Akron factory was operating at about 50 percent capacity, and it didn't make sense to build another. He decided the only thing he could do was to absorb the Akron jobs into the four other General plants in the United States, return the money held in escrow to the workers—without interest—and cut his losses.

And so, on March 1, he made what he called the most painful announcement of his life. But the pain was not his alone. The decision affected thousands in Akron. Not just those who were losing their jobs, but also those who had taken pride in being residents of an industrial capital, only to see it degraded to minor-league status. "My father worked for [Firestone] thirty-seven years, and I had a special concern for rubber workers," Mayor Ray said. "You didn't want to be the man on watch when the last rubber job left Akron, and I was. We closed the door quietly."

Rust Belt. The words burned in the throat. With Akron's unemployment rate approaching 15 percent, tire builders who had made nearly $13 an hour were taking whatever work they could find. At the end of the year, seven thousand people applied for seventy-four minimum-wage jobs at the Land O' Lakes dairy factory in Portage County.

The General plant closed in August. With it went Trachsel, a hose builder for more than two decades. "I stuck around in Akron for a few months," Trachsel said. "It was hell. I didn't know what to do with myself. I guess I just tried to hide. . . . That was devastating. That's a point I never want to return to in my life." Trachsel drifted to Islamorada, Florida, where he lived for almost eleven years, working as a maintenance man, a meat cutter, a pastry chef. When he finally returned, in 1994, to help his daughter through the University of Akron, the city was a different place.

O'Neil's company had moved to Fairlawn, had changed its name to GenCorp, and was no longer in the tire business. The General Tire unit had been sold to Continental AG, a German company, in 1987, and was about to move its headquarters to Charlotte, North Carolina. Firestone, after massive layoffs and other cost-cut-

Workers gather near the main gate before the 3:00 PM shift change the day the plant closing was announced. (*Akron Beacon Journal*/Ron Kuner)

ting moves, had been purchased by Bridgestone Corporation, Japan's oldest tire company. Bridgestone had moved Firestone's headquarters from its once-proud home in south Akron to Nashville, Tennessee. Goodyear, bloodied by a 1986 takeover attempt by British-French financier Sir James Goldsmith, had thrown out all the ballast it could to stay aloft, selling Goodyear Aerospace and other non-tire operations. Goodrich merged its tire operations with Uniroyal in 1986, and the combined company was bought by Michelin of France three years later. Michelin moved the tire company to Greenville, South Carolina, in 1994. Goodrich, now a chemical and aerospace company, moved first to suburban Bath Township, in 1986, and ten years later to Richfield, halfway between Akron and Cleveland.

Akron was littered with people who called themselves survivors—the optimists—and with victims. Yet Akron remains awash in monuments to its fabled rubber past. Stan Hywet Hall, the historic home of Goodyear founder F. A. Seiberling, welcomes visitors to its serene splendor on North Portage Path. The grand Tudor mansion on West Exchange Street that was the boyhood home of Trachsel's former boss, O'Neil, is now a bed and breakfast. The world headquarters campus of Goodyear, the Rubber City's last claim to fame, dominates east Akron, stretching for a mile and a half from East Market Street down Martha Avenue and Seiberling Street. Scarred, battle-weary, and much leaner, Goodyear still is Akron's

Richard Mayo pauses as he builds the last tire working its way through General's Plant 1 on August 20, 1982. Mayo, who worked nearly thirty years for General, moved back home to Tennessee a few days after the plant closed. (*Akron Beacon Journal*/Marcy Nighswander)

A worker's face is obscured by sparks as he cuts a fallen girder beneath a ruined smokestack at the former site of General Tire's Akron manufacturing plant. The bias tire plant, built in 1915, was a multistory relic when it closed in 1982. (©Daniel Mainzer)

A new sign is prepared for the exterior of the General Tire headquarters building by Bob Greathouse of Century Sign in Cleveland. The company's tire division was purchased by Continental AG of Germany in 1991. The headquarters is now being marketed for lease; Continental moved Akron operations to Charlotte, NC, its US headquarters. (*Akron Beacon Journal*/Paul Tople)

largest corporate employer, with about forty-seven hundred people on its local payroll. Goodyear's blimp, the *Spirit of Akron*, regularly drones in the sky from its home base at nearby Wingfoot Lake in Portage County.

The other fortresses of glory tell different stories. In the late 1990s, General's massive, 150,000-square-foot office complex sat mostly empty with a colorful "For Lease" sign hanging from its side. Goodrich's labyrinth of buildings, filled for years with trash and graffiti, was slated for destruction in the late 1980s. Hollywood once asked if it could implode one of the factories to promote the film *Demolition Man.* Now, the fifty-two-acre site is called Canal Place. It houses a beehive of small businesses, standing as a testament to Akron's ingenuity. It tells the story of a place that has found new use for what was no longer needed. In the Firestone parking lot on South Main Street were the cars of the 950 people who still worked there, designing experimental and race tires. Across the way, Clouser's Restaurant, once bustling with hungry Firestone workers, was mostly empty stools and tables. A short distance up Wilbeth Road was the monument of Harvey Firestone, the Ohio farm boy who came to Akron and manufactured a legend. The bronze statue was dedicated with international fanfare on the fiftieth anniversary of the Firestone Tire and Rubber Company in 1950. Flashbulbs popped as the five Firestone sons posed before the monument meant to immortalize a man of great honor.

In early 1997, it stood in disgrace. Human figures sculpted in granite behind the statue, intended to represent such virtues as contemplation, invention, and leadership, were defaced with phallic drawings, their noses and toes broken off. "I love Jenn" was smeared on Mr. Firestone's right lapel. "Jake" was scrawled across his forehead. Bridgestone/Firestone had the statue cleaned up later that year, but the image of decay seemed to reflect a mood that settled in hard after the Rubber City's demise.

∽

In the years that Trachsel lived in Florida, Jerry O'Neil worked hard to ensure that the future of his father's company was in good hands. He found a suitable successor, William Reynolds, who was appointed GenCorp's chief executive in 1984. O'Neil stepped down from the company's board, in 1993, into a comfortable retirement, spending eight months of the year at his home in tony Jupiter, Florida, and the remaining months at his comfortable West Akron condo, closer to his grandchildren. O'Neil retired a rich man. In his last year as chief executive of GenCorp, he drew a compensation package valued at $650,000 and owned nearly 245,650 shares of company stock worth more than $2.7 million. He settled into his golden years golfing for sport and jetting around the country in a plane he flew himself. His car of choice was a late-model Cadillac; his primary business activity was watching over his investments. He remained a man of considerable personal warmth, a proud Republican, clear-voiced and resolute in his opinions about capitalism and American industry.

Trachsel scratched for a decent job after he lost his position at General. He spoke freely, even jokingly, about the jobs he held in Florida. "I learned to make a great Key lime pie," he said. But in 1996, he was not at ease discussing his occupations since he had returned to Akron. His resume ended in 1983, with his last job in the rubber industry.

A dyed-in-the-wool Democrat, Trachsel was living in a duplex in Green, a city south of Akron, and driving a 1983 Buick. As a younger man, he had wanted to go to college, but his family could not afford to send him. His father, who worked for Goodyear for thirty-seven years, pushed Nate to take a rubber industry job. Trachsel went to work directly after graduation from Garfield High School, in 1956, landing at General in 1961. He was, in his mid-50s, a proud man and a hard worker who had been humbled by circumstance.

These two men whose lives oddly intersected lived in different worlds. Yet they called each other by a name that crosses all boundaries: friend. Over the years and the distances, they kept in touch. In August 1996, O'Neil was busy with the details of everyday life. He had to take his car in for an emissions test. While his car sat on the rollers and the workers watched the meters, the former CEO noticed a "help wanted" sign. He asked about the job; it paid about $5.50 an hour, just above the prevailing minimum wage. He requested an application, chuckling at the notion that people might think he was looking for work.

But the application wasn't for him. When he got home, he stuck it in an envelope. On the front, he wrote the name of Nate Trachsel, his old friend.

2   The Rubber Barons

THE MAPMAKER would tell you that Akron sprang up at the junction of 41.04 N and 81.31 W. The historian's view would be different. The historian would insist that Akron came to life at the place where luck and leadership intersected more than a century ago, long before job-hungry cities floated loans, land grants, and tax abatements to bring jobs to their doorsteps.

Today, a monument to that luck stands largely ignored in a park between the Summit County Courthouse and the Oliver Ocasek State Office Building on High Street. The life-size bronze statue depicts Charles Goodyear, chunk of rubber in hand, looking as if he had just strolled out of the Massachusetts kitchen where he accidentally discovered Akron's future more than 150 years ago. How Goodyear accomplished this bit of serendipity is the subject of conjecture. He was either a sloppy man or a sneaky husband. Forever fooling with rubber to the point where he was always in debt, Goodyear either spilled onto his hot stove a batch of sulfur-laden rubber or hid it in the oven so his wife wouldn't catch him playing with it again. He had promised to give up rubber before it became his family's ruin. He couldn't.

Charles Goodyear was addicted to solving rubber's secrets, and, regardless of

A view of Akron around 1855 shows the Ohio & Erie canal as it cuts through the future downtown area. (The University of Akron Archives)

how it happened, he won his place in Akron's history that day in 1839. Heating rubber into which he had folded sulfur made the substance "useful," as the plaque on his statue puts it. His rubber became less brittle in winter's cold, less prone to turn into a puddle of goo on a hot summer's day. His bit of kitchen chemistry would prove more durable for the manufacture of shoes, raincoats, hoses, and other rubber goods. The process became known as vulcanization, honoring Vulcan, the Roman god of fire.

Goodyear's stovetop discovery brought luck to Akron but none to himself. He died penniless in 1860. Though he never set foot in the city, his shrine is perfectly placed at Akron's convergence of luck and leadership. Akron owes much of its evolution as an industrial city to a clever deal that secured the surrounding land for public use.

In 1825, Akron's founder and one of its principal property owners, General Simon Perkins, donated various parcels of land to the State of Ohio to assure that state officials would route the Ohio and Erie Canal through Perkins's newly platted Akron. He benefited handsomely; so, too, did the nascent community. Of the canal's forty-four locks between Akron and Cleveland, twenty-one would be located along a two-mile stretch of what would become the City of Akron. As canal boats worked their way through the locks, passengers got off and patronized the businesses that began to spring up along the waterway. When the canal linked the Cuyahoga and Ohio Rivers, in 1832, Akron was able to steadily ship and receive raw materials and finished goods. With construction of the Cascade Race, in 1833, Akron had the cheapest water power in the state, attracting operators of distilleries, furnaces, and mills.

On March 12, 1836, the Ohio Legislature granted a charter to Akron, then a city of nearly 1,350 people. By 1840, Akron's second canal, the muddy Pennsylvania and Ohio, connected the Ohio and Erie to the Ohio River at Beaver, Pennsylvania. The Akron region quickly became one of the leading manufacturing centers in the state. First canal boat building, then flour, coal, clay products, matches, cereals, and agricultural equipment. And three decades later, the thriving industrial base and cheap supply of canal water caught the attention of Akron's first rubber baron: Dr. Benjamin Franklin Goodrich.

A Civil War surgeon, B. F. Goodrich had given up on the practice of medicine to try oil-drilling and real estate before turning to rubber. Goodrich needed a more prominent place to locate his fledgling business, Hudson Rubber Company of Melrose, New York. Hudson Rubber was about to fail without new investors to supply working capital. Goodrich's partner, John P. Morris, refused to put up more money unless the company moved west of the Alleghenies, where there was no competition. But Goodrich wasn't inclined to give up on rubber; he had learned through early experience that adversity sometimes precedes opportunity.

Born on November 4, 1841, in Ripley, New York, Benjamin Franklin Goodrich was orphaned by age eight. He was raised and educated by an uncle, John Dinsmore. At fifteen, Goodrich went to boarding school in Austinburg, Ohio, and, at sixteen, to the private Academy in Fredonia, New York. Before turning twenty, he had graduated from Cleveland Medical College (which became the medical school of Case Western Reserve University). In 1870, Goodrich returned to Cleveland seeking assistance for Hudson Rubber. But Cleveland leaders, wrapped up in mining and oil and showing new enthusiasm for steel, had no interest in rubber.

Exactly how Goodrich hit upon Akron is not known. According to one popular account, Goodrich came across a copy of the Akron Board of Trade's report for 1870, a one-page promotional handbill boasting of the city's 18.7-mill tax rate, rich coal veins, flour mills, and agricultural works. Akron, the report exulted, "is but at the beginning of her greatness" and stood ready to nurture new business.

It is known that Goodrich came to Akron in November of that year. He found a city that was 3.5 miles square and one of the fastest growing in Ohio. Signs of economic might were everywhere. Tons of coal were being dug and hauled away on the railroad lines that had begun to link Akron to an ever-widening consumer market for its cereal products, sewer pipes, and farm machinery. Bucolic Glendale Cemetery, in the middle of a $20,000 beautification program, was considered one of the city's showplaces. Construction either was under way or had recently been completed on ten major churches, including St. Bernard's, St. Vincent's, St. Paul's, and First Congregational. Children learned in eleven grade schools and one high school. The most fashionable shops were along South Howard Street, the first street in the city to be paved in stone. The wealthy among Akron's ten thousand citizens lived in showy Victorian homes in the East Market-Fir Hill section, and the poor in shantytowns near Furnace Street. Everyone breathed air toasted liberally with oats from the cereal mills and coke from the coal furnaces.

Newspapers backed all business activity without question. The May 24, 1870, edition of the *Akron Daily Beacon* carried this commentary: "One needs to visit Akron pretty often to keep up with the rapid stride of progress of that vigorous city. . . . The rapid and enormous growth of manufacturers in Akron is a standing marvel, and shows the power of productive industry to grow upon its own growth and strengthen itself upon its own strength."

Goodrich asked to meet with the Board of Trade to explain his business plan. They gathered at Akron's premier hotel, the Empire House, which hugged the Pennsylvania and Ohio Canal. Over several hours, Goodrich fielded questions about rubber patents and operating expenses. He urged the group to put up $15,000. With that and $20,000 of his own, he could build a factory and meet the payroll. The loan would be backed by a mortgage on the factory paying 8 percent interest.

Before committing money, the Board of Trade sent Colonel George Perkins, a banker and grandson of Simon Perkins, to Melrose to check out Goodrich's operation. Within a week, Perkins returned to recommend the loan. Lewis Miller, inventor of the Buckeye Mower and Reaper, put up $1,000. John F. Seiberling, who manufactured farm equipment and operated Akron's Academy of Music, also invested $1,000. At last on the table was $13,600, a sum worth more than $250,000 in 1997.

"These confident and successful businessmen were willing to take a chance on a new industry that didn't threaten any of them," said historian George Knepper, author of *Akron: City at the Summit.* "This guy wasn't going to be a competitor. But he might be a customer and contribute to the well-being of the economy."

Goodrich didn't get as much as he had asked, but it was enough to convince him he was wanted by Akron's business community. He bought four lots near the Ohio and Erie Canal for $1,800 and opened his shop, a partnership organized as Goodrich, Tew and Company, with capitalization of $40,500. Goodrich, Tew's early Akron years weren't smooth. "The doctor," wrote Goodrich's partner in Hudson Rubber, John Morris, "had a long and hard struggle with the Akron factory to make it succeed." In 1874, Goodrich, Tew was reorganized as a new partnership, B. F. Goodrich and Company. Still, Goodrich twice had to find new capital and turned for cash loans first to George Perkins and later to industrialist George W. Crouse, who became a company vice president. The B. F. Goodrich Company was incorporated as a publicly held entity on May 10, 1880, with authorized stock of $100,000.

Goodrich, a pale, mustachioed man, long suffered from tuberculosis, and his health finally failed at age forty-six. On July 11, 1888, he spoke for the last time to his management team. "The only anxiety that I have—the things I conceive that might break up this concern—are just what I talked with you about the other day," he said, referring to his poor health. Goodrich went on to instruct his production superintendent, Frank H. Mason: "The details of the business . . . I must

Benjamin Franklin Goodrich, who was convinced by Akron's Board of Trade (and a loan of $13,600, worth about $250,000 today) to move his fledgling rubber mill to Akron. It was the first rubber-manufacturing plant west of the Alleghenies and made fire hose and rubber belts. (The University of Akron Archives)

now drop entirely, but I do not want a change of any kind made in the policy of the manufacture without first consulting me."

The company had just begun to succeed on a grand scale—sales had more than doubled from $319,000, in 1881, to $696,000, in 1888—when Goodrich died on August 3, 1888, in a room at Barker's Hotel in Manitou Springs, Colorado. His family learned of his death while celebrating the eighteenth birthday of Goodrich's oldest son, Charles, at a Silver Lake party. George Perkins became president of the company, and Crouse continued as vice president. Goodrich's two sons eventually joined the company.

Charles C. Goodrich served as a company director from 1912 to 1932, but for the most part eschewed the executive suites for rubber research. He opened and for many years directed the first rubber company laboratory in Akron, which ultimately led to the Goodrich company's prominence in plastics. David M. Goodrich preferred the executive track and enjoyed many of the perks that came with it. As B. F. Goodrich Company chairman, from 1927 to 1950, succeeding Bertram G. Work, David Goodrich ran the company from New York City. Historians Mansel G. Blackford and K. Austin Kerr describe David Goodrich's chairmanship as "chiefly ornamental" until the 1930s, when he "emerge[d] as one of the strongest directors. . . ."

The B. F. Goodrich Company eventually grew into a diversified $2.4 billion

The entire workforce of the B.F. Goodrich factory stands outside for a portrait in 1876. (The University of Akron Archives)

The Rubber Barons

The press room of the B.F. Goodrich company, September 1890. (The University of Akron Archives)

company with an impressive list of firsts, including the first pneumatic tires for automobiles and the first de-icer for airplanes. Though Benjamin Franklin Goodrich did not live to see these achievements, other companies grew up in the likeness of his creation. A decade after Goodrich's death, Frank and Charlie Seiberling, sons of John F., started Goodyear Tire and Rubber Company on borrowed money. By the turn of the century, Harvey S. Firestone had sold his carriage tire business in Chicago and come to Akron. His reason was simple.

Akron had become the Rubber Capital, the scent of rubber and its jobs in the air. In the end, Akron would be influenced by four rubber barons: Goodrich, Seiberling, Firestone, and William F. O'Neil, founder of General Tire. In the belly of each burned an entrepreneurial fire hotter than any curing press in their tire plants. These were the men who put the tires on the cars and the money in Akron pockets. Together, these risk-takers made the city stink of rubber—and stinking rich.

Patsy McGinnis, a lad from Akron's "Dublin" neighborhood, could have warned everyone in the rubber business what to expect from F. A. Seiberling: Frank Seiberling was a fellow who would come out for round two. Patsy found this out the hard way, in the early 1870s, when he and Frank were just boys. Frank had moved from Norton to Akron, in 1865, at age six, with his parents, John F. and Catherine. Patsy was the third generation of Irish living in shanties along Furnace Street. His ancestors had come to build the Ohio and Erie Canal and had stayed.

On Decoration Day—now better known as Memorial Day—Frank had taken the family's cow, Old Pet, to munch grass near the canal. Henry Upson, son of Congressman William Upson, tagged along, and both boys tossed off their clothes and went for a swim. That's when the trouble began. The boys were skinny-dipping too close to the turf of Patsy and his gang. They tied the bathers' clothes in knots and threw them into the yellow canal water. To young Frank, it was a declaration of war. He lit into the older, bigger boy. Patsy's buddies piled on and gave Frank a "terrible drubbing" before a woman who lived nearby swooped in with a broom and swept the gang away. Nose bloodied, lip split, tears of rage streaming from his eyes, Frank pulled on his shirt and ran home to East Market Street, pants in hand, too knotted to untangle.

Later, Frank went to fetch the mail and ran into Patsy again, this time near Market and Howard streets. This was Frank's turf and, with improved odds, he went after Patsy to even the score. The town marshal, a man named Corbus, broke up the fight, but not before Frank had gotten the better of Patsy.

"That was the last of my fights with Patsy McGinnis," Frank said, "but it was far from being the last of my fighting."

F. A. Seiberling brought that same pluck and spirit to the rubber industry. He and his younger brother, Charlie, founded Goodyear with borrowed money, late in 1898, at the site of an old strawboard factory on the Little Cuyahoga River. F. A.'s eight-year-old daughter, Irene, tugged a cord for the ceremonial start-up of the buildings that became Goodyear Plant 1, and fifty men went to work making bicycle and carriage tires. At first, the Seiberlings struggled from one payroll to the next. On one occasion, F. A. even accepted a freight car full of bicycles in payment for some tires, then raised cash by selling the bikes to employees for $10 each. By 1910, nearly 460,000 cars were traveling the nation's road system, each one requiring four tires. Goodyear's work force exploded to twenty-five hundred. By 1916, Goodyear had become the giant of the tire industry, outselling all competitors.

People in the industry respectfully referred to F. A. Seiberling as the "little Napoleon." Seiberling was short, only five foot four. But F. A. Seiberling was a big thinker. He saw the need for quality, affordable homes for Goodyear workers and urged the company directors to support a housing development. When the board scoffed at the idea, Seiberling financed Goodyear Heights himself. He saw the need for preserving part of Akron in its natural state, so he donated thousands of acres that became Sand Run Park and served to prime the pump for the city's metropolitan park system. He saw the need for education for Goodyear employees, so he started Goodyear University. If five or more employees wanted to pursue a subject, the company found someone to teach it.

Goodyear, in 1920, found the country in a postwar recession and itself overextended—too much high-priced inventory in a declining market. E. J. "Eddie" Thomas, longtime Goodyear president, said the main problem at Goodyear "was that the record keeping was awfully bad. [F. A.] didn't know anything about fi-

nances. That's what got us into trouble." Rather than let the company fall into receivership, F. A. fought to secure capital, and the price of a bailout in 1921 by Wall Street bankers Dillon, Read and Company was his resignation.

At age sixty-two, F. A. Seiberling, with Charlie, who was fifteen months younger, started the 364th rubber company in the industry, Seiberling Rubber Company of Barberton. In little more than a decade, Seiberling Rubber would become the seventh largest tire company in the world. F. A. Seiberling was back in the fight, which would not have surprised Patsy McGinnis.

"In losing Goodyear," Seiberling said, "I felt that I had lost something that was as much a part of me as my heart or lungs. Anyone misjudges me who supposes I busied myself all those years for money. The building was the exciting thing, and, of course, I liked to be captain."

Goodyear quickly recovered from the financial crisis of the early 1920s. Dillon, Read returned company management to Seiberling's handpicked lieutenants, first George Stadelman, in 1923, and then Paul W. Litchfield, in 1926. Litchfield, whom F. A. Seiberling had recruited in 1900, influenced the course of the company for fifty-eight years as superintendent, president, and chairman.

The old Akron Strawboard Company plant, shown in 1875, became the first building of the Goodyear Tire and Rubber Company in 1898. The present Goodyear Plant 1 stands on this site today. (Goodyear Tire and Rubber Company)

Charles W. Seiberling, left, talks with his brother, F.A. Seiberling, in 1943. The two brothers founded the Goodyear Tire and Rubber Company in 1898. After F.A. lost control of Goodyear in the financial hard times of 1921, he formed the Seiberling Rubber Company, which he was running at the time this photograph was taken. *(Akron Beacon Journal)*

"And that's one of the reasons that Goodyear has had the reputation throughout its history of being a good place to work," said F. A.'s grandson, John Seiberling, a former congressman and Goodyear lawyer. "One of the things I observed as a corporate lawyer was how the personality and the morality of the founder shaped that company."

The founder of Firestone Tire and Rubber Company would never have countenanced the shenanigans that went on in 1950, the year of the company's fiftieth anniversary. *Life* magazine was publishing a special issue commemorating the occasion. NBC was planning a nationwide radio broadcast. A circus was coming. And, as the crowning event, a bronze statue of Harvey Firestone, who had died in 1938, was to be unveiled. It would be a grand thing, bigger than life, perched at the entrance to Firestone Park, overlooking the founder's empire of factories and office buildings.

But there was one problem. James Earle Fraser, the celebrated New York sculptor commissioned for the project, wasn't quite finished with the monument. Anxious phone calls were exchanged. The higher minds huddled. A plan was concocted.

The celebration's planners took Fraser's full-size plaster model, painted it bronze, set it in place, threw a big gray cloth over it and yanked it off at the climactic moment. Flashbulbs popped. Ten thousand observers cheered. Firestone's five sons beamed with pride. The world smiled back. And nobody was the wiser. A month later, in the dead of night, some trusted Firestone insiders slipped the plaster model from its pedestal, replaced it with the bronze masterpiece, and stole away.

No one ever found out. Harvey himself, though, would never have approved of such improvisation because, for him, planning was everything.

"I think the thing that was outstanding about Mr. Firestone was that he had long-term vision," said Robert Koch, a retired Firestone vice president and a pallbearer at Firestone's funeral. "I recall after I was made purchasing agent, I was in a meeting with a number of others, and he kept talking: 'If we do this, well, where will we be . . . and if that would happen, now, what would we do then?' After the meeting was over, I said to Mr. [John W.] Thomas, the president of the company, 'I don't think I can handle this job; I don't understand him.' He said, 'We don't either; he's just thinking out loud.'"

Koch said Firestone was cautious and conservative, characteristics that "really saved the company during the crash of 1920 when so many companies went broke."

There are really two Harvey Samuel Firestones. One is a farm boy from aw-shucks Columbiana, Ohio. Horses, in Columbiana, were for plowing. The other Firestone is a rubber king whose blood seemed far bluer than a pair of denim overalls. Horses, in Akron, were for polo.

Akron, at the turn of the century, was the kind of place where a farm boy could become a king, but something special was required of the farm boy. In Firestone's case, it seems to have been the way his mind worked, the way it digested an idea slowly and carefully. It was the mind of a thoughtful man, of a gentleman.

The blue-eyed, diminutive Firestone—he was five feet six inches tall—would spend his mornings walking the grounds of his estate, Harbel Manor (named for Harvey and his wife, Idabelle), now the site of Georgetown Condominiums and environs. His body was there, walking among the flowers and trees, but his mind was on the rubber company as he thought through his daily plans. By the time he arrived at the office, usually around 10:00 AM, he was already hard at work.

When he got there, he would confer with J. W. Thomas, his right-hand man. Thomas already would have been on the factory floor, overseeing operations there. Firestone would remain behind his desk and ask Mr. Thomas—never "John" or "J. W."—for his report. Firestone would reserve his comments until the end.

"When you went into his presence for a discussion, you'd better know what the subject was. He was a good listener and might not say anything till you were through, then he'd point his finger and give you his answer," Koch said.

Firestone arrived at his position of power in a buggy. He got his start as a salesman in Detroit for his uncle's buggy company, a job that jostled him into

This famous group took time out from a 1918 camping trip to stop at a grist mill in West Virginia. Standing from left are Thomas A. Edison, Harvey Firestone Jr., naturalist John Burroughs, Henry Ford, and Harvey S. Firestone Sr. Seated is R.J.H. deLoach, a director of the Armour Company. These jaunts were caravans that included cars and trucks carrying servants, equipment, and a fully-equipped kitchen. The dining table carried with them had room for twenty. *(Akron Beacon Journal)*

thinking about how to soften the ride. Rubber tires were the answer. Firestone demonstrated their worth by driving the first carriage equipped with them around Detroit's streets. By the time the buggy company went bust, in 1896, the wheels of entrepreneurship—rubber-tired, of course—were already turning in his brain.

He headed to Chicago with $1,000 in his pocket and the notion to start selling rubber carriage tires. Within a few years, he refined his plans. He couldn't shake the memory of the day back in Detroit when a fellow named Henry Ford had wandered into his shop and purchased a set of newfangled rubber tires for one of his horseless carriages.

In 1900, Firestone moved his young family to Akron, which by this time was the place to get into the rubber business. He took the money he had earned in Chicago and put it into a new venture, the Firestone Tire and Rubber Company. By 1903, he was making his own tires. Even after getting into the manufacturing side of business, Firestone retained the salesman's creativity. He was the type to come up with an idea, then let his engineers find a way to make it work. When, in 1908, he concocted the notion of a "non-skid" tire with a diagonal tread pattern, he sketched out the idea on a note pad in his office. Why not use the words "Firestone non-skid" to form the tread? It would be a great marketing tool and serve the function of helping the tires grip the road. The designers made it work, and the company still points to the non-skid tire as one of its proudest developments.

Firestone became the most famous of Akron's rubber barons. The company that bore his name was one of the largest rubber companies in the world, always battling but never surpassing Goodyear for the crown.

A reserved, stately man, Firestone even wore a tie on camping trips. An ad man is said to have sat down once with Firestone to talk about the broadcast time of *The Voice of Firestone,* a classical music program sponsored by the company. The consultant suggested the show air on Sunday afternoons, a good time to harness a classical audience.

"Good God, no," Firestone is said to have responded. "Everyone will be at the polo grounds."

The story may be more myth than fact. But Harbel Manor did, indeed, include a polo field, perhaps the only one ever in Akron. While Firestone's fortune was newly minted, there was a sense the family came from old riches. Part of that,

Harvey Firestone Sr. is shown, in 1937, at the family's Columbiana County farm with three of his grandchildren. From the left are Martha Firestone Ford, who married William Clay Ford and lives in Grosse Pointe Shores, Michigan; Harvey S. Firestone, III, who died in 1960; Harvey Firestone, Sr.; and Anne Firestone Ball, who is married to John F. Ball, and lives in Greenwich, Connecticut. Firestone used the farm as a retreat to entertain visiting dignitaries, a place to confer with company executives, and a destination for testing the road-worthiness of his early automobile tires. (Harriet Myers)

no doubt, stems from the Firestone family's demeanor: aristocratic and dignified, the family moved as much in New York's social circles as Akron's. And part comes from the founder's associations with the elite. The relationship the young man had forged with Henry Ford blossomed; Firestone was the primary tire supplier for Ford's cars, and the two men became close friends.

Their camping trips have become the stuff of legend, but they were nothing a backpacker would recognize. These jaunts, which also included Thomas Edison and noted naturalist-author John Burroughs, were caravans that included cars and trucks carrying servants, camping gear, and a fully equipped kitchen. The dining table they hauled with them had room for twenty. Presidents Harding and Coolidge were among those who sometimes tagged along.

Firestone was a man whose fortune allowed him the finer things of life, but there always remained his Columbiana background. He loved the family farm and spent considerable time there, using it as a retreat to entertain visiting dignitaries, a place to confer with company executives, and a destination for testing the road-worthiness of his early automobile tires. It also helped inspire him to lead the movement to put farm equipment on rubber tires.

In the end, then, Harvey Firestone's death was really the death of two men—the farm boy and a prince of the Industrial Revolution. He died in his sleep on Sunday, February 6, 1938, at Harbel Villa, his oceanfront retreat in Miami Beach, at age sixty-nine. The next night, the popular *Voice of Firestone* radio show played Schubert's *Unfinished Symphony* across the nation, presumably to commemorate a life cut short.

Late in the week, on a cold, snowy day, the city's wealthiest and most famous citizen returned to Akron in a solid bronze casket so heavy it required twelve pall-bearers. The plant and offices were closed. Hushed Firestone employees looked on as the casket was wheeled through the plant. The gray procession continued past the original factory on Sweitzer Avenue, past Firestone's former home on Fir Hill, and finally ended at Harbel Manor, where it lay for viewing.

At the funeral the next day, more than twelve thousand mourners came to pay their respects. A special refrigerated train car was required to bring flowers to Akron from mourners in New York City. Members of the Ford and Edison families attended the funeral, along with White House officials, captains of industry, and opera stars.

After two days of observances, the procession continued to Columbiana, where there was another viewing, this time at the brick farmhouse whose image was so closely tied to Firestone. When the pomp and circumstance ended, the king and the farm boy returned to the Columbiana soil.

There was nothing regal about Will O'Neil, in 1934, when General Tire's workers sat down and refused to work. Patience O'Neil's son, William Francis, was mad enough to spit fire. The robust Irishman, with an anger as sharp as his wit, didn't like unions, and he hated strikes.

He took this, the first sit-down strike against a major corporation in the history of American industry, as a personal affront. Hadn't he provided his workers with an excellent wage? Hadn't he given them a decent place to work? Hadn't he danced with their wives at the company parties? This is what they gave in return?

W.F. O'Neil, who founded General Tire, with one of the company's seven fleet planes used to promote the company and its products. O'Neil liked flying and airplanes, but he never took the controls himself because his distance judgment was not good. (Courtesy of Daniel Mainzer)

It was ugly. The strike dragged on for a month. Unpaid workers went hungry. General's plant sat idle. O'Neil looked deep inside himself and responded the only way he knew how. He invited the workers over to his house and ordered out for sandwiches.

There was never any need to guess how O'Neil, known alternately as W. O., Will, and Bill, felt about anything. He had strong convictions, and he expressed them freely, often in language that would have curled his mother's hair. So when it came time to settle a strike, he didn't hide behind corporate artifice. He chose to do the job in his living room, face to face, as if he were playing in a high-stakes poker night. This was no game, though. Unions had not yet established a strong presence in Akron's growing rubber empire, and O'Neil was in a position to set a tone for the rest of the industry. He wanted to do it right.

"Bill O'Neil was a down-to-earth man. You didn't feel uncomfortable in his presence. He was just a good-natured Irishman, except he could be real nasty, too, when he wanted to be. He was comfortable—or, we were comfortable with him, shall we say," said William Prather, who was in the O'Neil living room that night as a member of the labor negotiating team.

O'Neil played hardball with the men, but he also made sure they were treated well—he had sandwiches brought in from Portage Country Club, delivered to the room by Bill Jr., his oldest son. After twelve hours, O'Neil and the men finally came to terms. The agreement, which included a raise and increased union privileges, was ratified the next day by the rank and file. O'Neil ended the matter by throwing a beer bash on company grounds. Stories about O'Neil always end with a twist, though. This one was no different. Some joker pilfered a few of the celebratory beer kegs, once again lighting O'Neil's fuse.

In some ways, the success story of General Tire is more remarkable than any of the others. Goodrich, Goodyear, and Firestone, the founders of the industry in Akron, were all well established by the time General came along in 1915. O'Neil started his company during a second wave when Akron was armpit deep in rubber companies. Three hundred companies were making tires by 1920; more than twenty were in Akron. India Rubber. Falls Rubber. Lambert. Amazon. Mason. Virtually none of the latecomers survived. O'Neil and General did.

"He was one of the last great individualists and builders who gave this country both creative genius and rugged purpose," wrote former *Beacon Journal* Editor John S. Knight.

O'Neil was also a damn good salesman. In fact, he got his start selling tires—tires made by a company that would later be one of his competitors. Too restless to take the easy way out, he refused a job in his father's successful department store, the M. O'Neil Company. He wanted to sell goods around the world, not just in a local department store. The young man headed west, for Denver, where he latched on as a distributor of Firestone tires.

From there it was on to running a Firestone dealership in Kansas City with fellow Akronite Winfred E. Fouse as his partner. With accountant Fouse as the straight man and O'Neil adding the spark, they formed the Western Rubber and Supply Company, which later became the Western Tire and Rubber Company. O'Neil could charm the most resistant customer with a story. And he was not above a bit of trickery: when customers came in to inquire about replacement tires, he had a mechanic remove the existing ones for a free inspection. That way, the customer couldn't leave.

O'Neil and Fouse began to make and sell tire-repair kits as a sideline and, in 1915, decided to get into the tire-making business. W. O. approached his father, Michael, for help getting started. Michael, a conservative businessman, furrowed his brow. An insider who had supplied textiles to the local rubber shops, he had seen far more failures than successes in Akron's rubber industry. But W. O. the salesman was up to the task. He persuaded his father to put up money—the amount has never been revealed—toward General's $200,000 capitalization. In return, Michael was named president, though W. O. ran the show.

O'Neil, with his laughing blue eyes and trademark blue bow tie with white polka dots, quickly established himself as the Will Rogers of the rubber barons.

A hunting trip yields some ducks for General Tire's W. F. O'Neil, whose son M.G. "Jerry" O'Neil recalls him as not really caring for hunting or fishing and not normally taking the time. (Courtesy of Daniel Mainzer)

He was always ready with a good story and was nèver hindered by a lack of facts. He kicked pretense out the back door, refusing to have an executive dining room. He preferred to stand in line at General's cafeteria, filling his tray with chicken and chocolate cake—two of his favorites—but you didn't want to get behind him. "He never had enough money to pay for lunch," said Rita Dunlevy, a longtime member of the executive secretary pool. "He'd turn around: 'Do you have four cents?'"

On the back of General's success selling replacement tires, the company got into broadcasting—originally buying Akron radio station WJW, supposedly because O'Neil wanted a mouthpiece to rail against unions—and eventually buying RKO, an independent network of radio and television stations. O'Neil, an aviation buff, got into rocketry with Aerojet-General. And General did a brisk business in plastics and chemicals.

O'Neil's company made everything from girdles to rocket engines. But perhaps his greatest product was his family: three sons each took a significant role in the direction of General. Jerry O'Neil served as president from 1960 to 1987. Thomas F. O'Neil served as vice chairman of the board and as president of RKO General. John O'Neil, one of General's finance officers, also served on the executive board. A fourth son, William Jr., worked at General for a time before going into other businesses. A fifth son, Hugh, was killed while in the navy in World War II.

Jerry, at the time he stepped down from his chairmanship, in 1987, was the last member of a founding family to head one of Akron's rubber companies. William O'Neil, who died in 1960, lived to see that his company was in his son's good hands. He did not live long enough to see the foreign takeovers that eventually dismantled the rubber capital, put his tire company into the hands of German owners, and sent onto the streets so many workers who had come to Akron to find not only work but also a better life.

"He turned over; I saw him," Jerry O'Neil said of his father's reaction to the sale of General Tire to Continental AG in 1987. "He turned over in his grave."

3 Standing Room Only

SPENCER, WEST VIRGINIA, is a town of just under three thousand, the county seat of Roane County, population fifteen thousand. Its social hub is the White Oak Restaurant, the kind of place where gravy is a given and toothpicks provide entree to lazy conversation. The main street is called Main Street. There isn't quite enough action to fill an entire week, so much of the town just takes off Thursday afternoons to go fishing. It is also a place with an oddly intense connection to the Rubber Capital of the World.

For a visiting stranger from Ohio, "Akron" quickly becomes the ultimate icebreaker. The pharmacist at Staats Drugstore lived in Akron when his dad worked at Goodyear Aircraft. One of his coworkers was born and raised there. The city clerk used to live in Peninsula, north of Akron. The newspaper publisher's wife was born in Akron. An owner of a local funeral home has been there lots of times—in the hearse, to pick up those whose final wish was to be buried at home, in tiny Spencer, West Virginia.

The local newspaper, the *Times Record*, has 930 out-of-state subscribers. Of those, 151 are in Akron and its suburbs. Compare that with thirteen in Cleveland, eight in Columbus, and two in Toledo. It seems harder to find people in Spencer who never lived in the Rubber City.

During the boom years of the rubber industry—the first two decades of this century, and then during World War II—people came to Akron in droves from places in western West Virginia, eastern Kentucky, eastern Tennessee, western Pennsylvania, and southern Ohio. Appalachia. They came from places where coal mines had tapped out, farmland had soured, and oil wells had dried up to a place where well-paying jobs were as plentiful as crab apples in September. Historian George Knepper said the hill folks from states surrounding Ohio easily are Akron's largest ethnic group: "They had all the same characteristics: speech patterns, consorting with one another in common organizational groups, going to the same types of churches, looking for the same types of recreation, living in compact communities for mutual support because that is all they could afford. Well, that happened in Akron in a very, very big way."

It was especially easy to pack up and head north from Spencer, which is in the western part of the state near old Route 21. Phillip Obermiller, an expert on Appalachian culture who teaches at the University of Cincinnati, said West Virginians and Pennsylvani-

Cars decorated for a parade make their way through downtown Spencer, West Virginia in the 1920s. The town has an intense connection to Akron, as many residents migrated to find work in the rubber factories. (Roane County Historical Society)

ans were drawn to Akron because "it was close. They could go back home and visit if they needed; those industrial jobs were plentiful; and the collateral construction jobs and service jobs were also there." Migration from Appalachia occurred mostly along family lines, Obermiller said. "Word of mouth generally traveled back and forth. . . . If they were hiring at one factory, folks back in the region soon knew about it."

In 1910, according to U.S. Census figures, West Virginia natives accounted for 2,075 of Akron's 69,000 people. By 1920, Akron's West Virginian population had soared to 13,527. The city's total population was 208,435. Excluding West Virginia cities, Akron, in 1920, had more West Virginians than any U.S. city of 50,000 or more. The number of West Virginians living in Akron grew to 18,902, in 1930, before declining to 15,071 in 1940. Even with the shrinkage, Akron by then had more West Virginia natives than any U.S. city of more than 100,000. While the Rubber Capital was a magnet for people from neighboring states, the city also was a true melting pot. By 1920, there were more people in Akron who were born in other states or abroad than were born in Ohio. Foreign immigrants, with the greatest numbers from Hungary, Austria, Italy, Russia, and Germany, peppered the stew. Although Pennsylvania provided the largest number of migrants—22,963 lived here in 1920—West Virginians made the strongest impression on this bustling industrial city.

The jokes are well-worn:

What's the capital of West Virginia? Akron.

What are the three R's in a West Virginia education? Readin', 'ritin', and Route 21 to Akron.

Did you hear that the governor of West Virginia resigned? He got recalled to Goodyear.

The West Virginians simply stood out more than the Pennsylvanians. There was the accent, for one thing. The distinctive twang that turned "Akron" into "Ack-ern" and "Firestone" into "Far-stone" quickly established itself in Akron's growing Tower of Babel.

"Oh, West Virginians! Oh, Jesus, yes! Hillbilly—hillbilly language," exclaimed Olympia Mangli, a Greek immigrant who waited on lots of West Virginians when she worked at restaurants near the rubber shops. "I didn't understand them at first. Of course, nobody understood me either. Everybody's got an accent."

The rubber companies did their part to help the migration along. Betty Dunlevy, who worked in the personnel department at General Tire during World War II, recalled that recruiters would head south into the hills in a bus looking for potential workers. When they found one, they would take a little tag with the name of the rubber company and hook it through the prospect's buttonhole. At the Akron Greyhound station, company representatives would round up prospective workers according to the name on the tag. Others were even more direct, delivering new employees straight to the factory doors.

As recruits to the rubber army, West Virginians were attractive for a number of reasons. They were thought to be hard-working, strapping farmhands who could handle the physical work of tire building. Obermiller said there was a belief among management that Southerners would be less prone to communism than European recruits and that Appalachians, with their strongly independent spirit, would be less likely to unionize. He pointed to the success of the Mountaineer-intensive United Mine Workers, however, to shoot down the second theory.

The West Virginia transplants tended to settle together in places such as Lakemore, Ellet, and Rittman, but there was never a West Virginia neighborhood in Akron per se. Part of that, no doubt, was due to the shortage of housing—people lived where they could. Even so, as the West Virginians came to Akron, they made their mark. They celebrated their culture with exuberance, gathering to sing and play the songs of the mountains, maintaining their farming lifestyle with gardens, holding on to their religious traditions, and never losing pride in their roots.

It's an old joke: What are the three R's in a West Virginia education? Readin', 'ritin', and Route 21 to Akron and its jobs. In this case, the road marker sits at the side of the state highway just outside of Spencer, West Virginia. (*Akron Beacon Journal*/Paul Tople)

Some sociologists have said that Appalachians migrating to northern industrial cities tried to hide their background to fit in. That wasn't the case in Akron. One visit to the West Virginia Society annual picnic could tell you that.

❧

On the morning of Sunday, August 7, 1938, Tressie McGee, a native of Tall-mansville, West Virginia, was up with the sun. Twenty-two years old, she had married at sixteen, in 1932, the year she came to Akron to work at Goodyear. This was a morning like most for her—she was getting ready to work the first shift at the plant. But the rest of the day would be different, and it was hard to keep her mind on work as she brushed her hair and went through her morning routine. This was the day of the big West Virginia Society picnic. Once she finished her shift, Tressie and her family would head to Summit Beach Park for the event. Soon, though, her plans would change.

The day before, "our foreman took a piece of paper and put a note: 'All West Virginia people that want to go to the picnic can have tomorrow off.' He did it as a joke," McGee recalled. "So when it came to the day for the picnic, I was working from six in the morning until noon. My dad was working mornings. We all planned to leave for work in the morning, and then we'd all get together at noon and go."

But when McGee went to work, "there wasn't enough of us to run the department. They took it [the foreman's note] to heart. The ones that were from West Virginia, they stayed home to go to the picnic."

As her boss scowled, Tressie smiled secretly at her good fortune. She headed back home, and she and her husband, Clifton, put together a picnic lunch and got their four-year-old daughter, Dollie, ready to go. They got into their old Model T and headed to Summit Beach Park, the amusement park at Summit Lake. Others were arriving, too—members of the society, friends who worked in the rubber shops, and family members who had come up from West Virginia for the big party. In all, thirty thousand would turn out that day. It was a warm, muggy day, and Tressie and Clifton quickly staked out a picnic table for themselves and Tressie's dad and stepmother and her five sisters. Dollie and the other children shrieked as they ran off to the rides, and the adults gathered to greet old friends, some of whom they hadn't seen since last year's picnic. The air was punctuated by the sounds of mountain music and carnival barkers.

The West Virginia Society, formed in 1916, had been organizing these events for years, and they had quickly become one of the largest social gatherings of the year in Akron. As the parking lot filled and the picnickers unpacked their baskets, some folks buzzed with the news that Homer A. Holt, the governor of West Virginia, would be arriving soon to address the crowd. Others laughed again about the story of the picnic two years earlier, when a West Virginia senator had given a speech and was interrupted by an old heckler whose outburst was cut short when his false teeth fell out. Tressie and her family sat down to a lunch of fried chicken, homemade bread, pickled beans, and apple pie. When they were finished, they joined the others. The contests were under way.

These picnics had become famous for their myriad and far-flung competitions. Prizes were given to beauty queens in street clothes and bathing suits, the most freckled boy or girl, the biggest family, the homeliest person, and the man with

Tressie McGee followed her father to Akron from Talmansville, West Virginia, in 1931, landing at Goodyear and working there from 1932 to 1945. She recalls attending West Virginia Society events, which had quickly become some of the largest social gatherings in Akron. (*Akron Beacon Journal*/Jocelyn Williams)

the biggest feet. There were hog-calling contests, husband-calling contests, and contests for the woman with the most items in her purse. (The winner at the 1947 picnic packed an impressive—and improbable—235 items into her handbag.) Soon, the crowd drew together and fell quiet as the governor of their home state took the podium and lauded West Virginia's industrial achievements and thanked these Akronites for showing such loyalty to the Mountain State. This was no ivory tower politician, though. After his speech, Governor Holt made his way through the crowd, shaking hands and laughing with old acquaintances. "It's like a veritable homecoming to me," he said to a newspaper reporter as he rubbed elbows with those who had left home but had not forgotten what home was all about.

Around 6:00 PM, the crowd began to thin as the day's events drew to a close, and the tired revelers loaded their children into their cars and headed home, ready for another day at the rubber shops.

"They were lean days," recalled McGee. "That's why [everyone] looked forward to days like this. They'd save their money for days like this. Them picnics was special for your family. You could be with your family, and it was a special day."

The gatherings lasted well into the 1970s, though they shrank as time went by. In 1996, the club was down to just a few members and no longer held regular meetings. But the society served as one of the important markers of a culture that etched itself deeply into Akron's character. One Sunday a year, West Virginians looked forward to their celebrations. The other fifty-one Sundays, a different sort of celebration took place.

Dallas Billington, who gave his first sermon at Akron's Furnace Street Mission, in 1929, soon established himself as a fire and brimstone-style preacher. *(Akron Beacon Journal)*

Some were Baptist, some were Pentecostal, some were "shouting Methodists." Different strains with one thing in common: the Southern religious folks celebrated with a fervor Akron had never seen. And no one shepherded them with more skill than Dallas F. Billington. Billington, the son of a Kentucky farmer, born in a log house, sensed a spiritual yearning in all these transplanted Southerners when he arrived in Akron, in the 1920s, to take a job at Goodyear. "Akron," he once said, "is the wickedest place this side of hell."

Akron probably was no worse than any other industrial city its size during the Prohibition era, but the morals of its citizens did become relaxed to a shocking extent. Authorities looked the other way when laws on drinking, gambling, drugs, and prostitution were flouted. Women of good reputation avoided the Grand Opera House, which featured midnight burlesque shows. High rollers hung out at the Buchtel and Windsor Hotels, among Akron's finest. So Billington started preaching. His first sermon, at Akron's Furnace Street Mission in 1929, was delivered to a shabby gathering of drunks and whores. They were the people who needed him.

Soon he started holding revivals in churches and tents—wherever he could find a place. When a tent wasn't big enough, he arranged to use part of Rimer Grade School. But that wasn't big enough, either. So he gathered together his flock and built what would soon earn a reputation as one of the largest Baptist churches in the country: Akron Baptist Temple, dedicated on Easter Sunday 1938. The temple, on Manchester Road in Akron, had pews to seat twenty-six hundred worshipers, and on some Sundays, even *that* wasn't big enough. (The church has been rebuilt twice and now seats more than four thousand people.) The worshipers, most of them transplanted Southerners, came to hear this big man with a big voice and an even bigger message. Dallas Billington, six feet tall, with a square jaw, black hair, and black eyeglasses, bore a passing resemblance to Clark Kent. As a preacher, he was more like Superman, fully capable of slugging it out in prayer. He was hauled into court one time for disorderly conduct: his preaching, projected through a loudspeaker, was too loud for the neighbors.

Billington was a talented evangelist with the foresight to take his message beyond the church walls and onto the airwaves. During the 1940s, 1950s, and 1960s, Akron Baptist Temple's services were broadcast across North America. But

Dedication day, in 1938, for the Akron Baptist Temple shows parking lots filled with cars near Kenmore Boulevard. The church was founded by Dallas Billington. *(Akron Beacon Journal)*

it all began in Akron, in 1932, when Billington started broadcasting his ministry over radio station WJW (an acronym, he said, for "Watch Jesus Win"). From the first day, the phone at the station rang, as Akron residents called to say this was the evangelist for them. Old-time religion had found its place in Akron.

For people away from home, in a strange place with strange temptations, Billington and others like him provided comfort and direction. While the distance was only a couple of hundred miles, Akron was a far, far piece from West Virginia.

Shortly after the turn of the century, a few brave souls from Spencer made the journey up old Route 21 to Akron—in those, days, the drive took seven hours. They had heard about a new kind of work in the rubber factories up there. They quickly found that the jobs were plentiful and the money was good. So, one weekend when they went home to visit, they told their friends and family about the boomtown up north. Word spread quickly, as it does so well in Spencer. The grapevine was flourishing, but Akron wanted to fertilize it. This ad appeared on April 20, 1903, in Roane County's *Weekly Bulletin:* "Wanted. Strong active men for automobile and bicycle tire making and press work. Mill men and laborers. Steady work and good pay. Apply at Falor St. gate. The Diamond Rubber Company, Akron, Ohio."

The same newspaper, in 1909, began running an "Akron, Ohio Items" column and estimated there were six hundred Roane County natives in Akron. The pipeline flowed freely. Some went to Akron and stayed. Others went in the winter and returned to their farms in the spring. And most, whether they stayed or not, came home to visit as often as they could. The roads out of Akron were filled with cars bearing West Virginia plates every Friday night. Folks would head for the hills, cure their homesickness, and drive back in time for work on Monday.

In fact, Ray C. Bliss, former head of the Summit County Republican Party, is said to have arranged for the rubber plants' annual weeklong cleaning to take place as Akron held its 1935 mayoral election. The cleaning would close the plants, and Bliss banked on the West Virginians, primarily Democrats, eschewing polling places for their home state on the days off. He supposedly watched with delight from a hillside south of Akron as the heavy traffic flow confirmed his plan had worked. And the GOP candidate, Lee D. Schroy, won handily.

Appalachians in Akron, joined by immigrants from other places, found their niches. Though Akron near the millennium was a fairly homogeneous city, there were ethnic neighborhoods: North Hill, for the Italians; Barberton, for the Hungarians; Lakemore and Rittman, for the West Virginians. The immigrants had to deal with the jokes that are inevitable for outsiders. The Appalachians were teased, sometimes cruelly, called "snakes" and hillbillies. And newcomers, more often than not, found themselves at the bottom of a clearly defined ladder at the rubber factories. Many had to start in the hot, black, stinking environment called the mill room, or in the tire curing area, better known as "the pit."

Even in the darkness, though, there was a new life in Akron. For many, it was a better life. But it was still a life juxtaposed against the fantastic riches of the bosses. Evidence of that great difference was sprawled just a few miles from downtown, across the grounds of a castle called Stan Hywet.

4 A Seiberling Legacy

THE CAPTAIN of the Seiberling ship wore no braid on his cap bill, no insignia on his narrow shoulders. No symbols of rank were required. Son J. Penfield knew who was in command as soon as he stepped into the cozy wood-paneled room that juts from the northeast corner of Stan Hywet Hall like one half of the cross-arm of a clipper ship's mainmast.

The cozy room was the office of F. A. Seiberling, cofounder of Goodyear Tire and Rubber Company, and Penfield's father. Penfield, however, didn't feel too welcome on this morning in 1916. It was summer, and seventeen-year-old Penny had been to a dance the night before. He had gotten home about 1:00 AM, and at the Seiberling home, Penny's mother, Gertrude, ordered the doors locked at midnight. "I scurried around the house and finally found that someone had left the window into the swimming pool open," Penny remembered. "It was just a little skylight, but I could reach in and get it open far enough to get in."

That morning at the breakfast table, Gertrude Seiberling was visibly displeased by Penfield's after-hours adventure. "Later that morning," Penfield said, "Father asked me to come into his office. From the tone of his voice, I knew I was

Stan Hywet hall under construction. The sixty-five-room Tudor Revival mansion on seventy acres took four years to plan and build. (Stan Hywet Hall and Gardens)

in for some kind of upbraiding." F. A. asked Penny what he intended to do in light of the fact that his mother wanted the doors locked at midnight. Penny complained that he could not get home over poor roads from distant parties by such an early hour. Besides, protested Penny, fourth of the seven Seiberling children, other kids his age didn't have to be home at midnight.

F. A. told Penny that he could come and go as he pleased, as long as he took up residence somewhere else. "You think this over," F. A. told his son. "I want to know in the next twenty-four hours if you are going to comply with the rules of this house or are you not."

Penny complied—and would forever remember this conversation with his father, its circumstances and surroundings. "Father's office was like the bridge of a ship," Penfield said. In it, F. A. Seiberling relished picking up the telephone that connected him directly with Goodyear. To this room, F. A. liked to retire after supper to finish reading his evening *Beacon Journal*. From this room, F. A. meted out the love and lessons that provided a family foundation as solid as the rock on which Stan Hywet had been built.

Stan Hywet (pronounced *hee-wit*) is Anglo-Saxon for stone quarry. The house received its name because it is built in the midst of a quarry. From the beginning, F. A. Seiberling intended the splendid Tudor mansion to be more than a home for rubber's royalty. The Seiberlings had workmen cut into Stan Hywet's stone entryway the Latin phrase *Non Nobis Solum*—"Not for Us Alone." To the family, these were more than mere words. They were a way of life.

"Father's idea was that this home should be able to serve the needs of this expanding Seiberling family," said Irene Seiberling Harrison, the last surviving child of F. A. and Gertrude. "When that time and the need no longer existed, then he wanted something of an art value, an historic value, so it could serve the nation."

Stan Hywet Hall was the Seiberling family home for more than forty years. The mansion, on the National Register of Historic Places since 1982, is now operated as a historic home by the Stan Hywet Hall Foundation. But the family has not entirely left behind the estate: its quaint gatehouse has been home to Irene Seiberling Harrison and her daughter, Sally Cochran.

F. A. began planning Stan Hywet after the death of his mother, Catherine, in 1911. The sixty-five-room mansion on seventy acres off North Portage Path took four years to build, furnish, and landscape, at a cost of between $3 million and $4 million. F. A. Seiberling spared no expense. His sons asked for an indoor pool. F.A. said OK, even though it had to be blasted and hammered from rock. Irene and Gertrude wanted a music room. They got the entire southeast wing. "I wanted all of them to be proud and happy," F.A. said.

A tram road built to haul supplies runs alongside Stan Hywet Hall, under construction in 1915. The Seiberlings spent $3 to $4 million dollars—$49.5 million in 1998 dollars— to create the estate. (Stan Hywet Hall and Gardens)

The formal dining room seats fifty-six. But the more intimate breakfast room, with its hand-hammered copper fireplace, set the tone for the entire house. From the U.S. Naval Observatory in Washington, D.C., the Seiberlings obtained the angles of the sun at various times of the morning. "They wanted to have a breakfast room that would have sunlight at breakfast time for the maximum number of days [each year]," Penfield Seiberling said. "There was no use having a breakfast room in the shadows."

The family gathered by evening in the great hall, where interior decorator H. F. Huber played with the effects of light and shadow to create what Irene called the "dream room." Early in the design stage, the Seiberlings took their architect, Charles Schneider of Cleveland, to England to study manor houses and acquire antique furnishings compatible with the Tudor period. At Ockwells Manor in Berkshire, the Seiberlings discovered what became one of Gertrude's most cherished possessions—a harpsichord that George Frideric Handel once owned. F. A. paid his hosts twice the amount they asked for the harpsichord but never considered the purchase an extravagance. "Because of some queer, inexplicable satisfaction the instrument gave me," he commented years later, "I always felt I got a great bargain."

On a second trip to England, in 1915, the Seiberlings encountered two men from Persia who were selling rugs. The men said they could duplicate anything the Seiberlings wanted and accompanied them to the Victoria and Albert Museum in London to find patterns. The rugs, as beautiful as promised, arrived for the opening of the house in 1915. F. A. had sent acetylene lamps to Persia so the weavers could work through the night to finish.

The Seiberlings returned from England with part of the woodwork and ceiling from an English manor that was being razed. The woodwork contained a casement window that once looked out over an English courtyard. Architect Schneider intended the antique salvage for the master bedroom. That room, also known as Mrs. Seiberling's bedroom, has the only woodwork not carved on site from American materials. When he was drawing the room, Schneider asked Gertrude Seiberling if she wished him to seal off the window. "Leave it open," she said. "I can keep an eye on my children." Because it opened onto the great hall, the window came to be called the chaperone's window.

For their time, the Seiberlings were amazingly health conscious. Among its many amenities, Stan Hywet had outdoor and indoor swimming pools, a gymnasium, two tennis courts, five golf holes, a putting green, walking trails, and bridle paths. F. A. Seiberling loved fresh air, often sleeping on a small porch off the master bedroom suite. Weather didn't matter. "He used to wear earmuffs," Irene said. "He would sleep out there when it was down to zero. He would have hot jugs in the bed and wear a regular Teddy bear suit. The windows would be open. Sometimes snow would be in there. He loved it. Finally, when he was eighty, the family clamped down on him and said: 'We think it is time you sleep indoors.'"

Stan Hywet also was designed for the comfort of visitors. Over the vestibule hangs this message: "Welcome. As Thy Need May Be Find Here Happiness, Gladness, Peace Sanctuary." It has never been clear whether "peace sanctuary" lacks punctuation or is a single concept invented by Gertrude Seiberling, who wrote and placed poetry throughout the house. But guests often were overcome by

F.A. Seiberling dances in costume with Mrs. F. H. Huber, the wife of Stan Hywet's New York decorator, at the house's grand opening in 1916. *(Akron Beacon Journal)*

Irene Seiberling's wedding party at Christmas 1923. Because of financially hard times for the family, Irene planned the wedding over Christmas, since she knew the entire family would be assembled at Stan Hywet anyway. (Stan Hywet Hall and Gardens)

at least one of the sentiments in the greeting. Pianist Percy Grainger, for example, asked Gertrude Seiberling if he could run through the house because it gave him "such a sense of joy." Gertrude consented.

The Seiberlings hosted many diverse and distinguished visitors, from presidents (Warren G. Harding, Calvin Coolidge, and William Howard Taft) to artists to regular folk, including forty-two board members of the National Federation of Music, who stayed in the third-floor dormitory. But as much as she loved company, music, and the arts, Gertrude Seiberling refused to allow Stan Hywet to become a recital hall or a museum."We used the antiques as ordinary furniture," said John F. Seiberling, the first grandchild born at Stan Hywet. "Like most children, I probably damaged some—accidentally, of course."

At Christmas, as many as eighty-four family members came to dinner; children dined in the breakfast room and in the corridor between the kitchen and great hall. Christmas 1923, celebrated amid the financial hardship that accompanied the loss of Goodyear two years earlier, nonetheless was a day of special joy. Irene had scheduled her wedding to New York banker Milton Harrison for that day, knowing family members would already be assembled. The one extravagance was a wedding dress from New York. Married in the music room, with her five-year-old nephew John F. Seiberling serving as a page, Irene started a tradition within her own family. "I was married there," Sally Cochran said. "My daughter [Debbie Barr] was married there. And now I have a little granddaughter, Sarah Seiberling Fulton Barr, who I'm trying to hook up with some Akron baby."

The Dell, an outdoor garden, was the setting for the 1919 wedding of Virginia Seiberling, Irene's younger sister, to Jack Handy. Like the other gardens and landscaping, The Dell grew from the mind and eye of Boston landscape architect Warren H. Manning. A disciple of Frederick Law Olmsted, "the Father of American Landscape Gardening," Manning designed, planted, and cultivated the property before the house was completed. Afterward, he returned to stay with the Seiberlings to continue his work. "He would get up in the morning at the break of day," Irene said. "He'd have on old tweed pants and heavy tramping shoes. By 5:00 or 5:30, he'd be tramping. He tramped on practically every square yard of the three thousand acres that father piled up."

F. A. Seiberling amassed fabulous wealth during the early boom years of the

F.A. Seiberling (second from left) plays croquet on the grounds at Stan Hywet with Sam Miller, Ernest Pflueger, and William Chase. The estate sported an indoor swimming pool and gymnasium, two tennis courts, five golf holes, a putting green, walking trails, and bridle paths. (Stan Hywet Hall and Gardens)

Irene Seiberling Harrison, the only surviving child of F.A. Seiberling, sits inside her home in the gatehouse at Stan Hywet Hall as she looks forward to celebrating her 105th birthday in 1995. (*Akron Beacon Journal*/Robin Witek)

rubber industry and had hoped to leave an endowment for Stan Hywet to be operated as a public monument after his death. But the family had lived in the great manor for only five years when F. A.'s plan began to fall apart. In the recession of 1920–21, F. A. not only lost Goodyear, but his personal worth dropped from $15 million to nearly zero. A good deal of his fortune was in Goodyear stock, which had plunged from more than $100 a share to an all-time low of $5.25 a share.

F. A. still had children at home to support and borrowed heavily to start his next venture, Seiberling Rubber Company. Three of his five sons, J. Frederick, Willard, and Penfield, who had just graduated from Princeton University, helped run the new business. But first, F. A. had to settle some old business with Goodyear, which had accused him of intermingling $500,000 in company money with his personal funds and was demanding repayment. An old friend, Texas oilman Edgar B. Davis, loaned F. A. the money to repay Goodyear and also arranged for a $5 million line of credit for the new rubber company. Because of Davis's assistance, F. A. did not have to sell his depressed Goodyear stock to raise money.

In early 1928, F. A.'s finances took a decisive home bounce. Goodyear stock had rebounded nicely, to $68 a share. Cleveland industrialist Cyrus Eaton, who had been accumulating Goodyear stock and was a company director, made F. A. an offer he couldn't refuse. "He was willing to pay way over the market price for it," F. A. said, though he did not specify the premium. "I didn't given him a chance to change his mind." F. A. sold Eaton sixty thousand shares.

With the money from that deal, F. A. wiped out $5.5 million in debt. A few years later, Seiberling Rubber ranked among the top ten rubber companies in the world, but the Depression quickly put the brakes on additional growth. At one point, in 1933, the company had only $300 in its safe. The family never again enjoyed the riches that enabled F. A. and Gertrude Seiberling to build Stan Hywet.

F. A. Seiberling retired as chairman of Seiberling Rubber in 1950. He died five years later, at age ninety-five. In 1962, the family lost control of Seiberling Rubber to Toledo investor Edward Lamb who, three years later, sold the tire division to Firestone. There was no money, as F. A. had hoped, to endow Stan Hywet forever. "Many things happened," Irene said. "Three wars. Depressions. . . . It bothered him terribly."

Akron's rubber companies and others funded a study to determine how much money it would take to preserve Stan Hywet. The study recommended a $1 million endowment and an immediate $50,000 to build a parking lot. Corporate Akron concluded Stan Hywet could not be saved. But a cadre of women volunteers who loved Stan Hywet—Irene Seiberling Harrison among them—refused to believe this. They started Stan Hywet Hall Foundation on a shoestring. Ten years later, the hundreds of volunteers and their thousands of hours of work prompted the family to sign over the house, land, and furnishings to the foundation. Today, half a million people wander annually about the mansion and grounds for springtime mystery performances, antique and classic car shows, Shakespeare on the Terrace, madrigal dinners, and celebrations of Christmases past.

John Seiberling said he has been asked repeatedly why the family did not sell Stan Hywet instead of donating it to the foundation. "If you had grown up there, as I did," John Seiberling said, "you would know you couldn't have enjoyed the money because you would think about that treasure you had destroyed."

5 The Company Town

EACH WORKDAY EVENING in the spring of 1912, F. A. Seiberling would drive west on Market Street, turn north on Portage Path, and wend his way from the grime of rip-roaring industrial east Akron to the clear, bright prospect of Stan Hywet, both idyllic artwork in progress and future Seiberling home.

Behind him, Seiberling, president of Goodyear Tire and Rubber Company, left what his daughter Irene called Cinder World. Early Goodyear employees, to be near the factory, lived in Cinder World, fields covered with charcoal ash and row after row of houses that amounted to little more than inflated boxes, a regiment of cardboard soldiers marching in close-order drill. Few workers owned cars. Fewer still owned homes, which were in short supply in fast-growing Rubber City.

"This bothered Father very, very much," said Irene Seiberling Harrison. "There wasn't a single green tree or shrub or blade of grass."

Akron had been growing like an amoeba along with the burgeoning rubber industry. Between 1910 and 1912, Goodyear added one thousand employees, growing to sixty-eight hundred. By 1920, Goodyear employed about twenty-five thousand. Firestone grew from one thousand employees in 1910 to 19,800 in 1920. Between 1915 and 1920, B. F. Goodrich, Goodyear, Firestone, and upstart General, along with Akron's smaller rubber companies, would spend $20 million on new buildings and as much on additional machinery.

There were more people than houses. Sometimes, there were more people than beds. Laborers worked the factories in shifts and slept in rooming houses the same way, often on soiled sheets. Between 1910 and 1920, Akron grew faster than any city in the United States, from 69,067 people to 208,435.

"It seemed to me that if Goodyear wanted to avoid terrific labor problems," F. A. Seiberling said, "we would have to offer our workers more than just jobs." To prevent labor strife and worker turnover, Seiberling personally financed a housing project for Goodyear workers known as Goodyear Heights. Across town in south Akron, Harvey Firestone would match Seiberling's play with Firestone Park—but with corporate financing.

For Goodyear Heights, Seiberling proposed quality homes of structural variety to be sold to employees at cost. Seiberling argued that it would be to the advantage of both Goodyear and the city to have the allegiance of a small army of workers who owned homes in east Akron and paid taxes. Goodyear's board of directors, including the usually enlightened P. W. Litchfield, opposed him, almost mockingly. Seiberling found the only supporter he needed in his wife, Gertrude, who handed over a large number of Goodyear stock certificates as collateral. "I remember seeing them sit for two days, signing over their common stock," Irene Seiberling Harrison said. "It was a big undertaking."

Seiberling foresaw that the auto would make the work force increasingly mobile. He worried that unhappy employees might load up their cars and return to their homes in West Virginia, Pennsylvania, Kentucky, and Tennessee. Turnover could lead to inferior tires and other rubber products. Goodyear's good name could be at risk. But as Litchfield feared, some people suggested Seiberling's motives were sinister. In August 1925, *Industrial Pioneer* magazine published a story titled "Rubber Slavery at Akron." The author: "A Rubber Worker." The writer denounced Seiberling's housing plan as enforced servitude, predicting that Goodyear employees would be paying off their mortgages, in constant fear of losing their jobs, long after these inferior homes fell apart at the seams.

Some company towns indeed consigned workers to a form of slavery, occasionally with bloody consequences. One of the more egregious examples occurred in Pullman, Illinois, near Chicago. Built in the 1880s by George Pullman, inventor of the Pullman Palace railroad car, Pullman, Illinois, rented houses to its workers. In 1894, Pullman cut wages five times but refused to lower rents, and twelve people died in a worker revolt.

History, however, has proved wrong much of the anonymous writer's remarks about Seiberling and Goodyear. Unlike in Pullman, when times got hard and Goodyear workers' hours dropped, mortgage payments also were reduced or even waived. Initially, some homes sold for less than $2,000. The mortgages, for the most part, were paid off in fifteen or twenty years. The houses are still standing. Over the years, they have appreciated in value, albeit modestly; the average 1996 sale price for Goodyear Heights homes was $56,700, compared with $68,700 citywide.

Workers build the foundations and basement walls of Goodyear houses in the Goodyear Heights allotment, circa 1913. In the background, a farmer tills his field with a horse and plow. (The University of Akron Archives)

"I think they were well built," said builder Jack Heslop, who developed the last five hundred lots in Goodyear Heights. "They've been there a long, long time. More than seventy-five years. It is amazing how many of these neighborhoods still look pretty good."

F. A. Seiberling hired landscape architect Warren H. Manning of Boston, designer of Stan Hywet Hall and Gardens, to carve a community out of an east Akron hillside. Manning left trees intact. He created parks and routed streets with the contour of the land. Seiberling also donated thousands of fruit trees, a different variety on every lot so that neighbors could share. He paid for the workers' home insurance. He selected nineteen models to avoid monotony. Seiberling insisted that each Goodyear Heights home have a fireplace and interior oak trim—even an oak toilet seat.

By 1913, the first families were moving in. Houses built on the first 463 lots averaged $3,500 in cost, with no down payment. They were offered only to white Goodyear employees. In the second phase, 1,503 lots were developed on 350 acres along the east side of Brittain Road. The minimum price range at first was $1,800 to $2,500, but quickly climbed to $2,000 to $3,500. A 2 percent down payment was required. Nonemployees were eligible to purchase, provided they were white.

The August 25, 1917, issue of the *Wingfoot Clan*, Goodyear's employee newspaper, addressed the restriction on race: "No sales shall be made to colored people and this is rigidly followed. . . . This is not done with any view to discriminate against the colored man, but because it is thought best for the more rapid and thorough development of the section."

Because the homes were sold at cost, Seiberling took measures to prevent speculation. The semimonthly payments for the first five years carried a 25 percent surcharge, which amounted to the real estate or retail value of the property. At the end of five years, if the buyer remained at Goodyear, the difference between the two values and any interest was applied to reduce the mortgage, and all other payments were only for the builder's cost. By the time Phase Two opened in 1917, Seiberling had won the board of directors over—Goodyear had invested $2 million in infrastructure—and P. W. Litchfield had endorsed the project in an opening day speech.

As its founder intended, Goodyear Heights evolved into a workingman's neighborhood, largely because of its policy of no or low down payment. By the end of the century, it still was working class. Average household income in the mid-1990s was about $26,000 per year, compared with $35,000 citywide. Caveats on race, however, no longer existed—Goodyear Heights was 22 percent black; Akron was 25 percent.

In an essay called "The Corner Grocery Store," Jane Kaneas paid tribute to the Goodyear Heights neighborhood of her youth and a way of life that has largely disappeared:

A horse-drawn milk buggy stops by to make a delivery outside one of the first houses in Goodyear Heights in 1913. (Goodyear Tire and Rubber Company)

The inside of the neighborhood Acme grocery store in Goodyear Heights, patronized by a Mrs. Zeigler in 1921. (Goodyear Tire and Rubber Company)

My father selected the $4,500 model [home] in 1920 and spent the next twenty-five years paying for it. Neighborhood grocery stores, fifteen in all, dotted the landscape. No one had to walk more than a half mile to fill the family larder. There was Camp's and Ben Shine's, Acme and Abe's, Andy's, the IGA and the Square Deal. These corner grocery stores were cut from the same bolt of cloth and helped to make up the fabric of our lives.

We knew them all. They were nearly identical, two-story structures with an apartment overhead. Only one, Acme, was a single-story building, its mansard roof and arched entry-way distinctive. These small stores were constructed on standard city lots, with no parking. Nearly everyone carried their sacks of groceries home in their arms or pulled them in a wagon. . . .

Customers never served themselves. They presented a list to the proprietor, who would fetch and accumulate the purchases on the counter. The friendly grocer would gladly run a tab, payable on payday. Each family's name was neatly lettered on their individualized sales book. It was a great way to enjoy an ice-cream bar on a hot summer's afternoon. I'd announce to Mr. Camp: "Just put it on our bill." Then I'd deal with Dad later. . . .

Most of the neighborhood grocery stores survived until just after World War II, when gas rationing was lifted, and nearly every family owned an automobile. The A&P built a large new store on Goodyear Boulevard, and the Acme moved out by Six Corners. People drove their cars to pick up a week's supply of groceries to fill their refrigerators. One by one the little stores that had been an integral part of our lives closed their doors. Some stores were boarded up for a while. Eventually, some became beauty shops or apartments. A florist opened a shop in one. Another became a post office. Two have been torn down. . . . Now, the nearest grocery stores are located in suburban shopping centers, miles from Goodyear Heights. Even the A&P and Acme are gone.

It is ironic that the automobile, which spawned the rubber-neighborhood groceries, was, in the end, the same factor that led to their demise.

This Firestone Park street was a sea of dirt as it was constructed in 1917. (*Akron Beacon Journal*)

The houses look to be complete, but no trees or landscaping have been planted in Firestone Park near the intersection of Evergreen and Crescent in 1920. (*Akron Beacon Journal*)

Officially, the developer of Firestone Park was the Coventry Land and Improvement Company, which Harvey Firestone incorporated in 1915. Though Coventry was a separate legal entity, Firestone, the company as well as the man, stood behind the project.

To design the landscape, Harvey Firestone hired Alling S. DeForest of Rochester, New York, the landscape architect for Harbel Manor, Firestone's sixty-acre estate. Firestone ordered DeForest to provide public spaces in the thousand lots to be developed and also to design a park in the shape of the Firestone company shield. The prestigious New York firm of Alexander B. Trowbridge and Frederick L. Ackerman, architects for Harbel Manor, designed the plans for the Firestone Park homes. Buyers could select from one of twenty variations of "kit" houses manufactured by Sears, Roebuck and Company or hire a local contractor to duplicate the Tudor Revival, Dutch Colonial, Georgian Revival, and other styles available.

In October 1916, when 929 lots on six hundred acres went on sale, 177 houses were purchased, with a 5 percent down payment. By 1920, a thousand houses had been sold, many with stylistic treatments such as casement windows, paired entrance benches, and mural latticework. Buyers did not have to work for Firestone, but blacks and noncitizens were excluded initially. Because a higher down payment was required, Firestone Park became more middle class and less integrated than Goodyear Heights. In the mid-1990s, average family income in Firestone

Park was about $30,500. Homes sold in 1996 for an average price of $62,300. The black population was slightly more than 7 percent.

Clarice Finley Lewis, a retired schoolteacher, lived most of her life in Firestone Park and wrote *A History of Firestone Park*. Lewis said that, over the years, Firestone Park remained attractive to families because of its affordability. "People move in, see how nice it is, and feel guilty if they let it go downhill," she said.

C. P. Chima, owner of Chima Travel Bureau, grew up in Firestone Park as immigrants carved the company neighborhood and nearby areas into ethnic enclaves—Romanians on Moore Street and Stanton and Steiner Avenues, the Serbians around the Grant Street area called "Goosetown," and the Hungarians near Brown Street. Chima's father, Peter, a Romanian immigrant, was responsible for some of the immigration. Peter Chima founded Chima Travel after World War I to help eastern and southern Europeans come to Akron for work in the rubber shops. Peter Chima would even advance them money for the trip. "I never lost a penny," he told his son.

"At first," C. P. Chima said, "they planned to go back to Europe. If they could save a couple of thousand dollars, they could live like a king back home. But then, most of them decided they would stay here. Their concern was to get a job, buy a house, and become citizens. They wanted to go back home with an American passport. That was important."

∾

The Astor Avenue and Reed section of Firestone Park in 1918. The street-car line was extended to the new residential area in this year to serve the increasing number of residences in Firestone Park, developed by the Coventry Land and Improvement Company, which Harvey Firestone incorporated in 1915. The building at right housed an Acme grocery store. *(Akron Beacon Journal)*

After Goodyear Heights was under way, F. A. Seiberling began to plan a more exclusive neighborhood, Fairlawn Heights, and a 150-acre country club. In 1917, Seiberling brought Harold S. Wagner, Warren Manning's associate from Boston, to Akron, to design $1.5 million in improvements to a thousand undeveloped acres south of West Market Street, between Lownsdale Avenue and Miller Road. Then Seiberling formed a home-building company called the Fairlawn Heights Company. The upscale neighborhood quickly became a haven for professionals; the average family income in the late 1990s was $123,500. While the larger, older homes occasionally sell today for as much as a million dollars, the average sale price in 1996 was $188,465.

The original deeds to Fairlawn Heights homes formally prohibited resale "to any person or persons of African descent or belonging to any other branch of the Ethiopian race." In 1997, the neighborhood was about 4 percent black. The Fairlawn Country Club did not accept its first black member until 1987.

Frances H. Halbert moved to Fairlawn Heights after marrying Paul A. Frank, in 1921, two years after Fairlawn Country Club opened. Over seven and a half decades, Mrs. Frank witnessed many changes. In 1942, the Heights agreed to annexation by Akron to obtain city water. That same decade, C. Blake McDowell Sr. bought the Fairlawn Heights Company out of bankruptcy. Under new ownership, the development firm began building smaller, less expensive homes. In 1961, Interstate 77 cut a swath through the southern border of the Heights. When Mrs. Frank died in 1997, at age ninety-nine, she was the last original homebuyer in Fairlawn Heights. Her son, John, represented Fairlawn Heights as Ward 8 city councilman from 1978 through 1997.

"Everybody else is gone," John Frank said.

The neighborhoods, though, have stood the test of time. The rubber companies wove a cocoon of life within Akron's borders. They built athletic fields and gyms and then formed industrial league teams. They fed their employees in cafeterias, charging only for the cost of the food. Firestone baked bread and sold it in the company store. Firestone and Goodyear set up their own banks, welfare funds, stock purchase plans, and health clinics. Goodyear Heights even had its own bus line, the second established in the country after New York City's Fifth Avenue Coach Line. In 1918, rides cost two cents on buses equipped with Goodyear's newly developed pneumatic truck tires.

"Goodyear Heights, to my way of thinking," said F. A. Seiberling, in 1949, "had sufficient beauty and charm to make it remarkable alongside any community in the country."

He had even stronger points to make about the housing development:

> But the important thing about it was the workingmen could afford to live there. . . . Certainly my motives in establishing Goodyear Heights were not entirely unselfish. I was trying to make employment in the Goodyear Tire and Rubber Company to be desired by a great number of men. Nevertheless, I was also trying to help a group of fellow humans attain a better life than they could achieve unaided. There was no charity involved. The men I was seeking to help were fellows who would never take charity. What they got they paid for. The plan was not perfect in its conception or execution, but it benefited hundreds of workmen, a great rubber company and the city of Akron.

6 Rubber Shop Royalty

IF, AFTER SHIFT CHANGE one night, you happened into one of Akron's blue-collar bars, say the Elk Cafe on South Main Street, you could pick out the kings of the Rubber City. As the jukebox spilled its honky-tonk, you could look along the bar, and, in the neon light of the beer signs, you could spot them just by looking at the hands. Heavy calluses on the heels of the palms. Cracked fingers. Ragged cuticles. Swollen knuckles. Awful hands that spun a peculiar magic. The hands of kings.

Akron had its rubber barons, but the true royalty of the rubber shop, as just about anyone who worked in one will tell you, was the tire builder. He shared his court with a motley collection of princes—Banbury operators, mill room and pit workers, inspectors, mechanics, and electricians, among others. These people were the substance of Akron, the stuff that made it what it was, the character of the town. Rubber workers were to Akron what cowboys were to Texas and coal miners were to Kentucky.

For the scores who worked in Akron's rubber plants, the inside goings-on could be as mundane as watching rubber cement dry. But to those who never had a glimpse inside, the factories were full of mystery. How is a tire made? What

The callused, bandaged hands of a tire builder during a smoke break. Tire builders were the royalty of the tire shop, and among production workers, they generally earned the best money and the most respect. It was an individual craft, one that bonded a man with his machine. (©Daniel Mainzer)

kind of people make them? The truth is, tire building, especially in the days before automation, was a craft. A good tire builder could reach his quota, called "making out," in a few hours, hitting a quick rhythm as he deftly smoothed the layers of rubbery fabric. A less talented builder might work twice as hard and just barely make out. "There's an art to building tires, and you have to have a touch to lay everything on right," said Daniel Mainzer, who worked as a photographer for Firestone and General in the 1970s and 1980s. "You really had to have a good feel to build tires, and I would bet, especially, say, in the race area, you would know from the way the thing performed who built that tire."

Tens of thousands of people—mostly men—have worked as tire builders in Akron. Earthy, independent, hard-working, and well-paid, they defined the town for most of this century. Their work was intrinsically linked to the Rubber City—the tire-making process was refined here and still, even with the jobs gone, carries the indelible stamp of Akron. Tire building was different from most factory work. In Henry Ford's assembly line, for instance, each worker performed one function that eventually, after many hands, produced a finished product. Not so in the tire room. There, one man did almost all the work that went into producing a tire. It was an individual craft, one that bonded a man with his machine. The job was not easy. Most men will tell you they did it for one reason: the money. An efficient tire builder made top wages among production workers; only some calender operators, who processed rubber, made more. In 1976, a few years before the massive plant closings in Akron, B. F. Goodrich's maximum wage for tire builders was $5.50 per hour. The plant average was about $5.25 per hour. In an era when the national minimum wage was $2.30 an hour, Akron factory wages were 29 percent above the U.S. average.

The pay, in some ways, compensated for the pressures and for the hazards that existed before government agencies oversaw workplace safety. Tire builders were constantly prodded to keep up their pace, mostly by piecework quotas that forced them to crank out the tires. Piecework was a complicated system through which workers were paid according to how many tires, or portions of a tire, they produced in a given period. The fastest workers, therefore, made the most money. Sometimes, union members would pressure faster workers to hold back to keep the pace down for slower workers. Others paced themselves voluntarily, doing the bulk of their work early in a shift so they could take it easy later. In some cases, production workers could work furiously for the first few hours, make their quota, then sneak out to a bar or a secret sleeping place, returning to work in time to clock out.

Speed wasn't the only factor in the tire room, though. Each tire, marked with a sticker bearing the builder's name, was inspected for quality. Tolerance for mistakes was near zero. If a layer of rubber was off by even a fraction of an inch, the tire could be scrapped. Even one or two bad tires over a career, and the builder could find himself reclassified into a lower-paying job. So it's not surprising that few tire builders talk of piecework with fondness in their hearts. Piecework meant stress. As a result, according to University of Akron labor historian Daniel Nelson, these independent, confident tire builders tended to be the most militant unionists: "The sense of their own importance was aggrieved because of the constant pressure."

Carl "Bud" Lawley, the son of two rubber workers, built tires for Goodyear for forty years, spending much of that time in the passenger tire room. The passenger tire room was above the hot-as-blazes pit, and the heat of the curing presses rose through the concrete floor, turning the tire room into an oven. "The roughest thing was during the summertime," recalled Lawley, who retired in 1995. "In the summertime, you couldn't touch the floor with your hand. So they just fed you salt pills all the time. . . . But you wasn't allowed to sweat on that tire, because if water got in between those plies, that tire would blow, and it would be scrapped. So you tried to stay away from it, and guys wore rags on their heads; you try to keep the sweat off. Course, after two hours, you didn't sweat no more. All your sweat was gone."

Most Akron workers built bias-ply tires, which were constructed of fabric plies set at a diagonal and were the standard on American cars until the 1970s.

Row after row of workers are nearly elbow-to-elbow inside the tire room at the Diamond Rubber Co. in 1910. Diamond Rubber later was bought out by the B.F. Goodrich Company (*Akron Beacon Journal*)

A Goodyear tire builder stretches a semicured tread around the fabric body of a tire on a crude stand during the early days of tire building. The assembler then cemented and wrapped the two together and prepared them for final curing. Today, a tire is built on a machine with a collapsible drum. (Goodyear Tire and Rubber Company)

Radials, which replaced bias-ply tires, require even more precision in construction. As technology advanced, much of the work became automated.

But the basic process remained the same during the time tires were built in Akron. The builder stood facing his machine, which consisted chiefly of a drum about the size of a small beer keg turned sideways. As he worked, he periodically hit a control to rotate the drum. First, he pulled a thin sheet of rubber, called a liner, around the drum. The liner was about three feet wide. He cut the liner with a knife and sealed the seam with rubber cement. Over that, he laid a piece of rubberized textile—cotton in the early days, then rayon and later nylon. The fabric was laid with its fibers running diagonally and smoothed out. It, too, was cut and sealed. Wire hoops, called beads, were then placed on the outer edges of the tire. The edges of the fabric were folded over to hold them in place, then cemented. A second layer of textile was laid over that, with the fibers running diagonally in the opposite direction to the first. Its edges were folded over the bead and cemented. Finally, the tread was applied. This was a heavier piece of rubber put on in the same manner as the other layers. In many cases, the layers, called plies, were swabbed with a solvent—the volatile benzene—to make them tacky and keep them in place.

The tire builder's skill was judged by his ability to smooth each layer properly and make clean seams. The fibers in the rubberized fabric had to be straight; the layers had to be free of bubbles and debris. The drum rotated and the builder constantly ran his hands over the rough stock, pulling and smoothing. Because of the handwork involved and the danger of getting tangled in the machinery, he couldn't wear gloves. That's why his hands were such a mess. "After so many hundreds and thousands of tires, you start looking at your hands, and it looks like you've got red ink all over them," Lawley said. "What it is, your skin is getting thin, and the blood is seeping through your hands."

When the tire was finished, the builder hit a control that collapsed the metal drum, allowing the tire, still a barrel-shaped tube of rubber, to be removed. It was called a green tire at this point, not because of its color, but because it had yet to be cured. It was then placed on an overhead conveyor with hooks or tossed into a cart to be taken to the tire press. The press pushed the tire into its doughnut shape and molded the treads and sidewall lettering into the rubber. The press vulcanized the rubber, heating it to strengthen the compound. When it was removed, it was a tire.

Walter Reed, a thick-shouldered farm boy from Spencer, West Virginia, spent five years in the truck tire room at General's Plant 1, in the 1950s, golden years for Akron's tire industry. He worked the 5:30 to 11:30 PM shift. In the early part of his shift, tall windows in the factory walls maximized natural light. Later, the windows offered a view of the moon and the landscape of industrial Akron. About twenty tire machines, set in two rows with an aisle down the middle, filled the long, narrow room. The floors were wooden, well-worn. Everything in the tire room was worn smooth by the men who worked there.

Reed usually arrived a few minutes early for his shift, allowing time to change into the tire builder's uniform—"ratty old jeans and a T-shirt." Then it was straight to the machine, where he arranged his tools and solvents, preparing for the evening's work. As the builders took their places, one or two might holler that his machine wasn't set up properly. That was serious business: A worker was not docked if repairs exceeded six minutes, but, if he couldn't work, the company didn't get any tires. So a mechanic was called to fix the machine.

The shift began. Each builder found his rhythm. Rubber was spun into tires. Truck tires, because of their size, require more time to build than passenger tires. Reed might turn out three or four tires in a night; passenger tire builders such as Lawley might crank out a hundred tires in a shift. As Reed's hands worked the rubber and the machinery, his thoughts drifted to his day job as a carpenter, or to his home life. "The outside," he called it, in the way of a prisoner.

"I gave General Tire my body," he said, "but my mind was outside all the time." The work quickly eased into the subconscious, and voices rose above the machinery. "You could talk all night," said Reed.

> You see, building tires was a very monotonous job. It was so monotonous, you do that day in and week in and year in, and you would talk to your buddy, and you would agitate the daylights out of him. Many a night I went home, I was so hoarse, I couldn't talk. Because you was yelling. There was a certain amount of noise, but you

HOW TO BUILD A Tire

Tire building is faster and more precise than in the days when passenger tires were made in Akron.

Today's tire-building machines are more automated, handling some tasks formerly done by hand. Stiff, steel-belted radial tires have replaced the softer, fabric-reinforced bias tires made in the Rubber Capital of the World.

An inside look

The radial ply tire was first patented, in 1913, by Christian Hamilton Gray and Thomas Sloper of England. It was not produced commercially, however, until after World War II by French tire company Michelin.

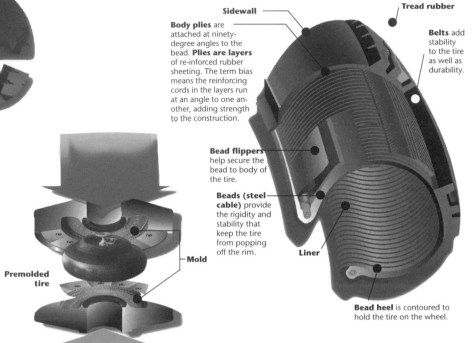

Sidewall

Tread rubber

Body plies are attached at ninety-degree angles to the bead. **Plies are layers** of re-inforced rubber sheeting. The term bias means the reinforcing cords in the layers run at an angle to one another, adding strength to the construction.

Belts add stability to the tire as well as durability.

Bead flippers help secure the bead to body of the tire.

Beads (steel cable) provide the rigidity and stability that keep the tire from popping off the rim.

Liner

Mold

Premolded tire

Bead heel is contoured to hold the tire on the wheel.

Into the mold

The tire before molding is soft and flexible. After the mold closes, pressure forces a curing bladder into the tire. Hot steam softens the rubber even more and forces it into the mold.

As the newly cast tire cures in the mold, the heat from the steam causes a chemical change in the rubber. This process, called **vulcanization**, does two things: first, it fuses the different layers of the tire into one unit, and second, it makes the soft, pliable rubber tougher and more durable, which is essential for good tire production.

The building process

- **Tire builders tightly wrap a layer of airtight rubber liner** around the drum of tire building machine.

- **Layers of cord fabric plies** are wrapped around the drum.

- **Wire beads are placed** around the rubber-coated fabric, which is turned up to hold the bead in place.

- **Sidewall rubber is wrapped** around the drum over the rubber-coated fabric.

- **The tire is placed on a forming machine,** which stretches it into a doughnut shape.

- **Steel-reinforced belts** are wrapped around the doughnut.

- **A layer of tread** rubber finishes the assembly.

- **The tire is placed in a mold,** which is heated to vulcanize the rubber. Compressed air forces the tire into its finished shape.

- **After vulcanization,** the cured tire is cooled and removed from the mold.

Technical assistance from Bridgestone/Firestone SOURCES: Firestone Tire and Rubber Company, Goodyear Tire and Rubber Company, Tire Business newspaper, *The Motor Car: Its Evolution and Engineering Development,* and *Beacon Journal* archives *Research by Beacon Journal staff writer* JIM QUINN *Design and illustration by* RICK STEINHAUSER

John Dunlop of Ireland was the first to patent a commercially practical tire in December 1888. His earliest tire was an air-filled tube enclosed in a canvas covering, then overlaid with a rubber tread. Dunlop and some investors formed Pneumatic Tyre and Booth's Cycle Agency, in 1889, after his tire proved superior to the solid rubber tires used on bicycles of the time. The company later went on to become Dunlop Rubber Company.

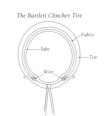

John Boyd Dunlop

The Bartlett Clincher Tire

William Bartlett of the North British Rubber Company, in an effort to find a means to securely attach a tire to the rim and yet easily mount and take off the rim, developed the "Bartlett Clincher" – the first detachable pneumatic tire, introduced to the market in 1890.

Winton Motor Carriage

In 1896, Cleveland automaker Alexander Winton commissioned B.F. Goodrich in Akron to manufacture pneumatic tires for his cars. The rubber company's financial success spawned new growth in the tire-making industry in the Akron area, soon earning it the title "Rubber Capital of the World."

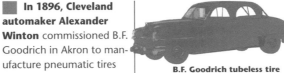

B.F. Goodrich tubeless tire

In 1947, B.F. Goodrich introduced the tubeless tire to the American public. Dunlop Rubber Company was the first European company to manufacture the tubeless tire, starting in 1953. Firestone introduced its first tubeless tire in 1954.

The first steel-belted radial was put on the market by Michelin in 1948. A radial in tire making refers to the reinforcing cords running in ninety-degree angles to the wheel. A restraining belt is then placed over the cords in order to keep the tire body from flattening out under a load.

The belts in a radial tire are made of fairly rigid materials (usually steel cord) and are commonly narrower than the old style cord plies.

The plies or layers of belts add resistance to puncture and additional strength to the tire.

Double layer of cord body plies are placed over airtight tire liner.

Radial tires

Steel-belted radial tires have been produced for at least fifty years. Radials didn't gain popular acceptance until the 1970s when U.S. automakers decided that, because of their durability and a 10 percent gain in fuel economy due to lessened rolling resistance, they should be installed on all new cars. The switch to radials brought the most costly production changeover in tire making history and, some say, the demise of tire building in Akron.

could talk to a guy across the wing; you could talk to guys in front or behind you or something like that. It was nothing to have an ongoing argument or conversation a total shift. Just to kill the monotony of the job.

You automatically built the tire; you didn't have to think at all. No concentration, no thinking of what to do. You just automatically did this and that like you was chained to a machine.

The talk was interrupted by builders calling out for more stock or hollering for their buddy to "tail"—to grab one end of the heavy tread stock when it was ready to be applied. One supervisor roamed the floor, checking on workers, responding to their calls.

"Repair!"

"More stock!"

A couple of hours into the shift, the first break was called. The men went into the smokers, where they could have a cigarette, safely removed from the flammable benzene. Some might stay at their machines, grab a bite to eat. Others might curl up in a corner for a nod of sleep. Then it was back to the rhythm of the machine. When the shift ended, most guys hit the showers. Those who had "made out" early could clean up and leave right when the whistle blew; others might have to clock out, then shower. But afterward, another Akron tradition took place—the tire builders went out for beer.

Akron was peppered with bars that catered to the cycles of the rubber shifts. In the industry's heyday, bartenders used to set up a series of shots and beers along the bar just before the whistle blew, allowing the workers to get straight down to business when they came in. It didn't matter if it was midnight or six in the morning. Not everyone drank, of course, but enough did to keep business booming at places such as the Cork and Bottle, across from General Tire. The blue-collar saloons were part of the glue of the Rubber City, a true forum for union politics, a place to jump-start the psyche after hours of mind-numbing work. And as Akron's fortunes went, so went the fortunes of the tavern keeper. The bar at the Cork and Bottle bore a concave groove worn deep into the wood by the elbows of a generation of General Tire workers. But when the plant closed, in 1982, business suffered. Money for booze was scarce, and the rubber workers were scattered about, looking for other jobs. The Cork, as true a marker of Akron's fortunes as any, closed in 1987, after nearly forty years in business.

The glamour and prosperity at the top of the industrial heap was sullied by the often harsh conditions inside the rubber shop. Chemical accelerants made it possible to build a better tire, but at the same time resulted in hazardous working conditions. Congress did not create the Environmental Protection Agency and the Occupational Safety and Health Administration until 1970, and, in the decades before, Akron rubber factories were smelly, dirty, and dangerous places. Rubber provided some of the best-paying industrial jobs in the country, but opportunity came with a price.

The smell came from the processing of crude rubber with chemicals and from reclaim operations. The dirt came from carbon black, also called lampblack, which gives tires their color. The smell and the dirt saturated workers' skin and clothes so thoroughly that no amount of strong soap and hot water could remove the

The vulcanizing room, in 1915, at Goodyear, where tires were lowered into pits for curing.
(Goodycar Tire and Rubber Company)

odors and stains completely. Some workers found it easier to buy secondhand clothes and throw them out when they got too filthy to use again.

The dangers were as run-of-the-mill as burns from steam, hot molds, and freshly cured tires, as traumatic as dismemberment, and as insidiously threatening as toxic fumes from aniline and ether. Toxic chemicals were used as far back as 1906, when Diamond Rubber Company chemist George Oenslager discovered that aniline oil, a cheap organic base, would speed the processing of rubber and make a tire stronger. "And it worked," said retired chemist Waldo Semon, who later worked with Oenslager at B. F. Goodrich. "But aniline oil was volatile, and when he tried it in the factory, it turned the workers blue. It was poisonous."

Aniline use ended in 1916, but exposure to dangerous chemicals and substances continued. Edgar Lyle, retired Goodrich tire builder and manager, made some of the first tires using synthetic rubber in the late 1930s. "The first synthetic rubber was real tough," Lyle said. "The only thing that would soften it enough to stick was ether. I had a machine by the windows that opened onto Bartges Street, and to keep from going to sleep, I would stop after I put each ply on and stick my head out the window."

Workers eventually turned to the court system seeking compensation for health problems. In 1986, more than twenty-five hundred rubber workers who claimed they had been damaged by exposure to asbestos filed suit in Summit County against two hundred asbestos companies in what became known as the Tire Workers Litigation Project. Overhead lines carrying steam to cure tires had been insulated with asbestos in Akron's rubber shops. In 1993, the first of the lawsuits came before Judge William Victor. Proceedings were held in the downtown Akron Masonic Temple.

"They went on for three or four years, and I was very busy with them during that time," Victor said. "There were a couple of thousand people involved. In terms of number of people, it could very well be the biggest case in Summit County." The workers lost the first two cases that went to trial. After that, most of the cases were dropped or settled. Some remained on the docket for trial in 1998. So far, the lawsuits seem to have proved that there was an abundance of asbestos in the rubber shops and that many rubber workers have suffered from impaired lung capacity. What they haven't proved is that asbestos was to blame.

Banbury operators had one of the

At Firestone, a worker operates a calender, which processes the rubber into sheets. Harsh conditions were often the rule inside the rubber shop, and the calenders were among the most dangerous equipment found there. Workers risked getting their hands and arms caught in the rollers. (©Daniel Mainzer)

The raw materials of rubber are dumped into a Banbury mixer at the B.F. Goodrich tire plant in Miami, Oklahoma. The early rubber industry had trouble blending chemicals into rubber on old-fashioned open-roll mills. The Banbury mixer changed all that, allowing for fast, efficient blending of rubber using an enclosed mixer that reduced worker exposure to chemicals. (The University of Akron Archives)

most dangerous and filthy jobs in the tire-building process. They were the cooks of the rubber shops, mixing five hundred pounds of rubber, one hundred pounds of carbon black, and fifty pounds of oil, to send off to the calenders, where the rubber was processed into sheets. The good Banbury operators could tell by the sound of their batch when it was too oily: it sucked. They could smell it when it got too hot, almost like baking bread.

John Nardella, who became president of URW Local 2 at Goodyear, began his career, in October 1943, in the mill room. He mixed rubber in open mills, predecessor of the Banbury, an internal mixer. "It was awful, awful hard work, dangerous work," Nardella said. On the open mills, with a fast roller in front and a slow one in back, rubber could stick. To free it, an operator had to risk his hands. "A lot of guys lost their hands, or part of them," Nardella said.

Bob Walker, director of health, safety, and industrial hygiene for Bridgestone/Firestone, said the rubber factory is a much safer place today. "I know what

A worker displays the brute strength required in some areas of the rubber shop, in this case rubber reclamation. The factories in the early years were smelly, dirty, and dangerous places, but the jobs provided were some of the best-paying industrial work in the country. (The University of Akron Archives)

those factories in Akron were like," Walker said. "In a lot of cases, they weren't designed to produce the products they ended up manufacturing, or the volume. Sometimes they weren't even designed for the rubber industry." Today's single-story plants have high ceilings that provide better ventilation. Chemicals formerly mixed manually in the open are now handled by enclosed, automated systems. Banburies and calenders are equipped with shields and systems that shut down if workers get too close. Carbon black, once handled directly by workers, is now loaded automatically.

Still, tire manufacturing is relatively hazardous. According to the U.S. Bureau of Labor Statistics, which compiles data for OSHA, 13.8 percent of tire and tube production workers suffer work-related injuries or illnesses each year. That compares with 36.4 percent of meat packers, who have the most dangerous job, and 2.7 percent of financial and real estate workers, who have the safest occupations. The least hazardous production jobs are in the manufacture of electrical instruments, which has a 4.5 percent injury/illness rate.

Even as improvements came to the tire factories, the smell and filth remained. And those things affected everyone, from the mill room to the executive offices. Before he became a congressman representing the Akron area, John F. Seiberling worked as an attorney for Goodyear, the company founded by his grandfather.

"When I first went to work for Goodyear, in 1954," Seiberling recalled, "we had to keep the windows open, and the fly ash would blow in and cover everything to the point we almost couldn't work. Sometimes, it was worse than places in the factory." One day, Goodyear President Russ DeYoung was touring the law department, and the window in Seiberling's office was open. The room was a contradiction. It felt like a blast furnace and looked as if snow had just fallen.

"Would you like to have air conditioning in this office?" DeYoung asked Seiberling.

"You sure could get more work out of me," Seiberling said.

A short time later, window-unit air conditioners were installed in Seiberling's and others' offices. Meanwhile, the rubber shops' scent and residue continued to permeate the city. They became part of the atmosphere. Whenever someone complained of the smell, someone else would remind them of the Akron adage, that it was the smell of money.

"My most vivid memory is the odor rubber produces on a warm summer night," said Rebecca Heisler Weissfeld, who took a job with Goodrich in the mid-1940s. "That odor covered Akron. How we complained of the polluted air and the smell of rubber. Now we would be so happy to still have the rubber shops and the prosperity of a working town."

7 Goodyear's Guiding Force

INDOMITABLE IN LIFE, Paul Weeks Litchfield now stands in front of Goodyear Tire and Rubber Company's Research and Development building immovable in death, a bronze monument to his interests, to his status, to his legacy. He looks ready to travel, topcoat on, hat in hand, prepared, eager even, to fly off on another of his crisscross-the-world jaunts. In his right hand, he holds a set of blueprints.

Over a fifty-eight-year career, Litchfield influenced the course of Goodyear more than any other, had more faces than Eve, more personalities than Sybil. He was an engineer and inventor, an administrator and aeronautical pioneer, a philosopher and teacher, an industrial relations innovator and writer, a leader and inspiration.

But how does a sculptor, in this case Walker Hancock of Massachusetts, mold such myriad qualities into a hunk of bronze atop a chunk of marble? Litchfield's family and friends fretted over this. They kept asking themselves: Who was Paul Weeks Litchfield and what did he do? How could his complexity be distilled?

"The thing that stands out is that he was a builder," said daughter Katharine Hyde. "He built up . . . and up . . . and up." When Litchfield left his native New

England, in 1900, Goodyear had $1 million in sales, one plant, and 176 employees. When he died, in 1959, still the honorary chairman of the board, Litchfield had turned Goodyear into a multidimensional company with $1.6 billion in sales, fifty-eight plants in twenty-three countries, six rubber plantations, and a hundred thousand employees, twenty-six thousand of them in Akron.

"I think that he should be considered a founder," said his protege and successor, E. J. Thomas. Of course, Litchfield wasn't a founder. P. W. Litchfield, the taciturn Boston-born descendant of Mayflower arrivals, sailed into Akron a few days before his twenty-fifth birthday and two years after F. A. and Charlie Seiberling had launched Goodyear. Litchfield no more founded Goodyear than did Charles Goodyear, but no one would know this by the homage Goodyear pays to him. Litchfield created a category all his own. And so did others, with respect to Litchfield. In the 1950s, Thomas established a funded retirement plan for salaried personnel. He attached to it a compulsory retirement age, first sixty-eight and, later, sixty-five. The retirement age was enforced with only one exception: P. W. Litchfield, who left the board of directors, which he had served as chairman from 1930 to 1956, on October 6, 1958, at age eighty-three. Little more than five months later, he was dead. But his legacy lives on. It is the legacy of opportunity.

"When I came here," Litchfield said in December 1958, "I was given the greatest thing a man can have—opportunity. Frank Seiberling gave me every opportunity to develop." The timing of Litchfield's birth on July 26, 1875, multiplied that gift of opportunity manyfold. "I sailed with the tide, just as manufacturing in America was setting off on an era of tremendous expansion," Litchfield wrote of his business career.

Sailing is no accidental metaphor. It could have been his life. Though he couldn't swim, Litchfield loved to sail the waters off Bath, Maine, the shipbuilding center where he spent summers as a youth with his maternal grandmother, Julia Weeks. The days of great clipper ships had dwindled to a precious few. But as he breathed the salt air, young Paul Litchfield witnessed the end of the sailing vessel and the shift to ships of iron. Hammered into his mind was the importance of being receptive to changes in transportation.

It was only one of the turning points of his life in Maine. When he was five, Litchfield came down with polio. It affected one of his feet, and for a time it looked as if he might be crippled for life. Then, at the suggestion of the dean of the Massachusetts Homeopathic Hospital, his grandmother massaged his foot with brine. "I can still see Grandmother Weeks massaging my foot day after day

Paul Weeks Litchfield poses on the deck of a sailboat, in 1900, just before starting to work at Goodyear in Akron. Litchfield spent his youthful summers sailing the waters of Bath, Maine, the home of his maternal grandmother, Julia Weeks. *(Akron Beacon Journal)*

until it was almost bleeding, while I struggled to hold the tears back and my mother had to leave the room," Litchfield wrote.

Before Litchfield arrived in Akron, on July 15, 1900, he took a month's vacation and sailed three weeks with a friend. "When he landed in Akron," Eddie Thomas said, "he was pretty well bronzed, and he had on a pink shirt. I don't know how that fit in with a conservative New Englander."

That Litchfield ended up in the rubber business, pink-shirted or otherwise, is somewhat remarkable. "It was the last thing I ever expected to go into," he wrote. Two reasons: one, the smell of rubber made him sick; two, he was a man who believed a person should plan his life. Rubber wasn't in his plan. As a chemical engineering student at the Massachusetts Institute of Technology, Litchfield visited twenty-eight industries to which his degree might open a door. He ranked rubber number twenty-eight. Hard times, however, softened his view. When Litchfield graduated, in 1896, a depression gripped America. For six months, he could find only part-time work. Then he landed at the L. C. Chase Company, which made rubber products, including bicycle tires, in Reading, Massachusetts. Litchfield got all the worst jobs—at first, he washed rubber—earning $9 a week. When F. A. Seiberling discovered Litchfield, he was an assistant superintendent of a Chase Company branch factory.

"I don't know whether P. W. Litchfield is aware of it even now," Seiberling would say almost fifty years later, "but I went after him as a collector would go after a rare species of butterfly that suddenly flutters into his presence." Litchfield was the missing component at Goodyear. "We had come to the conclusion," Seiberling said, "that we needed a chemist in our factory just as certainly as we would have wanted a bird dog in the field when hunting. You need a dog's wonderful sense of smell to locate the hidden partridge."

One of Litchfield's main tasks at Goodyear was to instill discipline. Workers were inordinately fond of the company first-aid kit, which included a bottle of whiskey. "I noticed that the calls fell off after I substituted spirits of ammonia," wrote Litchfield, a teetotaler. Then he cut piecework rates by one cent in the bicycle tire department. He believed the rates were so high that workers could take it easy and still earn what they wanted. The workers staged a sit-down strike. Litchfield knew the men were testing the new "Kid Super" from the East. He responded to the strike by cutting the rate another cent per tire. The men grudgingly returned to work. Litchfield also reduced the workday from eleven or twelve hours to eight and gave workers vacations and pensions. But he always would be sorely disappointed that he and labor found it difficult to agree on what was a good day's pay for a good day's work.

Still, he knew how to establish loyalties. Eddie Thomas, who became Litchfield's assistant secretary shortly after joining Goodyear, in 1916, liked to tell how Kid Super broke up the factory poker game. "Everybody in the factory was pretty much accustomed to doing as they pleased . . . ," Thomas said. "The boys used to sneak off and play poker. Finally, Litchfield found they were all off in some room somewhere . . . where they had a little poker game. It was a lot of his key foremen."

"This is the last poker game you're holding here," Litchfield told the foremen. "From now on, we'll play at my house every Friday night."

Litchfield chose Goodyear not for the $2,500 a year starting salary—a salary

only $500 less than F. A. Seiberling's—but because Seiberling was interested in tires. "While I was making tires for the Fifth Avenue Coaches and early automobiles at Chelsea [Massachusetts]," Litchfield wrote, "it came to me that rubber was destined to play a vital part also in transportation."

And transportation—by sea, by land, by air—lighted the fire of a man whose reserve bordered on shyness. In 1901, Litchfield crossed the Atlantic to observe a car race that would test a new kind of tire developed by Goodyear: the "straight-side" tire. It was Goodyear's answer to the Clincher tires that then dominated the market. Goodyear's straight-sides, though, blew out midrace. Litchfield went back to the drawing board. "We had sought strength rather than resiliency," Litchfield wrote. But it was resiliency that would allow the larger straight-side tires to withstand the heat generated by faster driving and the pounding on the roads. "A tire that would not fight the road but would yield and come back. That realization alone was worth many times the cost of the trip."

With the straight-side, Goodyear would rise from obscurity to stake its claim as number one in tires. Litchfield, however, saw opportunity in other transportation, specifically lighter-than-air craft such as balloons and dirigibles. In 1910, Litchfield journeyed overseas again, to air meets at Wolverhampton, England, and Rheims, France. After witnessing his first airplane flights, Litchfield led the redesign of Goodyear's airplane tire. More important, he decided that Goodyear should be in the airship business, too. Back in the States, he hired Ralph Upson from the Stevens Institute of Technology and R. A. D. Preston from MIT and told them to master airship building by beginning with balloons.

Paul Litchfield sits at F.A. Seiberling's left as the Goodyear "Old Guard" holds a luncheon banquet, October 8, 1912, atop the foundations of a smokestack that was the last remnant of the original factory. The "Old Guard" was a group made up of some of the earliest employees of Goodyear. *(Akron Beacon Journal)*

P.W. Litchfield, then factory manager, personally helped build Goodyear's 45 millionth tire in 1922. (Goodyear Tire and Rubber Company)

"Litchfield was a great comfort to Father . . . ," said Irene Seiberling Harrison. "He [Litchfield] had vision, like Father."

But in 1921, Litchfield and Seiberling stopped working together. The New York investment banking firm Dillon, Read and Company took over the financially troubled Goodyear and forced the founder out. Two years later, the firm chose George Stadelman, then head of sales, to become the new president. Soon, however, fate would thrust the presidency upon Litchfield. In the winter of 1925–26, George Stadelman and his wife, Gertrude, were awakened in the bedroom of their home at 732 West Exchange Street, now the Akron Woman's City Club. A man put a gun and flashlight in Stadelman's face. "It was a cold winter," Eddie Thomas remembered. "[The intruders] left the windows open. It was freezing. They ordered Stadelman to open the safe in his room, and he didn't know how. They thought he was bluffing and threatened to kill him." Stadelman's wife managed to open the safe, and the men fled, but they left wreckage in their wake. "That whole experience," Thomas said, "was a terrible shock and Stadelman wasn't a strong man physically anyway. He went downhill. . . ."

On January 22, 1926, at age fifty-three, George Stadelman died. To Thomas and those who knew Goodyear best, it seemed this sad opportunity could be meant for only one man. "There was no other consideration by the board," Thomas said, "except that Mr. Litchfield would be president."

By the time of his ascension, Litchfield had already launched what he considered to be among his greatest initiatives: Goodyear's Industrial Assembly to foster good labor-management relations, and the Goodyear-Zeppelin company to promote the airship industry. Ironically, these initiatives would also would lead to Litchfield's greatest disappointments.

Litchfield established the Industrial Assembly in 1919. The organization was modeled after the U.S. form of government. Workers elected representatives to two houses, and Litchfield had veto power. "The Industrial Assembly," concluded historian Daniel Nelson, "was not a toothless company union: During the 1920s it gradually expanded its activities to include potentially sensitive subjects such as wages and hours. In 1926, it struck for a week to reinforce its demand for higher wages. . . . Like other Akron employers, Litchfield was strongly anti-union; yet unlike many others, he recognized the importance of the individual worker in mass production."

The Industrial Assembly became irrelevant during the nationwide labor unrest of the Depression era. The United Rubber Workers gained recognition at Goodyear, in 1936, though the union did not win its first contract until 1941. But the Industrial Assembly dissolved in 1937; it was considered an illegal company union under terms of the National Labor Relations Act.

For years, Litchfield had dreamed of filling the sky with an aerial armada of huge passenger-carrying airships, "the heavens filled with commerce, argosies of magic sails." And in 1924, Litchfield had the opportunity to craft imagination into reality. Goodyear had supplied roughly a thousand balloons and 100 nonrigid airships to the Allies during World War I, building the Wingfoot Lake air station in Portage County in the process. But those were just models for a greater plan. Litchfield envisioned the massive, rigid zeppelin crafts—far larger than nonrigid blimps—as yachts of the air.

A postwar ban on German airship building left some of the world's great minds adrift in the ether. The U.S. Navy found a way to reel them in. An agreement was made with the German Zeppelin company to give its technology to the Americans. Goodyear won the contract. The company would inherit men and ideas. Zeppelin, in return, would receive a third of the profits. And so, in late October 1924, Ernst Lehmann, one of the greatest airship pilots of the recent world war, arrived in Akron from Germany to help launch the Goodyear-Zeppelin company. He would soon be joined by some of the greatest architects of the imagination the world had known.

Three days before Thanksgiving that year, thirteen engineers arrived in Akron from Friedrichshafen, Germany. The twelve disciples of Zeppelin, as they were called, were brought here as part of Litchfield's grand plan. Their leader was Dr. Karl Arnstein, a native of Prague, a quiet, scholarly man with a rare eye for beauty in function. He had been chief engineer of the Zeppelin company; now he would be at the forefront of Goodyear-Zeppelin. The disciples, having arrived by sea, took a train to Akron. The men, whose families had stayed behind until spring, looked at one another, anticipation and trepidation in their hearts. They had worked together for the Zeppelin company in Friedrichshafen. At home, many of them were heroes. But Akron was a strange, new place.

Their new landscape was brick and steel, with a pungent smell above the factories. In the small town of Friedrichshafen, one could look out the window at Lake Constance and see the Swiss mountains beyond. Here, there were smokestacks. As the train slowed, the men watched from their windows. Word of their arrival had spread through Akron's tightly knit German community, and a crowd had formed. The disciples buttoned their coats, gathered their belongings, and began to disembark to a hero's welcome. Arnstein and the other twelve dropped off their luggage at the Portage Hotel and headed straight for the Goodyear plant. There, they met with Lehmann, their old colleague, and Litchfield, their new one. Arnstein and Lehmann had been named vice presidents of the new Goodyear-Zeppelin Corporation.

"I am certain that the lighter-than-air craft industry of the world will be centered in America," Arnstein said in carefully measured English the day of his arrival. "You have here all the best conditions for dirigible manufacture—capital engineering talent and a favorable public spirit. I hope to make America my home forever."

For Arnstein, then thirty-seven, this was a return to glory. One of Europe's finest engineers, he had designed the bridge at Langwies in the Swiss Alps, a marvel arching between two mountain peaks. When the war broke out, he was pressed into service and assigned to build airships for the Zeppelin company, originator of the dirigible. He soon rose to chief engineer. An avid collector of fine art, Arnstein saw his mission beyond the lines on the blueprints. The dirigibles were the pyramids of his time, monuments to beauty and form.

Training balloons sit outside Goodyear's airdock at Wing-foot Lake in 1917. Litchfield saw opportunity in forms of transportation other than tires, particularly in lighter-than-air craft. (*Akron Beacon Journal*)

Hugo Eckener, center with cigar, head of Germany's Zeppelin Works, in October 1929, with Goodyear president P.W. Litchfield, left with hat in hand, and Dr. Karl Arnstein, head of Goodyear-Zeppelin. (Goodyear Tire and Rubber Company)

While they felt welcome in their new home, the men found their own friendship to be a precious commodity. Strangers in a strange land, they stuck close together. Some of the bachelors took up residence in an apartment building on West Exchange Street, where they quickly discovered an unusual pastime—watching through binoculars the comings and goings at the house of ill repute across the street. Yet to be joined by their families, the disciples spent their first Christmas together, sharing wine and song and memories of Germany. The event was the foundation of a bond that would last several years, as the group gathered regularly.

But, while most of the disciples found that their new situation suited them, Lehmann, the popular vice president who had preceded the disciples, did not. He returned to Germany in 1927. His personal mission had been to prove to Americans that lighter-than-air was the future of commercial travel, a goal shared by Litchfield. But as Goodyear-Zeppelin got under way, Lehmann became frustrated by the lack of financial support from the government. The ban against German airship building was over; he saw possibilities back in his homeland. Upon his departure, he said: "Perhaps the huge ship I hope to help build in Germany, and then to fly, will convince the United States of the possibilities of the air."

Steel framing shapes the Goodyear Airdock as it goes up in 1929. The building was known as Plant A in the Goodyear Aircraft days. Today, the airdock is owned by Lockheed Martin Tactical Defense Systems, which continues to seek blimp or balloon business that would reinflate the lighter-than-air industry. (*Akron Beacon Journal*)

Those words would later haunt those who had known Lehmann.

The rest of the engineers remained optimistic. Arnstein oversaw the construction at Akron Municipal Airport of the Goodyear Airdock, at the time the largest structure in the world without interior supports. Kurt Bauch designed the massive doors, still referred to as "Bauch doors." They all poured their expertise into the design of the world's largest zeppelin, to be named *Akron.* The great ship, 785 feet long and 146 feet tall, would carry more than passengers and cargo. She would carry hope. But rigid airships had their critics. Some European crafts had crashed, others had exploded; one a year had gone down from 1920 to 1924. Detractors called them suicide devices. American airships were safer, proponents argued, especially because they were filled, not with flammable hydrogen, but with helium, a gas available only in America. But the *Shenandoah*, America's first rigid airship, crashed in 1925 in a storm over southern Ohio, leaving the air full of doubt.

Litchfield stuck to his mission, backed by powerful support from President Herbert Hoover and Rear Admiral W. A. Moffett. On August 8, 1931, the *Akron* was christened when first lady Lou Henry Hoover released forty-eight doves into the sky. Amelia Earhart was among the honored guests in Akron. On October 21, throngs of Akronites looked to the sky as the ship left her hangar for the voyage to her base in Lakehurst, New Jersey. The great ship lifted, then dipped in salute to the people who had given her birth. Her departure opened the hangar for con-

struction of a sister ship, to be dubbed the *Macon*. Hopes soared; the sky was the limit. The great black airdock in southeastern Akron buzzed with activity as work continued on the *Macon*, and the *Akron*, the largest craft ever to fly, gave wings to the imagination.

Then, on April 4, 1933, with the *Macon* less than a month from her christening, the dreams fell from the sky—the *Akron* crashed in a wicked electrical storm off the New Jersey coast. Among the seventy-three dead was Rear Adm. Moffett, one of the airship's greatest proponents. With pessimism growing, the *Macon* was perhaps the last vessel of hope. In April 1933, she was launched, a reporter wrote, "with understanding born of tragedy." Two years later, she crashed and sank to the bottom of the Pacific Ocean. Two men died in the accident, and so did the dreams of Karl Arnstein and Paul Litchfield.

The navy had yet to build a successful rigid airship. Debate swirled in the aftermath of the tragedies, but the future of America's zeppelin production looked bleak. The Germans, meanwhile, continued in their quest to make the ships a viable form of air travel. Their *Hindenburg*, with a Nazi swastika on her tail, had become a luxury liner, soaring across the ocean with a cabin full of celebrities, millionaires, and dignitaries. Litchfield was one of the privileged few, late in 1936. But her fabled end brought an end to all hope of passenger travel by airship. On May 6, 1937, the world would listen in horror as NBC radio announcer Herb Morrison, at Lakehurst, New Jersey, where the ship was about to land, could find

Workers begin to cover the duralumin frame of the USS *Macon* as the dirigible takes shape inside the Goodyear Airdock in May 1932. Sister ship to Goodyear's *Akron*, the *Macon* met a similar fate, crashing in 1935 to the bottom of the Pacific Ocean, killing two crewmen. (Goodyear Tire and Rubber Company)

only three words to describe the colossal fire that suddenly filled the sky: "Oh, the humanity!" Passengers and crew burned to death; others were killed when they tried to jump from the cabin. One of the Nazis' greatest zeppelin pilots, the man who had been at command when the ship exploded, stumbled, dazed, from the wreckage, cloaked in flames.

It was Ernst Lehmann, Akron's "little captain." He would die the next day.

The *Hindenburg* disaster disturbed Litchfield almost as much as if it had been a Goodyear failure. The incident even came up subtly at a dinner party one night at Litchfield's Merriman Road home, the Anchorage. In the absence of Litchfield's wife, Florence, who was in Arizona, daughter Katharine Hyde played hostess to guests of honor who were aeronautical luminaries. The great German airship, the *Graf Zeppelin*, was visiting Akron. Dr. Hugo Eckener, head of Germany's Zeppelin Works, and Lord Trenchard, British air marshal during World War I, were guests. "One was on my right," Mrs. Hyde said, "and one was on my left. Of course, they had been deadly enemies during the First World War. When the cigars were passed around at the end of the meal, they each took one. As Dr. Eckener lighted his, he looked at the cigar and said: 'It's shaped like a zeppelin.'"

Lord Trenchard looked at his old enemy.

"Yes," he said, holding his cigar, "and it burns like one."

Paul Litchfield waves from the gondola of the blimp *Mayflower* in August 1930. (Goodyear Tire and Rubber Company)

P. W. Litchfield's fingerprints can be found on every inch of Goodyear's businesses. He placed Goodyear's first domestic factory outside Akron in Los Angeles. He and F. A. Seiberling built Goodyear Hall for the recreational and educational use of employees. Litchfield solved, at least in part, a shortage of cotton from Egypt by buying desert land near Phoenix so Goodyear could grow its own. He directed the development of the Supertwist cord, which gave Goodyear tires improved resiliency. He advocated that other industries follow Goodyear's lead during the Depression with six-hour shifts that enabled more people to work. "Management did that over the [Industrial Assembly's] objections," Eddie Thomas said, "and later regretted it." After the Depression, retention of the six-hour day became a union rallying point in negotiations up to the day most Akron tire shops closed.

Over time, Litchfield even became accustomed to rubber's stench. He wrote, in 1954, when the factories still pulsated: "I have not been conscious of the smell of rubber for thirty years."

8 Hometown Heroes

EDDIE THOMAS didn't break the mold; he made it. Rising from a modest east Akron neighborhood to claim the most important office on the Goodyear Tire and Rubber Company's mahogany row, Thomas established an Akron pattern. For forty-three years, a hometown boy ran the world's largest rubber company as either president or chairman of the board. The tradition began in 1940, when Paul W. Litchfield guided Thomas' election as Goodyear's eighth president. Russell DeYoung succeeded Thomas as chairman, and Charles J. Pilliod took over from DeYoung. Even when this remarkable run by local talent ended, in 1983, Goodyear continued its tradition of promoting its leaders from within.

Pilliod espoused the Goodyear philosophy this way: "I never believed in professional management running from business to business. I think you develop your own."

Goodyear's own was Akron's own. And as much as any reason, it is why Goodyear's headquarters remains here while Goodrich, Firestone, General, or their latent corporate embodiments have moved to the South. When Goodyear's leaders could choose Akron for projects without consequences that affected stockholders, they did so. The O'Neils and Firestones ran General Tire and Firestone Tire and Rubber for years, but market conditions and foreign interests broke those family dynasties. Goodrich's Akron ties were loosened much earlier by one of its own. Bertram G. Work, the son of an early Goodrich manager, moved company headquarters to New York City when he became president in 1907.

Thomas would not have launched the remarkable hometown run, however, had his predecessor and mentor, Litchfield, made different choices, in 1921, during a meeting with Goodyear President Edward G. Wilmer. Wilmer was an outsider, a financial expert installed by the New York bankers who took control of Goodyear in 1921. "He didn't know a tire from a doughnut," Thomas said. Litchfield was not an Akron native, but he had been with Goodyear since 1900, two years after its founding. As he entered Wilmer's office, Litchfield was concerned about his future under the new management as well as Goodyear's ability to recover from its financial difficulties. He was thinking about forming his own tire company. "I would have followed Litchfield, as would six or eight other Goodyear men," Thomas said.

But Wilmer's meeting with Litchfield was conciliatory. "I'm not familiar, as you men are, with the rubber business," Wilmer told Litchfield. "There has never been anything wrong with Goodyear's manufacturing and selling. You men continue to run these affairs. I, as president, will back you in what you want to do and see that the money is available." Litchfield left and called his group together. "Our future," Litchfield said, "is at Goodyear."

∽

Among the many stories about Eddie Thomas, there is one in his unpublished 1981 memoir that reaches the core of both the man and his success. Thomas had been sent to Los Angeles to run Goodyear's factory there, its first U.S. plant outside Akron. He succeeded Harry Blythe as general superintendent.

"There was one division superintendent whom Blythe wanted to discharge before he left for Akron, but I told him this man was now my responsibility," Thomas wrote. Thomas called the man in and told him what Blythe had perceived his weaknesses to be. Then Thomas suggested they "wipe the slate clean and that he try to overcome his difficulties." The man's performance improved. Then, just as suddenly, he reverted to his previous unproductive ways. Thomas had to fire the man. It was the first time he'd ever had to dismiss anyone.

"We did, however, remain friends and played some golf together," Thomas said.

"I do not know of anyone," Litchfield said, "who went up as fast without making bad friends along the way."

Jean Mercer, the daughter of Eddie and Mildred Thomas, said her father's working-class background prepared him to get along with people from all levels of industry and society. Thomas was born in a small frame house at 937 Johnston Street. He described the neighborhood as "made up of decent hard-working people, with no hunger or poverty, but no abundant riches." Eddie's father, Richard, a postal worker, was "a fine, jolly, even-tempered, hard-working, religious man seldom angered." Eddie's mother, Nettie, meted out the discipline. The Thomases attended the Grace M.E. Church, where Richard Thomas served as a lay official.

Eddie Thomas sits on a lumber pile during his growing-up days on Akron's east side. A talented piano player, Thomas also lettered in basketball and track at Central High. *(Akron Beacon Journal)*

The Thomases didn't drink, smoke, play cards, or dance. "Yet our home was not an oppressive place," Thomas wrote.

When Eddie Thomas was young, the toilet was in the back yard. He ran barefoot from the day school ended until the day it began again in the fall, playing beneath arc lights at the corners of dusty, unpaved streets. He roamed nearby woods and claybeds. "One of the old claybeds was a dump," Thomas said, "and we spent many a day there shooting rats and searching for scrap metals to sell to Jakie Wolf, the scrap merchant who lived at the top of Johnston Street hill." The best dump, however, belonged to Goodyear. In it, Eddie and his buddies would occasionally find the rarest of treasures: a ball of discarded Brazilian rubber.

That was only a part of his practical east Akron training. To raise money to buy baseball uniforms for their team, the Nationals, Thomas and the other boys went into business. The boys cleaned out an abandoned shed near a marble factory and converted it into a candy store. The boys' mothers made the candy. Thomas became bookkeeper and banker. Their best customers were young women from the marble factory. "It was in this connection, that I learned early about extending credit," Thomas said. Though most of the women paid faithfully, a few didn't. They are, Thomas said in his memoir, "still on the books."

In high school, Thomas earned letters in basketball and track but was even more talented at the piano. From the time he was ten or eleven, his mother made him practice while his friends shouted outside for Eddie to come out and play ball. He became skillful enough to play in the high school orchestra and give lessons for fifty cents an hour to neighborhood children.

Much of Thomas' grittier education occurred away from the classroom, athletic field, and recital halls. He hung out with the guys at the Wilson and Hawkins Cigar Store and Pool Room and learned to dance at Roberts Dancing Academy on Case Avenue. "My parents would never have approved of such 'goings on,'" Thomas said. "I am sure they learned of it, but they never spoke to me about it."

Young Eddie was a teenager when he met the man who would become his boss and benefactor, Litchfield. It was an inauspicious encounter at a Boy Scout lodge that Goodyear was building for the sons of employees. "I went over there one day during the noon hour to see how the building was progressing," Litchfield said, "and got to talking with a fifteen-year-old youngster who had ridden over on his bicycle on the same errand. This was my first meeting with E. J. Thomas."

At Central High School, Thomas began learning most of the commercial skills that would lead him to Goodyear's top job. On the first day of classes in 1912, Thomas was sitting with three or four other boys on the rail fence across from the school. They had to decide what course of study they would pursue. Among the choices were manual training and a commercial course, which included shorthand, typing, commercial law, English, math, and a foreign language. "When one of the boys said he had heard the commercial course was the easiest," Thomas said, "that was what we decided to sign up for."

Shortly before Eddie Thomas earned his diploma, in 1916, K. M. Johnson, Central's commercial teacher, recommended Thomas for a job at Goodyear. Thomas was hired as a clerk for $25 a month, part time, until the school year ended, and $50 a month thereafter. Thomas did so well that, in 1917, chief chemist C. R. Johnson recommended him for an opening as assistant secretary to Litchfield, the head of production. In that role, Thomas gained a breadth of experience, often at his own initiative. With Litchfield's approval, Thomas would end his office workday, go to the Goodyear gatehouse and buy a box lunch, change to work clothes, and head over to the factory. "For two years, I worked every night," Thomas said. "I built tires. I ran mills. I ran tube machines. I did everything and learned all about how things were done."

Eddie Thomas and his wife, Mildred, with their children Jean and Richard on shipboard. Thomas was then managing director of Goodyear England, a job that broadened his production experience to include finance and sales.
(*Akron Beacon Journal*)

In 1918, near the end of World War I, Thomas left Goodyear to join the Army. When only months later peace came and Thomas was discharged, he rejoined Litchfield. "I have always preferred men secretaries, thinking that contact with the things that went through my office would be good training in business for anyone who could absorb it," Litchfield explained in his writings. "Thomas used the opportunity to good advantage. . . . He did not tell me about this until long afterward, but it seems that when a problem would come up in my absence, he would try to figure out what my decision would be, and for what reasons. It became sort of a game with him, and one more useful than crossword puzzles. When he guessed wrong, he would try to think out why, and sometimes asked me. However, as time went on, he found himself guessing right a good many times, so finally he got up his courage to make tentative rulings himself when something was really urgent."

In 1922, Thomas became Litchfield's assistant rather than his secretary. When Thomas was twenty-nine, he was running Goodyear's Los Angeles plant, and by thir-

Goodyear president E.J. Thomas, right, dons work gloves and personally assists employees in lifting out of its mold the 600 millionth tire built by the firm. The giant earth-mover type tire is used for heavy construction vehicles. (*Akron Beacon Journal*)

ty-six, he was managing director of Goodyear England, a job that broadened his production experience to include finance and sales. When he returned to Akron from California, in 1932, with his star on the rise, Thomas received an offer from another Akron rubber company. Now an assistant vice president and in charge of production at Goodyear, Thomas was intrigued. The other company was offering a fancier title and more money. He went to Litchfield.

"Mr. Litchfield," Thomas said, "I have an offer from another rubber company and I'd like to talk to you about it."

The conversation was brief.

"Any time you think you would be better off someplace else than you are here," Litchfield said, "the thing for you to do is go."

Thomas went for advice to Bill Stephens, Goodyear's general superintendent, whom everyone called Steve. Thomas told him of the offer.

"Yeah, yeah, I know," Stephens said. "What are you going to do?"

"Well, Steve, I guess I'll stay here."

"I think that's right," Stephens said.

"But you said you knew about the offer. How'd you know?"

"I recommended you."

"Do you think I ought to leave?"

"No, I thought you'd make the right decision and stay here. But let me tell you, kid, they'll think a lot more of you around here now."

And Goodyear did. Thomas had value beyond East Market Street. So, in 1940, when Litchfield reached age sixty-five and wanted to eliminate some of his corporate duties, the presidency went to Thomas. He was forty-one.

"Someone was looking after me in making these decisions," Thomas said years later. "If any of those had gone the other way, I never would have been president."

At almost the same time Eddie Thomas became president of Goodyear, across town on Firestone Parkway, John W. Thomas was moving up from president to chairman of the board at Firestone. Though not related, the Thomases shared a homeboy heritage. J.W. Thomas was a blue-eyed farm boy from nearby Tallmadge. From the start, J. W. Thomas was on a more obvious track to the top. J. W. graduated from Buchtel College, in 1908, and was hired by Harvey Firestone to set up the first chemistry lab at the burgeoning Firestone Tire and Rubber Company. Very quickly, J. W. Thomas became Harvey Sr.'s right-hand man, the one who made key decisions. "The most powerful guy in those days, in my view," concluded Akron historian and Firestone alumnus Jack Gieck, "was not Harvey Firestone but J. W. Thomas." Retired Firestone executive John Moore, who served under Thomas, concurred: "He was a colossal, tremendous leader. Firestone became great because J. W. was great."

J. W. and Eddie were equally well-matched on the golf course at such places as Portage Country Club. Eddie regularly won father-son club championships with

Akron native John W. Thomas, center, with Leonard Firestone, right, and Harvey Firestone, Jr., left, in a photograph that hearkens back to Thomas's days in the chemistry department he was hired to set up by Harvey Firestone. A graduate of Buchtel College, in 1908, Thomas was moving up to chairman of the board at Firestone around the time Eddie Thomas was named president of Goodyear. (*Akron Beacon Journal*)

Eddie Thomas gestures during an interview in his home in 1984. The Akron native rose at Goodyear from a part-time clerk while still in high school to president at age forty-one. His career spanned more than fifty years. (*Akron Beacon Journal*/Marcy Nighswander)

the considerable help of his son, Richard; J. W. was considered one of the better golfers among Akron's executive elite. Portage, with the opening of its new club-house on Memorial Day weekend 1923, became not only the gathering place for the great captains of the rubber industry—the Firestones, Seiberlings, Goodrichs, and O'Neils—but also for lieutenants and successors. The talk they made in the clubhouse would influence the future of rubber. Long into the night, the spirit of the industry would be bent through the prism of a brandy snifter on the clubhouse bar, floating on the smoke of a sublime cigar.

In the front office at Goodyear and in the smoky private club backrooms, Eddie Thomas groomed his designated successor, hometown boy Russ DeYoung. And from DeYoung came his successor, hometown boy Chuck Pilliod. Both De-Young and Pilliod presided over a Goodyear torn by labor strife and plant closings and threatened by European radial superiority. Pilliod, the first president and board chairman from Goodyear's international side, strengthened the company's bond to Akron, even as he closed Plant 2 in 1978. Goodyear's last tire plant in Akron became the Goodyear Technical Center, and the company built a tire test track across the street. When Pilliod announced that decision, the retired Eddie Thomas thought of all the strikes and plant closings, and said: "All we've had for so long is negative. Now we've got something really positive . . . and I love it."

Despite Akron's loss of production jobs, Pilliod said he hoped that Goodyear's decision regarding the Technical Center would serve as a signal that "Akron is the Rubber Capital of the World, and we're going to keep it that way." He also had the offices refurbished, which additionally cemented Goodyear's bond to Akron. "We felt we put it in a position that Goodyear would never move," Pilliod said. "So we accomplished our purpose."

This sense of purpose can be traced to Eddie Thomas. "He grew up here, same as Russ and I," Pilliod said. "A lot of workers went to school with him."

Eddie Thomas was president of Goodyear for seventeen years, longer than any other man, and was chairman of the board for another seven years. Under his leadership, Goodyear survived a takeover by the navy during World War II, expanded its influence in the air, made the transition into use of synthetic rubber, agreed to the first companywide contract with the United Rubber Workers, and kept Goodyear in its position of sales leadership. Most of all, he promoted the Goodyear Spirit by maintaining contact with the workers. "You have to subject yourself to constant exposure," Thomas said. "Don't lock yourself up in a tower somewhere and not be easily seen." On days when work went wrong and he felt low, Eddie Thomas knew what to do. "I'd just shut my desk," he said, "and I'd walk out through the office and factory and talk to everybody in sight. I always came back believing in what we could do."

Shortly after Thomas returned from Goodyear England, in 1936, workers struck to establish the URW. Litchfield sent Thomas and personnel manager Fred Climer out of the strikebound plant to join attorney Lisle Buckingham in negotiations. Times were tense. "There was a policeman at our house all the time," said his daughter, Jean Mercer, who was seven years old then. "I don't remember it, but I know he was there, outside." The police even changed the license plates on the Thomas car. Just in case. But nothing bad happened to Eddie Thomas, who died December 30, 1986. Not at Goodyear. Not in Akron.

"He had Akron at heart in most everything he did," said Jean Mercer. "He was the *real* hometown boy. I don't see his sort of history happening anymore."

9 Rubber Workers Unite

MORE THAN THE REST of the men, John D. House felt the raw hurt of the cold that Monday night in 1936 as he climbed the stairs to the room above the east Akron pool hall.

It was February 17. The mercury curled up in its little ball. Thirteen degrees. White knobs of ice formed at the edges of the Little Cuyahoga River. John House's ears warmed as he entered a room hot with talk, with anger, with anticipation. More than one thousand men were gathered in the headquarters of the United Rubber Workers Local 2, the newly formed union of Goodyear's factory workers. House was their president.

Trouble was on the agenda, and House didn't know whether he would lead his troops into it or out of it. Some of the men had stopped working on Friday, three days earlier. They had sat down at their machines and refused to build tires. They were trying to protect their coworkers and, ultimately, themselves. The company had posted layoff notices for seventy workers. Goodyear wanted to reinstate the eight-hour day, meaning fewer people would be needed to produce the same number of tires. It was an ironic stab at takeback: Earlier in this decade of economic

A sign during the 1913 rubber industry strike leads people to the Industrial Workers of the World (IWW) or "Wobblies" relief dining room. The strike began after the introduction of machinery that made tires easier to build and resulted in lower piece rates for the workers. After five weeks of striking, the workers had made no gains and never managed to shut down the rubber companies. (The University of Akron Archives)

pain, the company had started the six-hour shift on the theory that more people would remain employed. The men feared that with a return to the longer work-day, they would lose money and have to speed up production. By one estimate, a tire builder making $122 a month on the six-hour shift would make just $125 a month on an eight-hour day.

As House took his seat at the front of the room, he was burdened with not only the immediate turmoil, but also with a deadweight economy. The Depression had worn away the good feelings and prosperity that had flourished in the first two decades of the century. In 1932, the trough of the Depression, Akron's industrial unemployment rate hit a staggering 60 percent. The national economy, with unemployment of 23.6 percent, looked robust by comparison.

That same year, Goodyear posted an $850,000 loss, its first in more than a decade. (B. F. Goodrich declared a $6.9 million loss, its third straight annual loss. Firestone weathered the economic storm rather well, showing a $5 million profit.) Meanwhile, industry overcapacity had given rise to vicious price wars. "Akron was particularly vulnerable to this cutthroat competition," Litchfield wrote in his memoir, *Industrial Voyage: My Life as an Industrial Lieutenant*, "since it paid the highest wage in the industry, ranging up to 50 percent higher than that paid in some places."

Goodyear consistently recorded profits in the years after, but, in 1936, Litchfield was still looking for ways to keep costs down. Goodyear had fired the 137 tire builders who sat down at their machines, and additional layoffs were threatened, igniting tensions further. Fighting words bounced off the walls of the union hall. John House called for reason. Sure, management had turned him down when he asked for a meeting to discuss the issue. He was angry, too. But he did not want to be the president of a mob.

House was an ordinary man dealing with extraordinary circumstances. Like so many before, he had traveled from the South for a job in Akron. When the seventeen-year-old Georgian stepped off the train, in 1922, the first thing he saw was a huge billboard: "Welcome to Akron, City of Opportunity." A succession of jobs took him from B. F. Goodrich to Firestone to Goodyear, giving him an intense education in the workings of the industry. By the time House became a union official, in 1933, he had developed a strong sense of fairness. He wasn't a radical—he was shunned by Goodyear's small Communist element. He believed in working to change the system from within.

The angry talk he was hearing this night threatened his own intention: to work within the rules, take a strike vote, and maintain a dialogue with the company. "I was scared and wanted to suggest to the meeting that we postpone the establishment of a picket line and try again to set up a meeting with management," he wrote later.

He never got the chance. Cibert "Skip" O'Harrah, a member of the union's executive board, jumped onto the table. He grabbed the American flag from the speakers' platform and tossed the match into the powder keg.

"Come on, boys! Let's go!" he shouted.

A cheer tore through the room. With O'Harrah at the lead, the men stormed down the stairs to East Market Street. Above them loomed the brick walls of the Goodyear complex. Above that hovered the black, snow-filled sky and a cold moon. Winter whipped the faces of the men as they moved up the street toward Plant 2, but something primal burned inside them. This was revolution.

House moved through the confusion of bodies. He tried to call for order. This was not what he had wanted. His breath quickening, desperate to stay in control, he put his arms around a lamppost and shimmied up. Below him, the men were falling into haphazard formation around Plant 2. Workers began to join them from inside the factory. A picket line was forming. House could only watch.

Shortly after 11:00 P.M., the strikers formed human blockades in front of the factory entrances. Coal fires were lighted in big metal drums. As the flames lapped at the frigid air, cars pulled up. Men got out and joined the line. The midnight shift arrived. Some joined the pickets. The rest went home. The temperature dropped lower and lower, toward zero and below. Singing rang in the sky: "The picket line goes 'round and 'round. . . ."

By the time dawn broke, five hundred bundled-up forms surrounded the buildings.

❧

For a day, Paul Litchfield stewed. The president of Goodyear was furious at the prospect of mutiny. That first day, the company released a statement that began, "We do not know what the men are striking for." Litchfield was convinced the

A week into their 1936 Goodyear strike, United Rubber Workers members at a picket post on Kelly Avenue, nicknamed House of David, show off a week's growth after vowing not to shave or have their hair cut until the strike ended. *(Akron Beacon Journal)*

picket lines were dominated by outside union agitators and Communists. He was convinced that Goodyear's employees were being prevented from doing what they really wanted to do: work. And so, with the strike thirty hours old, he arrived at the factory gates at 5:30 Wednesday morning.

A tall man with a thick neck, Litchfield had grown into an imposing figure. But he was hardly the brawler to muscle his way through a throng of ruffians. Still, these were desperate times. With his coat buttoned up tight and a hat above his high forehead, he pushed through the strikers in the predawn and stood before the gate. He demanded that the first-shift workers be allowed in, demanded that the police, who were out in force, help him. In the end, he went in alone.

Around him were idle machines and workers. About a thousand men and women had stayed inside to work—not very many in a place that employed sixteen thousand. A man could feel lonely in there, especially when he was surrounded by the potential wreckage of his life's work. In 1919, Litchfield had formed a union of his own, the progressive, company-sponsored Industrial Assembly. Even with the rapid unionization of the rubber industry by organized labor, Goodyear's Industrial Assembly had succeeded and was lauded as one of the best-designed company unions in American industry.

But the Industrial Assembly took worker empowerment only so far. The company ultimately could decide what to do with its workers. And it was becoming increasingly difficult to keep them from forming a union of their own. In 1933, workers won the right to organize with passage of the National Industrial Recovery Act. The act, an attempt to boost the economy from the depths of the Depression, included a number of worker-friendly codes. Small rubber unions had existed through the years under the umbrella of the American Federation of Labor, but there was no industrywide organization. The NIRA changed that.

American industrial workers were growing up, and, in their adolescence, they were developing a sense of independence, often rebelling to express it. It was in that context that a convention was held in Akron in 1935. In the Portage Hotel, at the crossroads of downtown, an important block was laid in the foundation of the Rubber Capital. The United Rubber Workers of America was formed. The birth was not an easy one—proponents of a rubber union had tangled with the hard-nosed organizers of the AFL, who were pushing for divisions along trade lines. The argument was raucous, but, when the dust cleared, the URW was born.

Industrial workers in those days, though, were often split on the issue of union loyalty. The initial excitement surrounding the union's formation fell off, and so did membership. In 1933, twenty-five thousand Akron rubber workers were AFL union members. Although rubber workers remained affiliated with other unions, by late 1935 URW membership in the U.S. had plummeted to less than four thousand. This strike against Goodyear could make or break the URW, just as it could make or break Litchfield's Industrial Assembly.

Now inside his factory, Litchfield dug in. The couch in the room adjoining his private office became his bed. He would remain holed up in the plant for twelve days. He oversaw the minimized plant operations, addressed the press, and took to the radio airwaves. "Approximately sixteen thousand employees have been forcibly prevented from engaging in their usual occupations," he said over the airwaves, "by a group of men violating the laws of city and state."

Litchfield refused to negotiate with striking workers; federal mediators entered the scene to close the gap between the two sides. Three days after the strike began, federal mediator P. W. Chappell speculated on its effect on Litchfield: "I imagine this has broken the old man's heart."

Litchfield was not alone inside the plant. The boisterous ranks outside suggested otherwise, but there were Goodyear workers who disagreed with the union. They wanted to keep working. Albert J. Lucas showed up for his six-to-midnight shift the night the strike began. He had heard the rumblings, and when he arrived at the Plant 2 gate, the guard warned him there could be trouble.

"Let 'em strike," he shot back.

Under the most unusual circumstances, he was reporting for work. Before Lucas's shift ended that night, he became a virtual prisoner in the plant. He would spend the next five weeks inside. "I was young, wasn't married. So I thought, I'll

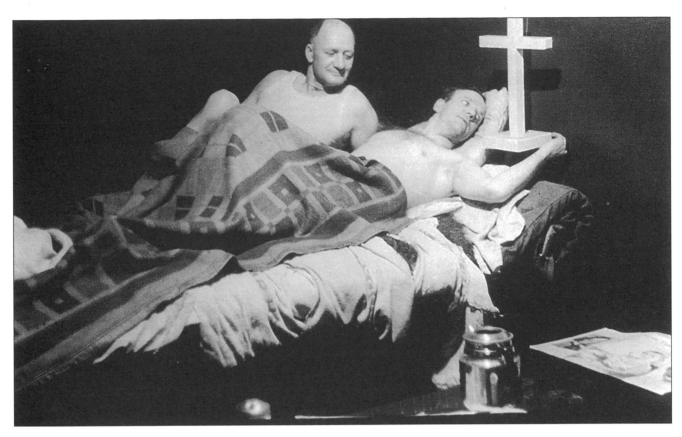

During the 1936 strike at Goodyear, many employees never left the headquarters building and found themselves doubling-up in makeshift beds. A skeleton staff helped the plant continue some semblance of operation. (Goodyear Tire and Rubber Company)

see if I can get in, and I'll stay in. I got in," Lucas recalled. "Well, I was called a scab a couple hundred times."

With a skeleton staff, the plant continued some semblance of operation. Truth being the first casualty of labor war, reports of the number inside ranged from seven hundred to more than a thousand, depending on the source. Some got in by rushing the gates whenever they cracked open; others posed as office workers, who occasionally were allowed to cross the line. Still others climbed fences. Once inside, they were able to fashion a sort of lifestyle. Workers—most of them men—slept on cots, many right next to their machines. There were showers and food and coal for heat. The workers passed the idle hours playing bridge and a card game called tong. Precious few tires got built. "After awhile, you realized you were making the money," Lucas said. "The other guys weren't making [any]. You kind of enjoyed it. I was working in the cafeteria and getting all the food I wanted to eat—ice cream, cakes."

The strike lasted nearly five weeks. Men warmed themselves around barrels and erected shanties with names such as Camp Roosevelt, John L. Lewis Post, and House of David. Those stationed at the latter declined to shave until the strike ended. The kitchen at the union hall was supplied by sympathetic farmers and butchers and staffed by wives and friends. Coffee fueled the strikers.

Men wielded baseball bats, some bats doctored with wooden spikes or razor blades; others carried bowling pins or sawed-off cue sticks. After a judge issued an order against mass picketing, police threatened to form a human wedge to drive their way through the strikers. The police backed off at the last moment. A skir-

Members of the six-month-old United Rubber Workers and their supporters cheer the end of the month-long strike against Goodyear on March 23, 1936. *(Akron Beacon Journal)*

mish broke out when sanitation workers and police tried to remove strikers' shanties. But deadly violence—the kind that happened in other strikes in other cities—never exploded.

With the aid of the outside mediators, the strike finally ended on March 21. The company agreed to maintain the six-hour day and the thirty-six-hour workweek, an arrangement that ended, for the most part, only with the closing of Akron plants in the 1970s. The company agreed to meet with union representatives on the behalf of employees. And it agreed to allow all employees to return to work "without discrimination." The union gave up its demands that the Industrial Assembly be abolished and that the company sign a contract with the union. Instead, an agreement was drawn up; Local 2 would not have a formal contract with Goodyear until 1941.

But the URW claimed victory, having kept the plant idle for more than a month and having established itself as a force that quickly would rise to dominance, particularly once company unions such as the Industrial Assembly were outlawed by the National Labor Relations Act in 1937. URW international membership rose sharply after the strike, reaching forty thousand by September 1936, a tenfold increase from a year earlier.

In the heat of the moment, none of the principals seemed to realize the significance of the strike. The Rubber City was fast becoming known as Strike City. Walkouts would continue into the 1940s and beyond. Akron's reputation as a hot labor town became a source of pride for some unionists and a source of anger for many company leaders.

For more than half of this century, the URW was an Akron institution, one that stood as proud as the big rubber companies and directed more lives than any one of those companies. It was a group that intimately reflected the rise and fall of the industry, that produced some of its most

An Akron police officer fires a repeating tear gas gun in front of Goodyear's main gate during the 1938 URW strike. *(Akron Beacon Journal)*

flamboyant characters, and that defined the tough blue-collar character of places such as Kenmore, Goodyear Heights, and Firestone Park. Its members filled bowling leagues and diners and shabby little bars.

Even as tire companies moved out of town, in the late 1980s and into the 1990s, the union kept its headquarters here. But change had become too much a part of the Rubber City. The URW would be the next victim.

At one minute past noon on July 12, 1994, the URW, as it had done countless times in its brawny past, called a strike. The target was a new one—Bridgestone/Firestone, a company formed, in 1988, when the Japanese tire giant bought the streamlined Firestone Tire and Rubber Company. A few days earlier, in the final negotiating session, both sides had refused to budge. The usual rhetoric—talk about "fair and equitable" treatment and the company's need to "remain competitive"—was batted back and forth as the working men and women, the guts and soul of the union, carried picket signs outside five Bridgestone/Firestone plants around the Midwest and South. A handful of the union members—165 of the forty-two hundred strikers—worked at the company's Akron facilities, most of them building race car tires.

Weeks of picketing rolled by, snowballing into months. The Akron workers, who in the past had hurled insults at the suits who lived a few miles away, now trained their sights on bosses from across the world.

"I think what you've got is a lot of people still upset that a Japan-owned company would treat its people this way," Local 7 President David Yurick said on the strike's second day.

The URW fired away with rallies and pickets; in late August, Bridgestone/Firestone announced it was hiring replacement workers. This company weapon, rarely wielded in the past, had become more common since the early 1980s, when

Striking B.F. Goodrich workers rally outside the Summit County courthouse on March 21, 1938. That strike led Goodrich to sign its first agreement with the United Rubber Workers. *(Akron Beacon Journal)*

President Ronald Reagan fired striking air traffic controllers and replaced them with nonunion workers. Bridgestone/Firestone, echoing the terms it had proposed to the union, offered new workers 30 percent less than the prevailing hourly wage of $15 to $18, with the promise of raises in three years. The company also put the new workers on twelve-hour shifts. The offer was enough to lure a teeming pool of applicants—four thousand people applied for 110 jobs at plants in Des Moines, Iowa, Decatur, Illinois, and Oklahoma City.

"Scabs," the strikers cried in disgust. The veterans knew this never would have happened twenty, thirty, or forty years ago. Then, unions were mighty armies. In 1954, 35 percent of Americans belonged to labor organizations, with heavy political weight and the force of public approval. Forty years later, the figure was less than 15 percent. URW membership had fallen from 194,000 in 1974 to 98,000 in 1994, a decline that can largely be attributed to the wave of rubber plant closings across the country. And now the union was against the ropes. By November, its $14 million strike fund was nearly depleted. Strikers' health benefits had expired in October. By December, the strike had become the longest in rubber industry history, with no end in sight. And in early January, Bridgestone/Firestone hired another two thousand replacement workers.

As the union stumbled, Akron fell. In the first days of January, with the looming threat that they would lose their jobs if they didn't return to work, members of Local 7 set down their picket signs and, one by one, filed back into the south

Akron production facilities. Some got their jobs back; some did not. To those left out in the cold, the company said it had offered no guarantees. But Bridgestone/Firestone had cornered them into having to decide between personal survival or the survival of the cause. It was an unfamiliar choice to face in labor-proud Akron.

Then a stranger thing happened. The day after Akron threw in the towel, Bridgestone/Firestone, its key plants up and running with replacements and returned workers, left the ring. It saw no reason to negotiate and declared the fight over. It had what it wanted. The battered union continued swinging away, but it had no target except its own shadow.

In late May 1995, the URW finally surrendered. It sent a letter to Bridgestone/Firestone offering to send its members nationwide back to work unconditionally. Union President Kenneth Coss called it "simply a change in strategy." Technically, the dispute was not over. The URW vowed to continue working for a master contract. But, as in Akron, Bridgestone/Firestone offered no guarantees. It said it would take back employees on an as-needed basis.

"We didn't expect the United Rubber Workers would collapse and get bankrupted," Bridgestone/Firestone President Kenji Shibata said, in 1997, in his prominent Japanese accent. "We thought the URW [would make] some compromise with us without committing suicide. . . . We were ready to talk with them, and we also tried to have some compromise with them, but they selected to die and to be merged—that was one of the most surprising things. So we learned American worker do not like to be defeated, but rather prefer to die. That good lesson!"

George Becker had been watching this fight from ringside. He was the hard-boiled president of the United Steelworkers of America, a union with six hundred thousand members and tens of millions of dollars in the bank. He was watching a smaller, weaker union being pounded by a big, multinational corporation, and he couldn't stand to watch any longer.

In February, at a meeting of the AFL-CIO in Bal Harbour, Florida, Becker's star crossed with that of URW President Coss. Becker, a wavy-haired ex-Marine, began his career at age fourteen, working alongside his father in an Illinois steel plant. He had risen through the labor ranks as a straight shooter and an aggressive organizer, a burly, old-school unionist. Coss, silver-haired and soft-spoken, was of labor's new breed—lawyerly and less confrontational. Secretly, he was opposed to his union's strike against Bridgestone/Firestone: he feared the company was trying to bust the union, and he wasn't sure the URW could survive.

When he and Becker began to talk and the conversation turned to merger, Coss ushered Becker into a quiet corner. Merger? The URW could sure use one. And if it happened now, it could save the fight against Bridgestone/Firestone. The Steelworkers had a $166 million strike fund and tactical resources that would pump new life into the URW's tired troops. Coss returned to Akron and proposed a merger to the URW board. He was given permission to move forward. Almost immediately, he and Becker began a series of secret meetings in Youngstown.

"During the fight with Bridgestone/Firestone, we sought help from the entire labor movement," said John Sellers, then Coss's right-hand man and now the top rubber official in the Steelworkers' union. "The Steelworkers offered not simply words, but resources. This was well ahead of the merger. But as we began working more closely, it became clear that this was really a natural fit. The two really went hand in hand."

The leaders of URW locals, from huge tire plants and tiny belt-making shops, arrived in Pittsburgh the weekend before Independence Day 1995. Pittsburgh was the home of the Steelworkers union, and eighteen hundred rubber workers had come to the city, to the David L. Lawrence Convention Center, to vote on their future. The outcome was far from certain. A two-thirds majority—614 votes—was required to approve the merger, and no one could tell which way it was headed.

"I'm a rubber worker, and I want to stay a rubber worker," proclaimed J. R. Countryman, president of Local 12 in Gadsden, Alabama, one of the largest URW locals in the country.

After three days of debate, the voting finally began. "We need a unified industrial union for these times!" Becker cried out as ballots were cast. But the time for talk was over. A few hours later, the ballots had been counted.

In favor: 617. Against: 304.

The merger had been approved with three votes to spare. The URW dissolved, becoming the Rubber/Plastics Industry Conference of the United Steelworkers of America. The new name didn't have quite the same punch as "URW," the three letters that said so much in Akron for so long. But industry was changing, and so were unions.

The new body's first order of action was to resolve what remained of the Bridgestone/Firestone dispute, the unusual battle that was now well over a year old. The Steelworkers unleashed their soldiers on Nashville. They erected a tent city called Camp Justice on a lawn near the company's headquarters in an industrial park. They held rallies, portraying the tire company as an enemy of the American worker. They sponsored boycotts of Bridgestone/Firestone products. And, wherever they went, they waved "Black Flag Firestone" flags. The second anniversary of the walkout was commemorated with a rally called "International Days of Outrage," a raucous event that bore the fiery Becker's trademark.

Bridgestone/Firestone brushed it off as "corporate harassment" and continued chugging along. The former Akron company showed its first, slender profit in 1993 and grew stronger over the course of the unrest, posting net profits of $130 million in 1995 and $172 million in 1996. The strike, the tried-and-true weapon of the rubber workers, seemed to have had little effect.

The unresolved contract continued to gnaw at the union. The long drama took its final odd turn in November 1996, when the company and union, meeting on the sly, emerged from a secret meeting place in Chicago with a surprise announcement. The two parties had settled the contract, twenty-seven months after the dispute began. Both sides had compromised— workers got a raise, a bonus, amnesty, and free health care; the company got twelve-hour shifts, twenty-four-hour plant operation, and wages tied to produc-

Two of hundreds of black flags, each with the name of a fired or laid-off Bridgestone-Firestone worker, dot the landscape at Camp Justice, a United Steelworkers encampment within sight of the company's headquarters in Nashville, Tennessee. (*Akron Beacon Journal*/Ed Suba, Jr.)

tivity. Instead of giving cost-of-living raises, the company would give raises when it made a profit. In what seemed like a footnote, the longest dispute in rubber history, the one that had killed the URW, was over.

A long road leads to the earthy little headquarters of Local 1055 in LaVergne, Tennessee, where Bridgestone/Firestone has a plant. A metal sign out front still bears the fading URW logo. Local union officials brush off the irony, explaining that they just haven't gotten around to changing the sign.

The same holds true in Akron, where the former world headquarters on White Pond Drive still has a marker out front that says "United Rubber Workers." The building signs, though, have been changed to USWA. The place is the office of the rubber and plastics division of the Steelworkers.

The signs, in some ways, are irrelevant. Rubber workers are still united in their goals. But to stand, they have realized that they need to be united with more than just themselves. By the year 2000, the USWA intends to join the UAW and the International Association of Machinists to form a so-called "mega-union" with two million members, people whose jobs will have little relevance to their union affiliation.

In an America homogenized by Wal-Marts, lookalike political parties, and cable TV, the survival of the URW, a tough little union based on maverick individuality, was perhaps bound to fade.

But history will know that it went down fighting.

Members of the United Steelworkers picket outside a Bridgestone/Firestone store in Nashville, Tennessee in July of 1996. Those in the foreground pound on the front door. The Nashville protest was part of the "International Days of Outrage," which marked the second anniversary of a strike and bore the trademark of fiery Steelworkers President George Becker. (*Akron Beacon Journal*/Ed Suba, Jr.)

10　Synthetic Rubber

THE B. F. GOODRICH COMPANY handed Mission Impossible to the one man in Akron for whom no mission had ever seemed impossible. The year was 1937. Germany owned the secret of synthetic rubber. Waldo Semon, Goodrich's research ace, was ordered to get it. America's future might depend on it. World War II loomed. In Asia, the Japanese could cut off much of the natural rubber supply by seizing rubber plantations. An army might travel on its stomach, but it rolls on rubber. And Germany, with its advanced synthetic rubber, Buna-S, in large-scale production, was ready to roll.

Every major Akron rubber company was working on synthetic rubber; some already had made runs at the Germans to learn more about Buna-S, but to no avail. Semon's boss, Goodrich President James D. Tew, and Goodyear's director of research, L. B. Sebrell, both returned empty-handed from separate trips to Germany in 1937. Semon, one of Akron's premier chemists, had proved his research ability time and again since joining Goodrich on June 1, 1926. Working with a range of chemical compounds called antioxidants, Semon found ways to prevent certain cheaper grades of rubber from aging so quickly. He devised ways to strengthen adhesives, the materials that

An early lab of the B.F. Goodrich company, which set the pace for technical research early on among the rubber companies. (The University of Akron Archives)

bound rubber linings to metal tanks. Semon's work with adhesives led to his signature discovery, polyvinyl chloride, and, decades later, to his seat in the National Inventors Hall of Fame. With adhesives and antioxidants on Semon's resume, Goodrich turned to him to head up its synthetic rubber research program, and, if possible, to unlock the secrets of Buna-S, the synthetic rubber that looked most promising for use in tires.

Semon, fluent in several languages, for six months studied all the existing French and German literature on synthetic rubber. He concentrated on the German patents and recommended that Goodrich buy a license from the German chemical industry to use the Buna patent. But Adolf Hitler, Germany's chancellor, refused. As far as Hitler was concerned, synthetic rubber was a natural resource to be hoarded for Germany's exclusive use. Goodrich President Tew, therefore, decided to have Semon work through his contacts on the technical side of the German rubber industry. Tew figured Semon could exploit the German interest in vinyl in exchange for information about Buna-S. Thus, Goodrich sent yet another emissary to Germany in 1937, this time Semon.

Dr. Waldo Semon, in shirtsleeves, works with other B.F. Goodrich scientists on the development of synthetic rubber in 1940. Germany, which had touched off World War II a year earlier, had developed its version, while Japan loomed as a threat to natural rubber supplies in Asia. (The University of Akron Archives)

En route, Semon, at age thirty-nine, made his first trip to Paris, where he dined on what he thought was steak, only to discover it was horse meat. From Paris he went on to Frankfurt and Berlin, traveling in a car with synthetic rubber tires. The tires, he decided, were "satisfactory." The trip, however, was not. His German hosts learned more from Semon about vinyl than he did from them about synthetic rubber. "They worked on me in shifts," Semon said. "They found they could get certain information, but I wasn't very successful in finding out more about synthetic rubber."

On his return, Semon acknowledged his failure to the Goodrich board of directors but recommended the company continue to develop synthetic rubber anyway. "We have bright chemists in the United States," Semon said. "I see no reason why we shouldn't be able to make synthetic rubber that's as good as the Germans have made, maybe better than they have made."

Other U.S. companies, though, still thought the simplest route would be through Germany. In 1938, Ernest T. Handley was managing a Firestone plant in Switzerland, close enough to what was happening in Germany to feel the coming war crawling on his skin. Handley brought to Akron a small square of Buna-S, which he delivered to John Street, Firestone's research director. Street loved it and wanted more.

That was no simple matter. Standard Oil of New Jersey already had the U.S. patents for Buna-S and Germany's other synthetic rubber, Buna-N. And German rubber companies were providing small samples of Buna-S directly to U.S. companies in hopes of generating future licensing agreements. But without the technical procedures guarded so closely by Hitler, Americans could not produce Buna-S. So Handley went through other channels. He bought chemicals for his Swiss plant from I. G. Farben laboratories in Leverkusen, the heart of Germany's government-sponsored synthetic rubber program. Handley wangled an invitation to Leverkusen and its labs and production facility. Waldo Semon had tried the same thing a year earlier, but Handley had better connections. He got inside.

"I was able to get a good look at the way Buna-S and Buna-N were made—the reactors, the drying," Handley said.

In the name of a Swiss company with which Firestone was associated, Handley ordered 100 kilograms (about 220 pounds) of Buna-N, a synthetic made primarily with butadiene and acrylonitrile that the Germans invented during World War I. But Handley really wanted Buna-S, a superior synthetic made primarily of butadiene and styrene, and leaned on a Farben salesman to return a favor. Handley had helped the salesman get Swiss francs in exchange for German marks, a transaction Hitler had made illegal. Now Handley wanted something in return. The two men sneaked to the large drums containing Handley's shipment of Buna-N. They replaced the Buna-N with Buna-S but left the drums labeled Buna-N. The drums were sent to the Swiss company and then on to John Street in Akron.

"I didn't want the name Firestone involved," Handley said.

Handley, though, wanted the credit, as did many others, for the eventual development of American synthetic rubber. Identifying individual contributions, however, is nearly impossible. Dozens of scientists, researchers, and chemists stood tall in the program, including Semon and Handley; Benjamin S. Garvey, Semon's colleague at Goodrich; and Edward R. Weidlein of the Mellon Institute.

By the late 1930s, Waldo Semon already had accumulated an impressive list of contributions to a war effort. During World War I, he worked at the University of Washington laboratories on a method for bringing out messages written in invisible ink without destroying the paper. He also sought an alternative to TNT, which took its principal ingredient from Germany. "I tried a lot of things," Semon said of his explosives work. "There were explosions. *Plenty* of explosions. What finally worked was ammonium sulfate with sulfuric acid and toluene."

Semon might have continued an academic career at the University of Washington had it not been for a decision by the state legislature: it took away the money he earned for consulting with industry. "I was earning $1,800," Semon said, "and then they made me give anything I earned on the side to the university's general fund. I couldn't live on that."

Semon by this time was married to his college sweetheart, Marjorie Gunn. They had two daughters, Mary and Beth. So Semon listened hard to a job offer from Harlan Trumbull, a former University of Washington chemistry professor who at this time was Goodrich's director of research. "I didn't know anything about Akron," Semon said. "But I knew something about Dr. Trumbull." Semon trusted Trumbull enough to gather up his young family and make the 2,354-mile trip from Seattle to Akron in a 1918 Ford Roadster. "We didn't make very good time," Semon says. "The car's top speed was twenty-five miles per hour. The tires were about the size of bicycle tires. The rims would come off. They were held on by bolts. We'd pick up nails. Screws were the worst. The road was just an old trail that wagons had used. These things fell off wagons and we'd run over them, and I'd have to repair the inner tube and sometimes the casing, as well."

Over the sixteen-day journey, Semon repaired fourteen flat tires. By the time he got to Akron, he knew what his first priority should be. "I resolved that if I did nothing else for Goodrich, I'd help make good tires," he said.

The Akron he found, in 1926, was a city indelibly linked with its principal product. "Akron *was* the rubber industry," Semon said, "and it was sort of a wild industry, with Firestone, Goodyear, and Goodrich competing." He could smell it from Wooster, thirty miles away. "Rotten eggs!" Semon said. "The wind was blowing from Akron, and that's what it smelled like. Rotten eggs."

From his home in Cuyahoga Falls, Semon rode a double-decker bus to downtown Akron and the Goodrich complex. Trumbull assigned Semon to "stick rubber to metal so it wouldn't come loose under high temperatures." The assignment led Semon to the discovery that he and others regard as the greatest of his 116 patents: polyvinyl chloride, commonly called vinyl. Polyvinyl chloride was Semon's ticket to the Inventors Hall of Fame, the Plastics Hall of Fame, and the Charles Goodyear Medal of the Rubber Division of the American Chemical Society. And, like other successes, the discovery of vinyl was something of an accident. "Most of the work that I've done has been based on mistakes," Semon said. "You have to look at something many ways, and expect the unexpected."

Searching for a synthetic rubber adhesive, Semon substituted chloride when he ran out of bromide as a base substance in his experiment. His result was a gas, not synthetic rubber. Finally, he was able to produce a powder that, when combined with a boiling solvent and treated with zinc or a strong organic amine, yielded a flexible gel that turned out to be vinyl. Semon molded a batch into a golf ball. He made a shoe heel from it and coated electric wire with it. Vinyl was durable and waterproof and would not conduct electricity. There was only one problem with vinyl: it wouldn't bond with metal. It wasn't what Semon was supposed to be making, but his vinyl, marketed as Koroseal, became immensely profitable for Goodrich.

Polyvinyl chloride found its way onto raincoats and shower curtains, onto the tops of cars and furniture, onto tool handles, floor mats, stockings, and hundreds of other products. Most important, however, may have been its use as insulation for electrical wiring, one of several ways Semon's work saved lives in wartime.

Patton's tanks moved on treads bonded to metal by one of Semon's processes. Eisenhower's Jeep rolled on tires of synthetic rubber from a government project to which Semon contributed. MacArthur's troops returned to the Philippines in ships protected with vinyl-coated wiring, which replaced the rubber-asphalt coating in common use. The rubber-asphalt composition, when hit by shell or torpedo, could ignite a fire that would race through the wiring and engulf a ship.

Looking exactly like the conventional automobile tire, casings like these have been made with a content of from 50 to 100 percent Ameripol, the synthetic rubber developed by B.F. Goodrich from ingredients found in petroleum and other American raw materials. In 1940, Ameripol tires were the first synthetic tires to be sold to the American public. (The University of Akron Archives)

But none of Semon's discoveries came at a more critical juncture for the country than Ameripol, the substance used in Goodrich's first commercially viable synthetic rubber tire, the Liberty tire. After Semon returned from his wasted trip to Germany, he headed up the team that created Ameripol. Working on a floor in Goodrich's old Plant 3, Semon and his colleagues formulated 14,492 types of petroleum-based synthetic rubber. Ultimately, a blend of 70 percent butadiene and 30 percent methyl methacrylate produced a synthetic rubber that, combined with natural rubber, became Ameripol. The name means "a polymer of American materials".

Goodrich rolled out its Liberty tire in 1939. But even with Europe on the brink of war, it was a bumpy road trying to persuade the U.S. government to put its financial weight behind synthetic rubber production. Time, and the nation's stockpile of natural rubber, were running out. In peacetime, the U.S. consumed an average of six hundred thousand tons of rubber a year. In 1940, the U.S. government formed the Rubber Reserve Company, which had the authority to buy up to 150,000 tons of rubber. That amount, along with the rubber held by private industry, would tide the country over for about a year. Finally, in 1941, before Japan's attack on Pearl Harbor, the U.S. government organized a Technical Committee of representatives from the rubber, chemical, and petroleum industries to choose a synthetic rubber recipe for GR-S, Government Rubber-Styrene, and to devise a plan to produce it.

The government had to put its clout behind the cause. Left to the individual rubber and chemical companies, synthetic rubber was being produced under different methods at an agonizing pace. In 1941, U.S. companies produced about eight thousand tons. By 1942, the amount had increased to twenty-two thousand tons, but the U.S. would require at least 574,000 tons in the next year just for military use. When Japan seized Asian rubber plantations that year, cutting off 90 percent of the natural rubber supply, the synthetic initiative became even more urgent. President Franklin D. Roosevelt exhorted Americans to collect and turn in any rubber they could. In Akron, people began donating everything from tires to teething rings. Reclaimed rubber was turned into civilian tires, but they were not quality products.

"If you got ten thousand miles out of them at 35 mph, you did well," said Firestone retiree Alvin W. Warren, a chemist during the early synthetic work.

Tires for military vehicles required stronger synthetic rubber. Roosevelt told his adviser, financier Bernard Baruch, to form a committee to decide what priority synthetic rubber should have and how many plants and materials would be needed for its production. The Baruch Committee issued its report in September: "Of all critical and strategic materials, rubber is the one which presents the greatest threat to the safety of our nation and the success of the Allied cause," the committee concluded. "If we fail to secure quickly a large new rubber supply, our war effort and our domestic economy will both collapse."

Goodyear Chairman P. W. Litchfield said the government nearly acted too late. The nation had only a two- to three-week supply of natural rubber "when synthetic began to come in quantities." By peacetime yardsticks, however, synthetic production accelerated rather swiftly. Within a year of the Baruch report, synthetic production reached 230,000 tons. In 1944, it reached 750,000 tons and stood at a million tons at the end of the war.

Because of his Ameripol credentials, Goodrich's Waldo Semon was elected by representatives of the collaborating companies to head the GR-S team. Semon quickly realized that too many egos were at stake and decided to step aside. "We got together in Akron . . . and it was quite a meeting because every company had done some work on synthetic rubber, and each company thought it had the best method for making synthetic rubber," Semon said. He recommended that the committee be led by an outsider. Into this thicket walked Edward R. Weidlein, director of research at the Mellon Institute in Pittsburgh and of chemical research for the U.S. Office of Production Management, which later became the War Production Board.

Weidlein insisted on two conditions to take control of the program. "We've got to have the complete cooperation of the rubber industry," Weidlein warned after meeting with Secretary of Commerce Jesse Jones and Stanley T. Crossland of the Rubber Reserve Company. That meant getting antitrust dispensation from the Justice Department for the rubber companies to work together and a cross-licensing agreement so that Standard Oil of New Jersey would have rights to any improvement resulting from use of its Buna patents. With that accomplished,

Weidlein decided to get the scientists from all the rubber companies together to inspect each other's processes. "They're going to spend the day going to each plant," Weidlein said. "They didn't know how [one another] operated, how they made the rubber, their equipment, how different it was—one from the other."

It was a revolutionary idea, because rubber's culture of secrecy ran deep in Akron. Rubber recipes, natural or synthetic, came in code. Ben Kastein, who started his thirty-eight-year career at Firestone in 1940, regarded as inviolate the little book in which he recorded recipes. "You didn't dare write the recipes and take them out of the office," Kastein said. "The recipes themselves were kept under lock and key. Everyone was very conscious of secrecy and security."

After just one meeting in Akron, Weidlein moved the Technical Committee sessions to his home turf at Mellon Institute in rubber-neutral Pittsburgh. It didn't prompt instant cooperation. "Everybody had a different formula and an idea of what we should do with it," Weidlein said. Finally, after one three-day meeting, Weidlein had had enough. He ordered the scientists to return to the University Club, where they were staying in Pittsburgh. There, they were to examine all the formulas and separately put together one that a representative from each company would write on the blackboard the next day. "You're not to get in touch with each other at all," he warned.

But that night, Ernest Handley, who with John Street was managing Firestone's synthetic program, met with representatives from Goodyear and U.S. Rubber. "The only one who wouldn't meet was Goodrich," Handley said. That meant Waldo Semon, who looked at the competitiveness differently. "There were always claims," Semon said of the credit-seekers. "I didn't pay too much attention to them. I was more interested in doing a good job than in the claims of who had done what."

Not Handley. Years later, during interviews Ben Kastein recorded for the Rubber Division of the American Chemical Society, Handley still insisted that Weidlein had settled "on my formula."

"It doesn't make any difference," Weidlein shot back. "When we came back the next day and each one of you put your formula on the blackboard, we found they were so nearly alike, that is the formula that was adopted."

But it wasn't the Firestone formula—at least not exactly.

"As I remember it," Semon said, "the OEI came from Naugatuck Chemical Company [a Standard Oil subsidiary] and the potassium sulfate initiator came from Firestone."

And it all came from the Germans.

The OEI Semon spoke of was the acronym for One Essential Ingredient. The collaborators weren't permitted to use the name of the ingredient, which was dodecyl mercaptan, a garlic-smelling hydrosulfide that contributed to the final molecular weight of GR-S. More than anything else, it separated American synthetic rubber from the German Buna-S and made it easier to process. The Germans knew of the OEI but didn't use it. Akron's rubber companies wanted a synthetic rubber that could be processed in their machines without an extra heating step that the Germans used.

Goodrich's Ameripol formula was not the choice for the mutual recipe, in part because styrene was more available than methyl methacrylate. But Semon's work with Ben Garvey, who tested or supervised the testing of Semon's synthetic rubber variations, was key to the later success of GR-S. "Ben Garvey brought to the synthetic rubber program an exceedingly important concept . . . that processibility of the rubber before cure was equally important to the properties of the rubber after cure," Semon said. "Events proved that it was because of this philosophy that the American synthetic rubber, as it was finally developed, turned out to be superior to Buna-S."

Garvey said Goodrich researchers sought a synthetic rubber specifically for tires. "We promoted and pushed the idea that it was tires that were important and not pounds of rubber," he said. "The Germans, on the other hand, made their synthetic rubber on the basis of the theoretical concept to give the best quality of rubber. The German Ph.D. apparently did not get out into the factory to see what happened to his product when it actually went into use."

The mutual recipe worked so well that it changed little throughout World War II. Members of the Technical Committee were able to turn their attention to the design of plants to produce GR-S. Fifteen plants were built with government financing.

And Ernie Handley finally got to be first—though not without a struggle. Firestone sent him to get a GR-S plant up and running in Baton Rouge, Louisiana. In what *Time* magazine referred to as "One of the great races in U.S. industrial history," Firestone was pitted against U.S. Rubber of New York, which was about to get a GR-S plant on line in Institute, West Virginia. Handley had the Firestone operation ready, in April 1943, but couldn't start it up. "I got every-

A building that will store completed latex is constructed, in June 1943, as part of a huge synthetic rubber plant which the Goodyear Tire and Rubber Company is building near Houston, Texas for the Defense Plant Corporation. *(Akron Beacon Journal)*

The master control room at United States Rubber Company of New York's Institute, West Virginia synthetic rubber plant during WWII. The plant was one of fifteen financed by the government to ensure that the United States would not be without vitally needed rubber products during the war. (*Akron Beacon Journal*)

thing all set but didn't have any steam," Handley said. "We got our steam from Standard of New Jersey, across the lot. They wouldn't turn it on. They needed to check it a few more times. Well, I couldn't listen to that."

Handley told Louisiana Governor Sam H. Jones of the Firestone plant's need for steam for its reactors. The governor phoned the president of a small Louisiana railroad company, who moved a steam engine onto tracks near Handley's plant. The engine pumped out 250 pounds of steam, but Handley had only a one-inch line to bring it into the plant. "Once I started operating one reactor with the steam engine," Handley said, "everybody forgave everybody and they turned my steam on. . . . We had so much flak [because] we had designed these plants without knowing they would work."

Other plants followed Baton Rouge on line. The rubber companies took on the operation of as many as three each. General Tire, the smallest of Akron's rubber companies, operated one, even though it had refused to pool its synthetic research to develop GR-S. Bill O'Neil believed the other rubber companies were still withholding their best, most secret processes.

In 1955, with the crises of World War II and the Korean War behind the country, the government sold the synthetic rubber plants to the rubber, petroleum, and chemical companies at a profit of $10 million. Including the plants' inventory, the government received $415 million. American scientists took Germany's synthetic rubber and made it better, turning it into a postwar industry that assures the United States will never again be held hostage by a lack of natural rubber. In 1996, the United States consumed 2.2 million metric tons of synthetic rubber, up 1.5 percent from 1995. The Rubber Manufacturers Association pro-

A Goodyear worker handles kernels of synthetic rubber in 1973. The synthetic rubber industry, given impetus by WWII, now dominates the US market. In 1996, consumption of synthetic rubber was more than double that of natural rubber. *(Akron Beacon Journal)*

jected that would increase to 2.22 million tons in 1997. Meanwhile, natural rubber use fell 1 percent, in 1996, to 981,000 tons and was expected to drop again, to 980,000 tons, in 1997.

More than fifty years after the war, history, especially in the hands of pop historians, celebrates the Manhattan Project. There have been documentaries, TV movies, and big-screen movies concerning the development of the nuclear bomb. The truth is, after a faltering start, the development of synthetic rubber outranked every World War II priority—including the Bomb.

"In retrospect," said R. E. Harmon, vice president of the Washington Rubber Group, a professional organization, "it seems apparent that without [the Synthetic Rubber Program] there would have been no completed Manhattan Project, no Polaris submarine, no man on the moon, since [synthetic rubber] paved the way to our victory in World War II."

The Washington Rubber Group and the Rubber Division of the American Chemical Society revisited the importance of synthetic rubber during a 1978 symposium, in part to bring attention to what research and development personnel have known for years.

"From a technological viewpoint," said Arthur M. Bueche, who was vice president for research and development at General Electric Company in the 1970s, "the most successful 'Project Independence' this country has ever carried out was the World War II synthetic rubber program. . . . The success of the synthetic rubber program was fantastic by any standard. The speed with which synthetic rubber tires were perfected and mass-produced was so great that it made other wartime efforts—including the much more famous Manhattan Project—look slow by comparison."

This was the accomplishment everyone in Rubber City could share.

"I don't care who says they were first or who says they did it best," said former Goodyear Chairman E. J. Thomas. "The whole industry did one terrific job. I say there is credit enough from that . . . to cover the waterfront."

As if to acknowledge as much, the 1943 Award for Chemical Engineering Achievement, established by the professional journal *Chemical and Metallurgical Engineering*, was awarded not to an individual but to the American Synthetic Rubber Industry as represented by sixty-five companies, including Goodrich, Goodyear, Firestone, and General.

In other words, they all did it. Waldo Semon. Ed Weidlein. Ernie Handley. And many, many others.

At his home in 1975, Waldo Semon pours into his hand powdered polyvinyl chloride that has been processed from the gas form contained in the labeled bottle. Vinyl has found its way into a myriad of products, generating a $30-billion-a-year industry. (*Akron Beacon Journal*/Paul Tople)

11 A War Brings Progress

MAYBE ARISTOTLE WAS RIGHT when he said we make war that we may live in peace.

Wartime in Akron forced the issue of diversity, pushing different types of people together in ways that they had not been pushed together before. As white males shipped out to fight in World Wars I and II, women poured into the rubber shops, joined by African-Americans from the rural South and by deaf people from around the country. By necessity, they learned to work shoulder-to-shoulder. In the first half of the century, particularly during the wars, Akron was a boomtown, a place people came to find work, a place that rang with different languages and dialects, and a place that was colored with different shades of skin. Black men looking for an even break on the factory floor challenged gnarled old attitudes. Women threatened male dominance in the shops. Deaf workers forced people to confront their attitudes about disabilities. Sometimes the roiling mix opened minds. Other times, the melting pot boiled over.

This was particularly true in issues of race. Even when they were covered in carbon black, all men were not the same color. Underneath the mess of rubber work, white men were still white and black men were still black, a difference often painfully evident in Akron's factories. For at least the first half of this century, African-American workers found themselves trapped in the worst jobs, in the heat of the pit, the soot of the mill room, held back by hard-cured attitudes about race. But early Akron had no choice except to look diversity in the face as more and more newcomers arrived in the Rubber City.

In 1910, there were 657 African-Americans living in Akron, less than 1 percent of the population. Migration beefed up those numbers significantly in the next few decades, with one of the most dramatic increases occurring during World War II, when Akron's black population nearly doubled to 23,878 in half a decade. By 1950, African-Americans made up 8.7 percent of the population.

In the early years, black workers in the rubber shops were relegated to the lowest jobs. They cleaned spittoons. They scrubbed toilets. They swept floors. During World War I, when blacks arrived from the South to help with the war effort, they found jobs, good ones compared with the low-paying agricultural jobs many had left in Alabama and Tennessee. But the work they had in Akron was still the worst in the rubber plants. Even as Akron thrived, many blacks lived in relative squalor. Akron's oldest black neighborhood, and one of the city's poorest, was in the Little Cuyahoga Valley along North Street. Another black neighborhood formed between Euclid Avenue and the Ohio Canal, near the B. F. Goodrich factory complex. Black migration accelerated during World War II, but the newcomers still settled mostly in the established neighborhoods. By this time, though, enough African-Americans had made Akron their home that things began to change, albeit slowly.

William R. Miller joined Goodyear, in 1952, and became the company's first black executive, in 1980, when he was named vice president of governmental personnel relations. Among other duties, he was director of equal employment opportunity, from 1974 through his retirement in 1984. Miller said Goodyear "was a stubborn old company," and the rubber industry in general was "slower to bring about change. There was a pattern of practices [and] it was harder to get them to change." By virtue of their product lines, Miller explained, tire companies are conservative. People don't choose tires based on corporate practices; most consumers "don't give a darn about tires." So the tire companies were less susceptible to social pressure.

Over the years, prospects did improve for African-Americans, but the improvement was relative. When production jobs opened up for blacks, there was still a glass ceiling. Otis Spurling walked into the mill room for his first day of work at Firestone, in 1944, to find brown faces stained black. The mill room is the place where raw rubber is mixed with carbon black. Carbon black is a fine, powdery filth that gets into the pores and stays there. Jobs in the mill room were not necessarily an improvement over spittoon cleaning. But they were a step closer to the more lucrative production jobs upstairs, building tires. To get to those jobs, one often had to work through the mill room and the pit, the hellishly hot place where tires were cooked into the final product. Like Spurling, most of the men in the mill room were black. They all knew black men didn't work as tire builders. Across Akron, the line was drawn.

"We was paying union dues but were not allowed to go further than the mill room, the pit, and janitorial service," said Spurling. He worked in the mill room for eleven years with little more than hope for something better. In 1954, he was laid off, despite the fact that there were job openings for tire builders. Finally, in 1955, Spurling and one other black worker cracked open the door to the tire room. The auspicious occasion called for a special meeting in the personnel department. "The boss told me we were going to have trouble," he recalled.

Spurling and his coworker showed up for their first day as tire builders to find no one else working. The white workers had sat down on the job, saying they wouldn't work if the company was letting blacks in. Spurling looked across the room. He saw hard faces; he saw hard men with brittle patience. And he saw a hard future for himself. But he saw something else more clearly than all these things. "I seen where the money was," Spurling said.

To hell with the racists, he figured. This was his chance to make some of the best wages in American industry. "I smiled at them," he said. "I knew I would overcome. I just wasn't afraid." The company stood up to those who had sat down. Firestone gave them a choice: Go back to work or hit the road. They went back to work, many grudgingly. Spurling got down to the work of building tires. He got no support from his coworkers. The fellow assigned to train him for several weeks left after half an hour. Spurling ate lunch alone. He heard muffled insults. He went home the first night with bleeding hands.

"Honey," he said to his wife, Minnie. "I can't do this job."

"Isn't there other men who are doing this?" she asked.

"Yes."

"Then you can do it, too."

He returned the second day. Making his own way was tough. To learn the complicated job of building tires, Spurling read the specification manual backward and forward. He slept with it, determined to succeed. After that second day, the other black man who had come on the job with Spurling quit. Spurling kept on. Some days, things were OK. He'd chat with a white coworker. Other days, he was told to go back to Africa or called hateful names. He stayed at the job twenty-one years. He was a pioneer of sorts. But, like many blacks who worked in the rubber shops, he said he wasn't fighting for civil rights so much as to make a better living. The jobs that for years were closed to blacks were the jobs that paid the most.

Many blacks say they encountered racism at every level—in hiring practices, in the unions, and in their everyday dealings on the shop floor. They were the first to be laid off and the last to be rehired during the Depression, according to a 1934 Family Services report. Goodyear had a policy, Miller said: "Don't bring any blacks into responsible positions." Besides opportunities for advancement, African-Americans often were denied some of the most basic considerations in the rubber shops, including a decent place to eat lunch.

When Clark Smith joined Firestone, in 1941, black workers in the company's mechanical building were forbidden to eat with the whites. While some areas of Firestone had segregated cafeterias, the mechanical building did not. So, at lunchtime, one of the black workers would go up to the company cafeteria and bring back lunch for the rest. While the white workers ate at tables in the lunchroom, the black workers sat on backless benches in the basement locker room, eating their food where they would later shower and change their clothes. "There was a time that blacks believed that they had a place—this is our place," recalled

Ray Dove, right, with Vito Giulitto, shown as they managed the chemical stores at Knight Hall at the University of Akron. Dove found it almost impossible to secure a job as a rubber chemist, despite an excellent academic record. In 1953, Goodyear hired Dove into its research department, breaking the color barrier. When Dove retired, in 1986, he had advanced to senior research chemist and, finally, section head, overseeing people with whom, thirty-four years before, he wasn't allowed to work. *(Akron Beacon Journal)*

Smith. "At the time, they were satisfied just to have a job. But I always wondered why—why you can't have this job, why can't you have that job? 'Well, this is a white man's job.' That's what they would tell you."

One day, Smith was sent to get the food. When he returned, he looked at the locker room full of black faces and said, "You fellows are crazy." The next day, he and another black man went up to the cafeteria at lunchtime. They sat down and ate their lunch. Nobody said a word. The following day, Smith went up to the cafeteria again. As he got his lunch, he noticed some new faces. Not Firestone workers, but Akron policemen in plainclothes, watching. As tension rose, a meeting of labor and management, white and black, was held. It was decided that the black workers from the mechanical unit could use the cafeteria. From then on, the black workers and the white workers ate in the cafeteria. They ate at separate tables, not because of any rule, but because, says Smith, "that happens anyway."

Some will argue that work in a rubber shop, even the worst work, was better than an uneducated worker could find elsewhere. But even education and high credentials didn't seem to make a difference. Ray Dove got a job at Goodyear, in 1941, as a freight elevator operator. He worked the six-to-midnight shift and attended college classes during the day. Like many of those who made their lives in the rubber shops, he was an extraordinary man doing an ordinary job. His daughter Rita would later win a Pulitzer Prize for her poetry and twice become a U.S. poet laureate. She was guided in part by the example of her father, who earned a bachelor's degree in chemistry from the University of Akron in 1947. The degree did him no good. He continued performing menial factory jobs.

In 1953, Dove got his master's degree in chemistry. He knew that chemists

A black worker for B.F. Goodrich in Los Angeles stacks rubber readied for milling in 1942. Once production jobs began to open up for blacks, they still faced a glass ceiling, filling jobs in the mill room and the pit. While the jobs were little improvement over janitorial service positions, they were one step closer to the lucrative tire-building jobs. (The University of Akron Archives)

were needed for rubber research, but he was a black man, and no black man had ever worked in any of the Akron companies' research departments, apart from sweeping the floors. "I had the candid notion that once I got all of this training, it was going to be duck soup," said Dove. "Just walk right through and get gainfully employed." It didn't happen. Dove had graduated second in his undergraduate class at the university, the only African-American in the group. He watched, with growing frustration, as one after another of his classmates got jobs in their field. In the early 1950s, he was still punching elevator buttons.

Finally, he decided to make a big push. Through connections, he secured an interview with a Firestone vice president. Dove found himself looking across the desk at the vice president. Dove's credentials were excellent. And Firestone needed good rubber chemists. But, to Firestone's eyes, Dove had one indelible drawback. "His decision was no, they couldn't hire me because he was afraid of what kind of reaction they would get," Dove recalled. "They were not going to make any decision on their own about incorporating a black within their organization for the first time."

Dove, a trim man with glasses, a thin mustache, and a well-receded hairline, tells the story in measured speech, in syllables carefully formed and empty of resentment. Instead of rancor, he moved on with deeper resolve. His former principal at East High School, Arthur Dillehay, a white man, talked to some people he knew at Goodyear. Doors creaked open and, finally, after months of prodding, Goodyear decided to break the color barrier in its research department. And so, in 1953, Ray Dove put on a tie and began the work he was meant to do. Goodyear wasn't sorry; Dove was a productive analytical chemist, and by the time he retired, in 1986, he had advanced to senior research chemist and, finally, section head, overseeing people with whom, thirty-four years before, he wasn't allowed to work.

He said he never once encountered prejudice from his white colleagues in the chemistry department. But he never saw them socially, either. They moved in white circles; he moved in black circles. In many cases, Akron was the kind of place where a black rubber worker could own a home alongside a white lawyer and eat in the same cafeteria with white workers without being equal.

The Civil Rights Act of 1964 forced corporations throughout the country to amend their hiring practices, and racial balance in the workplace improved dramatically. So did the standard of living for blacks. According to Hugh Davis Graham, author of *The Civil Rights Era,* the percentage of minorities living in poverty dropped from 55 percent in 1959 to 34 percent in 1970; during the same period, blacks saw their income increase 40 percent faster than whites. The unemployment rate for blacks averaged 9.8 percent in the decade prior to the Civil Rights Act, but had dropped to 3.8 percent by 1969. In the wake of legislation, large corporations drafted official policies regarding equal opportunity.

From 1987 to 1997, as Goodyear reduced its Akron work force from seventy-six hundred to forty-seven hundred employees, it maintained black employment at 9 percent. In 1986, the company, the city's largest corporate employer, had one black vice president. In 1997, there were three. But there never has been a black president of a major rubber company. And workers, to the very end of rubber's reign in Akron, saw incidents of discrimination and heard the occasional ugly slip of the tongue. In 1980, long after the civil rights movement had painted over

The director of a new 1969 program to develop more managers from minority groups for B.F. Goodrich retail stores explains a tire's construction to the first group of trainees. Following completion of the twelve-week classroom and on-the-job-training course, the trainees entered the company's regular retail management training program leading to a store manager's position within two years. (The University of Akron Archives)

some of the blatant racism of the past, Clark Smith found a card tacked to a bulletin board at Firestone. He pulled it down and stuck it in his wallet and carries it there to this day as a reminder. The card says: "Racial Purity is America's Security. Invisible Empire Knights of the Ku Klux Klan."

❧

If the challenges faced by black workers in the rubber plants were social, the challenges to women were more often personal.

So it was one day during World War II, as Violet McIntyre White crawled into the long, narrow tail of a Corsair, dragging her wrench along. White was skinny, hardly more than 100 pounds. That's why she had gotten the job. She could fit into the small space at the rear of the tail to finish assembling the wheel there. Her ribs, as she shimmied along, scraped against the ribs of the plane. The tail narrowed. She felt as if she were being choked by the steel.

The rivets fired in from the outside. A hard, metallic *rat-a-tat . . . rat-a-tat . . . rat-a-tat*. Her head ached with the sound. She squeezed herself farther into the tail. The riveting continued. As she inched her way along, she again considered quitting. She'd been thinking about it a lot lately. She was sick of the claustropho-

4027

Women who had original-
ly worked in the gas mask
department build tires at
Goodyear in 1918. Op-
portunities for women
typically peaked during
wartime labor shortages.
(Goodyear Tire and Rubber
Company)

bia, the sound of rivets in her head. She wanted to be home with her two young
children. But she continued moving along, into the most remote part of the fighter plane. Finally there, she installed the last part on the wheel, a boot that hadn't
been put on before. She was careful, thinking about her brother in the Pacific, all
the men from Akron fighting in the Second World War. Their lives depended on
this difficult job.

When she was done, she called for Mr. Brown, the one-legged man who was
her partner on the assembly line, to pull her out. Mr. Brown reached in and took
hold of her ankles, helping her along as she eased back the way she had come. Violet stepped back down onto the floor of the Goodyear Airdock and brushed herself
off. Another plane was waiting.

Across the room, she could see a military officer talking to one of the older
women, nervously handing her a piece of paper. The officers appeared with dread-
ful regularity, always with a piece of paper and a pained expression. The woman,
old enough to be Violet's mother, put her hand to her face. Her shoulders shook.
This was the second time she had received a visit in less than six months. Three
sons had gone to war; now only one was left alive.

That's when Violet decided not to quit.

Violet McIntyre White had come to Akron from West Virginia as a young girl, as her father joined the tens of thousands from Appalachia who made the trek north for work in one of the Akron rubber factories. She had never worked, might never have worked if not for World War II. But when fighting broke out, Akron became an important cog in the war machine, and Violet stepped in to do her part. She was not alone.

The employment rosters ballooned at Akron's rubber factories as Goodyear, Firestone, Goodrich, General, Mohawk, and Seiberling took on contract after government contract. Goodyear, with its large aircraft division, got the bulk of the war business. But the others underwent considerable expansion as well, turning out rubber goods that included barrage balloons, observation blimps, life rafts, gas masks, hoses, "Mae West" life vests, airplane tires, and waterproof clothing for soldiers. When America entered the war in December 1941, more than one-fourth of the rubber companies' production was for the war effort.

In 1939, 33,285 worked in Akron's rubber plants. By early 1944, 72,890 were employed. And a great many of them were new employees, called in to replace the men who had gone off to battle. Some men were excused from military service to work in essential jobs, such as tire building. But as the war dragged on, more were sent to battle, replaced by women from Akron and men and women recruited from the South. Akron experienced another growth spurt and another housing shortage; a string of shanties sprang up on South Arlington Street.

The rubber factories expanded their vision, moving beyond their traditional functions. Firestone designers reengineered the carriage and mount for the Bofors antiaircraft gun, and workers made them in a plant built for that purpose. The most notable contribution of Goodyear's aircraft division, formerly Goodyear-Zeppelin Corporation, was the Corsair, a small fighter plane used by the Navy. The plane's wings folded up so it would occupy less space on an aircraft carrier. Goodyear made just over four thousand Corsairs during the war; more than half of the workers on the project were women.

Despite the wartime rationing that reduced the production of passenger tires, Akron boomed during the war. The consumer tire market, always cyclical, had kept workers on a seesaw of layoffs and re-hires. War goods, on the other hand, provided steady, lucrative work. So much so, that just about everyone did well. The companies made a lot of money. In 1944, Goodyear posted a profit of $15.2 million, compared with $6 million in 1938. Membership in the United Rubber Workers union surged, from just more than three thousand in 1935 to nearly 190,000 in 1945. Production workers in Akron's rubber shops averaged just over $1.27 per hour in 1945, compared with about a dollar an hour for all U.S. production workers. World War II yanked Akron straight out of the Depression. Workers who had been on public assistance suddenly found an abundance of jobs—of the 13,500 men and women hired by the Ravenna arsenal, five thousand had been on relief. For part of 1942, Goodyear's aircraft division was hiring a thousand people a month; its roster soared to more than thirty-three thousand.

War rationing meant people had to use coupons known as Red Points and Blue Points to buy groceries, and gasoline rationing restricted travel. The government banned the sale of new tires, Akron's bread and butter, from 1941 until

1946. But there was no rationing of movies, restaurants, and the like. Residents spent money freely on entertainment, and the town rolled in clover as it hadn't since the boom years between 1910 and 1920. Among those finding new wealth were the Akron women who had taken their places at the hard machines building war goods and turning out traditional rubber products, such as tires, hoses, and belts. Many Akron women referred to themselves as Rosie the Riveter.

"It had a lot to do with your feelings. You feel you're working for a purpose, the same as the soldiers out there," recalled Tressie McGee, who built B-6 bomber gas tanks at Goodyear during the war. "They knew they had to get out there and hold their line and fight. We knew if we didn't supply the material, they couldn't do their job."

These plants, which had been so much a man's domain, rang with voices of a different timbre. Restrooms were altered. Women, some of them, wore pants for the first time. By 1943, the Akron Metropolitan Housing Authority had established day-care centers in four Akron housing projects for the children of female workers. The local Office of Civilian Defense helped find baby-sitters for the chil-

Female workers perform a final check on nine convoy balloons lined up in the balloon room of the B.F. Goodrich Company on June 3, 1943. The Akron-made "convoy balloons" were flown from ships in convoy and from vessels used in landing operations to protect ships and men from dive-bombing attacks. The cable-tethered balloons keep the planes high. *(Akron Beacon Journal)*

dren of female rubber workers. Women's presence in the factories provided a true variation on the Akron theme. And the change was felt halfway around the world.

When Navy Seaman Elgin Staples found himself in the drink near Guadalcanal, in 1942, he quickly slipped on his life belt, which had been made at Firestone, where his mother was an inspector. Later, when the information on his belt was checked, he learned that it had been given the thumbs-up by his mom.

"It was like having Mother's arms around me," he said.

Women were not an entirely new presence in Akron's plants. Kathleen Endres, a University of Akron associate professor of communications and author of *Rosie the Rubber Worker*, points out that women had been employed by the rubber companies since the turn of the century. But, come World War II, they made a deep and distinctive mark. Jewel Vanke of Barberton, for instance, found herself at Goodrich, in 1944, building tires, a strenuous task that fatigued many men. The work may have been the same, but the dynamics were different. Where the men chewed tobacco ("West Virginia coleslaw," in shop lingo) and hung up racy pictures, women shared recipes and angled for nylons. Stockings were scarce because nylon was needed for parachutes. So whenever O'Neil's department store got a shipment, long lines of shoppers would form on State Street.

Women who worked at Goodyear could buy special uniforms at the company store with emblems reading, "Remember Pearl Harbor." Their outfits in the shops ranged from belted coveralls to slacks and blouses with buttons in the back for safety. With their new incomes, though, some of the women opted for finer attire. "We'd see them coming to work in slacks and high heels and fur coats," recalled Rita Dunlevy, a retired General Tire executive secretary with nearly forty years' service.

In the factory, the men talked rough. They sometimes made rude comments. Many were unaccustomed to working around women. But the female rubber workers say they generally were treated well.

Henry Haas supervised a group of older women building life belts on the night shift at General Tire. The women, many of whom had sons fighting in the war, achieved the highest production output of any shift at General. They shared letters from the front, bolstering one another with the news that their work in Akron was making a difference. Five decades later, Haas still spoke respectfully of his female colleagues: "Those women would come in and there was no fooling around. They'd work," he said. "I was very lucky to be with those older girls."

The work was not without hazards. Women were exposed to the same perils as men had been, and some of the new work brought new danger. One woman quit her job at Goodyear Aircraft after a coworker was killed by an errant rivet; another recalled a colleague losing four fingers in a die machine. A third was partially scalped when her hair caught in a drill.

In December 1943, Mary Snader took the second train ride of her life and her first trip to New York City. The forty-six-year-old Akron woman had been chosen to represent the rubber industry at a ceremony honoring women who were supporting the war effort. As the passenger car rattled along the tracks, the dimpled, blue-eyed mother of five had time to settle into her Pullman berth and think about how true an honor this was.

Snader had not had an easy time of it. Like most female factory workers, she was holding down two forts. Her twenty-year-old son was off in the navy. Two of her children lived at home. And her husband, who had been disabled years earlier in an industrial accident, required much of her attention. She was also the first woman to be a supervisor and instructor in Firestone's tire-building division. So, though humbled by the attention, Snader was proud to represent her city, her industry, and the other women who were serving on the home front. When she arrived in New York, she found herself whisked from appointment to appointment, including several appearances on radio shows, where she told of her work overseeing the building of military aircraft tires.

"My oldest boy, Richard, is in the navy," she told radio announcer Jim Backus, the master of ceremonies. "He's a fine boy, and we're very proud of him. My job makes me feel like I'm also in the navy, because lots of the tires I build are used on navy planes."

Mary Snader, a Firestone airplane tire builder, was the first woman to be a supervisor and instructor in Firestone's tire building division. Here, she proudly exhibits a finished tire after it had been removed from a mold. (Richard Snader)

One interviewer after another asked her about her work, about how she managed a household while working the graveyard shift at Firestone. "It's not hard," she told one. "But you do have to plan ahead. . . . We get along fine. We had a big garden, and we canned all the vegetables we'll need this winter."

As she spoke, a young sailor, two hundred miles off the coast, relaxed in the galley of a merchant ship with a cup of coffee. Some of the guys wanted to hear the news from New York, so he fiddled with the radio and happened upon the program. Suddenly, the sailor heard a familiar voice. A very familiar voice.

"I wasn't paying any attention. Then [the host] introduces my mom," recalled Richard Snader. "I thought, 'What the hell is this?'"

It was five hours before the ship docked. Richard watched in excitement as the New York skyline grew larger off the ship's bow. When the ship dropped anchor, he grabbed his gear and lit out for the Shelton Hotel. "They mentioned on [the radio] where she was staying," he said. "So I caught a subway and went straight up to Times Square. I walked in there, and she was in her room. So I knocked on the door. She about dropped when she saw me."

That night, mother and son, separated and reunited by war, had dinner together.

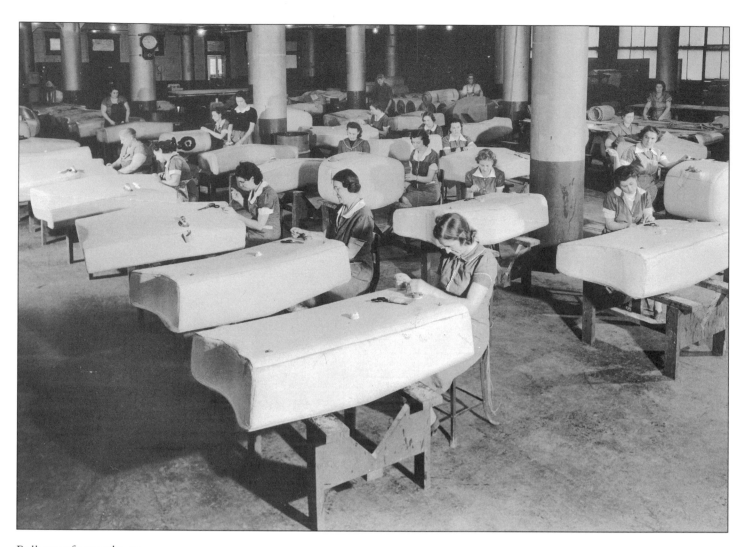

Bulletproof gas tanks are constructed, in December 1940, by female employees of the B.F. Goodrich Company (*Akron Beacon Journal*)

Victory over Japan was declared on August 14, 1945. An air raid siren sounded from the city hall roof, and downtown Akron spontaneously combusted in a confusion of dancing, horn-honking, cheering, crying, kissing, and flag-waving. Men ripped the shirts off one another's backs. The sky opened with a dog-day downpour, and nobody cared.

A day later, though, the realities of peace began to set in. Thirty thousand Akron workers would be laid off, half of them from Goodyear Aircraft. The War Manpower Commission figured half of those laid off would be women. In some places, the layoff rate for female workers was much higher. When Firestone released twenty-seven hundred employees from its aircraft division, 75 percent were women who, the company said, could not be placed in rubber factory jobs. Those jobs were for the men.

Some—maybe even most—women preferred to return to traditional occupations. But others were not given a choice. The Soldiers and Sailors Civil Relief Act of 1940 guaranteed returning veterans their old jobs, provided they reapplied within a short time after their discharge. And there were only so many jobs to go around. Still, plenty of women managed to hold on to jobs in the local factories. The women who stayed, though, were treated differently from the men. The 1941

Goodyear contract with URW Local 2 lists the minimum wage for new hires: seventy cents an hour for men; fifty-five cents an hour for women. And with incremental steps up in wages, the gap widened. Women, it seems, were not worth as much as men.

Their legacy is indelible, though, in each rivet of a Corsair, each life vest that saved a soldier's life.

A different legacy, but one equally remarkable, was left by the deaf workers who came to Akron.

On an April morning in 1945, Clyde D. Wilson walked into the Firestone Tire and Rubber Company personnel office, pulled a piece of paper and a pencil from his pocket, and wrote a simple request: I'd like a job.

The man behind the desk opened a pad and scratched down a question. Did he have any experience?

Yes, Wilson wrote back. My father owns a tire shop. I know how to work with rubber. I'm a hard worker.

I'll start you out at seventy-five cents an hour, the man wrote back. He led Wilson to the tire inspection department and put him to work.

Not a word had been spoken.

Wilson was deaf. In the tire inspection room, that didn't matter. With the help of pencil and paper, he learned the job quickly. His work was good. At the end of the day, the man from the personnel office came to check on him. He smiled and wrote Wilson another note: We'll pay you $1 an hour.

If the job interview was unusual, its outcome was not. In the first half of this century, Akron became home to one of the largest deaf communities in the United States. And, like so many Akron stories, this one wouldn't have existed without the rubber industry. Akron's rubber companies, most notably Goodyear and Firestone, had begun hiring deaf workers during World War I. Deaf people were not eligible for military service, but they could serve nonetheless—in the factories. And so, like thousands of others, they flocked to Akron.

By 1920, Rubber City had earned another nickname: Crossroads of the Deaf. Akron was said to have the largest deaf population in the United States. By 1918, an estimated eight hundred deaf workers were employed in Akron industry. At the end of World War I, there was a drop-off, as men returned from battle to reclaim their old jobs, displacing the new workers. In the 1920s and 1930s, Firestone had about thirty deaf workers, Goodyear about eighty-five. Still, those numbers were well above the national average for industry. Then World War II hit. Men and women came from all parts of the country, all walks of life, to fill the fast-growing need for labor. The old notion had grown roots—Akron was a good place for deaf people to find work. Word spread. By mid-1943, Firestone had approximately three hundred deaf employees; Goodyear had about 135; and the booming Goodyear Aircraft had more than five hundred.

The story of deaf migration to Akron mirrors that of the Appalachian workers who came to the city in droves early in the century: a few people tested the waters, found good jobs, and spread the word to their community, and the gold rush was on. With the hearing-impaired, though, the migration was not regional. People came from as far as California, Montana, Texas, and Florida for jobs in the rubber shops. Many of them were graduates of Gallaudet College, a school for the deaf in Washington, D.C.

"The deaf people who knew each other at Gallaudet were a good networking group," explained Luella Cordier, whose father, Philip Heupel, worked at Goodyear for more than thirty-seven years, beginning in 1920. "College friends told my dad there were jobs in Akron. Akron was known as the city of opportunity."

By most accounts, the first deaf workers were hired with reluctance. "We were rather skeptical as to whether this would prove successful or not, fearing accidents," P. W. Litchfield wrote, in 1918, when he was Goodyear's factory manager. "We were most agreeably surprised at the result, finding that these men made up by quickness of eye and quickness of hand what they lacked in other senses. . . . We most sincerely hope that their numbers in the Goodyear family will continue to increase."

As their ranks grew, deaf people earned a reputation as some of the hardest workers in the plants. They were kept out of some jobs where their lack of hearing could put them in danger. In the curing room, for instance, deaf workers couldn't hear the hissing of the hydraulic equipment that announced the tire press was about to come slamming down forcefully. But deaf workers found jobs as tire builders, chemists, inspectors, and human resources officers. Firestone and Goodyear each had personnel offices for the deaf. "Akron was the first city in the country to offer equal pay for equal work" for the deaf, Cordier said.

The deaf workers, with their unique finger language, made an impression inside the plants. But it was outside the factories, on athletic fields near and far, that they left an even more profound legacy.

On an October day in 1918, a deaf man, new in Akron, wandered into a cafe near Goodyear. He scratched a question on a piece of paper and handed it to the counter man: Where are all these deaf people I've been told about?

The Goodyear Silent (Mute) Flying Squadron in front of the Mute Athletic Club, the only one of its kind in 1919. The building had reading and social rooms and was the recreational center for the Silent workers at Goodyear. It was located where today's visitor parking lot is located, next door to Goodyear Hall in east Akron. (Goodyear Tire and Rubber Company)

All the mutes are in Lorain, the man wrote back matter-of-factly. At the football game.

The team was the Silents. Its celebrity was anything but. Made up of Goodyear factory workers, the team began humbly, in 1915, losing every game it played in its first two seasons. Then, slowly, things began to change. The Silents beefed up their ranks with players from Gallaudet and shut out the Akron Bulldogs 48–0 in the first game of the 1918 season. Their next opponent, the Kenmore Cadets, forfeited—perhaps sensing a change in the autumn air. The deaf team roared through its season, beating up on now-forgotten opponents—the Akron

Philip Heupel stands with his wife, Julia, next to the statue dedicated to the founder of Gallaudet University in Washington, D.C. The deaf couple met and fell in love at the school. After their marriage, Philip ended up working thirty-seven years as a tire builder for Goodyear. (Luella Cordier)

Marlowes, the Goodyear Regulars, the Silent Scrubs. Its record that year was nine wins, one loss, and a tie.

The team's leader was Smiling Joe Allen, an unlikely football star. Just five-foot-six and 145 pounds, the twenty-three-year-old quarterback was a skilled and crafty passer. He wrote the plays on pieces of tape stuck to his pants, pointing them out to his teammates in the huddle. (The football huddle had been invented at Gallaudet, born of necessity by deaf players who needed to hide their hand signals from their opponents.)

The methods were sometimes unconventional, but the results proved wildly successful. The Silents became known around the country. When they traveled to

6152

Deaf Goodyear workers made up the "Factory Mute Football Team" as they pose for a team picture at Seiberling Field in 1919. Led by star quarterback Smilin' Joe Allen (front row, second from left), the team won nine games by shutouts and soon gained national recognition. (Goodyear Tire and Rubber Company)

other towns, many fans turned out for the sake of novelty, then were dazzled by the team's skill on the field. The men endured a tough life to win cheers they couldn't hear. On one occasion, they were turned away from a motel after a game because they were covered with mud. They often left the field bloody and bruised. They were sometimes taunted by low-minded fans who made fun of their inability to hear. But they were heroes, enjoying a fleeting wrinkle of fame. They continued their winning ways through 1923. Then, as hard times caused Goodyear's deaf ranks to dwindle, the team began losing some of its talent. The Silents disbanded in 1927, after four disappointing seasons.

Sports provided a bond among Akron's deaf workers, a way to share rough-and-tumble weekend afternoons. And it gave the hearing public a chance to see them not as people who were different, but as people who could thrill crowds with their talents. Goodyear had Silent baseball and basketball teams. And there were deaf bowling teams in the leagues that peppered Akron. As time passed, the name "Silents" moved into the public domain, and teams continued with workers from places other than Goodyear.

Akron, in the glory days of the rubber industry, was a city of clubs, a place that bounced with social interaction. The deaf community was especially close, drawn from around the country by a common desire to find decent work and held together by a common language. And so the hearing-impaired gathered at places such as the Akron Club of the Deaf, which now is on Manchester Road. Shortly after its formation, in 1943, the club had more than four hundred members. In the 1940s, there were four different deaf clubs in Akron, in addition to the sports teams and other, less formal groups. There was even a Silents Grocery.

"I think they liked being with deaf people that they knew," Luella Cordier said of her deaf parents. "There was a lot of socializing." Like any other group, the deaf gathered for drinks and to talk, their hands flashing with grace and agility as hours passed into the night. They danced, some of them, feeling the vibrations of music in the floor. They found, in Akron, a universal thing: friendship.

They found a way to worship, too. In 1954, a young Catholic priest in his early thirties was assigned to the Church of the Annunciation, a stone's throw from Goodyear's east Akron headquarters. The Goodyear Heights area was a bastion of the deaf—Clyde Wilson figures there were ten deaf people living on Watson Street alone. And so the Reverend John Dalton, who had previously worked with deaf children, decided to offer a monthly Mass in sign language. At the time, it was the only deaf Mass for Catholics in Summit County. "I'd say Mass in Latin, which was just as much known to the deaf as it was to hearing people," joked Dalton, who is now pastor emeritus at Holy Name Church in Cleveland. Dalton also formed a social club called the Catholic Deaf. Annunciation became a focal point for the deaf community. Dalton would adapt church tradition for this special audience. He would explain a prayer in sign language before speaking it in Latin. Sometimes, a hearing parishioner would stand near the altar and interpret for the deaf, as well.

Dalton offered the deaf an opportunity to feel close to one another. He removed one of the many layers of alienation felt by these closely knit citizens of Akron. Their community here thrived, and its importance was felt across the country. Several Akronites went on to serve as national deaf leaders. Benjamin Schowe, for instance, a labor economics specialist at Firestone, was national president of the Gallaudet Alumni Association.

Akron's deaf population has dwindled over the years. Like so many other communities within Rubber City, it suffered from the loss of tire making in the 1970s and 1980s. In 1997, according to figures from Summit County's Community Services for the Deaf, 762 deaf people lived in Summit County; another two thousand were categorized as having hearing impairment with serious communication loss.

Clyde Wilson, the last deaf employee to leave Firestone when Plant 1 closed, in 1981, said he's glad he was born when he was, in 1920. At the rubber company, where he spent thirty-six years, he had opportunity, he had community, he had a good life. His father, who was also deaf, found work at Goodyear in the early part of the century. Now Wilson is not so sure how he would make a living. So much in Akron has changed. He remembered teaching sign language to his coworkers. He remembered the deaf workers gathering in the lunchroom, eating quickly so their hands would be free to talk. He figured he knew ten thousand people over his years at Firestone.

But that was a long time ago.

12 Lighter than Air

IN A DIM CORNER of a drafty, remote warehouse at Goodyear's Wingfoot Lake blimp facility sits a coffin. Packed in a fifty-year-old wooden crate, it was stashed away years ago by a fellow named Jack LaFontaine. The coffin was built by Goodyear during World War II, under one of those myriad government contracts that had Akron's rubber companies making everything from life vests to, well, coffins. LaFontaine, a thin, soft-spoken man who strolls around the monumental blimp hangar in a Goodyear racing jacket, jokes that he'll be buried in that coffin someday. It would be only fitting. When he passes back into the earth, this humble soul will take with him some of the greatest secrets of Akron's most strange and wonderful icon: the blimp.

When LaFontaine joined Goodyear, in 1948, Akron's factories, streets, and taverns overflowed with the knowledge behind these nonrigid airships. The war had just ended, and young men tossed around stories of how they had built the blimps, flown them, fixed them, and helped to make them better. Goodyear, the navy's only supplier, delivered 132 blimps during the war. Most of the ships were used as submarine spotters, floating lazily along the East and West Coasts, their mere presence enough to keep the enemy at a distance. They were the "search" half of search and destroy—if an enemy

Goodyear Aircraft, which made caskets during World War II, continued to do so after the war, as this May 1947 photo indicates. Its products were not limited to aviation-related items. *(Akron Beacon Journal)*

sub was sighted from the sky, it became an easy target for the navy ships that patrolled the shorelines. Wherever the blimps went, they served as unlikely, skyborne ambassadors for the city whose name means "high place."

"Akron was the focal point of all airship building for our country," said Goodyear retiree Vince Rubino. Rubino is the president and a charter member of the Lighter Than Air Society, an Akron-based group of airship and balloon enthusiasts with about seven hundred members around the world. Like some of the knowledge behind the blimps, the group is aging; a great many of its 150 or so Akron-area members are World War II veterans.

Rubino was a year out of North High School when he went to work for Goodyear Aircraft in 1941. With a shock of black hair and a dimpled smile, he was somewhere between a boy and a man.

Most of Akron's plants were taking on war work, with much of the focus turning to the air. Firestone launched an aircraft division, in July 1941, put Harvey Firestone's son Leonard in charge, and began taking on government contracts to build airplane tires, tubes, self-sealing fuel tanks, buoys, pilot seats, and airplane wheel and brake units, among other things. General Tire contributed barrage bal-

Goodyear retiree Jack LaFontaine, sixty-eight, has been a part of the company's blimp program for almost fifty years, first as an employee and today as an advisor who still puts in hours at the Wingfoot Lake Hangar. He has been called on to help build and maintain airships around the world and has become an expert on the nuts and bolts of blimp construction. (*Akron Beacon Journal*/Matt Detrich)

Goodyear workers hoist Glen Wallace in a boatswain's chair to allow him to prepare for painting the top of the *Spirit of Akron* in Goodyear's Wingfoot Lake Hangar in Portage County's Suffield Township. (*Akron Beacon Journal*/Matt Detrich)

Vince Rubino helped build blimps while he was stationed at Moffett Field during WWII. Now, he is a Goodyear retiree and president of the Lighter Than Air Society, a group of airship aficionados. He is shown holding a K21-type airship, the kind he worked on in California. (*Akron Beacon Journal*/Paul Tople)

loons, and its aircraft division—Aerojet—cranked out rockets at its California plant. B. F. Goodrich Company resisted the temptation of government contracts for aircraft-related goods. But the company did make airplane tires, wing de-icers, and self-sealing fuel tanks.

Goodyear Aircraft Corporation, in its alphabet soup of plants, employed more wartime workers than any other Akron company. It was one of the largest aircraft companies in the country. In Plants A, B, C, D, E, and F (G followed after the war), workers built airplane parts, lighter-than-air ships, and helicopters. Plant A was the massive airdock originally built to house Goodyear's zeppelins; the other plants were built alongside it.

Vince Rubino went to work as a metalsmith in Plant A, building gondolas for the blimps in that cavernous, clamorous hangar. Soon, though, he and many of his buddies would be called up for more pressing duty. Airship bases had been established at Moffett Field in California and at Lakehurst, New Jersey; smaller bases were added as the war intensified. Men and women from Akron were vital, as the city was the mother lode of experts in the country on repairing and maintaining dirigibles. Rubino, eager to serve, was recommended for direct enlistment into the Navy's Lighter Than Air program, meaning he would bypass basic training and be

sent directly to Moffett Field, which was named in honor of Rear Admiral William A. Moffett, a casualty in the crash of the *Akron,* the Goodyear-built zeppelin.

In November 1942, Rubino, who had never been west of Ohio, boarded a train and arrived, alone, in California. "As I entered the base, the main gate was well guarded by Marine sentinels, and the base administration was sandbagged," he wrote in his memoir, which is kept at the Moffett Field Historical Society Museum. "Several machine gun nests around the base were visibly sandbagged as well. Being newly exposed to this military environment direct from civilian life was somewhat of a shock to me, and I naively felt that I was in a war zone on arrival."

The next day, Rubino found himself in a navy uniform, assigned to the base's metal shop, doing work similar to what he had done in Akron. After a few months, he volunteered for duty in the engineering department, where he would spend the next three years as a design draftsman, working mostly on the K-21, an experimental airship.

"We non-coms were in most part very knowledgeable in our line of work, and most of us were from Akron, Ohio," Rubino wrote. "At one time, there were approximately fifty men who were former Goodyear employees, who took part in the

The Goodyear Blimp

The Goodyear blimp is one of the most recognizable symbols of the company today. The Goodyear Tire and Rubber Company operates three blimps: the Eagle, the Stars and Stripes, and the Spirit of Akron; the latter is based in Goodyear's Wingfoot Lake facility near Akron.

Specifications

Name	*Spirit of Akron*
Type	GZ-22
Length	205.5 feet (68.5 yards)
Width	47 feet
Height	60.2 feet
Volume	247,800 cubic feet
Maximum weight	15,000 pounds
Maximum speed	65 mph
Cruise speed	30-40 mph
Envelope pressure	1.3 inches of water (.04693 lbs./sq. in.)
Fuel tank capacity	426 gallons (jet fuel)
Passenger seats	Eight, plus two pilots

On the starboard (right) side of the blimp is a network of colored lights. Each of the 4,032 lights is a light bulb in front of a reflector. A colored filter gives it a blue, green, red, or yellow color. This network can be seen only during the night, and the messages and animation can be shown in only one color at a time.

Tail

The control surfaces on the *Spirit of Akron* are aligned in an "x" formation as opposed to a "+" formation. In a "+" formation (found on the other Goodyear blimps), the vertically aligned "rudders" control the left-to-right movement and the horizontal "elevators" control up-and-down. On the *Spirit of Akron,* however, all four control surfaces (also called "ruddervators") work together to control both types of movement.

"+"

"x"

Flight

Airdock

As blimp rises, the helium in the envelope expands, increasing the internal pressure. The ballonets (air bags inside the blimp) are deflated to compensate.

Blimp cruises at 1,000 to 3,000 feet going 35 mph. The higher the blimp rises, the more air that must be released from the ballonets to compensate. The blimp can rise as high as 10,000 feet.

Ballast (bags filled with twenty-five pounds of lead shot apiece) adjusted to bring blimp to desired takeoff weight. Ground crew members hold the blimp down with ropes connected to the nose cone and by holding gondola railing.

Features

1. **Control surfaces:** Also called "ruddervators, " these fins control the direction of the blimp.

2. **Envelope:** The largest component of a blimp, it holds the helium that makes the blimp lighter than air. It is made of two-ply neoprene-impregnated polyester fabric.

3. **Helium valve:** This device allows the pilot to let helium escape, if necessary.

4. **Aft ballonet:** Air bag inside the envelope helps maintain a constant pressure in the envelope.

5. **Forward ballonet:** Air bag inside the envelope helps maintain a constant pressure in the envelope.

6. **Catenary curtain:** Cemented to the inside of the envelope, it supports the gondola through cables.

7. **Nose cone battens:** They support the nose of the blimp and are also used to help moor the blimp.

8. **Secondary mooring:** Small attachment can be used to secure blimp to the top of the ground crew's bus.

9. **Air valves:** Outlets let air escape from forward and aft ballonets to maintain envelope pressure.

10. **Gondola:** Passenger compartment.

11. **Railing:** Rail allows ground crew to hold blimp during takeoff and landing. Crew also uses it to "weigh" blimp before takeoff to determine the amount of ballast needed to compensate for fuel that will be burned during the trip. Crew grabs railing on both sides of gondola and lets go in unison – if the blimp rises, it is light; if it drops, it's heavy.

12. **Landing gear:** One retractable wheel helps steady the blimp during landing procedures.

13. **Turbine engines:** Engines provide blimp's thrust. They rotate, giving the pilot greater control over the blimp's movement.

On the port (left) side of the blimp are 3,854 boards such as this one, holding a total of 82,656 LEDs. Of these boards, 1,036 are configured to be seen from the ground during the day. To form the nighttime display, the day boards are reduced in intensity and added to the rest. Day or night, the LED display is capable of thirty thousand colors, allowing it to achieve shading and photographic effects. This LED display has been in use only since 1996.

As blimp descends, envelope pressure drops and ballonets are inflated—air scoops behind the turboprop engines funnel the air pushed out of the engines into the ballonets. The retractable landing gear is released.

Members of the ground crew grab the two ropes attached to the nose cone to help secure the blimp. Once it is close enough to the ground, other members grab the railing on both sides of the gondola. The blimp is docked to a portable moor.

Moor

SOURCES: Don McDuff, senior pilot, *Spirit of Akron;* Goodyear Airship Operations; Goodyear Tire and Rubber Company.

Navy's patrol against enemy submarines in the Pacific. Goodyear was a key player in the Lighter Than Air efforts at Moffett."

By the time the war ended, Moffett had become home to sixty-four airships, all built in Akron. They lolled about the skies, creating a heady, surreal skyscape when they flew in formation. The ships' long range allowed them to keep watch as far as two hundred miles out to sea. Their hovering ability made them excellent hawks, with a perspective that those on seabound vessels could only dream about. The blimps performed brilliantly. Only once near Moffett did an enemy sub fire a shell toward land. It exploded harmlessly on an unpopulated beach.

A single Goodyear airship was lost during the war, on the opposite coast. In July 1943, near Key West, Florida, a surveillance blimp spotted an enemy sub on the surface. A gunbattle ensued; the docile airship turned bird of prey. The blimp—hardly equipped for battle—took the worst of it. The damaged airship struggled toward shore but crashed, and the crew was rescued at sea.

The blimps, which now seem such flights of fancy, served a serious purpose at Moffett, Lakehurst, and the other bases. Rubino spent forty months at Moffett, "the most carefree time of my life." He returned to Akron, in 1946, and spent the rest of his career with Goodyear's aircraft—later aerospace—subsidiary. He retired in 1985. But Rubino has never lost his sense of fascination with airships. He owns a bookshelf-full of blimp models, about a dozen of them. They hover over a set of black binders—bound volumes of *Buoyant Flight*, the bulletin of the Lighter Than Air Society. Rubino's mission as president of the society is to try to attract more young people. The attraction ought to be magnetic—kids seem to run and shout whenever the blimp passes overhead. But Rubino admits his worry.

"It's become almost like a lost art," he said.

The time when Akron was a part of a great war machine seems like a wrinkle in the past. Tens of thousands of people worked in the rubber companies' defense units, but large numbers of them were laid off when the war ended; Goodyear Aircraft, the largest and most active, released fifteen thousand workers just days after victory was declared in Japan in 1945. Still, those days are indelible, both in the memories of those who worked there and in the lasting effect the war divisions had on the companies.

Goodyear Aircraft evolved into Goodyear Aerospace. The subsidiary, which employed more than five thousand workers, made defense electronics systems—radar and tactical weapons—and wheels, brakes, and antiskid equipment for military aircraft. It remained a highly profitable arm of the company until 1987, when it was sold to help offset debt incurred in warding off the takeover attempt by Sir James Goldsmith. GenCorp has jettisoned its General Tire unit, but the Aerojet division is still responsible for about one third of GenCorp's annual sales, despite cuts in military spending. In 1996, GenCorp Aerojet had $494 million in sales, and its profit increased 40 percent over the previous year. Aerojet brings in the company's highest-profile contracts, with projects that include the Titan missile program and the Minuteman missile line. The bulk of its manufacturing is done on the West Coast, but the corporate heads remain in GenCorp's Fairlawn headquarters.

B. F. Goodrich's aerospace unit remained basically a footnote to the company's

Planes are constructed at Goodyear Aircraft in 1946. The company employed more wartime workers than any other Akron company. (*Akron Beacon Journal*)

core businesses of tires and specialty chemicals until the 1980s. Since then, however, the unit has blossomed. Goodrich Aerospace now accounts for more than half the company's $2.2 billion in annual sales, thanks to nearly a decade of acquisitions in the industry. The division, which makes fuel systems and flight instruments and handles maintenance and repair for a wide range of aircraft, has bought twenty-one companies in the past nine years. Like GenCorp, its top management is based in Akron-area offices, with manufacturing elsewhere.

Firestone Aircraft Company was short-lived. It ceased production in Akron in August 1945, putting twenty-seven hundred workers—most of them women—out of work. By that time, some of the most significant chapters of Akron's aerial legacy had been written. Others were still forming.

〜

The blimp has become, perhaps more than anything else, the symbol of Rubber City. Akron kids always got colorful little blimp erasers in their Christmas stockings. People from Akron hear that distinctive drone and know without looking up that the blimp is aloft. But they always look up.

Jack LaFontaine has ridden in blimps hundreds of times. But he can't stop being around them. They are too much a part of who he is. Forty-eight years after he took his first job with Goodyear, the Mogadore resident was still putting in his hours at the Wingfoot hangar. "It's interesting work, and it gives me something to do. That's what I've been doing all my life," LaFontaine said. "A helium head is always a helium head." These days, the atmosphere around Wingfoot is loose. Jokes are tossed around like a game of pepper; laughter echoes through the hangar. The stiffness that, years ago, surrounded the military work has softened, and LaFontaine's stories, endless and fascinating, fill the air above the smoking area. People here know their main function is to give people a thrill—one Goodyear employee called the blimps "giant, puffy grandmothers."

A grand part of LaFontaine's formative years was spent just across Wingfoot Lake from the hangar, at Wingfoot Lake Park, which, from the 1930s through the 1950s, was operated by his father, Ray "Red" LaFontaine. In the early years, the park, which the elder LaFontaine leased from Goodyear, was known as Fontaine's Landing. Later, it was called Goodyear Recreational Park, before being dubbed Wingfoot Lake Park in 1970. In 1948, Jack's dad helped him get a job at the Wingfoot Lake hangar, building storm doors for Alsco Aluminum, which contracted with Goodyear to build its products. Goodyear was finding creative ways to keep all this wartime space busy: Montgomery Ward leased part of another Goodyear Aircraft plant to build kitchen cabinets. LaFontaine backed into his blimp career in 1949. He was working in maintenance at the time and had started to fancy the idea of becoming a truck driver.

"The driver at that time was getting into trouble—he was mouthing off," LaFontaine recalled. "And the supervisor had been on vacation, and they said to me they wanted me to go with Luke, the truck driver, and learn the route—that they were gonna transfer Luke off the truck and get him into the plant. Lo and behold, Harold Capes [his supervisor] comes back from vacation and asks what I'm up to."

"I'm learning the route for truck driver," LaFontaine told him.

"'No, no,' he says—'You ain't gonna be no truck driver.' He says, 'There ain't no money in that.' He says, 'You got too good an education.' He says, 'You go over there and work on the airship.'"

LaFontaine did. His first job was helping to treat the inside of envelopes—the blimps' "balloons"—with a paraffin compound that made them airtight. Soon, he moved deeper into the fold, working as a crew member on the airships and a supervisor of their construction. For ten years, LaFontaine's education continued. He learned the quirks of these magical ships, listened to the pilots and the riggers, watched the way the ships went together. Even without a war, Goodyear Aircraft kept about three thousand employed at its plants in the early 1950s. The navy was still interested in the defense aspect of the airships and continued pumping money into their development. As technology advanced, Goodyear developed larger airships designed to haul and employ radar gear. By the late 1950s, the company was building giant ZPG-3W ships; at 403 feet in length, they are the largest nonrigid airships ever built.

Then, early in 1960, the bottom dropped out. The Department of Defense could no longer justify the expense of its airship contract and severed its ties. La-Fontaine was working the day that last 3W eased through the giant retractable doors of the airdock for her delivery flight to Lakehurst. On board was a pensive Karl Arnstein, leader of the elite group of engineers who had come from Germany a generation earlier to launch Goodyear's rigid airship program. That program had failed, but from its ashes had risen the blimps. Now Arnstein was bearing witness to the end of yet another era. LaFontaine, looking skyward, was wistful about this last flight; a few weeks later, his dejection took a further dip. On June 10, 1960, the majority of the blimp workers were laid off.

When LaFontaine was recalled, in January 1963, to be a crew member on Goodyear's blimp in Miami, he was part of a more elite group than ever. Goodyear maintained just a few blimps, keeping afloat one of the most recognizable corporate symbols in history. But the more practical uses of airships apparently had ended forever. Back in the 1920s and 1930s, Goodyear President P. W. Litchfield had dreamed of airships dominating the skies like massive luxury liners. But the repeated spectacle of rigid airship wrecks dashed those dreams. The blimp era revived them, but no one has found a way to bring them to fruition. Yet the dream goes on. Every year or two, it's pitched as a certainty—airships will be the next big thing. Headlines since the 1960s have trumpeted the news that blimps were about to make their resurgence. The hopes rise, but they always have landed empty.

That's not to say the blimp serves no purpose. It's just that its chief practicality is its novelty. The blimp is to Goodyear what Mickey Mouse is to Disney. And for that reason alone, Jack LaFontaine and his few aging colleagues are a vital link to a time when the airships were cranked out by the dozens. LaFontaine has been a part of the streamlined blimp program through the decades, called on to help build and maintain ships around the world. By osmosis, he has become an expert on the nuts and bolts of blimp construction. But because the airship program has been in a relative holding pattern since the navy contracts dried up, there is no new generation of Jack LaFontaines.

"We have a situation that's a little unique—we don't have a lineup of people that are understudies on a day-to-day basis," said Tom Riley, Goodyear's manager of airship operations. After the navy mothballed its blimp program in the early 1960s, Goodyear didn't build another completely new ship in Akron until 1987, when it unveiled the *Spirit of Akron*. A number of ships had been rebuilt and repaired in Akron, but this technologically advanced blimp, built strictly for advertising and public relations purposes, was the first in two decades to go from blueprint to finished product. It was based for five years in Pompano Beach, Florida. Other companies have entered this decidedly specialized field since the years when Goodyear dominated. And Goodyear no longer owns the technology behind the blimps; that was sold, along with the rest of Goodyear Aerospace, to Loral Corporation in 1987. Then Loral sold the operation to Lockheed Martin Corporation in 1996. All Goodyear owns now are its blimps, the Wingfoot Lake facility, and a lot of memories.

As with tires, Akron is no longer the center of the airship industry. A staff of seventy-eight is dispersed across Goodyear's three airship bases in Akron, Pompano Beach, and Gardena, California. Riley manages to hold together a cadre of retirees whose knowledge is invaluable, and he is working to make sure that a new generation is groomed. But there will never be the kind of gritty experience gained in wartime. That isn't necessary, of course, but it creates a certain breed—people with an organic sense of how the ships work.

∾

So much of Akron's pride has headed south over the past twenty years. But one day in 1992, a big hunk came back. Stanley Gault had just taken over as chief executive officer of Goodyear. The company was still recovering from the debt it had incurred fighting takeover artist Sir James Goldsmith. Gault was looking hard at every aspect of the company, at ways to save money and eliminate waste. Insiders' hearts quickened when they thought about what might happen to the blimp.

Blimps cost money. They don't make money—at least, not directly. From a bottom-line standpoint, they look awfully bloated. John Perduyn, Goodyear's vice president of public affairs, remembered the statement Gault made at a gathering to announce his appointment as CEO: "I don't know whether we need any blimps—or whether we need five blimps."

Recalled Gault: "My point was: Unless we can find a way to make them more productive and can merchandise this corporate icon better than I believe we have, then [the blimps] will go on the block like every other thing."

Not long after Gault was appointed, he pulled Perduyn aside. "Why are the blimps silver and black?" he asked. "Why not more colorful—blue and yellow?"

The blimps were staying. They now have blue and yellow side panels. As discussion continued, the decision was made to close Goodyear's airship base in Houston, sell the valuable land it occupied, and move the *Spirit of Akron* from Pompano Beach to its birthplace. Gault couldn't see much purpose in keeping a blimp in Texas, where two of the major sports facilities—the Astrodome in Houston and Texas Stadium in Irving, near Dallas—come with roofs, full or partial, blocking the blimp's signature bird's-eye camera view. In neighboring Louisiana, the Superdome offers another view of a roof. And Gault could see plenty of reasons to move a blimp back to Akron. Basing it in the hangar at Wingfoot Lake in Suffield Township, Goodyear could save $750,000 a year. The change would leave the company with three blimp facilities to maintain instead of four and allow it to sell the Texas land. The move made financial sense. For Akron, it made metaphorical sense, as well.

Perhaps more than anything else that defines Akron, the blimp, its big lit-up presence floating fancifully above town, represents hope. For a long time, all that Akron residents had was hope. As plant closing after plant closing and foreign takeover after foreign takeover humbled the city's residents, one thing bonded them: dreams.

Dreams of a better future, dreams of a fruitful past, and one small dream that many people who have lived in this city share.

To ride, just once, on the blimp.

13 The Radial Invasion

IN THE 1960s, a leash of fear stretched from Detroit to Akron: fear of radial tires, the superior European product. Radials had the U.S. auto industry running scared. Re-engineering and retooling for radial tires would eat into Detroit's profits. Akron's tire industry faced the same pressures. It, too, would have to retool for the more precise and costly construction of radials. And that would chew into Akron's profits.

At the B. F. Goodrich Company, Gerard "Gerry" Alexander was attempting to put the brakes to fear of radial tires. Alexander, president of International B. F. Goodrich Company, knew from his experience in Europe that radials would soon be the future of American drivers. Radials also might be the future of Goodrich's tire division, which sorely needed a product with cachet. Infatuated with chemicals, especially polyvinyl chloride, B. F. Goodrich had failed to reinvest in its tire operations. In U.S. tire sales, Goodrich trailed Goodyear, Firestone, and Uniroyal. In a few years, Goodrich would have to decide: in or out of tires. Radials might give it reason to stay.

In Europe, Alexander already had vaulted the internal wailing wall of opposition from the corporate bean counters, who feared any major capital expense, and from others who simply feared the unknown. John Ong, who retired, in 1997, as

Goodrich chairman, worked with Alexander in international operations in the 1960s. "By force of personality, almost without authority," Ong remembered, "Gerry started a line of radial tires in our German and Dutch plants in the mid-'60s."

Goodrich got into the radial game late by European standards. Michelin of France had been building radials exclusively since the late 1940s. But Goodrich's tardy entry worked to the company's advantage because it resulted in capital investment in state-of-the-art operations in such places as Koblenz, Germany. Goodrich's European radial, the GT100, yielded a store of knowledge that the American side could use to facilitate the successful conversion of domestic plants. But others at Goodrich did not share Alexander's enthusiasm.

Many domestic tire people considered the radial "a freak product [that] isn't going to go anyplace," Ong recalled. "They were thinking about the tremendous investment they would have to make to reequip to produce radial tires. I think they were concerned about where the hell the capital was going to come from."

The radial proved to be the line of demarcation in the rubber industry. Radials caused the industry to contract. Companies merged and disappeared, one inside the other like Russian nesting dolls. Plants closed. Jobs vanished. Titles such as Rubber Capital of the World began to ring hollow. "I say today that the reason the rubber industry left Akron is radial tires," said Alvin Warren, a retired Firestone manager.

Early on, though, Gerry Alexander staked the future of Goodrich's tire division on this product. A textile engineer and graduate of Lowell (Massachusetts) Technological Institute, Alexander understood the fibers—rayon, nylon, fiberglass—that were being tried in U.S. rubber shops as alternatives to the steel belts used to reinforce European radials.

The radial has plies of rubber-coated fabric placed at ninety degrees to the direction of travel and a rubber-coated steel belt inserted between the plies and tread for strength and shape. It offers more advantages than the bias tire, which was the standard in the United States for decades. In the bias tire, plies are set at an angle to the tread and crosswise to each other. Consequently, the bias tire's plies twist more as the tire rolls, creating friction and heat and causing a rolling resistance that reduces fuel economy. Radials were far more fuel-efficient and lasted twice as long as bias tires. But radials cost more to make and required a technical precision heretofore unknown in U.S. tire plants. Also, the ride on radials could seem rough compared with that of cushy bias tires, particularly at lower speeds. In Akron, many tire executives contended that Americans weren't ready for a rough ride and would be unwilling to pay more for it.

But Alexander, with his global outlook, realized that Goodrich's competition wasn't just in Akron and, on the foreign front, it wasn't just Michelin. It also was Bridgestone of Japan, Pirelli of Italy, and Continental of Germany, all of which had been building and selling radials in Europe and Asia for years. So, in 1965, largely due to Alexander's efforts, Goodrich test-marketed a radial tire for the U.S. market. The Silvertown Radial 900 debuted in Dallas to good reviews from dealers and customers alike and won Goodrich a contract with Ford Motor Company to supply the 1967 Mercury Colony Park station wagon. Because Goodrich was a comparatively small tire maker, Ford wanted a backup contract with another tire

A B.F. Goodrich employee operates a radial tire curing machine in 1968. Goodrich gambled on introducing radials to the U.S. market in the late 1960s, but bias-belted tires instead became the rage. (The University of Akron Archives)

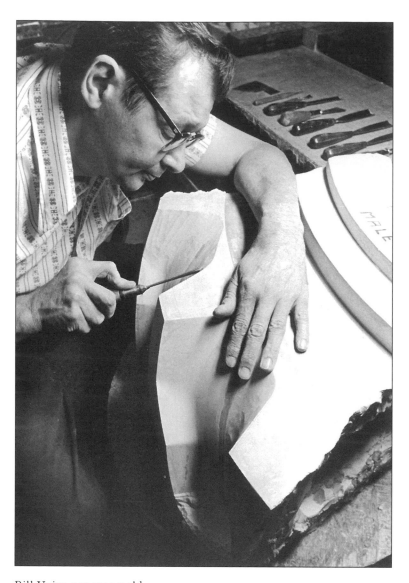

Bill Vujas, a master mold carver, uses a variety of chiseling tools to turn a block of plaster into the pattern for an aluminum mold that will shape and vulcanize a Goodyear radial farm tire. *(Akron Beacon Journal)*

company to ensure an uninterrupted supply of tires. Goodyear, then the world's largest tire company, with the industry nickname of The Gorilla, refused to be a secondary supplier. So did Firestone. Without a secondary supplier, Ford canceled the contract for Goodrich radials.

Goodyear then seized on the auto industry's hesitation and consumer ignorance. In November 1967, Goodyear introduced its response to the radial, a bias-belted product called the Custom Wide Polyglas. Constructed with diagonal plies but overlaid with radial-type belts, the bias-belted tire rode the middle ground in price and performance. The bias-belted tire, for example, lasted thirty thousand miles compared with forty thousand for radial and twenty-three thousand for bias. Most important, the bias-belted tire could be built on existing tire-making machines. The rubber companies could depreciate their machinery and equipment before retooling for radials, at an average cost per company of $500 million. U.S. manufacturers were simply buying time with a "transition" tire, according to University of Akron history professor Daniel Nelson. "They knew they would have to make the transition to radials, but they expected that it would take fifteen years."

To its credit but never to any avail, Goodrich wasn't deterred, at least initially, by The Gorilla's bias-belted product. In 1968, Goodrich launched the largest advertising campaign in its history, seeking with its "Radial Age" story to convince consumers that radials were the tires they had to have. Radials needed heavy promotion if the American public was to accept them. U.S. cars were larger than Japanese and European vehicles and did not have radial-friendly suspension systems. To get the optimal ride on radials, consumers had to replace all four tires at once, at an expense at the time of about $300.

Goodyear responded with its own advertising campaign, outspending Goodrich by a four-to-one ratio. Goodyear bought its largest TV advertising package ever, cosponsoring coverage of the Winter Olympics and Summer Olympics. It pounded an estimated 140 million viewers with sixty-six minutes of commercials that were nothing short of negative. They excoriated the radial, primarily for its ride and cost. The campaign worked. Detroit jumped on the bias-belted bandwagon with all four wheels and a spare. From 2 percent of the original-equipment market in 1968, bias-belted sales rose to 87 percent in the early 1970s.

One Wall Street analyst said, in 1971, that Goodrich's rush into radials "was one of the major errors ever made by a manufacturer in the judging of a market." John Ong attributes any market miscue to Goodyear. "They came up with this bastard product," Ong said, in 1996. "I think they knew, and we certainly thought, that it was not a product that had a lot of merit. But they put the power of their advertising and sales promotion budget behind it and were very, very public in their scorn for radials. It stalled the industry's move to radials."

Moreover, it allowed foreign companies to increase their U.S. market share just as the domestic tire industry was becoming vulnerable. Michelin, the world's leading maker of radials, was penetrating the U.S. market with private-label sales through Sears, an arrangement that began in 1965.

Detroit, for its part, gave off a signal that seemed forever amber. Charles Brady was the head of GM's Tire and Wheel Group in the early 1970s. He had trouble getting a green light for radials, even with the support of his boss, Ed Cole. Cole was GM's president when GM still sold more than half of the new cars in America. "I ran into a great many problems with our own company," Brady said. "Radials cost 45 percent more [than bias-belted]. The financial people said: 'You can't just put 45 percent more in costs on our cars. You're going to drive people out of our price range.'"

Nearly everyone in the U.S. rubber and auto industries, it seemed, was hedging bets, stalling, or otherwise tossing carpet tacks onto the fast track to the radial future. With no original equipment contract, Goodrich could not continue to push a product for which there was no market. And the other major American tire companies were content to follow Goodyear's lead. After all, what was the rush? Gasoline was cheap in the United States, and Americans could afford to operate the "sofas on wheels" that were hostile to radials.

Conflict in the Mideast, however, stopped America's motoring public as quickly as four flat tires. In 1973, members of the Organization of Petroleum Exporting Countries reduced oil production and distribution. Gas prices soared overnight from thirty cents per gallon to more than a dollar. Lines at the pumps stretched for blocks. Americans began demanding more fuel-efficient cars. Gas sippers from Europe and Japan replaced gas guzzlers from Detroit. That year, imports represented 15.3 percent of U.S. auto sales. By early the next decade, that figure had climbed to 28 percent. Imports usually came equipped with radial tires, often made by Bridgestone, the leader in Asia, or Michelin, the dominant company in Europe.

Actually, U.S. carmakers became interested in radials before the gas crisis handed them an imperative. The Ford Motor Company made the first significant move, signing a contract with Michelin to supply radials for the 1970 Lincoln Continental and Mark III models. After the OPEC embargo, Detroit had more leverage than ever, and the implications for Akron were indeed grave. Rubber companies got little more than cost for original equipment tire sales to Detroit—replacement sales on the retail level to consumers are far more lucrative. But with longer-lasting radials, a larger percentage of tire sales would be to the original-equipment market. And profit margins in Akron would shrink even more.

Richard S. Tedlow and Richard S. Rosenbloom from Harvard's Graduate School of Business Administration and Donald N. Sull from the London Business

School studied the fix in which the rubber companies found themselves. "Tire makers faced three alternatives," they concluded in a paper titled "Managerial Commitments and Technological Change in the U.S. Tire Industry":

> They could choose to exit from the business by selling their brands, distribution channels and manufacturing facilities to one of the foreign producers then trying energetically to gain a foothold in the U.S. market. . . . They could confront their large customers and make their investment in radial production contingent upon guarantees of adequate prices for the new products. . . . Finally, they could invest in radials without changing terms of business, with predictable economic consequences.

Goodyear chose to stay in the business without changing its terms. In truth, Goodyear hadn't been ignoring the radial tire. Like other domestic tire companies with international operations, Goodyear produced and sold radials overseas. In 1967, the same year it introduced the bias-belted tire, Goodyear was making a tire for limited distribution in the U.S. called the Power Cushion, essentially a knock-off of its European radial. Then, in 1972, Charles J. Pilliod became president of Goodyear, after spending most of his career on the international side. Like Gerry Alexander at Goodrich, Pilliod knew Goodyear's most serious competitive challenges would come from abroad. But convincing his colleagues, particularly Goodyear's marketers, wasn't easy. Goodyear's surveys indicated customers didn't want to pay more for tires. Goodyear tested radials in one market. The response was tepid. Pilliod said: "We're going to have to ignore all these studies." He went to Chairman Russ DeYoung to make his case.

"How much will it cost?" DeYoung asked.

"We're probably looking at $1½ billion to $2 billion," Pilliod said.

"If you feel that strongly about it," DeYoung told Pilliod, "I guess you'd better do it."

"That was a lot of money then," Pilliod recalled with a chuckle. "We didn't have it. It would have to come out of earnings."

Goodyear engineers and designers went to the drawing boards. A model plant was built in Lawton, Oklahoma. Seven older plants were updated for radial production. "He was the guiding light on turning Goodyear into a radial company," said Alan Ockene, a former Goodyear executive, "and he was tough about it. A lot of people were second-guessing him. He really is the savior of Goodyear. Without him there, I doubt if Goodyear would have made it." By 1977, Goodyear had its breakthrough radial, the Tiempo, followed by the Arriva in 1980.

In a twist of irony, the only rubber company that made an early but quiet decision to get out of tire making was the one that had been best positioned technically to take advantage of the radial revolution—Goodrich. In 1971, Goodrich was producing its fourth-generation radial while other American companies were still trying to get their first ones on the road. Gerry Alexander predicted that, by 1980, more than half the tires produced for American cars would be radials. His prediction was too conservative. By 1981, Detroit had gone 99 percent radial. By 1983, a driver couldn't find a bias-belted or bias tire on a new American car.

That didn't save Goodrich's tire division, though. In January 1981, Goodrich announced it was leaving the original-equipment market and would build tires only for sales to consumers. The move made it the most profitable tire division

among the Big Five but did not position it as the big-ticket original-equipment and replacement provider it needed to be to survive over time. By the mid 1980s, Goodrich had sold off all tire operations to Uniroyal and had staked its future on aerospace and specialty chemicals.

Goodrich survived because it knew when to say enough was enough and concentrate on business segments that had a future. Firestone's early radial experience, on the other hand, nearly drove the company out of business.

Harvey Firestone's proud old company rolled out the 500 Steel Belt tire, in January 1972, with its biggest-ever advertising campaign, identifying itself as the

Richard Riley, Firestone's new president in 1972, began a series of visits to the company's tire plants by visiting Akron's Plant 2. At the final inspection station for the new Radial V-1 tire, he chatted with Elliott Robinson, a Firestone employee. (*Akron Beacon Journal*)

"People Tire Company." A bias-belted tire, it was joined by a radial 500. Both employed steel-belt construction. Publicly, the 500 was an early success. *Consumer Reports* loved it. The magazine's October 1973 issue rated the radial 500 "well above average," placing it at the top of the heap with a comparable tire from Bridgestone of Japan in an intensive test of radials. A 1974 Firestone survey revealed that "500" was the most recognized brand name in the industry. Inside the Akron headquarters, though, ulcers were developing.

One month after the 500 hit the market, A. J. "Tony" DiMaggio, a Firestone quality control executive, learned that the cords in the steel-belted tire were not adhering properly to the skim, a rubber compound. The internal layers of the tire were liable to come apart, which could cause road failures. DiMaggio told his boss about this, word spread, questions were asked. Alvin W. Warren, who worked in the tire-testing division, sent a memo to the tire development manager: "I believe the poor adhesion problem is handled, but it is something we must continue to watch very carefully."

Production continued. Firestone engineers worked to improve the tire, but they didn't have the luxury of time that they might have had a decade before. And time proved to be the biggest problem with the 500—its technical flaws did not surface until a tire had been on the road for many thousands of miles. The new tires were tested extensively, but they were tested in the old way, the way bias-ply tires had been, for about four months. The adhesion flaw, though, was related to aging, not mileage, and didn't appear until a year or more after production. Firestone was not accustomed to testing a tire that would last this long and, according to many observers, the testing didn't go far enough. By late 1973, the problems were coming back to haunt Firestone in the form of returned tires. A large number of 500 owners were taking their tires to dealers, complaining of tread separation, a condition in which the tread pulls away from the rest of the tire. The number of tires returned for warranty replacement was more than double the number for Firestone's nonradials.

The early problem with the 500, according to *Beacon Journal* reports based on company documents, was that moisture existed in the bond between the steel cords and the rubber around them, damaging their adhesion. Firestone engineers worked doggedly to correct the chemical flaw, but the company did not interrupt production until 1978, when the tire left the market. The adhesion problem, because it was chemical, could take place whether the tire was on the road or in a warehouse. But its result—blowouts, tread separation, distortions in the tire's shape, etc.—showed up only after the tire was in use.

"I never quite believed the tires were so bad," said Bill Terrall, a forty-year Firestone employee who retired, in 1977, as manager of advance planning. Then, one day in 1976, Terrall slid into the driver's seat of a Firestone company car for a trip to the company's Hamilton, Ontario plant. Between him and the road was a set of radial 500s. As he neared Buffalo, he began to hear a thumping sound that turned into an awful racket. The sound soon went away, and he continued driving. In Buffalo, Terrall stopped for gas. When he got out of the car, he noticed a problem with one of the front tires. A chunk of tread the size of his hand was missing. "Here was what they were screaming about," Terrall recalled.

He took the tire off, put on the spare—also a 500—and continued on to

Hamilton, where he checked into his hotel. When he went out the next morning, the spare was flat. Terrall summoned a serviceman, who took one look at the car and issued his prognosis: "He said, 'Well, they're all radial 500s; they're no good.'"

"I've got to get back to Akron," Terrall said.

"I wouldn't go around the block on those," the man said.

Terrall believed. By then, a lot of other people were beginning to believe, too. General Motors had already threatened to drop Firestone as a radial supplier, and Atlas, a tire distributor, had written the company a letter saying, "it appears Firestone is coming apart at the seams."

"We were sweating blood," said Alvin Warren. Much of the sweat formed under the hot glare of Joan Claybrook, a hard-nosed consumer lobbyist in prominent black-framed glasses, nicknamed "the Dragon Lady" by auto industry insiders. Claybrook, the first of Ralph Nader's proteges to work her way into the federal government, became head of the National Highway Traffic Safety Administration in 1977. She was focused on one thing in the mid-1970s: the Firestone 500. The traffic safety administration had discovered an in-

Firestone engineer James Gardner checks a 500 radial, in August 1978, during a free safety inspection offered at area Firestone stores to counteract consumer doubts about the tire's reliability. Firestone offered consumers a trade-in policy, allowing them to get Firestone 721 steel-belted radials as replacements if defects were found during the inspection. (*Akron Beacon Journal*/Lew Stamp)

ordinate number of problems with Firestone's bias-ply 500. *Consumer Reports*, which a year before had given high marks to the radial 500, called the bias-ply 500 "not acceptable" after a 1974 test in which seven of the nine tires tested showed tread separation. The traffic safety administration declared a million of the bias-ply tires unsafe and, in 1975, demanded a recall of 350,000 of them.

Firestone fought back. The company's management decided to take its case to court and filed for an injunction. Firestone won that battle—the Washington agency dropped the case—but Claybrook immediately took up a new fight, against the radial 500. The traffic safety administration's early attacks on the radial prompted a Firestone recall of four hundred thousand of the tires, with the company stingily admitting "possible noncompliance" with federal standards in a "limited number" of the tires. Still, it was the largest recall to that point in Firestone history.

Firestone officials led by Bernard Frazier, right, public relations manager, and Richard Riley, chairman, are about to announce the recall of the Firestone 500 at a news conference in October 1978. The largest recall in the history of the United States, some 8.7 million tires were replaced at a cost to the company of an estimated $150 million after tax write-offs. (*Akron Beacon Journal*/Ted Walls)

But Claybrook was just warming up. Her agency sent out a questionnaire to about eighty-seven thousand owners of all brands of radial tires, asking if they were having problems. The survey included a question specifically asking about the performance of the Firestone radial 500. The response was damning. Claybrook's office was swamped with complaints about the Firestone tire, far more than any other brand. Meanwhile, lawsuits had begun pouring in from owners of the 500 claiming injury, damage, and death caused by blowout-related accidents. Firestone's legal department, led by vice president, secretary, and general counsel John Floberg, declared war.

"I believe strongly in cooperating with government agencies," he once said, "but I refuse to be bullied by them." By 1978, that refusal was becoming nationally known. Boldly, perhaps arrogantly, Firestone gave no quarter. It took the fight all the way to the nation's capital and, simultaneously, drove itself headlong into the public spotlight. The national news networks, along with other large newspapers and magazines, latched on like pit bulls as Akron's homegrown tire giant began to look like a monster. Night after night, lights glowed in the public relations office of the company's Firestone Parkway headquarters, as the PR team tried, sometimes desperately, to deal with the nightmare. "It had grown to the point that it was encompassing and engrossing everything we did," said Bob Troyer, a former Firestone public relations manager.

Firestone poured every resource it could into the battle. The only problem was that, in taking on the government, Firestone was pitting itself against people the public could perceive only as victims. As the traffic safety administration pounded away at the corporation, lawsuits poured in, some legitimate, some perhaps not—at least forty-one deaths and seventy injuries were blamed on the tires.

In October 1978, Firestone finally agreed to recall the radial 500. It was an agreement that would involve a potential thirteen million tires and $234 million, far and away the most extensive recall in the history of tire making and one of the most notorious consumer cases in American history. In the end, 8.7 million tires were replaced, at a cost of $150 million after tax write-offs. Worse was the damage to the company's name—the industry joke about the Firestone 721 radial, the

Green steel-belted radial tires await curing at Firestone's production facility in Wilson, NC. About 64 percent of the replacement market, in 1982, was predicted to be taken up by radials. *(Akron Beacon Journal)*

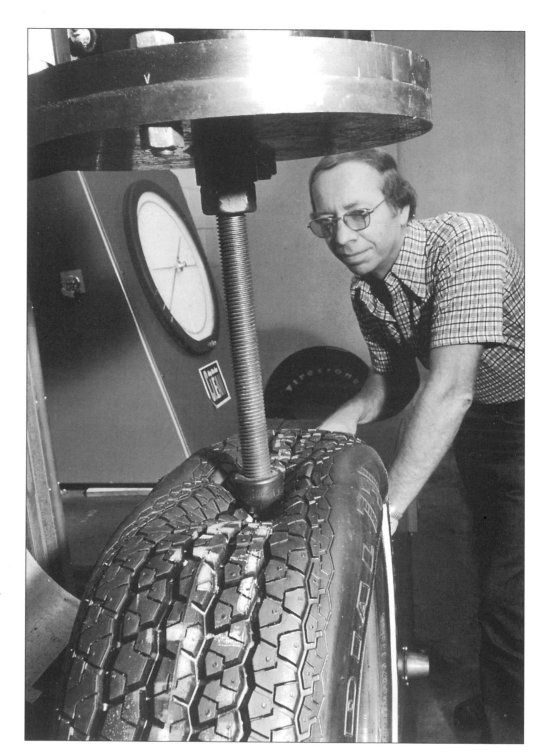

To test resistance to impact damage, a quality assurance technician at Firestone plunges a specially tipped steel rod into an inflated steel-belted radial 721 tire. Firestone's successor to their flawed 500 design was a success in both safety testing and in the marketplace, helping the company survive the 500 recall and aftermath. *(Akron Beacon Journal)*

500's successor and a success in safety testing and in the marketplace, was that it was guaranteed for seven days or twenty-one miles. "I believe, in hindsight, that it was looked at as a legal problem when it should have been looked at as a legal-public relations-marketing issue," said former company spokesman Troyer.

The Firestone 500 was one of a series of high stakes dramas of the 1970s. But it wasn't the only one—especially not after the arrival of a gunslinger named Peter Bommarito.

14   Triennial Passion Plays

COLUMBUS, OHIO. LABOR DAY 1976. The candle of the night had burned down to a nub, and everybody was tired and ready for bed. The longest strike in rubber industry history was coming to an end. Labor negotiators who had been going at it for months had finally, in these early morning hours, hammered out the last matters of the truce. Their nerves were bleached, and they all needed sleep. But Peter Bommarito was not tired.

The Bomber, as he was called, never seemed to need rest. Straight-backed and muscular, clear-voiced and clear-eyed, the United Rubber Workers president was the fighter who grew stronger as the bout wore on. And now, at two o'clock in the morning, two hours from Akron, the battle over, he wanted to get home, to be ready for work when the sun rose again. His union colleagues rolled their tired eyes and shook their heads. Go home? Now? He must be crazy. Besides, they'd all flown to Columbus; no one had a car. Bommarito turned to Stu Feldstein, the *Beacon Journal* labor writer who was at the hotel covering the negotiations. Feldstein had filed his story for the next day's paper. He was done for the night, as tired as everyone else. But he had a car. Under Bommarito's movie-star mustache, his lips curled into a smile, stoking the furnace of his charm.

Half an hour later, Columbus was shrinking in the rear-view mirror as Feldstein and Bommarito cruised northward in the reporter's Ford Pinto. Another negotiation won. As Feldstein focused on the road, Bommarito chatted away, his bright eyes reflecting the street lights and road signs they passed in the night. They neared Akron. And then, suddenly, a flash of gray-white came from—where?—the bridge above, disappearing into a spiderweb of shattered windshield.

Feldstein hit the brakes—instinct—squeezed the steering wheel and managed to bring the car to a halt on the roadside. His heart racing, he looked at Bommarito. Then the two men realized what had hit them: a bundle of *Beacon Journal*s thrown from the overpass. Staring them in the face was the Page One story Feldstein had just written about Bommarito's fight.

That was Peter Bommarito: so aggressive, he not only beat the news to his own doorstep, but sometimes got hit in the face with it. Confrontation was the Bomber's greatest talent. He understood its nuances and worked it like a pump organ. A gentleman, Bommarito possessed a grace that was animal, sleek, and sharp-clawed. He would offer an opponent a cup of coffee across a particularly contentious negotiating table, an act that could be seen only as generous, yet must have left the other side wondering: human kindness or strategy? As the head of the Rubber Workers, from 1966 to 1981, Bommarito ruled during a pivotal era and had nearly as much influence over the city's course as the men who had founded the tire companies. Akron, after Bommarito, would never be the same.

Peter Bommarito was born in the middle of a war, on May 1, 1915. His father was an Italian immigrant who had settled in Detroit, the harshest battlefront in America's labor war. Even as a boy, Peter was devilishly handsome, with black hair and snake-charmer eyes. His father was a street sweeper; young Peter delivered newspapers and worked as a shoeshine boy, playing baseball and football in the streets. He was a fine athlete, lithe and muscular, with a passion for winning. As a teenager, he became a Golden Gloves boxing champion, gleaning the strategies of man-to-man competition, learning to negotiate around weakness in himself and others. The young man took his father's blue-collar pride to work with him in the factories of Detroit, moving through a few jobs before settling into a position with U.S. Rubber Company (later Uniroyal), operating a web fabric machine.

The Second World War erupted when Bommarito was in his mid-20s, and he volunteered for the fight. In 1942, he joined the toughest group, the Marines, and shipped off to the war in the Pacific, where he manhandled flamethrowers, bazookas, and heavy machine guns. He became known as the Bomber. While in the Pacific, Bommarito met another Marine, a fellow from Akron named Bill Lepley. As the men were preparing to board a ship bound for Cape Gloucester off the island of New Britain, word spread that someone had a canteen full of brandy. The canteen was passed around, each Marine taking a belt. It came to Lepley.

"If you drink it all, you are chickenshit," Bommarito told him. Lepley tipped his head back and drained the canteen. Bommarito's muscles tensed; his eyes narrowed. A fight broke out. When it was over, Lepley had a black eye. The next morning, Lepley challenged Bommarito to another fight, saying Bommarito couldn't whip him again. Bommarito accepted. But he wanted to eat breakfast first. Afterward, he blackened Lepley's other eye. They were friends for life.

The URW was maturing when Bommarito rejoined its ranks after World War

Peter Bommarito, president of the United Rubber Workers, leaves a Cleveland hotel after a URW meeting during the strike of 1976. Bommarito earned the nickname of the Bomber while in the Marines, and it fit during his pivotal reign in Akron from 1966 to 1981. Bommarito excelled at confrontation and engaged in it repeatedly at the negotiating table, ending a period of labor calm by leading the URW into strikes every three years from 1967 through 1976. (*Akron Beacon Journal*/Marcy Nighswander)

II. The rubber companies were making money, and the union was becoming more adept at getting its share. In the mid-1950s, U.S. Rubber's Detroit plant became a combat zone, peppered with so many illegal, wildcat strikes that labor and management talked about forming a committee to bring them to an end. Amid the melee, Bommarito rose to power. By then, there was no question about his skill as a fighter, but other talents were emerging. He could recite poetry to a bunch of factory workers and hold them captivated. He could meet a man once and recall his name months later. He could send electricity with a handshake. He became president of URW Local 101, an old and powerful branch of the Akron-based union, in 1957. His ideals about human dignity were growing sharper. So was his fighting spirit. If he saw an injustice on the shop floor, he would confront the fore-man right there and then. He won new rights for black workers. He made a strong impression on just about everyone he met. And, in 1960, he arrived in Akron.

It was an evening in late spring. A group of URW leaders gathered in a pri-vate upper room of the Brown Derby restaurant, next to Goodyear's world head-quarters. The future of the URW teetered on a pivot. The men ordered steak din-ners and began to talk. Joe Childs, the hands-down choice to be the next president of the URW International, had just died of a heart attack. Elections were to be held in September. Suddenly, there was a void on the ticket. The name that had come up was George Burdon, a Los Angeles man who was not well known in Akron but had a solid reputation in the URW. Burdon had been in Akron before, most notably at the 1935 meeting at the Portage Hotel at which the URW was formed. As the men ate, Burdon politicked, getting to know the group, sharing his ideas. And Bommarito, the handsome, wavy-haired Detroiter, surfaced as a possible running mate.

"He was up and coming," former Local 2 president John Nardella said of Bommarito. "He seemed like he had a lot of smarts." As the meeting progressed, the outcome became clear. Burdon and Bommarito formed the one-two punch that went to the URW convention floor in St. Louis that September and won big, each man beating his opponent by a ratio of nearly three to one. But even as the confetti was still settling, Bommarito was eyeing his next move. Second in com-mand was not his nature. He was looking to move up. Bommarito hit the road, visiting plants, attending conventions, making friends. He could shake hands with both hands at once, and he had a vitality that could energize a room. He had the intangible talent—charisma—that distinguishes the great leaders from the rest.

He wanted to challenge Burdon for the presidency in 1962. URW leaders held Bommarito back. He strained against them in 1964, but they held him back again. Finally, in 1966, Bommarito was turned loose. Burdon was under pressure from the union for the money he was spending to have his wife travel with him. His presidency had been relatively uneventful, and many said he had lost touch with the rank and file. He could see the support Bommarito had built for himself. Burdon pulled out of the race. In 1966, Bommarito became the URW's fourth in-ternational president.

If Burdon's reign had been the calm, Bommarito's would be the storm, cloud-ing the air with change. Akron was on the brink of a guerrilla war, when triennial strikes would riddle the town with victims, victors, and uncertainty.

Bommarito and his wife, Dorothy, had moved to Reservoir Drive in Brimfield Township, a middle-class area with wide-open spaces. They became part of the fabric of greater Akron. Peter and Dorothy had no children, and he was often away, traveling on union business or hunting and fishing with his nephews. The five-foot-ten, 170-pound Bommarito was made for the outdoors, tanned and rugged. Even in a business suit, the tendons of his neck suggested a man of raw power. "I thought the man was indestructible," recalled George Vasko, former URW general counsel. "If you ever saw him in a bathing suit, you would not have believed it. I'm talking about when he was sixty-five or seventy. What a physical

Peter Bommarito collects money for the Salvation Army in December 1973. At immediate right is Jack McIntyre, director of the United Fund labor participation department. (*Akron Beacon Journal*/Lewis Henderson)

specimen! We'd go swimming in Florida. He would go underwater the entire length of the pool and back."

Bommarito focused most of his energy on union affairs. But he also, by virtue of his role as the head of a major political force, found himself representing the union in campaigns for the United Fund—later United Way—as well as Salvation Army fund-raising efforts. Even in civic matters, though, Bommarito's ego shone through. Former Akron schools superintendent Conrad Ott recounted the time the URW lent its support to a school tax levy campaign. A newspaper ad endorsing the levy included photos of Bommarito and Goodyear Chairman Russell De-Young. DeYoung's picture was larger than Bommarito's.

"He called me and said, 'Take my picture out of the paper, and I am not supporting this levy,'" Ott said. "If my picture isn't the size of Russ DeYoung," Bommarito continued, "I am not supporting this levy."

The picture was enlarged, and Bommarito continued his support.

On April 20, 1967, seven months after Bommarito took office, the URW rocked the industry with the first major strike in nearly a decade, hitting the four major rubber companies and General Tire. When he discovered the companies had agreed to help one another weather the storm by pooling their financial resources, Bommarito hurled fire and brimstone, denouncing the arrangement as "an unholy alliance." When he felt that newspaper stories about the strike attempted to "smear the good name of the United Rubber Workers," he took out a full-page ad in the *Beacon Journal*, attacking the press on its own turf. While the plant workers walked the picket line, Bommarito fought for them across conference tables.

"He was different to different people. I liked him, and we got along," said Peter J. Pestillo, B. F. Goodrich's head of labor relations in the 1970s. "But it was always a roller coaster dealing with him. One minute, he would be quiet and reflective, the next, he would declare war over the interpretation of a sentence. You didn't know which you would get. And if you tried to figure it out, you would only be guessing."

Management could sense change in the air, a change that became clear over the course of a most unusual day in 1967. No one, at the time, could realize the symbolic significance of that day. But it wrapped itself around some of Akron's greatest changes.

Jefferson Ward Keener awoke shortly after dawn on Monday, June 5, 1967, shaved and showered, put on his gray suit and slipped his watch over his wrist. Keener was a tall man, straight-backed, fifty-eight years old, with prominent tortoise-shell eyeglasses and hair slicked back on his head. From his earlier days as a college professor at Ohio Wesleyan University, he still carried an air of inscrutable dignity, even in the name he used—J. Ward Keener.

He drank his coffee that morning, the one cup he always had before heading into the office. He went out the back door of his Fairlawn Heights home, got into his sea-green Cadillac with the big gull wings, curled down Hampshire Road and turned east onto West Market Street. There was a chill inside the car, the kind of early summer chill that burns off quickly in the rising sun. Even as summer's perfume returned, though, there was something missing from the atmosphere—the gray spice of burning rubber that normally came through the vents of Keener's Cadillac as he neared downtown.

Keener was the chief executive officer of the B. F. Goodrich Company. There was no smell this morning because the workers had been on strike for a month and a half. As he drove down West Exchange Street, thinking about the strike, Keener had lots of things under his control and lots of things beyond it. He reached for the button on the radio to catch the local news. There was talk of some kind of trouble at the plant.

Downtown, one of the strikers approached a Goodrich plant gate. His name was Phil Kaster. He was no troublemaker; he was simply swimming, along with thousands of others, in the current of circumstance. Forty-six years old, he had taken a job with Goodrich straight out of Central High School, fought in World War II, and returned to forge a life in the rubber shop. Kaster was a big man, six-foot-two, two hundred pounds, with big hands and friendly eyes. He was a mechanic. It was a good job. The strike, as he saw it, was a necessary evil. Kaster arrived early that Monday at Goodrich's Bowery Street gate, at the rear of the plant.

He was a strike marshal, a kind of field sergeant. He brought coffee to the pickets and helped keep order in the ranks. That day, his job was to make sure no one hurled a brick through the window of a truck trying to make a delivery to Goodrich.

As Kaster neared the gate, he could tell right away that something was up. The men were talking excitedly about the strike strategy that had been brewing over the weekend. The Thursday before, a gang of pickets had managed to block the gates over at Firestone. This day, the Goodrich strikers were going to do the same. At that moment, someone looked up. Another man shouted. Kaster turned his head. A long green Cadillac was making the turn onto Bowery Street.

Ward Keener's mind began to race. The radio had hinted at trouble; he had considered the possibility of confrontation. But now, as he pulled closer to the plant gate, the situation was no longer hypothetical. It was real. Keener eased his foot into the brake pedal. There was shouting. He was one man in a car. This was a whole gang of his employees. As he considered them through the windshield, one of them, a man he recognized, a tall fellow, stepped in front of his car. Phil Kaster.

Keener shifted the car into park. Kaster approached the driver's side window. Keener rolled it down. He demanded to be allowed to pass. "Ward," Kaster recalled telling him, "you might as well go back home."

Keener looked through the windshield, then looked back at Kaster. "I have a right to go to work," he calmly replied.

The men at the gate shouted and pointed. A Corvair convertible was pulling up beside Keener's Cadillac. It was Glen Sengpiel, Goodrich's corporate director of employee relations. Sengpiel furrowed his brow. Like Keener, he had gathered from the morning news that something like this was going to happen. But the number of men surprised him. Two or three dozen pickets were gathered there. A court order limited the pickets to only three. Sengpiel opened his car door and slowly stepped out. He nodded an uneasy hello to Kaster as he approached Keener's car.

"Stay with me," he recalled Keener saying. Keener was going to make his point. He was going to sit there until he was allowed to go to work. Sengpiel returned to his car. He closed the door and settled into the seat.

A company president's power is in his position. A union's power is in numbers. Over the years, the URW had matured into a major American industrial union, with membership rising to 171,000 by 1967. Those powers had been tested over and over. Sometimes the companies won, sometimes the union. Business had been good for more than a decade, and the pendulum had swung in favor of the URW—the companies couldn't afford strikes with all these orders to fill, and they could afford to give the workers a good deal of what they asked for. In many senses, the industry—labor and management alike—had been lulled into a sleepwalk, moving forward on momentum. But by the late 1960s, demand for tires had flattened, and the companies had stiffened in their negotiating. Bommarito recognized that the URW still had the upper hand, and he was set to push the pendulum harder. The companies were going to push back.

And so, on a summer morning in 1967, Ward Keener found himself sitting in his Cadillac, the engine at idle, his metaphorical shoulder firmly set against that pendulum. Word spread quickly down South Main Street—the old man was sit-

Akron police chief Harry Whiddon, left, and Mayor John Ballard try to persuade Goodrich president J. Ward Keener (in car) to leave after pickets outside the West Bowery St. gate at B.F. Goodrich blocked the entrance to the plant. A battle of wills ensued. (*Akron Beacon Journal*/Julius Greenfield)

ting in his car back at the Bowery Street gate. Pickets from the other posts went to see it for themselves. They kept their distance, but they made their show. A few taunted; some wondered loudly how long Keener's bladder could hold out. Someone grabbed a big piece of cardboard and set it against the Cadillac's grille, an attempt to make the car overheat. Another suggested it might be fun to tip over Sengpiel's little Corvair. By midmorning, many of the men were still betting that Keener would figure his point had been made and drive away. But Keener simply sat there with his windows rolled up. He lit another cigarette. A heavy smoker, he was well into his first pack. He had little else to do.

At noon, some members of the Goodrich medical department brought sandwiches to Keener and Sengpiel, along with several packs of cigarettes for Keener. The temperature was climbing toward eighty degrees, but the CEO still wore his suit jacket. Word of the standoff had spread through downtown Akron. By afternoon, some of Akron's leaders got into their cars and drove down to Bowery Street to see if they could bring this thing to an end. Mayor John Ballard came. Summit County Prosecutor James Barbuto came. Police Chief Harry Whiddon came. *Beacon Journal* Publisher Ben Maidenburg came. Several of the local union leaders came. The action of the strikers was illegal. There was no doubt about that. The temporary court order clearly limited the pickets to three per gate. Each of the visitors told the strikers this. The strikers refused to step aside.

A strike is a hard thing to endure. Its success demands a unified front, even when the troops grow tired. These rubber workers, who earned $3.25 to $3.70 an hour, were scraping by on $25 a week in strike pay. About fifty of them, proud workers, had gone on welfare. The $6.5 million URW strike fund was almost gone. Something was needed to boost morale, and strikers were fairly confident they could be defiant without consequence. The rubber workers swung heavy political weight in Akron. In theory, city police could have arrested the illegal pickets, and Keener could have driven through the gate. They didn't. On this day, and for a decade hence, theories were bouncing around like runaway tires.

The sun continued its journey and began to fall in the sky. J. Ward Keener looked at his watch. It was 5:00 PM. Time to go home. Sengpiel started his car and backed away. Keener paused, pushed his cigarette into the overflowing ashtray and stared through the windshield one last time at the men who worked in his plants. He flashed a wry wave at them, then clicked the gearshift into reverse. The pickets cheered, some say in victory, others say out of respect for the old man's conviction.

No one seems to know for sure.

The strike of 1967 lasted three months. It was the longest major standoff to that point in URW history. Bommarito walked away a winner. One of his greatest goals was to gain a guaranteed annual wage for hourly workers to protect them during layoffs. In the 1967 contract, the companies increased supplemental unemployment benefits from 65 percent to 80 percent, meaning laid-off workers would receive the difference between unemployment compensation and 80 percent of their pay. Bommarito had been tested, and he had won.

So, when the contract expired in 1970, Bommarito, the man who had given the same buddy two black eyes in less than a day, went at it again. The target this time was Goodyear; the key issue in that inflationary age was wages. Goodyear's workers struck for fifty days, joined by Goodrich's laborers for thirty-nine days. The rubber workers gained better pay; an agreement by management to study plant carcinogens; and a paid prescription program. The strike, for the companies, was reportedly the costliest in industry history. The rubber companies were starting to hurt, and the Bomber's reputation in Akron was growing.

"In some areas, Pete Bommarito is held up as a great icon," said John Ballard, whose tenure as mayor almost exactly mirrored Bommarito's term at the URW helm. "I must confess, he is not an icon of mine. . . . He had to show he's a man and all that ex-Marine crap and have a strike."

In 1973, Bommarito and the URW went on the attack once more. Goodyear settled the master contract without a strike, but Goodrich and Firestone workers

Summit County sheriff's deputies direct rubber union pickets onto a bus to take them to Summit County Common Pleas Court for refusing to obey a court order limiting pickets outside a Firestone gate in June 1967. (*Akron Beacon Journal*/Don Roese)

refused to accept it and hit the streets. Goodrich workers were out twenty-four days; Firestone's struck for three days. By using the strike as a weapon, each company's workers ended up with a better deal than Goodyear's. Not long after the 1973 contracts were hammered out, life soured for Akron's rubber workers. They had received 5.5 percent pay raises, the maximum allowed under President Richard Nixon's wage and price controls. But inflation was shooting into the stratosphere, reaching 12.3 percent in 1974. Tire prices were rising by about 16 percent a year. The wages weren't keeping up. Late in 1973, the lid came off the wage and price controls. Bommarito asked the tire companies to reopen negotiations. Management rejected the request. Rubber workers around the country were unhappy with their take-home pay, with their bosses, and with Bommarito. Then came 1976.

It began, as these things so often do, in a bar. The Crypt, in this case. Nighttime home to a punk rock band called the Rubber City Rebels, daytime haunt for a lot of thirsty rubber workers. Beer was cheap. The ambience, dark and unfettered, was true blue-collar Akron—some lovingly called it "the upholstered sewer." Right in the shadow of Goodyear, guys could talk there, curse their bosses, grumble about how they'd like to get back at the companies that were making so much money while the workers were just getting by. They'd flex their beer muscles and call for another bottle. And in the spring of 1976, there in the Crypt, they began talking about the coming war.

Bill Carpenter was all tangled in the conspiracy. The Crypt's co-owner, he helped provide a place for the talk. He was also a Goodyear production worker. By now, the Akron workers were getting pretty good at striking. This year, everybody knew, was going to be hot. What nobody knew then was just how hot it was going to be. These men were on the brink of the longest, most far-reaching strike in rubber industry history. Sixty thousand workers from the nation's four largest tire makers would march for four months.

So, as the big boys sat at the bargaining tables, shaking their heads and rubbing their temples as they realized just how far apart they were, the men at the Crypt got ready. Bill Carpenter went down to Champion Bowlers Supply and ordered up some T-shirts—orange, because everybody was a Browns fan—with the phrase "URW—Catch Up in '76." Nobody, but nobody, was expecting anything but a war.

From the opening days, the difference between the two sides was simple but vast. The URW wanted an inflation-proof wage, one that would flex with the volatile economy. The companies refused to give it, unwilling to grant a cost-of-living adjustment that would give momentum to a growing trend in industry. "Both sides were entrenched to the point it was very difficult," was the understated observation of William J. Usery, who eventually was called in to mediate a settlement as secretary of labor under President Gerald R. Ford. This was a tug of war with great strength at each end of the rope. Philosophies, personal agendas, and careers were on the line. So was the fate of 24,600 Akron rubber workers. Each team was dug in hard, and neither was budging. And the strike deadline was coming on fast.

Down at the Crypt, they drank pale beer, shouted epithets, and kept an eye on the clock. In other bars and in union halls—the outposts of the tire shops—the

Pickets kick off the boy-
cott of Firestone products
outside a Firestone store at
Chapel Hill on May 8,
1976. Joining striking
United Rubber Workers
members were representa-
tives of several other
unions, including the
United Steelworkers,
Teamsters, and the Amal-
gamated Clothing work-
ers. (*Akron Beacon
Journal*/Ron Kuner)

men and women who were Akron's soul drank and waited. It was late Tuesday
night, April 20. Bommarito had permission to call a strike at midnight. The rubber workers were waiting, not for a last-minute settlement, but for the strike to
begin. Bill Carpenter pulled the tap and drew another beer.

Just up the street near Goodyear, at the headquarters of Local 2, empty Pabst
Blue Ribbon cans were pushed aside and new ones were opened. These men, many
of them, had been on strike before. They lived in Akron, and strikes were as much
a part of life as garbage collection. The first night was like a high school football
game, an earthy community thing, charged with energy. This was the tailgate
party.

At midnight, the union hall's elevator doors opened and Pete Zaroka, a hard-
nosed, cigar-chomping Local 2 official, stepped into the loud, smoky room.
"That's it," he declared. "We're down."

At that same moment, in the bars and union halls around Firestone and B. F.
Goodrich, the announcement was repeated. Phones rang in homes around Akron.
Word was passed on the streets. Eleven thousand Akron workers—sixty thousand
nationwide—were on strike. Another thirteen thousand Akron rubber workers,
not legally eligible to join this strike, watched with keen interest. Zaroka went

A union rally endorsing the boycott of Firestone products is led by Pete Bommarito during the 1976 strike. This speech outside the Rubber Bowl, on May 8, marked the first time he had spoken to his troops in the two-week-old strike, which would last 140 days. *(Akron Beacon Journal)*

out to his Chevy Impala and cruised the streets around Goodyear, Akron's biggest rubber company. "We're out," he called to the men on the sidewalks. Cheers went up as the men—a few women, too—gathered in groups. Late-shift workers left their posts inside the plants and poured out into the night. Six-packs of cheap beer appeared. Barrel fires were lit. From South Main Street to East Market Street, thousands of people had given up their livelihood, and there was great joy. For this moment, they felt power. Downtown, horns honked and the rubber workers' bright orange T-shirts were illuminated in the momentary flash of firecrackers.

Early in the strike, the pickets buzzed with activity. The negotiators, though, were stuck in the mud. Bommarito focused on the Firestone talks, hoping to settle with that company first and set a pattern for the others. Firestone negotiations were held in Cleveland, while Goodrich negotiators met in Columbus, Goodyear in Cincinnati, and Uniroyal in New York City. Bommarito was asking for a huge boost in wages—30 percent by some estimates. Rubber workers always measured their wages against those of the United Auto Workers. Under their latest contract, the rubber workers were earning $5.50 an hour, $1.26 less than the auto workers. In the early weeks, company negotiators offered slim cost-of-living allowances. Bommarito held firm. The prospects of a short strike withered.

As April faded and the game settled into its slow rhythm, people began to scribble down numbers, calculations with dire consequences. Auto executives in Detroit counted the number of tires stockpiled for the next model run. URW officials counted the dwindling number of dollars in their nearly six-million dollar strike fund. Tire company leaders tallied the days and profits lost. And the hard-working families of Akron watched their savings swirl down the drain. A few days after the strike began, Goodyear and Firestone stopped paying unemployment benefits to previously laid-off workers. Bommarito was furious.

"This is a pressure tactic; we aren't denying that," a Goodyear official said. "But so is a strike."

Late in May, a month into the standoff, the URW revealed that it had spent everything it had available for strike benefits, including $900,000 earmarked for a new headquarters in Akron. The last of the checks—$25 each—came with a letter from the URW: "Strike benefit payments will be suspended with the issuance of this check." The Rubber City had a mature work force. Many of the strikers were second- or third-generation rubber workers. They knew how to prepare for a strike; they knew to put off big-ticket purchases and sock away some money in a contract year. Because they were in their forties and fifties, many Akron workers had paid off their mortgages. They could struggle through this dry spell. By 1976, the two-income family was common. Striking men could rely on their wives' paychecks. But there was plenty of hurt. Proud working men and women had to swallow their pride—about a third of the striking workers began receiving food stamps. Applications for Aid to Dependent Children increased. Consumer spending was down more than 10 percent by midstrike. The excitement of the first days faded into boredom. Bill Carpenter started selling beer at the Crypt for next to nothing. Maybe a quarter a glass, just to pay for the kegs. He had a full house of people with no money.

By late June, the automakers had begun shipping new cars with four tires and an IOU for the spare. National unemployment figures bore the troubling burden of sixty thousand striking rubber workers. As the White House prepared for a massive celebration of the nation's bicentennial, President Ford sat at his desk in the Oval Office, thinking about Akron.

"Because of the impact of that shutdown to the economy as a whole, it was obvious to me and to Secretary of Labor Usery that something had to be done to try and negotiate an end to the conflict," Ford recalled. "The impact of that industry is broad, and that many people out of work on a strike just necessitated the maximum effort by my administration to get the parties to agree to a settlement. I had been pressured by people all over the country, and especially people like Ray Bliss, who was our national Republican chairman, who came from Akron, to do something beyond the Federal Mediation Service."

Ford dispatched Usery to Cleveland, where negotiations were being held with the target company, Firestone. Federal mediators had been involved since spring, but now the nation's highest-ranking labor official was on the scene. Usery got a firsthand look at the Akron way, the decades of calluses that had been built up over the years. He learned what Akron already knew—that a Peter Bommarito strike was filled with thorns. The labor secretary stayed in northeast Ohio from June 28 through July 6. As the nation celebrated the bicentennial of its independ-

ence, the rubber industry remained in the chains of the strike. Talks broke off and didn't resume until July 27, when Usery summoned the two sides to Washington.

Nineteen seventy-six was the Rubber City's longest summer ever. As the nation watched, Akron grew more like a small town than a big labor capital. Pickets got to be friends with the cops dispatched to keep peace on the strike lines. Workers who had never shared more than a "hello" in the tire shop's cafeteria became like brothers. Strikers, still wearing their "Catch Up in '76" T-shirts, put up Christmas trees at their posts—they said they were prepared to stay out until winter if they had to. Restaurants donated food; drivers from the local beer houses dropped off six-packs of beer and pop. Men and women made sandwiches in the union hall kitchens. Union leaders persuaded banks and utility companies to go easy on strikers behind on their bills.

Not all of Akron's rubber workers were part of this communal experience. May 15, the expiration date for General Tire's contract, had come and gone. General stayed in, on orders from Nate Trachsel, president of Local 9 at General Tire. Bommarito was not pleased. He believed that taking out all the workers at once would neutralize the companies' "mutual aid pact," an agreement among the rival companies that, if one was struck, the others would provide economic assistance.

Triennial Passion Plays 169

Pickets outside the General Tire complex in east Akron confront and turn away a white-collar worker attempting to get to the headquarters building on June 21, 1976. Despite General Tire's refusal to strike, URW members from the other rubber companies picketed outside. (*Akron Beacon Journal*/Ott Gangl)

By bringing production to a virtual standstill, he was certain the companies, facing a tire shortage, would cave in to the URW's demands. Solidarity was a must. But General, the fifth-largest tire maker, was staying in.

Trachsel was a rising star closely allied with Bommarito. He was being groomed for the URW international vice presidency and was believed by many to be Bommarito's eventual successor. But now Trachsel was trading that future for what he felt was right in the present. He did not believe General Tire's workers could help the cause by striking. "The vast majority of our membership supported what we did," Trachsel said.

The rest of Akron did not. In Akron, a lot of the feeling that striking was the right thing came from the fact that everyone else was doing it. This was not a good place for a voice in the wilderness. It was a good place to follow the crowd. In late June, workers from the other three companies picketed General, hollering "Scabs!" and preventing workers from entering the plant.

This public division within the URW had its roots in a private clash. Trachsel said he had received a letter before the strike from Bommarito and URW negotiator Francis "Pooch" Maile, saying it wasn't necessary for General to strike. Because General's plants made tires mostly for the replacement market, its union members couldn't help with Bommarito's strategy to cut off the supply of original-equipment passenger tires to Detroit. But when May 15 came and General stayed in, Bommarito said publicly that the decision was "not in the best interests of the URW."

Trachsel feared that a long strike would weaken the companies and eventually lead to a loss of jobs in Akron. He was sure he could, fairly quickly, negotiate a pattern settlement at General that included every demand Bommarito was after. Bommarito's reply: Get me what I want, and I'll just ask for more.

Trachsel, disillusioned, went back to the bargaining table. His relationship with the powerful URW president had changed forever. General's talks dragged on lethargically. Trachsel knew a settlement would be worthless—Bommarito would shoot it down.

In Washington, Usery managed to whittle away at the differences between the companies and the union. Slowly, penny by penny, he managed to edge the parties closer together. Finally, on August 24, the first of the four struck companies settled: Goodyear had a tentative agreement. Firestone followed suit, then Uniroyal, and, finally, Goodrich. The agreement included an 80-cent-an-hour raise in the first year (eighty-eight cents for Firestone), with thirty- and twenty-five-cent raises in the following two years. The cost-of-living allowance, computed at 6 percent average inflation, was seven cents in the first year, twenty-seven cents in the second, and thirty-eight cents in the third. There was a substantial increase in pension benefits.

General Tire, the company that refused to strike, emerged as the biggest winner. A month after the other companies settled, General's workers received a contract that matched that of the strikers, with bonuses that included raises retroactive to May 15—the date General could have struck, but did not—and pension increases in the first year that the strikers would not get until the third year of their contracts. At General's ratification meeting, Local 9 negotiators received a standing ovation. But Trachsel's fate outside his own union hall was blackened.

To this day, other local union leaders begrudge their quietly rebellious colleague.

Usery had helped negotiate a compromise between the URW and rubber's Big Four, but the winner of the strike was not clear. Maybe there was no winner. The tire makers had not reached red alert—every car sold in the summer of 1976 rolled out of Detroit on four tires. And now, with stockpiles almost nil, the companies would run at full capacity for months. But they had given in on a cost-of-living allowance, something against which they had taken a hard line. Their labor costs would escalate just as foreign competition was breaking loose. Bommarito and his negotiators had gained, in one fell swoop, one of the largest economic packages in recent American labor history. But the union president had miscalculated the power of his take-no-prisoners strike. He had not brought the industry to its knees, as he had hoped. He had not expected his followers to suffer through four months of this mess. And his swagger had finally caught up with him. Bommarito had promised the moon in return for the rubber workers' sacrifice. So, even though he had gotten them an excellent contract, it wasn't everything he had said it would be. There was division in the ranks. And the ranks were tired and broke. They survived, but something was taken out of them.

"A strike, you're never going to get anything back," said Kenny Rinesmith, a Goodyear retiree who picketed in 1976. "I mean, when you lose wages and so forth, I don't care what kind of money you get in return, you're never going to get it back. Something that is lost is gone."

This was the last stand of the old-style URW, the union that proudly claimed "responsible militancy" as its legacy. No one wanted to strike like this again. Contracts in 1979 were settled without a strike for the first time in more than a decade. Negotiations continued to go smoothly through the 1980s. But rubber had bigger problems. As European companies ravaged the industry, the union dwindled, from a postwar nationwide high of 137,000 members, in 1974, to 84,400 in 1990. The next major strike, in 1995, against Bridgestone/Firestone, led to the URW's merger with the United Steelworkers of America.

The last details of the 1976 contracts were ironed out early in the morning of Labor Day, with Goodrich negotiators in Columbus. Ratification meetings were held in late August and early September.

On the muggy morning of August 27, about half of Goodyear's sixty-three hundred Local 2 members gathered in the Akron Armory to vote on the contract. Many, their hopes having been raised on the wings of Bommarito's promises, grumbled about the terms, but planned to vote "yea" anyway, wanting to be finished with all of this. John Nardella, Local 2 president, grew hoarse as he explained the complicated terms of the contract. When Bommarito's name was spoken, boos filled the rafters of the cavernous hall. The vote was taken.

"All in favor . . ."

A chorus of yeas.

"Against?"

A smaller rumble of nos.

It was done. Autumn was approaching, the bitter summer fading into the sluggish Akron afternoon. The men began to filter out of the hall, off to find one last drink before they returned to work, a drink to raise in celebration or to stare into, wondering.

George Clark, Jr. plays the saxophone on the picket line outside the Archwood Avenue entrance to Goodyear's Plant 5 during the strike of 1976. (*Akron Beacon Journal*/Marcy Nighswander)

Some went home to tell their families they had a job again. Others went to the Crypt, reaching deep into their pockets for the last remaining coins. One man scowled, his young face beginning to show the wear of wisdom and remorse. It was an Akron face.

His orange T-shirt had faded. He had scratched out one of the words on the front and replaced it with another:

"URW—Beat Up in '76."

༄

The Bommarito legacy had been written. One industry observer referred to Bommarito's first decade in office as an era of "triennial passion plays." There was an average of ninety-five rubber strikes per year between 1965 and 1969, roughly a 30 percent increase from the previous four-year period. That number grew to 117 per year between 1970 and 1974, with a high of 143 in 1973—the most in a single year since 1951. From his office downtown, Bommarito proctored the most tumultuous period in the labor history of a city that had seen its share of tumult.

"Pete never understood there was a problem," said John Ong, former chief executive of B. F. Goodrich. "Pete just thought it was like the old movie *Key Largo* with the gangster Rocco, and Humphrey Bogart finally says: 'I know what you want, Rocco. You want more.' He says: 'That's right. That's right. I want more.' Well, that was Pete. Pete wanted more."

In 1989, Peter Bommarito knew he was dying. He had cancer, a disease he had chosen to leave untreated, figuring chemotherapy was not worth the loss to his vitality. In September, he arranged what would be his final fishing trip, with his nephew, John DiGuiseppe. They went to Alaska. Bommarito was in pain; DiGuiseppe knew it, even though his uncle didn't show it. They went out on a boat to fish for salmon. The Bomber was in a wheelchair. At seventy-four, he was, for the first time in his life, beginning to look like an old man, withered by the disease.

Out on the water, he hooked a salmon, a big one, a fighter. The reel screamed; Bommarito tensed and pulled back on the rod. DiGuiseppe hurried over.

"Let me reel it in," DiGuiseppe said.

Bommarito brushed him aside. He had not come this far to have someone else land his fish. Maneuvering in his wheelchair, Bommarito furrowed his brow and fought the big fish, sensing its moves through the line, reacting and attacking. He beat the fish, and, as he reeled it in, he may well have known that he had just won his last fight.

He died a week later.

15 What Went Wrong

BIG SLICK WAS ON A ROLL, huffing and puffing and trying to blow away with choice and coarse language this negotiator whom Goodyear Tire and Rubber Company had dared to send to the bargaining table with proposals for work-rule changes. John Nardella looks his nickname. He's a big man—six feet, two inches—and slick as a used dragster tire. "I don't know who started that crap," Nardella said. "Maybe Breslin. I never did a dishonest thing in my life."

Nardella's nickname had nothing to do with his character and everything to do with being a character. Nardella used a comb the way Old West gunslingers used six-shooters. After he pulled it through his thick black hair, the hair didn't dare to move. Big Slick was Pat Riley before the Miami Heat basketball coach ever thought about gunking-up his 'do. Nardella, president of Local 2 of the United Rubber Workers union, had four other union members by his side at the bargaining table. They were big men like Nardella. They looked like an NFL offensive line.

"Our local always elected big fellas," said Bill Breslin, another former Local 2 president who was in the room that September day in 1976. Across from Nardella sat Ernie Fortney, one of Goodyear's principal negotiators. Fortney was tall, bald,

When a load of used tires headed for a reclaim plant threatened to topple this truck in downtown Akron, in 1950, police cited the driver. Decades later, when myriad problems combined to topple Akron as the Rubber Capital of the World, company executives, the United Rubber Workers, and government leaders did not rescue it. (*Akron Beacon Journal*/Jim Root)

and new to Akron. Nardella's members had been out on strike for four months. It had been the industry's longest walkout ever. The URW had won a master contract for all Goodyear's union plants that included raises and cost-of-living allowances. Now it would hammer out issues at the local level.

Fortney admitted he didn't know how these talks were supposed to go but suggested that Local 2 go through its proposals without interruption. On the second day, Fortney and other members of Goodyear's negotiating team would ask questions and make sure they understood what the union wanted. Then, on the third day, the company would present its proposals, again without interruption. Nardella, according to Breslin, reached under the table, snatched a wastebasket, and slammed it down in the middle of the table.

"You're goddamn right you don't know what goes on here in Akron, Fortney," he said. With that, Nardella lambasted the company with dates and details of alleged offenses against his hard-working members. Finally, Nardella gestured toward the wastebasket.

"You can shit-can your proposals," Breslin recalled Nardella saying.

"Well, John," Ernie Fortney said, "I appreciate your comments."

Charles J. Pilliod, chairman and chief executive officer of Goodyear, did not appreciate Nardella's comments. The company proposals included an offer to rebuild old, multistory Plant 2 and equip it with new radial-tire technology, the lifeblood of a rapidly changing industry. In exchange, Goodyear wanted some concessions. Pilliod was not present at these negotiations, but he received reports from Goodyear's men at the table. He tells the same story as Breslin, down to the infamous trashcan quote. Pilliod remembers it well because at that critical juncture, the last of Goodyear's regular tire-building jobs began an inexorable march out of Akron. Other companies had already closed some Akron tire operations or would soon do so.

Instead of converting Plant 2, Goodyear built a $300 million, state-of-the-art, nonunion plant in Lawton, Oklahoma. Because he was a homeboy, reared in Cuyahoga Falls, Pilliod would find a way to save Plant 2. He turned it into the Goodyear Technical Center, where Goodyear's radial racing tires still are built and where new tires of all stripes are designed. But most of Akron's tire-building jobs would be gone, like so many ghosts in the night.

Why? What went wrong?

The drama of rubber in Akron has all the elements of a classic Greek tragedy.

Groundbreaking ceremonies are held for a new plant to be built in Los Angeles for the B.F. Goodrich company in July 1927. After 1917, the rubber companies had not built a major tire plant in Akron. Between 1960 and 1979, thirty-one tire plants were built in the United States, twenty-four of them in the South because of the more favorable labor climate. The inefficient, old plants in Akron were allowed to crumble away, without significant investment or modernization. (The University of Akron Archives)

Like King Oedipus, who in solving his father's murder unexpectedly discovers that he is the killer, Akron's rubber workers and the companies make a similar discovery. Who was responsible for driving rubber from Akron? They both were, with major assistance from events beyond anyone's control. Among the causes for rubber's departure: triennial strikes in the 1960s and 1970s; union work rules, wages, and benefits; aging, inefficient factories; union politics; management complacency; lack of government incentives; foreign competition; and basic economics.

The union wanted too much money, too many costly benefits. The companies wanted too many givebacks, specifically regarding working conditions that management had instituted in the first place. If together the union and management had made a mess of rubber in Akron, they also had advanced tire making too far for their own good. John Nardella, asked two decades later about his intemperate gesture and remark, bristled with denial.

"No, no, no," Nardella said. He did not slam any trashcans onto the negotiating table. "I'm too smart for that," he said.

Nardella preferred another nickname that Local 2 members gave him—the Godfather, because he tried to help his people. Personal problem or professional, it didn't matter. He even got his people out of jail. "My philosophy was to give a person a chance, no matter how bad he is," Nardella said.

For a number of Nardella's twenty-three years as president of Local 2, however, his attitude toward Goodyear was not so accommodating. He would later change, helping to create a less hostile atmosphere. But in 1976, a pivotal year in Akron labor history, Nardella was willing to concede little.

"He's the one who helped drive them out," said Don Stephens, president of the Akron Regional Development Board from 1978 to 1988. "He and Pete Bommarito. They hung on to those old contracts."

To rebuild for state-of-the-art radial production in Akron, Goodyear needed, more than anything else, for production workers to agree to an eight-hour shift. For better than forty years, production workers in Akron's rubber shops worked six-hour shifts. It was an anomaly initiated, ironically, by Goodyear brass during the Depression, on the theory that the scarce work would be spread among more people. Other Akron rubber shops followed suit. At the time, workers argued the concept made little sense, and they were right. During the Depression, it just saddled more people with economic misery. Afterward, the companies discovered that operating on four shifts drove up labor and production costs. But once the shorter shift was in place, workers clung to it as if it were an entitlement.

Day after day, negotiating session after negotiating session in 1976, Fortney began his presentation by telling the Local 2 negotiators that Goodyear needed the eight-hour day to keep Plant 2 open. "We didn't have a lot on the agenda except that," said Del Salzer, a retired Goodyear manager. It didn't matter.

"John didn't listen," said Robert Kidney, former president of the Akron Labor Council. "I'm not saying John did the wrong thing. He was looking after his people. But John didn't listen."

Bill Breslin represented the skilled trades—such as electricians, welders, and plumbers—at Goodyear. His union members already worked eight-hour days. As he carried Nardella's briefcase to the union hall after a negotiating session, Breslin wondered aloud: "John, why don't we just give them the eight-hour day?"

"We can't do that," Nardella replied.

"Why not?" Breslin asked.

"Because if we give them the eight-hour day, they will lay off a fourth of our people," Nardella said. "That's about three hundred or so people."

"If we don't give them the eight-hour day, and they shut down the plant, we're going to lose twelve hundred jobs," Breslin replied.

"Yeah, Bill," Nardella said, "but it's the company doing it—not us."

Breslin said that kind of thinking was characteristic of union leaders. For his part, Nardella categorically denied making those remarks. He took issue with almost every word out of Breslin's mouth—and they were on the same side. Those on the other side, as well as those with no personal stake in the negotiations, cited union politics as a pernicious force in the decline of Akron's rubber industry.

Peter Pestillo experienced such forces as a Goodrich executive in the 1970s. "We have seen good contracts rejected by membership because of a lack of nerve by union leadership," Pestillo said in a 1979 magazine essay. "Too often, union leaders have been too slow to accept changes necessary to keep a business competitive. . . . Leaders chose only to do what was most politically expedient."

"None of them was flexible enough," the Akron Regional Development Board's Don Stephens said of the union leaders. "They just couldn't give up."

In 1976 contract talks, the URW was determined to get wage parity with the United Auto Workers union, and to win a cost-of-living escalator and pension improvements. But the URW's strategy was ill timed, given the prevailing economic conditions. In Akron, wages were already higher than the rubber industry average—production workers made fifty cents an hour more in the mid-1970s. At the same time, the factories of Akron's three top tire manufacturers (Goodyear, Firestone, and Goodrich) were, according to *Business Week*, "only 50 percent to 75 percent as productive as similar rubber plants in other areas." The tire industry overall was in a slump. In 1973, the rubber companies sold nearly 239 million tires, a record to that point. By 1976, they were three years into a seven-year slide in which sales declined an average of 4.7 percent a year.

World events also affected the bargaining climate. The Yom Kippur War of 1973 had led to reduced production by the Organization of Petroleum Exporting Countries (OPEC). This led to gas rationing in the United States, in 1974, as well as to higher prices for the oil used in tire production. And that wasn't the worst of it. The new emphasis on conservation convinced Detroit automakers that they should put energy-saving radial tires on more new models. Radials meant costly retooling in U.S. tire plants, which built bias-ply tires. Even under such adverse circumstances, the URW made gains in 1976. But first, Peter Bommarito took sixty thousand rubber workers out on a 140-day general strike that hardened Akron's image as Strike City.

Jim Walker, a teacher at Jackson High School, worked for Goodyear as a pipefitter from 1968 to 1976. He criticized the union's emphasis on winning wage gains and improved benefits: "We should have been looking at job security, retraining issues, transfer rights," Walker said. "But the head of the local running for office would say: 'Yeah, but that would get me three votes in the next election, and a $1-an-hour raise will bring me three thousand.'"

As the U.S. tire industry began to abandon bias-ply tires in favor of radials,

(left to right) Goodyear Chairman Russell De-Young, Ohio Development Director Fred Neuenschwander, Goodyear Executive Vice President Walter H. Rudder, URW Local 2 President John Nardella, and Stow Mayor Roger Howard, break ground for Goodyear's Stow Mold plant in April 1969. (*Akron Beacon Journal*/Julius Greenfield)

the least productive plants with the most restrictive work rules became targets for closing. New plants would be built in places with the "most cooperative and productive" employees, Pilliod said. Ground was broken at Lawton, Goodyear's premier tire operation, on June 14, 1977. Lawton built its first tire in February 1979 and, by the late 1990s, was producing up to sixty thousand radial passenger and light-truck tires daily. In 1978, a $69 million expansion for radial production went to Goodyear's Gadsden, Alabama, plant. "We could have put the expansion in another spot for $20 million less, but the labor was attractive enough that we decided to spend the extra money to go to Gadsden," Pilliod said.

Nardella got the message this time.

"I kept noticing that . . . we were going to be in trouble if we didn't do something about the old plants in Akron," said Nardella. "I'd talk it to the membership at meetings, but I'd never get any response." Nardella took the lead anyway. He worked eagerly and cooperatively to facilitate construction of a mold plant in Stow and an air springs plant in Green Township by securing work-rule concessions from the membership.

"He accomplished a lot of good things," said Bob Young, former Local 2 member and head of the Akron Labor Council from 1979 to 1992. "But it was always my feeling that the company had made a decision before they asked anybody if it was all right. I just feel these companies felt: 'It's our company. We've looked at the situation, and this is what we're going to do, and nothing is going to change that.'"

Management often had little choice in such matters. Its options were limited by the union contracts and work rules. The bidding-and-bumping system allowed a more senior employee to take the job of one with less experience, regardless of skill. The profusion of job classifications prevented a worker from encroaching on another's turf.

"In our nonunion plants, we had two classifications: electricians and maintenance men," said Pilliod. "At Goodyear in Akron, I think we had about fifty classifications."

Walker, the former Goodyear pipefitter, explained why multiple classifications were inefficient: "I recall waiting two hours as standard operating procedure for an electrician to show up to disconnect a couple of solenoid wires so I might replace the valve body connected to it." In the meantime, a machine sits, the operator sits, and no tires or other products are made.

Workers "owned" their machines. If their machine didn't work, neither did they. Not even if they might prove useful somewhere else until their machine was repaired. Many workers, not just tire builders, were paid under the piece rate system, which bred inefficiency and abuses. Janitors were paid by the number of toilets cleaned. At Goodrich, former Local 5 President Jack Moye recalled, "There was a young lady, Florida Hirt, who was paid by the number of water fountains she cleaned."

The more skillful production workers could meet their quotas, called "making out," within a few hours, then goof off. Former Mayor John Ballard tells one of the more egregious stories about "making out" early. Ballard was a young attorney in the 1950s, representing a rubber worker charged with driving under the influence. Ballard's client, who worked the 6:00 PM-to-midnight shift, had been involved in an accident with a truck at 1:00 AM.

"Obviously, he was drunk," Ballard said. "This guy would have had to have had nine or ten beers or shots to have this blood alcohol reading."

Despite the evidence, Ballard persuaded a jury that no man could consume that much alcohol between the end of his shift at midnight and the 1:00 AM accident. Years later, Ballard was running for mayor and handing out books of matches with his name on them. Ballard saw his former client sail past him on Main Street. It was 10:00 PM. Two hours later, he saw the man reenter the plant just in time to punch out on the time clock and leave. Suddenly, Ballard understood how the man could have drunk so much.

"I'd deceived the jury unwittingly," Ballard said. "All those years, some of these guys were getting paid for six hours and working four. I blame management for that."

Pilliod was a stranger to these home-front machinations, having spent much of his career in Goodyear's international operations. When he became president and chief operating officer at Goodyear, in 1972, he questioned why the company had agreed to a profusion of work categories and rules that made it less competitive. "I said: 'How in the blazes did you ever get in this situation?'" he recalled. Pilliod said he was told that the union would take issue after issue to arbitration. Because of the sheer number, the union would win its share, and the company losses mounted over the years. Historian George Knepper offers another explanation.

"For a quarter of a century after World War II," suggested Knepper, "we didn't have any significant competition, and labor and management played games. . . . Labor kept demanding more benefits. Management would resist. There would be a strike. Management would concede more benefits and more wages and then [pass on] higher prices to the consumer."

Sometimes, though, labor did budge. URW Local 5 at Goodrich became, in 1965, the first to give up the six-hour day. In 1972, Local 5 agreed to a package of concessions, called HEY MAC (Help Make Akron Competitive), to improve productivity. A year later, Local 5 accepted a smaller wage hike (15 cents an hour compared with 28.8 cents) than Goodrich workers outside Akron. But concessions didn't always buy security for workers. Product lines exited Akron despite improved productivity. Fire hoses, for example, left in 1982 for Oneida, New York. Workers felt betrayed.

"The HEY MAC program, to me, was a farce. They were less than honest with us," former Local 5 President Matt Contessa said of Goodrich management. Nevertheless, in 1982, Goodrich workers traded still more concessions for job security. The company had asked for $1-an-hour wage reductions over three years.

"I told Jim Berlin [Goodrich vice president and general manager of the industrial productions division] that there was no goddamn way we could do that," Contessa said. "We cannot sell that."

What he did sell amounted to a twenty-seven-cent cut per year. Local 5 agreed to give up the cost-of-living allowance in return for profit sharing and improvements in benefits. "It was a wash," said Contessa, who by this time was on the union's international staff.

A wash with a political price. By now, the rank and file was fed up. Local 5 President Paul Breese, who had helped to negotiate the job-saving concessions, lost his job, in 1983, to Wilmer Davis. Davis ran on a no-concessions platform. The consequences of holding to that position meant more losses for Akron. Late in 1984, Goodrich announced it would close its industrial products division, eliminating 850 Akron jobs. The next year, Goodrich asked Local 5 to forgo a negotiated forty-three-cent-an-hour raise. John Ong, then Goodrich chairman, was sending the message that marginal operations such as those in Akron—aircraft tires, missile and marine products, and molded rubber products—could not survive with the high wage scale.

Don Stephens, the Akron Regional Development Board president, and a city-wide labor-management committee approached Wilmer Davis. Swallow this concession, they urged, and Goodrich would guarantee the work and about nine hundred jobs, for at least three years. True to his campaign pledge, Davis refused.

"They're going to close this place down," Stephens exhorted Davis.

"I don't believe it," Davis replied.

At other times, union leaders boldly championed contract reforms and won them. But the reforms were either too little or too late to be meaningful. In December 1971, URW Local 7 rejected a proposal for the eight-hour day so that Firestone would build radial truck tires at Plant 1. A few months later, Firestone announced it was building a radial plant in Nashville, Tennessee.

"They weren't willing to give a thing up," recalled Gerald Gelvin, then the Local 7 president. Gelvin said many union members held two jobs, which might become impossible with changes in the work schedule. Even so, Gelvin again put the forty-hour week to a vote, in March 1972. He endured threats to his safety in the process. The vote drew thirty-six hundred to a union hall that held twelve hundred. A few union members had guns. Gelvin said he had a bodyguard for protection: "The whole union hall was surrounded. That was one of the few times in my life I can say I was scared."

In the end, Gelvin prevailed. The membership agreed to the contract changes but ended up only buying time for the Akron plant, which closed in 1980.

"I started at Firestone in 1951, and there were ten thousand members of our union," Gelvin said. "When I was elected president of the union, there were fifty-three hundred, and when I left the union in 1973, there were eighteen hundred members. I was a militant labor leader, and I felt strongly about the labor cause and everything else, but I couldn't convince the membership to do what had to be done to preserve those jobs."

Goodrich, as it was extracting concessions from Local 5 and nursing a few more years out of its Akron operations, was also milking its tire unit of money and preparing to sell it to concentrate on other products, specifically specialty chemicals and aerospace. Goodrich stopped making passenger tires in Akron, in 1975, and industrial tires three years later. Aircraft tires would be the last Goodrich tires out of Akron, in the mid-1980s.

"To have maintained Akron as a tire manufacturing center," John Ong said, "a lot of people would have to have done things very differently. Certainly by the time people like me got involved, it was too late."

Polyvinyl chloride (PVC), the creation of Goodrich's brilliant chemist Waldo Semon, distracted the company. "Certainly in the late '40s and early '50s, when PVC was minting money for this company and our stock price was going through the roof and a lot of people were getting wealthy, we should have reinvested in the tire business if we were going to stay in it. We barely reinvested at all," Ong acknowledged.

Goodrich wasn't the only Akron company to diversify beyond rubber. Competition—primarily domestic for years—drove the rubber companies into other product lines to improve profit margins. "Everybody in the rubber industry had to work like the devil to keep their place in the sun and try to increase it," said Edwin J. Thomas, the longtime Goodyear executive who retired in 1964. "So did we. Firestone was always on our tail. I think it was a splendid working of the American enterprise system."

Indeed, the free-enterprise system worked too well. Just as the rubber companies changed, so did their principal product. In the 1930s, the average bias-ply tire made with natural rubber would last five thousand miles. By 1970, radial tires, the standard in Europe and Japan, would last for forty thousand miles.

"They made the product last too long," said URW former general counsel George Vasko. "When you do that, you cut down on demand. You don't need so many tires. I think that was the paramount reason for the fall of rubber. They lost because of their own success."

Even so, the U.S. rubber industry cruised merrily along for decades, seemingly indifferent to threats from abroad. The wake-up call for Akron came from France in 1976. Michelin was adding to the North American factory beachhead it established in Nova Scotia, Canada, in 1971. In 1976, it opened a radial plant in South Carolina, just as Peter Bommarito was leading the URW on a national strike.

Chuck Pilliod's remark about Michelin's serendipitous timing has been quoted often: "How would you like to come into a country, open a factory, and have four of your largest competitors go on strike for the next four months? God must be a Frenchman."

Bommarito refused to allow the URW to be blamed for Michelin's gains. He maintained that the rubber companies had long ignored mounting evidence of radial superiority. "We are aware of the financial problems you have encountered in the '70s relative to the extremely rapid and, therefore, costly, changeover from bias-belted to radials," Bommarito told the company negotiators during 1976 master-contract talks. He continued:

> However, this problem, as we see it, was of your own making and choosing. As far back as the early [and] middle 1960s, it was very apparent, especially to those who had the opportunity to experience the ride and handling characteristics of the radial tire, that it was the tire that should be developed for the U.S. market, as it had been for Europe. Instead, each of your companies chose to ignore the facts and charged blindly after each other, pushing the bias-belted tire on Detroit and the uneducated consumer. As a result, Michelin, Pirelli, Dunlop and a couple Japanese firms began making serious inroads into the U.S. tire market.

Bommarito's remarks told only part of the story. The companies did not rush to radials because conversion would be expensive: Goodyear, for example, spent between $1.5 billion and $2 billion. Also, radials required 25 percent to 35 percent more labor than did bias tires, plus technical skills that U.S. tire builders had not yet acquired.

As foreign competitors became a part of the local equation, an always small profit margin shrank further. In the next two decades, Akron's remaining tire plants would close, and sixty thousand jobs melted away. When Bommarito retired in 1981, one of his Akron-area local presidents commented anonymously: "We [in the union] are as much to blame as the companies for what's happened here in Akron. [Union leaders] were looking at getting more wages and benefits for the membership. Maybe there was something more to it than that. . . . We closed our eyes until it was too late."

Many people in leadership positions disregarded the evidence that Akron was losing its rubber jobs. "We tended to take companies for granted," said Richard Erickson, ARDB president in the 1990s. "If the company was here, the probability of it moving or changing its product line, adding a plant or closing a plant wasn't a great concern. The rate of change was so low that we tended to think once we had something, it was always there."

In truth, though, Akron hadn't gotten a new tire plant since 1917, when Firestone built Plant 2. In the years since, scores of factories, each more technologically advanced than the last, were built in other cities in the United States and around the world. The explosion of activity at Akron's companies during World War II masked the fact that rubber production was headed other places. Firestone, for example, built five Akron plants during World War II. All were for war production; none was for tires, which were the company's future. In that same period, twenty-nine factories were built in other places, far from Akron.

Akron's sometimes nasty labor personality is almost universally cited as a reason the rubber companies began to expand elsewhere. But it was not the only reason. Goodyear, Firestone, and Goodrich opened plants in Los Angeles in the 1920s to widen their business across the United States as the popularity of the automobile spread. The movement away from Akron picked up steam, in 1928, when Goodyear announced it would build a large tire plant in Gadsden, creating twelve hundred jobs there. And, despite the company's somewhat improbable assertion that the plant was built elsewhere because Akron's water supply was dwindling, there was really only one conclusion to be drawn. "Gadsden's only advantage was a labor-cost differential," University of Akron labor historian Daniel Nelson wrote in his book *American Rubber Workers and Organized Labor: 1900–1941.* "There were fewer drivers in the South than in other regions, and most raw material costs were at least as high as in Akron."

Even with the lack of factory construction in the Rubber City, jobs remained plentiful into the 1970s. But little was done to secure them. Residents of the Rubber Capital of the World looked with pride at its smokestack-punctuated skyline, but paid little heed to its eroding foundation. The jobs had already begun to trickle away. The number of Akron-area jobs in the tire industry dropped from 37,100 in 1964 to 32,700 in 1974 to 15,400 in 1984. By 1997, Ohio ranked twelfth in the country in terms of tire production; nine of the top ten tire-making states were Southern. In 1997, Akron rubber companies employed only about six thousand in a city of about 222,000.

Occasionally, a rubber company would modernize an aging facility, but the plant still would not be viable. In the early 1960s, Goodyear spent $12 million to upgrade Plant 2 in exchange for union concessions on wages for some production workers. But it wasn't enough to improve productivity by the company's goal of 50 percent. Edwin H. Sonnecken, Goodyear's vice president of corporate planning at the time, said lower wage costs alone don't make a plant competitive. "It is a question of what you get in return for what you are paying," said Sonnecken. "It is a matter of total behavior, attitude, and cooperation. It is a mind-set."

Pilliod's 1976 offer of a tire plant was Goodyear's last for Akron. Goodyear closed Plant 2 in 1978. A new factory for General Tire died aborning in 1982.

Some political and civic leaders did observe the gradual job constriction, the shifting of product lines, and the lack of capital investment in Akron plants. But they took no action, believing city leaders should not intervene in the business arena. "It's hard to say what any city can do to solve the problems," said Pestillo, the former Goodrich executive. "Obviously it was in the community's interest to help [the rubber companies], and I think [it] genuinely tried. But it was a losing battle."

Steel pans, heavily reinforced and imbedded in the floor, will support new tire curing presses which are being installed as part of a 1966 modernization of Goodyear's Plant 2 in Akron. Old, multistory plants were inefficient facilities for all the rubber companies, and, with the anticipated conversion to radial technology, companies looked to close the least productive plants with the most restrictive work rules. *(Akron Beacon Journal)*

Robert Strauber, education director for the URW's international office in Akron and later deputy mayor for labor relations under Mayor Ballard, said city leaders felt helpless. "I don't think the city administration had any feeling that they could have an impact on decisions that had been made," said Strauber. "I think most of the cards had been dealt. They just hadn't been turned over yet."

Ballard opposed tax abatements for industry because they could create an unending cycle: "Say you bring in a company that will compete with a company that is already here, and you give [it] a tax abatement. Sure as hell I'm going to run into the CEO of the company [that] is already here and he says, 'Hey, John, you're a helluva guy. You are giving my competitor a tax abatement. Now how about giving me one?' What do you say to a man like that?"

Ballard's position, said current Deputy Mayor Jim Phelps, "was a deep Republican philosophy. It was hands-off."

That position has changed under Mayor Don Plusquellic, a Democrat. "The

Goodyear Tire and Rubber Company received our first tax abatement," Plusquellic said. "We've done tax-increment financing in the past. The companies paid the same amount of tax, but the tax went to make the development work possible—grading site, water, sewer, infrastructure of all sorts. Goodyear asked that we go a step further. We've given grants that had to do with racing tires and to keep tire development. This isn't a five-thousand-job tire plant, but I've told [Goodyear Chairman] Sam [Gibara] that if they want to do that, I'll do just about anything any other community would—and then some."

Prior administrations found other ways to serve the needs of the business community. Since 1955, the city spent more than $70 million on capital improvements that directly benefited the rubber companies. Projects included the East Expressway off-ramps at General Street and Brittain Road, in 1955, which benefited General Tire; Kelly Avenue construction between U.S. 234 and East Market Street in the 1970s, for access to Goodyear; the South Main Street Bridge, in 1978, for Firestone; and Opportunity Park parking improvements, in 1970 and 1977, for Goodrich.

"It's not just the companies and labor who have to learn," former Goodyear Chairman Pilliod said. "I think the cities and the people have to learn as well. If you want a thriving industry in your city, and you want to maintain it and see it grow, you have to support it. That doesn't mean you particularly favor business or labor, but you try to support the general theory [of] a competitive, profitable operation."

At times, however, it seemed the rubber companies ran every stoplight out of Akron whenever another city or state came along with a more lucrative financial offer. In 1975, the late Roger Cerasuolo Sr., a thirty-four-year Goodyear employee and union and retiree activist, testified before a House subcommittee about the loss of Goodyear jobs and five plants in Akron. He painted the loss as a betrayal.

"Here is a company that has built a billion-dollar corporation because of the sweat, tears, and muscles of Akron employees," Cerasuolo told the representatives. "Here is a company that feels it has the right to destroy the families of thousands of employees simply by saying: 'We're moving on.'"

It would be years before the city and its workers stopped checking the rearview mirror. In the 1930s, two-thirds of the nation's tires rolled out of Akron's plants, as

A reporter interviews Governor James Rhodes outside Goodyear's headquarters, in September 1977, after the Governor met with Goodyear Chairman Charles Pilliod about Plant 2's uncertain future. In 1976, Goodyear offered to rebuild the plant and equip it with radial technology, but could not get the needed union concessions. (*Akron Beacon Journal*/Tom Marvin)

(left to right) Mayor John Ballard, Goodyear Chairman Charles Pilliod, and US. Congressman John Seiberling, grandson of Goodyear's co-founder, look at cubes, in 1979, showing various sections of Goodyear's planned Akron Technical Center that would take over the old Plant 2. (*Akron Beacon Journal*/Dennis Gordon)

well as half the world's other rubber goods. The old plants painted the sky gray-black even on sunny days. They rained potash onto everything under the grayness. They wafted a sulfur-tinged smell that punched a person right in the nose. Times were good.

Now the only tires made in Akron ride the wheels of Goodyear's and Bridgestone/Firestone's racing customers. Products made or designed here are more likely to be polymer pellets than something that looks like a black doughnut. The rain is clear and doesn't require a broom in its wake. The air is clean, the smell neutral. Times are different.

During the ten years that Don Stephens presided over the ARDB, the nation lost nearly forty-six thousand rubber jobs, including fifteen thousand in the Akron area. A good friend of Stephens once jabbed him hyperbolically: "You know, Don, when you were president of the ARDB you did a hell of a job. You lost sixty thousand rubber jobs."

The inflated figure likely refers to the number of URW members who went on strike in 1976—Akron hadn't had that many jobs to lose since World War II ended. Still, Akron lost nearly 60 percent of its rubber jobs during Stephens's term, and he was often troubled by the prospect of another plant-closing announcement. "I used to wake up in the mornings . . . with a gut ache, because I knew what was going to happen," Stephens said. "Thank God somebody came up with the idea of polymers."

16 Akron Plants Close Down

IT WAS STILL DARK the morning of March 22, 1978, when Andrew Dakoski arrived for work at Firestone's Plant 2. Everything was in between—somewhere between night and morning, between winter and spring, between rain and snow. As Dakoski walked from his car, he could make out the dark hole in the north side of the huge, five-story factory building. Thirty feet across, it was hard to miss. The hole in the concrete wall had been torn there a year before by a wrecking ball. The message was just as hard to miss.

Six o'clock was not an early morning for Dakoski. That's when he arrived every day, seven days a week, pumping a fist in the air and flashing a bright smile as he marched into the tire factory. He was the production manager, a position he describes in football-coach terms: know your players, know what they need, know how to get them to do what you need. He knew the first name of every man and woman on the plant floor, a thousand people. He knew many of their birthdays, knew how to work their machines. He had been there himself, having started with Firestone, twenty-eight years before, as a machinist's apprentice. He had played quarterback on and captained the company's semipro football team, had come to

A handmade "For Sale" banner hangs on the side of the closed Firestone Plant 2, in March 1978, when the closing was announced. The plant was demolished rather than sold. (*Akron Beacon Journal*/Ott Gangl)

understand Firestone the way patriots understand America. In an age when words such as "unproductive" and "bloated" were being applied to Akron's workers—blue-collar and white-collar alike—Dakoski was running a tight ship. Plant 2's waste record, an important indicator of efficiency, was second best in the company, and productivity had been running at 100 percent.

But the ship had a hole in its side.

Dakoski entered the artificial fluorescent light of the plant. The musky smell of rubber filled his nose, as it had every working day for more than half his life—every day except one. It seems young Andy failed to get out of bed one morning back in 1953, suffering from a case of the brown-bottle flu. His dad, Andy Dakoski Sr., who had worked at Firestone since the 1920s, went off to work, returned home, shot Andy a glare, and didn't speak to him for two weeks.

"The next time you don't go to work, you're out," his dad said when he finally broke his silence. "Clothes and all—out. You're not gonna ruin my name."

Andy never missed another day. There was a sense in his father—a man who walked thirteen miles each way when he began working at Firestone—that a person owed something to the company, perhaps even more than the company owed to him. And so people in and around Plant 2 talked about the "Dakoski goal," one man's drive to get more out of an old factory building with a big hole in its side.

It was only March, but 1978 had already been a harrowing year for Akron's rubber workers. In January, Goodyear had announced its plans to close the venerable Plant 2. The building had every strike against it. It produced almost-obsolete bias-ply tires; it was multistory; and it was populated by workers whom managers considered overpaid and underproductive. When the plant closed in February, twelve hundred people lost their jobs. The Goodyear closing hung like a dark cloud over Firestone's Plant 2. It, too, was an old, multistory factory. It, too, produced the bias tires that soon would become industry relics. It, too, employed nearly twelve hundred workers in all. The only question about Plant 2's future was "when."

Back in January, Firestone Chairman Richard Riley had declared: "It is difficult to be optimistic about the outlook for our tire manufacturing operations in Akron, and we cannot rule out the possibility of substantial layoffs." Riley anticipated, also, that the company would be slapped with a hefty bill for the recall of its radial 500 tires. The next month, Firestone reported that its first-quarter profit plunged 68 percent, to $7.4 million, largely because of poor results in its tire division. Few had any delusions about the reason for that wrecking-ball hole. It was widely believed to be Firestone's attempt to begin devaluing the building for tax purposes. In the world of accounting, a building slated for demolition is worth more once a chunk has been taken out of it. Plant 2, a shiny new symbol of Firestone's progress and solidity when construction began in 1917, was a white elephant sixty-one years later, worth more if reduced to rubble. It was costing the company $75,000 a year in property taxes. There was no sense that it could be converted to new use. As long as business held steady, Akron's factories, all built before 1920, were useful. But in the late 1960s, as foreign companies began to chip away at American tire dominance, the old brick and steel symbols of the Rubber City started to become symbols of its demise. There were no new factories in Akron, just old ones, operated by some of the most experienced—and expensive—workers in the tire industry.

∾

Tony Fanizzi got ready for work as usual that chilly March day. A native of Conversano, Italy, he had lived in Akron since age thirteen and had worked at Firestone for more than twelve years, carefully saving his money to provide for his family. His wife, Maria, was pregnant with their fourth child, and Tony, every time he headed off for his 2:00–10:00 PM shift in the tire curing room, had no doubt in his mind what he was working for. Shortly after lunch, he drove from his house in Green to the factory building in South Akron. For years, going to work in Plant 2 had been, in part, an act of apprehension. Memos and newsletters had warned of the need to increase productivity. The threats were veiled, but thinly. Plant 2 was in trouble. The implication was that it was the workers' fault, that if they would only put their shoulders harder to the wheel, they could turn things around. That was advice Fanizzi and most of his colleagues took to heart.

"Everybody was working harder and smarter," recalled Fanizzi, who served the local union as a committeeman. "It seemed like we were clicking pretty good." The filing of petty grievances had fallen out of fashion. The practice of an entire shift walking out to protest a disciplinary action, common in the past, was a rarity. Fewer people were missing work, and managers and clock-card workers were communicating better than they had in the rough-and-tumble days of the recent past. The sense of uncertainty about the plant's future, coupled with some of the painful lessons learned from the 140-day general strike in 1976, made people willing to talk. Even, sometimes, to compromise. Dakoski had managed to get the company to spend some money on updating equipment. So, as Fanizzi arrived in the parking lot off Firestone Parkway that March day, his future should have held some scent of promise.

∾

At 1:00 PM, Dakoski was called into a meeting. About 150 managers from all areas of the factory gathered in a large office area adjacent to the manufacturing portion of Plant 2. A chilly silence hung in the room as Ted Veiock, the company's vice president of U.S. production, took out a piece of Firestone stationery and began to read. Within the next few months, Veiock said, Plant 2 would be phased out as a manufacturing facility. The building would be torn down. That was it. He had tears in his eyes.

The words everyone had feared for so long were now in the air. There was almost no movement in the room, save for stolen glances and a few people raising their hands to cover their eyes. It was like a tomb. Slowly, the men and women walked away, their heads already filled with questions and despair. Dakoski went back to his office. One by one, office workers came by, poking their heads around his door, asking if they could talk. They looked, Dakoski recalled, "like someone hit 'em in the head with an ax."

"What's going to happen to me?" they asked Dakoski.

"I would tell them, officially, 'I don't know.' Because I did not know," he recalled.

The company could try to place them in other jobs, he suggested. People who had once been in the union could return and try to get work in Firestone's Plant 1, which was still making bias-ply truck and airplane tires. Dakoski tried to help, to offer advice, to offer answers. But he also wondered: "What's going to happen to me?"

Production continued down on the factory floor, men running their hands over the rough stock that turned on their tire machines. The utility men, who served as the plant's bench players, filling in at idle machines, had begun to receive word—the news had spread downward, from the office building to the foremen to the supervisors. Now the utility men made their way through the plant's network, as messengers.

Tony Fanizzi was standing near a tire curing press, a big machine that clamps its jaws around a green tire, when one of the men came through. Fanizzi already knew. As a Local 7 committeeman, he had received word about an hour earlier. Everyone knew, really. News had leaked into the newspaper; rumors terribly close to the truth had snaked through the factory. But the official declaration, here, live, in the condemned plant, was hardest to bear. That's because it was shared, felt equally by everyone at the same time. The collective darkness that came over the tire makers was even worse than the reality that Fanizzi, for the past hour, had suffered alone. Some spoke aloud, some in whispers, some just with their eyes: "I can't believe it. I don't believe it. I thought we were doing everything right." Some claimed they just didn't care anymore. But they cared. The men and women kept working, their hearts in their throats, a joyless job to be done. As the shift came to a close, the rubber workers began to talk in groups—in the locker room, the showers, at the time clock, and out into the parking lot.

Cold rain swept across the pavement behind the steel gates of the plant. Fanizzi pulled on his beret and headed to his car, thinking. For years, it had been "us" and "them"—worker and company, union and management, the Man and the men. Now everyone was walking in the same shoes.

In and around Akron, the hardest announcements began as the plant closing curdled from news to reality. As some of his second-shift co-workers headed off to bars to share their sadness, Fanizzi drove straight home. Shadows filled his eyes as he came through the door. His wife, Maria, was waiting up for him. No prelude—he got straight to the point. The plant was closing. In a few months, no paycheck. They talked about the baby, about the mortgage. But Fanizzi felt a strange sense of comfort, of independence: "My old-world values and traditions kept me alive," he said. "I never relied on Firestone or anyone else." He had saved some money, invested some. He had job skills and, more important, hope. But for others, he says, "everything collapsed." He would soon see "For Sale" signs pop up like weeds in front of colleagues' homes. He would hear of coworkers who filed for divorce, of broken men leaving town.

Dakoski went home late that night, making the same announcement to his wife, Evelyn. "It's finally over," he told her. He didn't sleep. He didn't sleep for a long time.

The numbness of that night quickly turned to anger in these men and women who felt they had worked so hard to turn around Plant 2. Bitter words planted in the spring grew ripe in the summer as workers and union officials voiced their disgust. The city was hurting, too. When Firestone razed Plant 2, about $75,000 in property tax—about two-thirds of which benefited Akron schools—was lost. And the city income tax lost as a result of the Firestone and Goodyear layoffs totaled about $430,000. By midsummer, unemployment hung around 6.5 percent; the area's average jobless rate that year was a significantly lower 5.7 percent.

Andrew Dakoski, meanwhile, was stuck somewhere in the middle. Workers continued to ask for his help. They knew he understood their plight, knew he was someone they could talk to. But his directive from the company was to prepare for demolition. He made arrangements to have usable machinery unbolted and shipped to other Firestone plants, to have the place cleaned up in preparation for the wrecking ball. He was in charge of closing the plant where he and his father had worked together for fourteen years.

June 16, the last day, passed like a sigh. The doors were supposed to close forever at 10:00 PM, the end of Tony Fanizzi's final shift. But everyone was finished at six. They were bid farewell and sent home. Some, by then, had already secured new jobs. Others began the hunt in earnest. Unemployment forms were filled out. But the competition was about to heat up.

On August 16, Mansfield Tire, an hour away in Mansfield, announced it was phasing out production, eliminating 750 jobs.

On August 26, Firestone asked Plant 1's thirteen hundred workers to take a pay cut to help keep their jobs, but made no promise about the factory's future.

On November 13, Mohawk Rubber announced it was closing its aging, unprofitable Akron plant. Three hundred and eighteen workers would be out on the street.

On December 20, General Tire announced plans to close its tire plant soon. Workers were asked to make pay and work-rule concessions, with the thin promise that the company would consider building a new factory in Akron. The plant was never built.

Firestone took it on the chin financially that year, losing 3 cents on every $1 in sales. For fiscal 1978, the company reported a $148 million loss, attributed mainly to the 500 recall and the plant closings in Akron and elsewhere. The only ray of hope that shone on Rubber City that awful year was Goodyear's announcement

Goodyear employees display their "Bad Attitude Worker" T-shirts, in 1978, to vent their anger after company CEO Charles Pilliod declared that poor labor attitudes of blue-collar workers in Akron were a determining factor in jobs being phased out. (*Akron Beacon Journal*/Lewis Henderson)

that it would convert its empty Plant 2 into a technical center, a $75 million investment. The move would create five hundred jobs. All white-collar. By the end of 1978, the profession that had defined Akron since early in the century—the building of car tires—was virtually gone.

Andrew Dakoski and Tony Fanizzi were two of the lucky ones. Dakoski secured a position as manager of a Firestone plant in Kentucky, and Fanizzi got a construction job. Their resumes, from there, read like road maps, as each man had to move from state to state to remain employed. Both men had enjoyed stable work and stable lives in their earlier Firestone careers. Before 1978, Dakoski had put in twenty-eight years with the company, Fanizzi had put in twelve. In the decade that followed, they bounced, between them, through seven jobs.

Akron lost more in 1978 than perhaps any other year. The ugly subtraction would continue with plant closings over the course of the next four years. But some things could not be removed, chiefly the sense of resiliency, the result of years of fighting, hard work, and bitter lessons. The buildings crumbled, but a foundation remained.

Demolition of Firestone's Plant 2 began in 1979. Members of the crew from Eslich Wrecking watched in semidisbelief as they dropped the six-ton wrecking ball thirty feet onto the roof and it bounced off like a child's toy. It took them two years to bring the castoff factory to the ground.

Demolition work at Firestone Plant 2 in 1979. The five-story building had been a symbol of Firestone's progress when it was built, in 1917, but six decades later, the building and the bias-ply tires its twelve hundred workers produced had become industry relics. The building, which was made of steel and concrete, was almost indestructible and took two years to tear down, about twice as long as demolition of a normal building the same size. (©Daniel Mainzer)

Workers at ground level are dwarfed by concrete skeletons, all that remains of a portion of Firestone's Plant 2 as demolition continues. Despite the removal of interior supports, the floors of the building remained intact, forcing Eslich Wrecking, the demolition company, to keep pounding with the wrecking ball until the building finally came down. (©Daniel Mainzer)

One worker said it was the toughest building he had ever seen.

As devastating as the closing of Firestone's Plant 2 was, it was still an act that could be explained in cold business terms. The news became harsher when people called their company "family"—and meant it. Such was the case with The Mohawk Rubber Company, a smaller firm with a rich Akron history. There and at Sun Rubber Company, another small company, the sound was somehow different when the ax fell. For Mohawk, that sound came a few months after the closing of Firestone's Plant 2.

From a window in the old Mohawk Rubber Company plant on Second Avenue in Akron, purchasing manager Beech Fannin watched the final act of the saddest human drama he had ever seen. If it had been just about business, as it was supposed to be, the scene unfolding in the cold of a late November would not have chilled him beyond the bone and into his soul. But it wasn't just business. This was Mohawk, and Mohawk was family, perhaps the closest-knit rubber family in Akron's milieu of plants and neighborhoods and households in which men and women found their identities and gave one to a city. After sixty-five years in busi-

ness, Mohawk had given its loyal and productive work force nine days' notice that the plant would close the day before Thanksgiving 1978. The little rubber company had posted the notice above the time clock on Monday, November 13. Now, the clock was ticking not only on jobs but also on personal and civic identities. If these men and women were no longer to be part of the Mohawk family, then who were they, what were they?

The questions haunted the 318 Mohawk workers who read the announcement. They reacted with shock and disbelief, uncertainty and bitterness. They had improved productivity in the dilapidated truck tire plant that began its industrial life at the turn of the century. Labor and management got along well. Workers had struck the company only once, earlier this same year, an anomaly in Rubber City. "The bosses were fair. They listened to us. We listened to them," said Ed Wilson, who worked at Mohawk for twenty-nine years. "It was probably the ideal situation."

After Mohawk had locked the plant doors, some workers kept returning. Beech Fannin said these workers were so humiliated and upset about losing their

Joe Oppihle of Akron and other Mohawk employees clock out for the last time at 5:45 PM on November 22, 1978. The 318 workers had received notice of the closing only nine days earlier. Radial conversion of Mohawk's out-of-state plants had siphoned off money that might have been invested in remodeling and modernizing in Akron. (*Akron Beacon Journal*/Ron Kuner)

The stone nameplate of the Mohawk Rubber Co. plant lies like a gravestone along a sidewalk, in June 1983, after the building on Second Ave. in Akron was razed. The site became a parking lot for Goodyear's East Market St. complex. (*Akron Beacon Journal*/Dennis Gordon)

jobs that they could not bear to face their families. So each day, they returned to their other family, the one that knew their pain. "They'd get dressed, drive down to the plant, and sit at the gatehouse until their shift was over," Fannin recalled. "It was so sad to see."

By this time, all of Akron knew how the workers outside Beech Fannin's window felt that Thanksgiving. "It was like a punch right to my heart," said Wesley Lake, son of a Mohawk man and one himself for thirty years. "I never got the chance to get my fists up."

Radial conversion at Mohawk's out-of-state plants siphoned off money that might have been invested in remodeling and modernizing in Akron, where the plants were old and workers costly. "That was tough on us, a real financial burden," said Henry "Hank" Fawcett, Mohawk president and chief executive officer. "Our workers were good workers, but our facilities were just beyond repair."

Mohawk eventually was bought by Yokohama Tire and Rubber of Japan, a full decade after the Akron plant closing. For Akron, the takeover was merely a postscript in the saga. By then, Mohawk had removed every trace of itself from the city of its birth. The old Akron plant on Second Avenue had been torn down and made into a parking lot for Goodyear, back in 1983.

Darkness had fallen on Sun Rubber Company of Barberton earlier, in 1974. At one time the world's largest manufacturer of rubber toys, Sun, like Mohawk, was squeezed by foreign competition and by pressures resulting from the area's high union wage scale. There the similarity mostly ends.

The end for Sun's nearly three hundred employees came on the eve of a potential settlement of a four-and-a-half-month strike by URW Local 58. Labor and management did not coexist peaceably at Sun. Both sides seemed to accept that regular strikes were a necessary, though regrettable, part of doing business. That reluctant acceptance began to change, in 1969, when ownership of Sun shifted from local hands to Talley Industries of Arizona. Sun Rubber was the only unionized company Talley owned. In April 1974, Talley executives B. Paul Barnes and Ted Ryan Jr. showed up in Barberton. By then, the walkout by Local 58, which had begun in December, had left Sun without any business orders. During a bargaining session, the Talley executives announced that Sun would close in Barberton and operations would be moved to Georgia.

"There was silence," recalled Richey Smith, Sun's president. "We were stunned. We were just a hair away from settling."

"I never dreamt the plant would go down," said Catherine "Kitty" Garlock, president of Local 58 at the time. "I can't remember them saying we weren't competitive."

For many workers, Sun Rubber was the only job they had ever known. They built friendships with their colleagues over the years. They grieved when the plant closed. Many of them did not qualify for pensions. They had spouses and kids to support. They had to search for new work. But Sun never represented a second family to its workers the way Mohawk did. Sun workers did not have that loss to overcome.

According to Garlock, union negotiators asked whether Barberton workers could transfer to Georgia. Possibly, the negotiators were told, but the Barberton workers would have no seniority. "So I went back to the picket lines. That was a very hard thing to do. There were a lot of tears and anger, and of course they didn't say it to my face, but you hear it later—the union did it."

Filled with ambivalence, Richey Smith, the son of the company founder, helped relocate a smaller Sun Products to Carrollton, Georgia. "I'm not too proud of the fact that we couldn't settle the strike," Smith said. "When you have three hundred people working for you, you are really responsible for their livelihoods. I didn't feel at all sorry for the union leadership, but I did feel sorry for the

Rena Grand, Ella Young, and Ann Ketenach handle doll heads on the assembly line at the Sun Rubber Company in 1956. *(Akron Beacon Journal)*

Newly unemployed members of United Rubber Workers Local 58 talk, on April 22, 1974, outside the shack that served as their strike headquarters near Sun Products in Barberton. Three days earlier, the 134th day of their strike, Talley Industries had closed the plant. (*Akron Beacon Journal*/Ott Gangl)

people. . . . I hated that persons who had been there thirty and forty years got hurt."

In the end, Richey Smith lined up with the workers to fight Talley in court when it refused to honor the pension rights of Sun workers. The case went all the way to the Ohio Supreme Court, which ruled Talley owed lifetime pensions to thirty former workers and one-time payouts to 242.

The plant closing proved historic, not just for Sun, but for Akron. It was, in retrospect, the shot heard 'round the Rubber City, the first of a volley that, within a decade, knocked down virtually all major rubber production in Akron. But there is still a major passenger tire plant in Ohio. It is in Findlay, Ohio, owned by Cooper Tire, another small rubber company that formed in boomtown Akron. This one has thrived.

17 A Niche Company Survives

ONE HUNDRED and twenty miles west of Akron, over a ribbon of concrete, across rich Ohio farmland, past Mail Pouch barns lies a near-mythical rubber company where all the workers are above average and in all the bosses beat hearts of gold.

"Brigadoon," J. Alec Reinhardt, a boss, calls it.

Yet this is no mythical eighteenth century Scottish village that appears out of the mist for just one day every 100 years. Findlay is on the rubber map, and Cooper Tire and Rubber Company put it there with the last full-scale tire plant in Ohio.

Once, Akron was the Rubber Capital of the World. Now, it is not even the rubber capital of its own state. If any place owns that distinction, it is Findlay.

Akron has Goodyear's headquarters, technical center, research and development facility, and radial race tire manufacturing. Akron also has Bridgestone/Firestone research and development and design facilities and the U.S. portion of its radial race tire manufacturing. Findlay has Cooper, its first plant and its headquarters. Some sixty-two hundred people work for Akron's rubber companies—2.7 percent of Akron's population. Findlay, the seat of Hancock County, has about thirty-eight thousand people. Two thousand of them, give or take a worker or three, earn their paychecks at Findlay's singular rubber company. Cooper employs 5.2 percent of the Findlay area's population, almost twice the industry's share in the Akron area.

"Cooper is our biggest employer," Mayor John Stozich said. "They mean a lot to us."

The Cooper story is one of feelings and relationships, of a small company in a small town doing big things. "You just can't imagine how neat it is to be in a small town," Alec Reinhardt said. *Neat.* The word, oft repeated at Cooper, rings of small-town America. They use such words at this small-town Fortune 500 company without a hint of self-consciousness.

The Cooper story is also one of survival. Cooper was supposed to be nowhere today, making nothing. Other companies its size were swallowed by larger rubber companies in the wake of the industry's costly conversion to radial tire production, in the 1970s, and its painful contraction because of overcapacity during the 1980s.

"When you go back to the 1980s when all the acquisitions, mergers, and takeovers were in process," said Patrick W. Rooney, Cooper's chairman of the board, president, and chief executive officer, "the pronouncement of the industry was that only four or five tire companies would remain in the United States. We weren't on that list by a long shot." Rooney attributed the company's survival to "our employees. The dedication. The culture. The independence."

On the cusp of the millennium, Cooper is a throwback in a move-up, move-on society. It is a place where a person is encouraged to spend a career and make a life. From president of the company to president of the union, from tire builder to plant manager, there is a feeling at the Findlay plant and throughout Cooper that abandoned Akron long ago. Small-town America knits a more seamless tapestry. Alec Reinhardt wended his way from Cleveland to Findlay, in 1976, to become Cooper's general counsel. He now serves as executive vice president, chief financial officer, and Cooper booster.

"It is the company involvement that really drives people's careers at Cooper," Reinhardt said, "as opposed to the more cosmopolitan, professional drive . . . where the person is first an engineer or a lawyer, and their idea of a job is to add something to their resume to leverage off of that for the next job at a little higher salary."

CEO Rooney is a volcano of small-town warmth rather than an iceberg of corporate self-importance. He grew up in Findlay, graduated from Findlay College (now University), and made good at Cooper. He rumbles and erupts with delight when he talks about the tire company, weighting and fusing the words "small" and "community" as if they were one. He roams often through the Findlay plant, greeting longtime friends who also have made good. Floyd Rader has put two children through college. He has built tires every way Cooper has found to build them, "from hand turn-up to space-age" with computer and laser to guide him.

"I hired in, in 1960, as a tire builder," said Rader, "and today . . . I'm still a tire builder. That has to tell you something: our employees don't leave."

Industry analyst Harry Millis has been in every company's tire plants around the industry. "You're talking to a conservative, old Midwesterner," Millis admitted, "but I've always felt there was an advantage in being in a small place. I think there is a little greater work ethic in smaller communities and a greater feeling of camaraderie, that we're all in this together, that we're all a part of the community. You just can't build that same type of feeling in a large urban environment."

Akron native James S. Kovac knows this as well as anyone. From 1957 to 1983, he worked for Firestone in Akron, then in Oklahoma City and, finally, in Memphis. He retired from Firestone when it downsized, and he joined Cooper, becoming plant manager and then vice president of Findlay manufacturing operations. "Akron is my hometown, and I appreciate it," Kovac said. "But companies got extremely big, and probably there wasn't the capability of communications. This is just neat. I'm telling you, it's refreshing. . . . When I first came here, I thought I'd died and gone to heaven."

Problems don't mushroom into grievances and arbitrations. Kovac just meets with Mike Saum, president of Local 207 of the United Steelworkers of America, the bargaining unit for Cooper production workers. People walk away feeling good about one another.

"Them days of beating on the table and saying: 'That's the way it's going to be!'—they ain't there anymore. You have to sit down and resolve it," said Saum. "I've been all over the United States at different locals' meetings. I've never found a management's relationship with a union as good as the one we have. When other people have been at arm's length, we've been at elbow's distance."

Cooper has both union and nonunion plants. In those that are unionized, such as Findlay and Texarkana, Arkansas, Cooper forges agreements based on local conditions rather than on an industry master contract. "The employees know their needs," Rooney said, "and together we can work them out."

That doesn't mean there aren't disagreements. In 1991, for example, Local 207 struck for twenty-three days over health benefits. A more usual outcome to negotiations occurred, however, in 1994, when a new contract was signed two weeks before the old one expired.

It is the kind of relationship and money—the average Cooper tire builder in Findlay earns $23 to $24 an hour, compared with the industry average of $18—that have people lining up for jobs at Cooper plants everywhere. Cooper employs ninety-one hundred in the United States and at a tube plant in Mexico. A few years ago, the company announced that it would expand its Findlay work force by fewer than 100. More than five thousand people applied, lining up the day before the hiring process began. For fewer than 100 openings in Albany, Georgia, Cooper received eleven thousand applications.

Once hired, Cooper employees can be fanatically dedicated. In 1978, one of the biggest blizzards ever to sweep across northern Ohio struck Findlay. Radio stations announced that Cooper was nevertheless open for those who could get in. Hundreds showed up. "Guys were getting in their four-wheelers," Saum said, "and picking up other guys and coming to work. Guys were getting on their snowmobiles and coming to work. Of course, they may have regretted it later. They were stuck there for three days."

Peer pressure dictates behavior in a different way from that found in Akron when rubber shops spit out tires. In Akron, a tire builder who exceeded the normal production rate faced reprisals from coworkers lest they, too, be required to do

Employees of a Cooper corporate ancestor, The Giant Tire and Rubber Company, are shown in Findlay, in 1917, shortly after the company moved from Akron. Executive Patrick W. Rooney says: "The move from Akron to Findlay was the right move. . . . Not being in Akron forced us to think independently." (Cooper Tire and Rubber Company)

more. Moreover, the companies often increased the production rates and lowered the pay when they found more could be done in less time. At Cooper, there is no quota.

"I think what has really helped is incentive rates," tire builder Doug Alge said. "They put rates out there and let people go get that middle-class lifestyle. If they see that people are making money, they don't just come out and say: 'We're going to change your rates.'"

Kovac remembers a time at Firestone when people got along, too. "When I first went to Firestone," he said, "it was a family operation. The Firestone family was there, and it felt very similar [to Cooper]. But it changed. They downsized so badly that it wasn't much fun. This is so different. This is a family, and I'm glad they welcomed me into it. We respect each other. We appreciate one another. We listen to one another. And, I believe, we trust one another. This is a great, great work force. A lot of that stems from the history of Cooper and the way they've treated people."

Ironically, Cooper's history begins in Akron, in 1914, when brothers-in-law John Schaefer and Claude E. Hart bought the M and M Manufacturing Company, a maker of tire patches, tire cement, and tire-repair kits. Schaefer and Hart added tire rebuilding to the business, in 1915, with the purchase of Akron's Giant Tire and Rubber Company. Akron was not, however, the place the merged companies would make their future in tire building. Too crowded. Too many big fish. Not the right facilities. There were 134 tire manufacturers at the time, forty of them in Ohio. Rubber companies had sprouted on every other block in Akron. Hart, company president, and Schaefer had a different idea for Giant Tire. They found in Findlay just the right facilities in the buildings of the failed Toledo Findlay Rubber Company and moved there in 1917.

"The move from Akron to Findlay was the right move," Rooney said. "Not being in Akron forced us to think independently."

Giant Tire's exodus did not rock Rubber City—Akron was exploding with people and rubber-related industry between 1910 and 1920 and would not be wrenched by plant closings and departures for many decades. But Giant's move is early testament to the flawless timing, when it came to taking leave of a city or product, of the company that became known as Cooper.

Even bad fortune turned into a blessing. When fire struck, in 1919, destroying Giant Tire's main multistory building, reconstruction began immediately on a more efficient one-story plant. Giant Tire began to build tires as the Cooper Corporation, in 1920, when Ira J. Cooper, a Cincinnati wholesaler of auto accessories, joined the company and attached his name to it. Cooper merged, in 1930, with Falls Rubber Company of Cuyahoga Falls to form Master Tire and Rubber Company.

By 1936, when the United Rubber Workers union was gaining strength in Akron, Master's tire operations also had ended up in Findlay, where relations were better even during the often violent years of the early labor movement. By then, the company already was firmly entrenched in the ideals and culture fostered by Ira Cooper—good merchandise, fair play, and a square deal for suppliers, employees, and dealers alike.

The company began operating under its current name, Cooper Tire and Rubber Company, in 1946. Through the years, the old-fashioned precepts of the Cooper Culture have been redefined thus, according to Rooney: "We're a company that has quality products, gives excellent service to our customers, and maintains a position as a low-cost producer."

Cooper is more than a company of warm-hearted, enlightened executives and dedicated workers. It also is a company whose leaders run it with an icy resolve when it comes to critical decisions. In the mid- to late-1970s, Cooper found itself a bias-tire manufacturer in a radial world. Led by original-equipment tire purchases of the automakers in Detroit, between two-thirds and three-quarters of all tires being sold were radials. "They came very, very close to going under back in the days when Mansfield and Mohawk and the

The Cooper Tire and Rubber Company Findlay plant is shown in an aerial photograph from around 1920. Today, Cooper has a modernized production plant, corporate offices, a research center, and warehouses on the site. (Cooper Tire and Rubber Company)

During WWII, the Findlay plant produced these inflatable landing craft as well as inflatable tanks as part of the Allies' effort to deceive the Germans about their real D-Day invasion target on the French coast. The company also produced tires for military vehicles. In 1945, it accepted the Army-Navy E Award for the excellence of its war work. (Cooper Tire and Rubber Company)

others went out," analyst Millis said. "Cooper had about 15 percent of its capacity in radial. They were really on the ropes."

But Cooper still had its gift for timing."We decided early on that we had to be in the radial tire business," Rooney said. "But we also made the decision that we were not going to vacate the bias market overnight." Cooper, a replacement-market supplier, did not build tires for automakers to use as original equipment; consequently, Detroit wasn't pressuring Cooper to rush into radials. The big tire companies began phasing out their bias-tire production to supply new cars with radials and, led by Firestone, dropped out of the private-brand bias-tire market. But the market for bias tires hadn't vanished and would not for some time: Radials did not dominate the replacement market until 1980. In the meantime, consumers still wanted bias tires because they were cheaper than radials. Cooper decided to fill that void.

"We were going to run out the life cycle of the bias tire," Rooney said. "If there was a time to turn out the light on bias tires, then we decided we might just be the last one to turn the light off. It was probably the right decision."

"They converted to radials in a very intelligent way," analyst Millis agreed. "They didn't make the mistakes that the guys who led the radial revolution did. They expanded gradually and at low cost."

Cooper expands only when it has sales to support the expansion. "Since the mid- to late-'70s," said Executive Vice President Alec Reinhardt, "there have been at least forty plants closed [by others in the United States]. We've only opened plants and enlarged existing ones."

Cooper, in 1984, even took an abandoned Mansfield tire plant that no one else wanted and made it successful. "Virtually everyone in the industry had looked at this old plant in Tupelo, Mississippi," Reinhardt said. "All they saw was a plant that had been closed down for five years and had a lot of old equipment in it. It turned out that this old equipment was the same old equipment that was in our plant. We had been able to convert it and modernize it with nominal capital investment. We were able to take a plant that five years before had employed seven hundred people making thirty-five hundred tires a day—primarily bias—and with 350 people produce seven thousand [radial] tires a day. We got that with a $30 million investment." Starting from scratch, a similarly productive plant would have cost Cooper between $100 million and $120 million, Reinhardt estimated.

Cooper executives made another shrewd move by allowing only a network of fourteen hundred independent dealers to sell Cooper name-brand tires—Cooper, Mastercraft, Roadmaster, and Starfire. This strategy ensured that the independent dealers would not have to compete against the mass merchandisers to sell the Cooper brands. At the same time, Cooper began to supply private-label tires for mass merchandisers, such as Sears, Pep Boys, and Winston Tires. In 1997, Cooper held 12 percent of the replacement market. The larger tire companies, including Goodyear, allow their name brands to be sold outside their own stores.

"We made the determination that the tire business was a service-oriented business and that the key player in the replacement tire business was the independent tire dealer," Rooney said. "We didn't have company stores. We didn't have the advertising budget of a Goodyear or Michelin. So the monies we spent were best spent on the local level with and through our dealers. Our growth . . . would be facilitated by keeping the channel clean as far as those house brands were concerned."

Cooper's net sales have more than tripled from $522.6 million in 1985 to $1.62 billion in 1996. It has consistently produced the industry's highest profit margins, reaching 14.86 percent in 1994. In 1996, its profit margin fell but still was 10.68 percent. Goodyear's margin, in comparison, was 9.3 percent.

Jerry O'Neil, former chairman and president of General Tire, had been among

Cooper Tire and Rubber Company fits snugly into the small city of Findlay, where it's the largest employer. The company encourages its employees to build careers there. A union steward says incentive pay rates allow workers to pursue a middle-class lifestyle. (*Akron Beacon Journal*/Ed Suba, Jr.)

Floyd Rader builds a radial tire at Cooper's Findlay plant where he hired in as a tire builder in 1960. He has built tires every way Cooper has found to build them, from "hand turn-up to space age" with computer and laser to guide him. (*Akron Beacon Journal*/Ed Suba, Jr.)

the doomsayers about the long-term prospects of the smaller tire makers, including his own. With the benefit of hindsight, he expressed admiration for Cooper's strategy. "It is very simple why they did well," O'Neil said. "You pick a little niche, which they did, and you stick to it. Get as good as you can from a manufacturing and quality standpoint. Then just stick with it. There is always room for somebody in the industry like this. If the niche is right, you can do it."

Cooper was profitable. It had a niche. Yet no one tried to buy it or to take it over.

"Maybe," Rooney said, "we didn't have what they were looking for: We weren't in Akron. We had a philosophy, a culture, of independence. We didn't have an OE [original equipment] presence."

More likely, analyst Millis said, the foreign companies came shopping in America to get into the high-price—and more profitable—end of radials. "It was like the days when Cooper was left in the belted-bias market, and no one else was there," Millis said. "They were left in the [less profitable] associate-label and private-label market, where only Kelly-Springfield was doing a good job. Cooper was again blessed by being where the majors weren't."

Moreover, Cooper never diversified to the extent the major companies did. Cooper's business is narrowly focused on replacement tires and engineered products—engine mounts, door and window seals, and hoses. It sells the engineered products to automakers and no one else in the aftermarket. During the takeover frenzy of the 1980s, Cooper was less attractive to the raiders who made runs at the Akron tire companies for their breakup value. "We haven't branched off into other areas that we didn't have the expertise in," Rooney said. "We figured we didn't have the ability to do it. We set our course and sailed it very steadily."

Given Cooper's negligible debt and low-cost, efficient operation, Reinhardt says any buyer "would have had to pay a premium [for Cooper stock] and feel they could improve the operation."

Even as it grows, however, Cooper is bent upon retaining its culture. Cooper's strategy includes everything from choosing a compatible spokesman for a high-profile media campaign—Arnold Palmer—to acquiring a British tire company—Avon—with a mirror culture. "They are recognizing," analyst Millis said, "that if they want to continue to be a rapid-growth company . . . they are going to have to move into the international scene. They are doing it the careful way."

For the past fifteen years, Cooper has been exporting its excess tire production. In recent years, it also found itself a strange bedfellow—Autobacs Seven, Japan's largest tire retailer. Autobacs Seven representatives called Cooper, in 1993, to say they wanted to meet with Rooney and others at Cooper.

"We didn't know Autobacs Seven from a hill of beans," Rooney said. Autobacs Seven knew Cooper, though. Because no Japanese tire maker had proved willing to produce a private-brand tire for Autobacs, the retailer began scouring the world market for the best qualified company.

"They found Findlay," Rooney said, "but they had to make a phone call to do it."

The relationship quickly blossomed. In 1995, one year after Cooper began shipping tires to Autobacs Seven's nearly five hundred stores, it was honored as Autobacs's Overseas Vendor of the Year, chosen from ninety suppliers in twenty-five countries. The award signaled Cooper's acceptance in the global marketplace. "One of the main reasons we received the award," suggested Tom Griffith, Cooper vice president of marketing, "is Autobacs's belief that Cooper's goals and culture are the same as theirs. We are both goal-oriented, customer-oriented, and flexible in responding to customer needs."

The relationship with Avon, the British tire company that Cooper bought for $110.4 million in February, 1997, goes deeper. In the mid-1970s, Avon helped Cooper develop its radial truck tire technology.

"It was not like we went clomping out overseas on an airplane, looked down and said: 'Well, let's buy something,'" Rooney says. "We knew the people. We knew the culture. We knew the way they operated."

Avon, which employs nearly twelve hundred, turned Cooper into a different player in the world market. No longer is it limited to exporting tires. Now it has a manufacturing base abroad, with distribution facilities and channels that will allow Cooper to grow. The purchase of Avon makes Cooper an original-equipment manufacturer by association. Avon supplies Rolls Royce, Aston Martin, and Land Rover.

Cooper's expansion of its engineered products unit is likely to be driven by following automakers as they open manufacturing facilities in other countries.

A Cooper store's sign is framed by the facade of a neighboring car wash business bearing Findlay's nickname, Flag City. Cooper executives advocate the benefits of the small-town atmosphere. (*Akron Beacon Journal*/Ed Suba, Jr.)

Meanwhile, Cooper will continue to look in tire operations "for opportunities that somewhat parallel Avon," Rooney said. In other words, for old relationships with which Cooper can feel comfortable. That's how golfer Arnold Palmer came to be Cooper's spokesman. Palmer said he agreed for reasons that go beyond money. He had money. He felt comfortable with Cooper's "loyalty to dealers and top-quality products."

Likewise, Cooper felt comfortable with Palmer, the man from another small American town, Latrobe, Pennsylvania, population 9,265. "We wanted to align ourselves with someone who would blend with our organization and would give off the culture of our organization," Rooney said. "I don't think we could have picked a better guy than Arnold Palmer."

So now, Palmer stands up for Cooper on television and in stores in his full-size cardboard persona, foot up on a Cooper tire. "Some of our dealers," said Patricia J. Brown, Cooper director of communications, "have even put them in local golf shops with the note: Find Cooper Tires at (the location of the dealer). People tell us: 'Oh, Cooper! That's Arnold Palmer's company.'"

Actually, Cooper belongs to Findlay, to small-town America. In addition to Findlay, Cooper has tire and engineered products facilities in such places as Auburn, Indiana (population 9,379), Albany, Georgia (78,122), Bowling Green (28,176), and Tupelo, Mississippi (31,685).

"In the industry," Rooney said, "we're a minnow swimming with the sharks. But in Findlay, Ohio, Clarksdale, Mississippi, and all the other locations where we have plants, we are a substantial part of the community."

Cooper's annual company picnic in Findlay is, indeed, a community affair. Cooper hires a firm to erect a carnival midway and rides. It provides free food. It even recruits civic organizations, such as the band boosters, to run the midway and benefit financially. It invites its employees and its retirees. They invite their neighbors. No one objects.

Reinhardt said the annual company picnic is a chance for the townfolk to mingle, an activity that occurs frequently in Findlay. Reinhardt lives on Orchard Lane. So do some plant workers. Pat Rooney is as likely to drop in at Wilson's, the hottest burger place in town, as he is at the Findlay Country Club. Mayor John Stozich got used to seeing Cooper executives, including Rooney, at Findlay High School's basketball games.

"They weren't real addicted to high school sports," Stozich said. "I think they felt that this was being a part of the community."

Stozich taught and coached basketball before entering politics. During his teaching career, Stozich worked summers at Cooper as a test driver and sometimes as a chauffeur for executives and directors. "No one sat in the back seat," Stozich said, "and they all wanted to talk. I think it's that nice, friendly overall attitude that is the reason Cooper has been so successful."

18 Philanthropy and Artistry

THEY CALLED HIM "Daddy." Tall, distinguished, with gray hair and a Vandyke beard, Edwin C. Shaw was the man the children in the Springfield Lake Sanatorium had come to rely on for almost daily visits. A talented gardener and collector of art, he understood life on a higher plane. He smiled as he made his way through the hospital's "Sunshine Cottage," greeting each patient by name.

The sanatorium's directors had come to rely on him, as well. Shaw, who had retired from his B. F. Goodrich vice presidency at age fifty-five, spent much of his time in the 1920s and 1930s traveling to tuberculosis hospitals throughout the country, returning with ideas for better care. But Shaw spent more than his time. He spent his money. Chiefly through his contributions, the Springfield Lake Sanatorium had become known as one of the best care facilities in the country for tuberculosis patients. Newspaper accounts never referred to Shaw as a former rubber executive. He was always "philanthropist Edwin Shaw." When the Summit County commissioners formally proposed to rename the sanatorium for Shaw, in 1934, he protested vehemently. He lost, and the Edwin Shaw Hospital stands as his legacy.

But that was only part of it. When Shaw died, in 1941, the bulk of his

Edwin Shaw, shown in 1938, resisted unsuccessfully the renaming of the Springfield Lake Sanatorium in his honor. Shaw spent much of his time in the 1920s and '30s traveling to tuberculosis hospitals throughout the country, returning with ideas for better care. *(Akron Beacon Journal)*

$300,000 estate was designated for a higher cause. The Edwin Shaw Foundation was established with that money, to help sustain health and education facilities in the Akron area. By 1955, Shaw's legacy had matured to $1 million, all of which was converted into the Akron Community Trusts, a fund to benefit the health, welfare, and cultural needs of the community.

"If it could ever be said of anyone," Akron industrialist Hugh Galt proclaimed at the time of Shaw's death, "it can certainly be said of him that he left his community better than he found it."

Akron had its share of millionaires. Barons, they were called, men who made fortunes through their shrewdness, through the windfalls of a thriving industry, and through the bitter sweat of Akron's manual laborers. But did these rubber magnates, too, leave Akron better than they had found it? It's a difficult question to answer, and perhaps the fact that there is no easy reply suggests that the answer is "no."

Shaw's foundation, which evolved into the Akron Community Foundation, had assets of $51.6 million in 1997 and gave away $1.3 million in 1996. But the two largest charitable trusts that benefit the Akron area—the $140 million GAR foundation, which gave away $5.7 million in 1996, virtually all in Summit and surrounding counties; and the $1.06 billion John S. and James L. Knight Foundation, which gave away $37.6 million in 1996, including $2.3 million in grants to Akron-area institutions—dwarf the rest of the area's foundations. And neither was established with rubber money. The GAR Foundation arose from the gilded estate of Galen and Ruth Roush. Galen Roush was the cofounder of Roadway Express. And the Knight Foundation—established in Akron, but since moved to Miami—grew out of the fortune of the Knight newspaper family, who founded the *Beacon Journal*.

For various reasons, the men who became fantastically rich from Akron's rubber industry did not endow the city in the way, say, steel magnate Andrew Carnegie did Pittsburgh. The Steel City reaps the benefits of Carnegie-funded li-

Springfield Lake Sanatorium, shown in 1921, became known as one of the best care facilities in the nation for tuberculosis patients, thanks in part to the efforts of retired B.F. Goodrich Vice President Edwin Shaw. His will provided for the hospital and established what had evolved over the years into the Akron Community Foundation, which had assets of $51.6 million, in 1997, and gave away $1.3 million in 1996. (Edwin Shaw Hospital for Rehabilitation)

braries, art and science museums, a music hall, and Carnegie Mellon University. Carnegie, who sold his steel company for $250 million in 1901, gave away $350 million in his lifetime—$3.5 billion in today's dollars.

This is not to say Akron's rubber families were stingy. Raymond Firestone, the son of the tire company's founder, left generous gifts to his hometown during his life and after he died, in 1994, and made perhaps the largest impact of any individual from the rubber families. But his family's best-known institution, the Firestone Library, is at Princeton University in New Jersey. And F. A. and Charlie Seiberling, Goodyear's founders, lost their fortunes before they had the opportunity to fold them into Akron's future. Those who had the most to give, the Firestones, scattered most of their money elsewhere. Those who history suggests might have been the most willing to give—the Seiberlings—had too little.

Summit County has numerous smaller foundations, many of them seeded by rubber; their generosity should not be taken for granted. And tire company executives have always had a strong presence on the boards of the larger institutions, providing leadership and support that has helped improve life here. But the industry that dominated the area for most of a century does not dominate its philanthropy. Akron attorney and prominent civic leader David Lieberth looks around his town and wonders, too: Where did all the money go?

"What bothers me most . . . is that Akron has been deprived of its birthright in terms of charitable contributions," he said. "What we have lost is the rubber fortune. We didn't ever benefit from the rubber fortune as we should have."

Perhaps the most notable case of that not happening is with the Goodrich family—the founders of the company that made Edwin Shaw rich. David Goodrich, B. F.'s son who served on the board of directors from 1912 until 1950, spent most of his time and money in New York City. The family showed little interest in Akron and has virtually no legacy here.

In 1889, Andrew Carnegie, the Pittsburgh steel baron and a forerunner to Akron's rich industrialists, wrote a two-part article for the *North American Review* titled, simply, "Wealth." Carnegie's intent was to explain his theory of scientific philanthropy, that is, how to distribute great personal fortune.

"This, then, is held to be the duty of the man of wealth," Carnegie wrote. "To set an example of honest, unostentatious living, shunning display or extravagance; to provide moderately for the legitimate wants of those dependent on him; and, after doing so, to consider all surplus revenues which come to him simply as trust funds which he is called upon to administer."

Carnegie went on to list, in order of importance, the seven beneficiaries he considered most deserving: universities, free libraries, hospitals, parks, public halls for use as meeting places or other events, swimming baths, and churches. While some members of the clergy complained about their place on the list, many people heralded Carnegie's thesis as an important blueprint for future philanthropy. The Akron industrialists who rose to princedom in the decades that followed may not have read the essays. But there is little doubt they knew of Carnegie's example. Were they obligated to follow it?

C. C. "Gibby" Gibson, the late Goodyear executive and civic leader, didn't believe so. "Who is there to criticize a man for doing his best?" Gibson said. "A man's philanthropy activity and generosity of spirit is strictly a personal thing. No one walks in someone else's shoes." Gibson defended the Akron industrialists—who, he points out, didn't achieve the wealth of Carnegie or other industrial giants of the day—for their leadership and their less public generosity. The Firestones, Seiberlings, O'Neils, and others served on boards and spearheaded public works campaigns, he said, which gave the city better-than-average public institutions and a higher quality of life.

According to historian George Knepper, "Akron never had a lead cow in charity giving, in the sense of a person who could be relied on to finance a large project. . . . These folks fell upon hard times in the '30s. Their money never had a chance to jell into fortunes. Akron did not develop anyone who had the combination of an interest in philanthropy and the resources."

Now that the decks have been cleared, with the purchase and removal of all but one Akron tire company, who is keeping the ship afloat?

F. A. Seiberling loved Akron. And there are plenty of indications he would have supported her generously. But he didn't have the chance. He did leave a legacy here, some of which bears his name and some of which does not. Stan Hywet Hall, F. A. Seiberling's voluptuous Tudor-style estate, is perhaps his most prominent and fitting legacy in Akron. While he intended to leave the castle for the enjoyment of the ages, the financial circumstances of his life meant that he also left the costs of the up-keep to others.

Seiberling also donated a significant amount of land to the city's park system. Five hundred acres of Sand Run Park in west Akron occupies land once owned by Seiberling. The rubber baron, a devoted naturalist, served on the park board in its early years. He was also the founder and first president of the board of directors of Peoples Hospital, now Akron General Medical Center. He spearheaded its first funding campaign, donating $20,000.

F. A.'s brother, Charlie, was even more public-spirited; he was often called Akron's "first citizen." But he, too, had relatively little to give. When he died, in 1946, he left a $100,000 estate, from which he gave $500 to the Akron Community Chest, a precursor to United Way, and $300 each to a number of other charities.

A lone car makes its way up a hill in Sand Run Metropolitan Park in October 1930. Nearly half the acreage in the 845-acre park, which opened in 1929, was donated by F.A. Seiberling, co-founder of Goodyear and builder of Stan Hywet Hall. The park is the first, the largest, and the most visited in the county system. *(Akron Beacon Journal)*

Nurses from the graduating class of 1973 at the Idabelle Firestone School of Nursing at Akron City Hospital toss their hats into the air outside the school's building. (*Akron Beacon Journal*/Ted Walls)

If the fate of Stan Hywet reflected the architecture of F. A. Seiberling's spirit, the same could be said of the fabled Columbiana, Ohio, farmhouse that was the birthplace of Harvey S. Firestone. In the early 1980s, the landmark was dismantled brick by brick, and reconstructed at Henry Ford's Greenfield Village in Dearborn, Michigan. The $1.5 million cost was bankrolled by the Firestone family. The old farmhouse followed the path of much of the Firestone legacy: out of Ohio.

Harvey Firestone was the wealthiest of Akron's rubber barons. But even as he made his home here, the company's founder often turned his attention to places with glossier postcards. He wintered in Miami Beach. He socialized in New York City. He relaxed at a Newport, Rhode Island, resort. He ran his company in Akron, but he loved other places at least as much as the gray-skied, brick-walled city.

"My own surmise is that, having not been brought up here like the Seiberlings were, who knew people and had two or three generations of background and had social standing in the early days, they [the Firestones] were kind of newcomers, new rich, and it was difficult to break into the old guard, and they never decided to do it," observed Bob Koch, a longtime Firestone executive who knew Harvey Sr. personally. "They would do it in New York or in Newport."

In the 1940s, the Firestone sons and their mother donated more than $1 million to build a library at Princeton, the alma mater of Harvey Sr.'s five boys. Family grants have supported expansion of the Harvey S. Firestone Memorial Library since then. It was a gift that, perhaps more than any other, symbolized the family's interest in places other than Akron, one that struck a sour note with many Akronites.

Even though most of the family moved away over the years, there is a considerable Firestone legacy here. The Firestones donated their west Akron polo fields to provide a place for St. Paul's Episcopal Church on West Market Street, earning it the nickname "St. Harvey's of the Polo Field." And over the years, the family provided considerable financial support to the church, including a charitable trust. The chapel there is named in honor of Idabelle Firestone, Harvey Sr.'s wife. The family name is all over town, from Firestone Park to Firestone High School.

Bob Troyer, the family's spokesman and a former company public relations official, pointed out that Firestone money was used to fund, in whole or in part, the Firestone Conservatory of Music at the University of Akron, the now-defunct Idabelle Firestone School of Nursing at Akron City Hospital, and Firestone High. Harvey Sr. built Firestone Country Club with his own money, and the NEC golf tournaments held there have generated millions of dollars for area charities. But the club is now owned by a Texas company. In 1996, the Akron Golf Charities Foundations (not connected directly with the Firestones) distributed $1 million. The Firestone Foundation, formed in 1947 by the founder's sons and based in Akron, provided money for Weathervane Theatre, Old Trail School, Walsh High School, the YMCA, Interval Brotherhood, United Way, and the Urban League.

But Bernice Vigar, Harvey Firestone Jr.'s longtime secretary, pointed out that the foundation's money was donated all over the country, with Princeton probably

The Firestone Country Club celebrates its grand opening in May 1930. Harvey Firestone, second from left in the foursome on the front steps, is joined by his company president, John Thomas, at right in the group. (The University of Akron Archives)

The O'Neil family has been generous to Akron over the years, but often privately so. Michael O'Neil (pictured), founder of O'Neil's department store, was a high-profile local merchant. His son, Will, founded General Tire, and, while the family fortune did not approach that of the Firestones or the Seiberlings in their heyday, the family's money found its way—usually in relatively modest amounts—into a number of local institutions. *(Akron Beacon Journal)*

receiving the most. Of the $5 million to $6 million the foundation gave away, about 20 percent went to greater Akron. The foundation dissolved in 1983, as the family dispersed geographically and the various members' philanthropic interests grew more varied.

Ray Graham, Harvey Sr.'s grandson, sat on the foundation's board. When the foundation disbanded, Graham, who lives in New Mexico, stressed that the family should continue to honor its commitment to the city that helped make its fortune. Graham, an honorary trustee of the Akron Art Museum, gives it about $10,000 a year.

Of the Firestone boys, Raymond left the most to Akron and Ohio. When he died, in 1994, he left $2 million to Princeton, but he also left $1 million to the University of Akron's School of Polymer Engineering. He left another million to the Cleveland Clinic. He contributed a Firestone room to the John S. Knight Center. And he sold his Bath Township estate to the Ohio State University for $5 million, which was at least $3 million less than its market value. He was a generous donor to Akron City Hospital—the auditorium and cardiac care center there are named in his honor. He also supported Pegasus Farm in Hartville, which runs an equestrian facility for handicapped children.

General Tire was perhaps the most Akron of the rubber companies. Will O'Neil, its founder and figurehead, was the son of a high-profile local merchant, and the company's top management, for much of its history, was homebred. The O'Neil family has been generous to Akron over the years, but often privately so. Family members, especially Jerry O'Neil, the founder's son and longtime company president, have been known locally to give quiet donations to charities and individuals. The spirit may be Carnegie-like, even if the level of recognition is not.

The O'Neil fortune has found its way—usually in relatively modest amounts—into a number of local institutions. Jerry O'Neil has a locally based foundation through which he gives charitable donations. Some money stays in the area, but a good deal goes elsewhere, depending on need. O'Neil makes all the spending decisions himself. Of the $525,000 donated in 1996, $185,000 stayed in the Akron area.

St. Thomas Hospital was started with a $100,000 gift from Michael O'Neil, the Akron department store giant who was the father of Will O'Neil. The family has supported the hospital over the years and is honored by an O'Neil Pavilion. The family donated Will O'Neil's 240-acre Bath Township farm to the Summit County parks system, in 1972, creating O'Neil Woods. And the O'Neils have supported a number of Catholic institutions, including Our Lady of the Elms school.

Jerry O'Neil, characteristically candid, throws shadows over the importance of his family's philanthropy.

"When you're active in business and you're working and you're part of the community, you're forced to [give something back]," he said. "Whether you want to or not, you find that people ask you to do things. You can't very well say no. I was born and raised here, and I give here, but I don't feel any compulsion to do so. Other people want to buy their place in history in Akron. You think I'd contribute to a baseball stadium, or a convention center, or an inventors hall of fame? That's not what I consider charity."

The rubber companies themselves, when they were located here, did provide support, both in terms of money and their executives' leadership. Tire company brass could always be counted on to spearhead United Way (previously United Fund) campaigns, school levy drives, and the like. The largest gift ever to the University of Akron, $3 million for a scholarship fund, came from Firestone Tire and Rubber in 1987. Goodrich donated nearly $4 million to help finance Opportunity Park, the urban renewal project, in the late 1960s. But, with the exodus of Firestone, Goodrich, and General Tire, some of the corporate support has dwindled.

The Bridgestone/Firestone Trust Fund, now housed in the company's Nashville, Tennessee headquarters, still supports Akron, but not as much as when the company was here. In 1990, the fund gave $656,000 to Akron charities and $35,000 to Nashville charities. In 1997, the trust fund budgeted $375,000 for Nashville and $337,000 for Akron. The GenCorp Foundation, based in the company's Bath headquarters, had assets of $52.3 million in 1997 and gave away $2.4 million the previous year. Of that money, $1.05 million stayed in Summit County. The foundation's local giving nearly doubled from 1990 to 1997. The B. F. Goodrich Foundation in Richfield had assets of $15 million in 1997 and gave away $1.2 million in 1996—about $325,000 in Summit County. Goodyear gave away $4.6 million in 1996; $1.35 million stayed in the Akron area.

Even without more Edwin Shaw-styled "Daddies," Akron has avoided becoming a Rust Belt wasteland. That has come in part through smaller but more numerous charitable donations, a grass-roots effort. And that may prove to be a more important legacy—that of community over individual.

The legacy of rubber in Akron is not measured only in dollars and cents, though. An industry whose factories spewed fire and poison into the sky, whose smoke blackened the snow, whose green windows cheated sunlight, and whose time clocks ticked away lives left its imprint in other important ways, influencing the intellectual and aesthetic tenor of the region. Beauty has proved to be one of the strangest of industrial byproducts.

Akron's most famous generation of artists rose from the ash, finding sweetness in the sulfur. From Akron, Rita Dove mined an embarrassment of poetic riches. Rock band Devo found vivid sarcasm in the sky and musical precision in the machines. And, under the fading facade, singer Chrissie Hynde discovered a gracious and romantic past.

As the blackened sandstone in downtown Akron attests, the mark of the factories is indelible. In each of these artists, that truth enforced itself. They all left Akron to make their art, but the Rubber City stayed with them. They did not have the pastel countrysides of Monet's France or the charming towns of Hemingway's Spain. They had Akron, a workaday place that, in Rita Dove's view, forces one to become a better poet.

With its blimps and tire shops, its penchant for bowling and strange passion for Tudor grandeur, Akron is an odd wrinkle in industrial reality. It is not a place that would attract artists, but it is a place that can groom good ones. Akron is unique in its usualness, surreal in its science. The first lesson in art is to use what you know. In Akron, people knew rubber.

Dove, Devo, and Hynde, all born after World War II, lived through the most crucial and degenerating period in Akron's industrial history. They grew up in a time of abundance, but matured in an era of decline. At the time they were blossoming as artists, the industry that defined their hometown was beginning to crumble. The alchemy could be toxic and intoxicating.

After Sunday evening suppers in the 1950s and 1960s, Ray Dove used to shoo his wife and children into the big old Plymouth for a visit to his parents. They wound through the city, from their home on Winton Avenue on the west side to Joseph Dove's house on Kelly Avenue, traveling past factories and neatly ordered neighborhoods. Young Rita would stare out the window. She did not know the factories were ugly. She did not know her father had been a pawn of racism, forced to work on the Goodyear shop floor despite having a master's degree in chemistry. She did not know that the Goodyear symbol, a shoe with wings, floated on poetry. She knew only what she saw: tire plants. And to her, they were beautiful.

Rita Dove, at about age three, celebrates Christmas in her parents' west Akron home with her brother. (Ray Dove)

"Especially at dusk," she recalled, "with the smoke coming out and the lights behind and the smudged green windows, you know, the way they kind of flipped open instead of opening out. It was a kind of perverse fascination, because it smelled horrible. . . . It wasn't a pleasant place, necessarily. But there was something so energetic, so modern, that it thrilled me to see it."

In grade school at Schumacher and through junior high at Simon Perkins and high school at Buchtel, Dove wrote poems, and when she went on to Miami University in Oxford, she began to realize that poems were writing her. And so she stayed with them, plowing the endless field of literature, and when she veered into the ground of her childhood, of Akron, she discovered the richest earth. She began to read a book by the German poet Rainer Maria Rilke, *Letters to a Young Poet*. And she found this advice: "If your daily life seems poor, do not blame it; blame yourself, tell yourself that you are not poet enough to call forth its riches; for to the creator there is no poverty and no poor indifferent place."

Rita Dove, two-time U.S. poet laureate, signs books during an appearance at the University of Akron in 1994. (*Akron Beacon Journal*/Robin Tinay Sallie)

Dove began to recall those smudged green windows and the place called Wingfoot Lake and the mysterious black zeppelin hangar. And she began to recall the stories of her mother's parents, whose lives spanned the early decades of Akron's rubber story. Realizing that Akron was no poor indifferent place, she began to write of those things. "If it was some place that nourished me," she figured, "then in a certain way, I was beholden to try to bring that nourishment to others."

As the seeds of poetry took root, she began to research her hometown, learning its secrets and obscurities. She learned how men, during the housing crunch of the early years of the rubber industry, rented beds in shifts, and how Akron was a Greek word for "high place." These things, mingled with the life stories of her grandparents, formed the poems that would become *Thomas and Beulah*, a slim and gentle book that, in 1987, won the Pulitzer Prize for poetry. Dove's success continued: in 1993, she was named U.S. poet laureate, a post she held for two terms.

Thomas and Beulah finds fascination in a city others chose to see as mundane. Like all poetry, it is specific in its detail but general in its effect. A detail such as Wingfoot Lake Park, where the Dove family attended company picnics, becomes the setting for a poem about the foolishness of racial division—white families on one side, black on the other, both "unpacking the same / squeeze bottles of Heinz, the same / waxy beef patties and Salem potato chip bags."

Behind the factory walls, Dove found beauty. And something more.

"I think that it's also partly knowing that human beings have managed to create something like this, that produces goods, and there's something about the human enterprise that's in there, too," she said. "You can almost see the human ingenuity and muscle and even hope. And failure, too. All in this factory."

In 1975, a group of young men approached the people in charge of the World of Rubber museum in Goodyear's Akron headquarters with a request. They wanted to shoot some film in there. For a fraternity prank, one of the young men explained.

No one, they were told, had ever been allowed to film inside the World of Rubber. But they seemed like nice kids. So Goodyear agreed.

The young men put on the yellow industrial jumpsuits they had bought at Portage Broom and Brush and set up their camera. They struck workmanlike poses in front of a mock-up of a rubber lab, then punched a Goodyear time clock and raced outside, camera still rolling, into a waiting beat-up blue Chevy. The car sped off, leaving the tire headquarters (actually a shot of the Goodrich offices) in the distance.

A still from Devo's film *The Truth About De-Evolution*, which the band filmed inside Goodyear's World of Rubber museum. The movie was part of a pre-MTV landmark in rock videos, one of the first conceptual films set to the music of a rock band. (Mark Mothersbaugh/photo by Eric Blum)

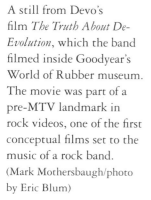

This was no fraternity prank. It was part of a pre-MTV landmark in rock videos, one of the first conceptual films set to the music of a rock band. The young men were Devo; the ten-minute film was *The Truth about De-Evolution*. Goodyear fit perfectly into their philosophy of de-evolution, their notion that, as humankind moves forward, it is actually moving backward. The rubber lab, even though it was old, looked futuristic. And the company, even though it was chugging ahead, was actually moving backward, about to come face to face with more forward-thinking foreign competition.

Goodyear didn't know how Devo it was.

The Devo aesthetic, blending cold, mechanical sounds and movements with the frenetic energy of New Wave rock, took form in the minds of Mark Mothersbaugh and Jerry Casale, Cuyahoga Falls natives who were studying art at Kent State University in the early 1970s. The pair had grown up in an American industrial setting, with polluted skies and rivers. The setting had gotten under their skin, and it came out as they formed a band and began to play in small clubs in and around Akron.

The rubber industry, Casale recalled, "sure helped create a monolithically depressing scene. When I was growing up, I remember the smell of rubber and this yellow stench in the air. It was kind of exciting and frightening, too—these rubber tire factories, when they were all in operation at once, wherever you lived in the city, at a certain hour at the end of the day, there were, like, yellow clouds and the stench of that sulfide—whatever it was—compound that was a byproduct of making tires, and it was something.

"You really knew you were somewhere," he said, laughing. "And it was hell."

Devo became part of the texture of a burgeoning, mid-1970s underground rock scene, playing most of its Akron gigs at a Goodyear-area bar on East Market Street called the Crypt, owned by a Goodyear production worker. They shared the murky limelight with other fledgling punk rock bands, including a group that called itself the Rubber City Rebels, whose singer used the stage name Rod Firestone.

Maybe there was something in that yellow air—this would be the era that put Akron on the musical map, as the Rubber City became perceived by the record industry as a New Wave mecca, spawning the careers of Chrissie Hynde, Rachel Sweet, the Waitresses, and Devo. Quite accidentally, the area became known as "the new Liverpool." The designation actually grew from a misunderstood comment Mark Mothersbaugh made to a reporter when Devo was in Liverpool, England, the birthplace of the Beatles. Mothersbaugh said the town reminded him a lot of Akron. But he wasn't talking about music. He was referring to the gray, depressing industrial landscape.

The band moved to the West Coast in the late 1970s. And even though the members, who still have relatives here, visit infrequently, the aura of Akron has stayed with them.

Mothersbaugh and Casale, the main songwriters, did not use the specific details of their hometown as Rita Dove has done. Instead, they adopted the atmosphere, bent through their own prism, as the setting for their musical science fiction. "It worked as an art-directed backdrop for this kind of music we were making," said Casale. "Because it had this hellish, depressing patina, this kind of a

Chrissie Hynde of the Pretenders performs at the Richfield Coliseum in March 1987. Hynde, whose grandfather and great-grandfather were the first Goodyear father-and-son duo to earn their twenty-five year pins together, left Akron in the early 1970s at age twenty-one. Now, she has become the best-known of Akron-born rock musicians. (*Akron Beacon Journal*/Ron Kuner)

dirty latex layer that fills the air, and the people in Akron seemed—their spirits were depressed; they were desperate. . . . They were so beaten down that they were gonna freak out. And it fit in with the early-twentieth century art movements that we were influenced by—German expressionism, Dada, and all those kinds of environments that came out of Germany and England.

"We had our very own backyard version of it; a rubber version."

❧

"I went back to Ohio, but my city was gone," Chrissie Hynde sings mournfully in the opening lines of the Pretenders' "My City Was Gone." "There was no train station; there was no downtown."

Hynde, whose grandfather and great-grandfather were the first Goodyear father-and-son duo to earn their twenty-five-year pins together, left Akron in the early 1970s at age twenty-one. She was an adventurous soul whose favorite part of her hometown was that train station she's singing about—the place that connected Akron with the rest of the world. She did a bit of wandering in those years, including a couple of stints back in Akron, where she played in a band called Jack Rabbit. (She had previously, briefly, played in a group with Devo's Mark Mothersbaugh.) Then she settled in London, formed the Pretenders, in 1978, and rose quickly to fame.

She has become the best-known of Akron-born rock musicians. And the city where she grew up—"beneath the burning sulfur skies," as she says in another song—has provided her with emotional material. In some ways, Hynde had to leave Akron to discover it—she speaks and writes with longing about the place she remembers and the parts of it that have disappeared. In the years since Hynde has settled in London, Akron has undergone a dramatic transformation through subtraction. The once-thriving downtown, the place she explored as a teenager, was boarded up in the 1980s, as rubber factories closed and other businesses pulled out.

"All of the places which to my mind were beautiful in Akron were allowed to just become derelict, and eventually torn down," she said. "So all of the things that excited me about Akron and the beauty of Akron, by the time I revisited over the years, had all been destroyed. I mean, certainly there's no question that Akron is in a very beautiful part of the world. And I guess that industrial aspect made it exciting because it made it seem urban. But when it stopped being urban and it became just a sort of sprawling metroplex . . ."

As a teenager, she used to go exploring with her best friend, Nita Lee (now Terzic), poking around places they found far more fascinating than the suburban west Akron neighborhood where they lived.

The downtown the two friends discovered was a place that had exploded outward from the rubber factories. When it began to crumble, its rubble landed in Hynde's songs, most notably "My City Was Gone" and "Downtown (Akron)." The latter song, with references to rubber, the Portage Hotel, and the Cuyahoga Valley, says downtown Akron "is where the future lies." But Hynde has found, whenever she returns, that it's really the residence of the past, a place in time that she loves.

"It's almost hard to describe how under my skin it gets when I'm there," she said. "If I ever smell burning rubber, you know what that reminds me of. That will never leave me."

The opportunity for the old Rubber City to fall under the eye of the artist has passed. The skies are clean now; the chemistry has changed for anyone who wants to make sense of this place.

One of the last chances to capture that city was not missed, though. In 1994, in the final days before Goodrich's old Building 41 was gutted and rebuilt as the headquarters of Advanced Elastomer Systems, Heather Protz, a young photography teacher at the University of Akron, turned her students loose inside the old factory.

The place, abandoned for several years, had become a favorite haunt for late-night graffiti artists, skateboarders, and the like. Its interior was a mix of the old factory aesthetic and the spontaneous combustion of spray-painted art.

Some of the young art students chose to focus on the pictures on the walls. Others found a certain gritty charm in the brick and steel erected early this century, at a time when factories couldn't go up fast enough to meet the demand for their products.

The students spent a brilliant Saturday morning inside, discovering for the first—and last—time the arcane beauty of the factory seen through a lens.

By then—1994—the utter decay in Building 41 was a relic of a lost era in Akron history. Enough of downtown had been rejuvenated to give a sense of hope. But the time was not long past when ailing rubber companies were being blamed for spreading their disease throughout the town.

19   The Changing City

SUMMER HEAT shimmered off Firestone Parkway. In south Akron, no one could drink the water, and tempers were rising. Mayor Roy Ray's job had become most sticky. As Ray walked out of Firestone Tire and Rubber, the company that had put bread on the Ray family table for all the years of his youth, it wasn't heat that was making the mayor hot.

"My father worked there for *thirty-seven years*," Ray said.

That was what made this confrontation on an August day in 1983 so traumatic. *E. coli* bacteria had made the water unsafe to drink for thirty-seven thousand people, primarily in the Firestone Park and Kenmore neighborhoods. The city responded by distributing water at three fire stations and sending its bad-water detectives in search of the culprit. They found it at Firestone.

Ray wanted Firestone to solve the problem quietly. But Firestone denied responsibility. It maintained it had checked its water system, and there was no *E. coli* bacteria to be found. Ray and his advisers thought otherwise. So Ray went to see Firestone Chief Executive John Nevin.

"I had a knock-down, drag-out with Nevin," Ray said. "We had found the problem, isolated it, and knew it was coming from industrial wells on the Fire-

J. Robert Kessler, Firestone's director of corporate engineering, looks at a section of pipe that was disconnected at the South Main St. plant. Industrial wells on the Firestone property with defective back-flow devices were leaking *E. coli*-ridden water into the city water system, leaving thirty-seven thousand residents with unsafe drinking water. (*Akron Beacon Journal*/Bill Wade)

stone property. They were leaking into the city system by virtue of defective back-flow devices on Firestone property. But Nevin wouldn't admit to the problem and shut the valves down. Finally, I reached the end of my line. I laid it all out for him. I told him: 'Here's what's happening, and you've got to cut the valves off. If you don't cut them off by twelve o'clock tonight, I'm coming out here with the city of Akron bulldozers and we're going to tear up Firestone Boulevard and I'm going to cut them off.'"

"All right," Nevin said. "Fine."

Ray left Firestone, went to his home on Malvern Road in west Akron, and waited. He ate dinner. He chatted with his wife, Frances, and his sons, Chris and Brian. His mind, however, was in south Akron. At about 11:00 PM, Ray's telephone rang. It was a Nevin lieutenant. The white flag was up. "They agreed to shut off the valves," Ray said. "After that, the problem cleared up. But it took weeks, and I was on the front page of the *Beacon Journal* every day, with people asking why in the hell I wasn't giving them potable water."

Water became a campaign issue that Democratic state Representative Tom Sawyer used to deprive Republican Ray of a second term as mayor in the Novem-

Fire hydrants were flushed on Firestone Parkway, in August 1983, after traces of *E. coli* bacteria made water unsafe for thousands of South Akron residents. (*Akron Beacon Journal*/Paul Tople)

ber 1983 election. There were other issues, of course. For most of Ray's single term as mayor, times had been tough in Akron, as they were everywhere in the country. Firestone and General quit making tires in Akron, idling thousands of workers on Ray's watch. Ray did not blame the rubber companies for his political difficulties, even though so much rubber-related misery visited Akron while he was mayor. "It never got so bad that I went out in the back yard, picked up a gun, and said: 'This is it.'"

Still, the economic data from that era offered staggering indicators of distress. The local unemployment rate in 1983, Ray's last year as mayor, stood at 12.1 percent, the highest level since the Depression. The city's population kept dropping, from an all-time high of 290,351 in 1960 to 237,177 in 1980. Ray had to cut the city payroll from thirty-four hundred people to twenty-four hundred and raise the city income tax from 1.5 percent to 2 percent.

The city suffered in ways that went far beyond the displacement of workers and a shrinking industrial base. Despite the coordinated efforts of city officials and rubber company executives, Akron's downtown ground to a standstill as laid-off workers tightened the purse strings. Remaining rubber resources, including the corporate sponsorship of recreational and professional sports, were shifted from frills to essentials, dealing another blow to community pride. Neighborhoods fell into decline. Families moved out or broke up. Women went to work in significant numbers, some by choice, some out of necessity.

The plant closings reflected a changing industry and a recessionary economy; other hardships probably coursed through the city as part of national trends. Even so, it became fashionable, though not always responsible, to blame most of Akron's institutional, civic, and social ills on rubber as it deserted the city.

"I think we had a victim mentality," Ray said.

In fact, rubber production jobs began leaving Akron several years before Ray became mayor. B. F. Goodrich closed its Akron tire operation in 1975, Goodyear did the same in 1978, and Firestone closed Plant 2 in 1978. When Ray took office, in 1980, the cutbacks continued in stunning succession. That year, Firestone announced it was closing Plant 1. Goodyear announced the closing of its Martha Avenue industrial products plant. In 1982, General Tire landed the final blow when it closed Plant 1, Akron's last full-scale tire plant. In less than a decade, Akron's rubber employment dropped from 32,700 before the first plant closing to 15,500 after the last, accounting for more than half the rubber jobs lost in the nation.

That Akron would ultimately lose most of its rubber company headquarters

Akron mayor Roy Ray concedes defeat to Tom Sawyer on November 13, 1983. From left are his children, Brian and Chris, and his wife, Frances. Ray didn't blame Firestone or the other rubber companies for his political difficulties, despite much rubber-related misery visiting the city during his watch. (*Akron Beacon Journal*/Marcy Nighswander)

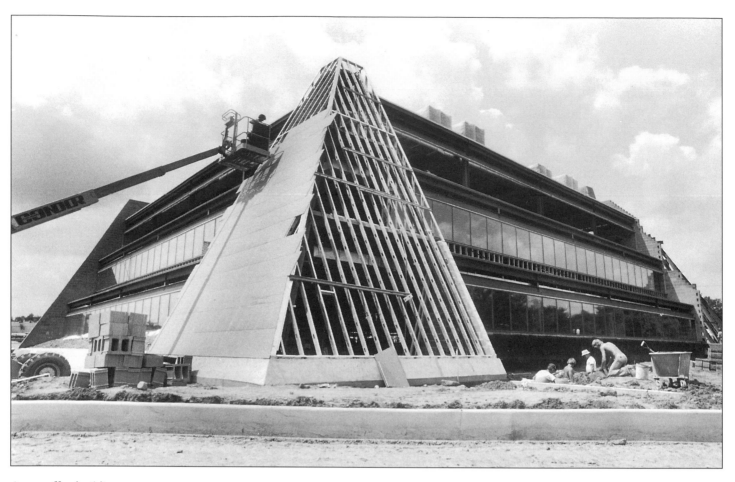

A new office building takes shape for General Tire on Ghent Road in Fairlawn, in 1981, dashing the hopes of city officials who tried to lure the company downtown. (*Akron Beacon Journal*/Bill Wade)

was another matter entirely. Bitterly ironic was the fact that the first two relocation decisions were made by executives who had long been devoted to improving Akron's economic infrastructure.

General Tire, under the aegis of Chairman Jerry O'Neil, was the first to move, though just to a western suburb. The announcement came in 1978, while John Ballard was mayor, at an Akron City Club luncheon of civic and political leaders, including Governor James A. Rhodes. City leaders were hoping that General Tire would move its headquarters from east Akron to the "superblock" of Main Street between Mill and Market streets. "We thought we were going to get it," recalled then-planning director James Alkire. General's presence downtown would mean a lot more than five hundred workers spending their lunch hours in downtown eateries, perhaps even staying after work to shop and take in a movie.

"Number one," Ray said, "it was important for the symbolism." It would mean General believed in downtown. And if General believed, perhaps others would believe.

At the luncheon, O'Neil unveiled a map of the Crystal Lake area near Interstate 77 and state Route 18 in Bath Township where General's new headquarters was to be built. Hailed as good news for the region by Rhodes and others, General's plan left Ballard nearly speechless. "I'm not very excited," Ballard said in his understated, uncritical way. "It isn't good news as far as I can see."

Three years later, high interest rates and a weak economy had stalled General's plan to build in Bath. Ray was now the mayor. He and Alkire tried again to persuade O'Neil to move downtown. "We told Jerry and his people that we had a piece of land—the site of the old Portage Hotel—and we'd work a deal if they'd bring their headquarters downtown," Ray said. "We were willing to do damn near anything."

But O'Neil asked for nothing. "I was not interested in going downtown," O'Neil said. Too expensive. Too little parking. Too little room for growth. Instead, General leased a building on Ghent Road in Fairlawn.

No one, according to Roy Ray, did more to boost downtown than Goodrich Chairman John Ong. Ray was no longer mayor when, in the end, even Ong left the neighborhood. In 1986, Goodrich moved its headquarters from South Main Street to the Bath property that General had owned. "John Ong," said Foster C. Smith, Goodrich's vice president for corporate communications, "doesn't want to be interviewed on the subject." A decade later, Ong said the move was strictly a business decision. There just wasn't proper space downtown for Goodrich, which no longer was large enough for a signature building.

Firestone left Akron for new headquarters twice—the first in 1987, when John Nevin moved the company to Chicago, his longtime home. Firestone returned, in 1989, when its new owner, Bridgestone Corporation of Tokyo, consolidated North American operations in Akron. But after only three years, Bridgestone pulled out for labor-friendly Tennessee, where Bridgestone/Firestone operated two major tire plants.

Samir F. Gibara, chairman and chief executive officer of Goodyear, was convinced that the bottom line was the same for the plant closings as it was for the decisions to relocate headquarters. "The city didn't do anything wrong," Gibara said. "The headquarters moved away because of the industry. The industry changed."

Weeks before Roy Ray began his term as mayor, he learned that the owners of O'Neil's Department Stores, the company founded by Jerry O'Neil's grandfather but no longer in family hands, planned to close the downtown store on Main and State Streets. The O'Neil's departure would leave no major retailer at the city's core; the Polsky's chain, which had operated a downtown store, had gone out of business in 1978. The city had to convince O'Neil's it had a chance to survive in Akron's changed environment. Rubber wasn't killing the downtown O'Neil's. Consumer trends were killing O'Neil's. Shopping was moving from Main Street to the suburban malls, as people moved in the same direction.

"The average Joe didn't care," said Alkire, the former planning director. "He didn't come downtown. He went to Summit Mall or to Chapel Hill. I'd go to neighborhood meetings, and it was not unusual for people to say: 'Why do we even need a downtown?'"

City officials had the answer. The downtown O'Neil's was to be the cornerstone of a redevelopment project known as the American Cities Corporation plan. The plan emphasized living, working, and shopping, and grouped those activities around the Ohio Canal, which wends through downtown. Without O'Neil's, the American Cities plan would disintegrate. Ray picked up the telephone and began dialing for dollars. The group he invited to breakfast, on February 13, 1980, consisted of business leaders and rubber company executives operating as the Akron

B.F. Goodrich Chairman Ward Keener, right, poses, in 1968, with the Goodrich board of directors in the middle of South Main St. near the B.F. Goodrich complex. Known as the Opportunity Park project, Goodrich joined with the city to redevelop a 404-acre area, which would include public housing, Channelwood and The Landings condominiums, a parking deck, and an industrial park. Goodrich built its new world headquarters in the area and contributed $300,000 during the planning stage and another $3.5 million toward the final cost. (*Akron Beacon Journal*/Dale Smith)

Priority Group. Ray asked the group for $10 million to jump-start the American Cities plan. The money would fund land purchases, including property for a mall that would keep O'Neil's downtown. It would guarantee a base price for a number of condominiums that would be known as Lock II. It would light the fuse for refurbishing the YMCA, turning its upper portion into apartments. "If we could have had a core of four hundred, five hundred, six hundred living units," Ray said, "that could have been a catalyst for other things."

Ray wasn't the first city official to turn to rubber to give Akron's downtown a shot in the arm. In 1964, when Edward Erickson was mayor, Goodrich and the city joined to create Opportunity Park, a 404-acre redevelopment area on the south edge of downtown. The $37.5 million, federal-local project included public housing, Channelwood and The Landings condominiums, a parking deck, and an industrial park. Goodrich, besides building a new world headquarters in Opportunity Park, contributed $300,000 during the planning stage and another $3.5 million toward the final cost.

Not long afterward, during John Ballard's first term, city officials, rubber company bosses, and community leaders gathered to solve the problem of Cascade Plaza. A group called Citizens for Progress, started by *Beacon Journal* Editor and President John S. Knight, in 1961, persuaded rubber companies and others to lease floors of Cascade One, the first office building proposed for the plaza. The

leasing commitment was necessary before Columbus developer John Galbreath would proceed with the project.

By the time Roy Ray was trying to move the American Cities plan forward, creating a downtown neighborhood had proved frustratingly complicated. Ray forged the textbook public-private project at Lock II: the state put in $2 million to help create Lock II Park on the canal adjacent to the condominiums. Akron Priority Corporation, the financial arm of Akron Priority Group, came up with $1.3 million to buy land. The city obtained a $1.5 million federal grant to subsidize mortgage rates, pulling them well below market level. In addition, the city, lenders, and Akron Priority Corporation created an independent corporation, Lock II Corp., to work with builders Irving and Steven Botnick. The first eighteen units of an intended 100 cost more to build than the Botnicks had anticipated and were priced too high ($79,000) to interest buyers. Only one sold. Lock II Corporation, guided by First National Bank President Howard Flood, lowered the price to $65,000. When sales remained slow, Lock II Corporation sought help from the real estate community. Marketing improved, and the banks stepped in with 5.5 percent financing. The units sold. More were planned.

"It was probably the first time in city history that there was a tremendous investment of the private sector along with the public sector to provide an economic incentive," Ray said. "I think it was an important thing to happen."

In 1979, the O'Neil's department store was slated for closure, which meant that downtown Akron would have no major retailer. The store was also supposed to be the cornerstone of a redevelopment project known as the American Cities Corp. plan. The plan emphasized living, working, and shopping, and grouped these activities around the Ohio Canal. Without the store, the plan would disintegrate. (*Akron Beacon Journal*/Ott Gangl)

The plan fell apart, in 1987, when Lock II's powerful neighbor, Children's Hospital Medical Center, announced it needed the very land on which the condos had been built for additional office space and parking. Children's got what it wanted. Lock II was razed. Downtown couldn't afford to lose Children's Hospital. The Lock II condos became the symbol of another failed plan, and downtown remained sick. The rubber companies could hardly be blamed. General had not moved downtown. Goodrich had moved out of downtown. But they had left behind money that had allowed O'Neil's to stay downtown and Lock II to commence, if briefly.

∾

For years, the rubber companies, especially Firestone and Goodyear, were the best sports in town, winning Akron a fat dot on the national sports map. Goodyear had auto racing. Goodyear had Industrial League basketball, until 1970, outlasting the National Basketball League and the National Industrial League. Firestone had disbanded its industrial basketball team, the Non-Skids, as long ago as 1941 and closed its bandbox of a gym, the Firestone Clubhouse, to high-level Amateur Athletic Union competition. But Firestone still had its greensward off Warner Road, where professional golf tournaments have been played since 1954, including the PGA Championship, the Rubber City Open, the American Golf Classic, and the World Series of Golf. Firestone also sponsored the Tournament of Champions, professional bowling's most prestigious event.

By 1980, Firestone was losing $1 million a day in the wake of its costly recall of the Firestone 500 radial tire. John Nevin had been hired to pare the troubled company down to a size that would be attractive to a buyer. Nevin told Mike Connor, former public relations executive, that he could not in good conscience close plants and put men and women out of work while continuing to subsidize a country club to keep fees to members low. No matter that those members were Firestone employees. Connor had the unenviable task of relaying this news to club members at their annual meeting.

"It was brutal," Connor said. "We needed the members' support in increased dues to help offset the expense."

The members refused to increase the dues, which were $35 a month for a family. Connor warned them what this would mean: Firestone Country Club would be sold. "For all the years, it had been theirs," Connor said, "and they didn't think that would ever change." But it did. Firestone sold the club to Dallas-based Club Corporation of America in 1981. Then Firestone withdrew as the big name in the World Series of Golf, remaining only as a corporate sponsor. NEC became title sponsor, keeping the NEC World Series of Golf at the only home it has ever known—Firestone Country Club.

The Tournament of Champions, on the other hand, did not survive rubber's changes in Akron. Bridgestone, which purchased Firestone in 1988, decided its sport should be Indianapolis-type racing, and it put Firestone back on the track. But racing takes money. "Every available marketing dollar they could get, they wanted to put toward the racing program," Connor said.

Bridgestone/Firestone gave the Professional Bowling Association nearly two years notice to find a new sponsor for the Tournament of Champions. Connor retired from Firestone at the end of 1991. He became the PBA's commissioner, in-

heriting the other end of the problem of what to do for a sponsor in 1993. Connor and PBA founder Eddie Elias went to another Akron rubber company, selling General Tire Executive Vice President Edward W. "Bud" Kissel and CEO Alan L. Ockene on keeping the Tournament of Champions in Akron. Elias was thrilled. "I love it," he said of the tournament. "It is a part of my heart. Take it, and you take that part of my heart."

General Tire signed a three-year agreement to sponsor the tournament. But more and more, the shots were being called by Continental, the German company that had bought General in 1987. So General wrote an escape clause into the contract with the PBA. The worst happened. After sponsoring the 1994 event, General bought out the remaining two years.

"Reallocating resources," Ed Kalail, General Tire director of communication services, called it.

❧

Among the city's major institutions, Akron's hospitals long had had an umbilical cord connected to rubber wealth. F. A. Seiberling of Goodyear helped found Peoples Hospital, later known as Akron General Medical Center. O. C. Barber of Diamond Rubber was behind Akron City Hospital. Then, in the 1950s, the United Rubber Workers won medical benefits that strengthened Akron's health care system.

"People who worked for the rubber companies had [some of] the better, if not the best, health care packages around," said Matt Contessa, Akron's deputy mayor

Ernie Pouttu, a volunteer and vice chairman of construction for the World Series of Golf, puts up one of the NEC banners on the grandstands surrounding the 18th green at Firestone Country Club in 1990. Firestone sold the club to Club Corporation of America, in 1981, becoming only a corporate sponsor, with NEC stepping up as title sponsor. (*Akron Beacon Journal*/Paul Tople)

for labor relations. Shortly after rubber workers began losing jobs and health benefits, the hospitals began to seek partners and mergers to reduce operating costs and eliminate excess capacity. Civic leaders worried that rubber wealth had overbuilt the local health care system to a point the city could no longer support. In fact, the hospital mergers and alliances had nothing to do with the declining fortunes of the rubber industry. Hospitals throughout the nation were forced to retrench because of cutbacks in government programs, inflation, and skyrocketing costs of medical technology. By this time, Akron hospitals no longer relied on rubber business anyway.

"City Hospital was profitable throughout the '70s and '80s," said Albert Gilbert, chief executive officer of Summa Health System, which comprises Akron City Hospital and St. Thomas Hospital. "The hospitals survived the transition because our . . . revenue was not dependent on local sources." By the late 1970s, City Hospital drew more than 40 percent of its revenue from Medicare, the national health plan for the elderly. In 1976, Medicare paid City 96.2 percent of what it charged a patient. By 1979, however, the figure had dropped to 85.5 percent, forcing hospitals to look to other sources for income. Gilbert said that, in 1997, Summa still made money, even though City Hospital's rubber company business had fallen from 12 percent of its total in the 1970s to 4 percent.

"The biggest concern we faced," said Isabelle Reymann, chief operating officer for Summa, "was losing employees who were married to rubber workers. It wasn't overwhelming. I do recall, however, that every time we would learn of a nurse leaving because 'my husband has decided to relocate,' it would bring tears to our eyes."

The hospitals managed their finances far better than some Akron residents who lost their homes, went on public assistance, or ended up in bankruptcy. Summit County foreclosures peaked at 634, in 1979, the year after Goodyear, Firestone, and Mohawk Tire closed manufacturing plants and Polsky's went out of business. The foreclosure rate in Ohio was running at twice the national average; in Summit County, it was the highest in twenty-four years. The plant closings and Polsky's probably weren't the principal causes for the spike in foreclosures, though. Experts usually cite the poor economy, high interest rates, and creative financing gone sour as the main factors. People familiar with Akron's working-class neighborhoods say there wasn't much turnover, either as a result of foreclosures or conventional sales.

"Most of the main neighborhoods," said Herb Stottler, District One representative for the United Steelworkers of America, "weren't affected by the rubber companies leaving because those homes belonged to workers who had seniority. Most of them had their houses paid for."

Ditto in minority neighborhoods. "No, you didn't see a lot of for-sale signs," said Art Minson, who worked at Goodyear for forty years and was president of the East Akron Community House. "Black people didn't move out. They weren't wanted out there."

For whatever reason, housing values throughout the city and some suburbs took a bath in this period. Between 1979 and 1984, the median sale price of an Akron-area home increased only 11 percent, to $50,400. Nationally, home values increased nearly 30 percent over the same years. Other evidence of hardship, particularly in blue-collar neighborhoods, was more subtle. Some residents chose to put repairs on hold because money was tight. "Everyone was holding close what money they had," said Goodyear Heights resident Earl Givens, who now sells real estate after a thirty-four-year career with Goodyear. "People were on pins and needles."

Gary Gappert, the late director of the Institute of Futures Studies and Research at the University of Akron, moved to the city in 1980. He brought with him expectations based on conclusions in his book, *Post-Affluent America*. But Gappert didn't find gloom and doom in Akron. The mood wasn't as bad as he'd expected. "I couldn't find the political and social anger I had written about," Gappert said. "These workers had saved well and had relatively low expectations."

As a generalization, Gappert's statement is largely accurate. But some folks—rubber workers and otherwise—did run short of money and turned to public assistance. In the wake of the 1975 layoffs, which idled nearly fifteen hundred workers, claims for Aid to Dependent Children in Summit County rose from 667 to 2,083 by early 1977. By the end of that year, ADC claims had dropped back to the 1975 level. After the succession of closings from 1978 through 1982 that furloughed nearly five thousand workers, claims for general relief peaked at 10,776 in mid-1983; ADC claims climbed to 1,628 in the spring of 1984. Still others took advantage of a 1978 change in the federal bankruptcy law that made it easier to seek protection from creditors in court. Personal bankruptcy filings in Akron more than doubled from 1,060 in 1978 to 2,168 in 1982.

Experts say bankruptcy filings crossed occupational lines. "Rubber plant closures was not a major cause of the increase in bankruptcies," said retired U.S. Bankruptcy Judge Harold White, who was on the bench in Akron during the 1970s. Ken Mayland, chief economist for KeyCorp in Cleveland, agreed. "We had two back-to-back recessions," Mayland said. "Recessions by definition are broad-based. It's not just one industry."

In Akron, however, the devastation caused by the rubber plant closures could feel quite specific when it came to the door in the form of U-Hauls and moving vans. Families moved away and, occasionally, broke up permanently. Earl and Marie Givens watched three daughters move away, and with each of them went a piece of their hearts. Candace Givens's departure, though, was the most difficult. She and her husband, Keith Fultz, had spent two years stationed with the military on the Pacific island of Okinawa. They had come home to Akron. Keith Fultz built tires for Goodyear in Plant 2. When Plant 2 closed, in 1976, Fultz's career took another route. If he wanted to continue building tires for Goodyear, he had to move to Madisonville, Kentucky.

"It was just horrendous for us," Earl Givens said. "Here you see someone every day or two, and then you know you'll see them once a year. It's heartbreaking. The job loss was bad, but the breaking up [of families] was worse."

The Madisonville plant closed in 1992. Candace did not, however, return to Akron. She took a job as a nurse in Washington, D.C. She and Keith Fultz have divorced. In Summit County, the divorce rate peaked during the period of plant closings. In 1979, nearly five thousand couples filed for divorce, annulment, dissolution, or legal separation. Charles Deitle, an Akron attorney once known as Mr.

Divorce, estimated that 20 percent of the divorces during the late 1970s and early 1980s may have been related to the loss of tire jobs.

"The guys would say: 'There's nothing left for me in Akron. I've got to go looking for a job,'" Deitle said. "But their wives wouldn't want to move."

With the national divorce rate peaking in 1980, when 1.2 million were granted, Akron attorney Howard Walton disagreed with Deitle's interpretation. "There were several other issues coming into play at the time: Less guilt about divorce. Society becoming more conscious of women being victimized. Women going back into the work force," Walton said.

But working women were hardly an Akron phenomenon, either. From 1975 to 1985, the percentage of women who worked outside the home increased by 9.6 points to 51.4 percent. In the preceding ten years, the increase had been only 4.9 points; in the decade after that, the increase was only 4.1 points. In some cases, women were doing more than just supplementing the household income. In Akron, Anne Berrodin became the main breadwinner for her family. Berrodin worked as a nurse at St. Thomas Hospital in the late 1970s. Her husband, Louie, had been laid off at Goodyear and went into the family business—the Bucket Shop bar on West Market Street. He was running the Bucket Shop full time when the plants began to close. It nearly closed his business as well. Rubber workers had more time but less money for beer.

"Those were tough times," Louie Berrodin said. "I was working day and night and taking home . . . $10 a week."

Anne kept the Berrodins and the Bucket Shop afloat. It was a heady new role. Anne still remembers being able to pick up her husband one night at work in a limousine and presenting him with flowers. "Most of the nurses were pretty positive about things," Anne Berrodin said. "Even if they were the sole breadwinner, it was feasible for the family to survive."

"I would credit the women for keeping the neighborhoods and homes together," said urban expert Gary Gappert. "Women kept up the mortgage during this time."

In 1982, Gappert took on the changing-Akron issue for a *Wall Street Journal* interview. For his assessment, Gappert received hate mail. "People really didn't get it for a long time," Gappert said, "didn't get that, in the postindustrial future, life would be different."

As Gappert told the *Journal:* "The buffalo will never return to Akron."

20   Goodyear Is Raided

TOM SAWYER chose his words the way a fencer chooses his foil. They became his pointed weapons, ones meant to cut, the verbal bloodletting of Sir James Goldsmith intended to incite and unite the masses in Akron and dozens of other Goodyear Tire and Rubber Company towns across the country.

They were words to "rouse the rabble," as Goodyear's William Newkirk put it. And they worked. All of them. Akron Mayor Tom Sawyer's words. Goodyear Chairman Robert E. Mercer's words. Akron Congressman John Seiberling's words. Goodyear employees' words. Akron citizens' words.

When Goodyear went to war with corporate raider Jimmy Goldsmith, in the fateful fall of 1986, it became a war fought with words and money. The money—$94 million—bought Goldsmith off, but the words, coming at him from so many angry mouths, convinced Goldsmith he should take the money and leave Goodyear to an afterlife of its own creation.

Newkirk, Goodyear's vice president of public affairs, stood at the arsenal door, passing out the verbs and adjectives and metaphors, marshaling his wordsmiths,

PROTECT OUR GOOD NAME

William Newkirk,
Goodyear's vice president
of public affairs in 1986,
became the company's
chief spokesperson during
The Goodyear War.
Goodyear speech writer
Gaylon White found him
so hard-nosed he nick-
named him "Thug." (*Akron
Beacon Journal*/Paul Tople)

then sending them into the streets. Newkirk went to Goodyear Chairman Mercer to discuss strategy when it was clear that Goldsmith, the multinational financier, was buying his way into the heart of Akron's largest employer. Goldsmith's intentions clearly were to break up the company and sell off its pieces for profit, shattering lives and communities in the process.

Goodyear had been taken over once before. In 1921, the company founded by brothers F. A. and Charlie Seiberling fell under control of the Wall Street banking firm Dillon, Read. If the company was for the second time to be taken over, it would be with Newkirk punching in the clinches and hitting below the belt.

"Hey, Bob, looks to me like we might as well go down kicking and screaming," Newkirk proposed to Mercer. "Do it," Mercer replied, wasting no words.

Mercer wasn't always so curt. He used the language skillfully, a talent that was genetic as well as enhanced by Newkirk's contributions. Mercer's father, George W., was "a great speaker . . . who could really tug at the heartstrings" as head of the Royal Arcanum, a fraternal, beneficiary society. Bob Mercer's twin brother, Dick, was for years considered "the best copywriter on Madison Avenue."

Throughout the ten-week Goodyear War, Mercer's words would serve dual purposes. He reassured employees and put Goldsmith on notice. "I tried to tell him that he was not just fooling with another company, another takeover target," Mercer said. "We've got 132,000 employees who want to see you go home. You bring nothing to the party."

Rufus Johnson did not work for Goodyear. But as handyman at the Goodyear barbershop, an independent operation, Johnson knew many people who did, including the chairman. Johnson coined the catch phrase, "It's Rambo time," spoken simply but urgently as he exhorted Mercer to hang tough against Goldsmith.

Former Congressman John F. Seiberling, the grandson of F. A. Seiberling and a former Goodyear attorney, played a critical role in the drama. During a congressional hearing on the takeover, he uttered the most memorable words of the siege when he asked Goldsmith: "Who the hell are you?"

"No one could have been better positioned, better suited, more knowledgeable—both by birth and upbringing," Sawyer said.

Sawyer was the surprise. His words usually did not start fires. During his years in the Ohio legislature and in a term as Akron mayor, Sawyer had developed a reputation for his intelligent, yet unexciting, rhetoric. This was different. In a New York City television studio that connected him by satellite to thirty-five Goodyear towns throughout the country, Sawyer turned into a combination Paul Revere and Lenny Bruce. He sounded the alarm with words that were spontaneously combustible: *crisis . . . devastating . . . caught in the cross fire . . . all the ethics and morals of a pack of sharks . . . dismembered . . . ambush . . . seizing control and breaking up . . . blitzkrieg . . . economic terrorism . . . predatory act . . . obscene . . . despicable.*

"There was no caution in the guy," Newkirk said.

Sawyer's satellite linkup with mayors and other leaders of Goodyear cities occurred on Thursday, November 13, 1986. It would be seven days before Sawyer would learn how effective his words were and, upon learning that Goldsmith had given up, would pronounce his benediction: "We sent the limey bastard home."

Goodyear hadn't seen Goldsmith coming, but the company knew *someone* might be stalking it, given the takeover tenor of the 1980s. So Mercer, in 1986, asked the investment banking firm Goldman Sachs to determine the odds that Goodyear would become a takeover target. Goldman Sachs assessed the value of the company's components, including Goodyear Aerospace, Motor Wheel Corporation, Celeron Corporation, and other holdings, and calculated Goodyear's risk of becoming a takeover target at just 15 percent. Yet a vague uneasiness gripped Mercer. In July, he sent his key financial personnel, including Vice President and Treasurer Oren G. Shaffer, and Newkirk and the wordsmiths, to Maryland's Eastern Shore for a working retreat with Goldman Sachs's experts. Talk takeovers, Mercer told them. Learn everything possible.

There was no sense of urgency at the retreat. The first order of business was deciding when to play golf and when to work. Shaffer's team and Newkirk's, including John Perduyn, Bill Fair, Gaylon White, and Robert G. Mercer (the chairman's son, better known as "Young Bob"), concluded they should golf before work to beat the heat.

"It was hotter than hell," Newkirk said.

It would get hotter in the months to come.

"You could see the storm clouds starting to gather off on the horizon," Young Bob Mercer remembered, "and you felt something could be imminent. The things we discussed helped to prepare us, at least emotionally and mentally, for the campaign."

Young Bob and Gaylon White, Chairman Mercer's speech writer, both emerged with a greater appreciation of Newkirk, the man who became the company's chief spokesman during The Goodyear War. "I referred to him as the Gang of One," White said. "For this type of fight, Newkirk was perfect: so hard-nosed that I nicknamed him Thug. He could get in your face."

Newkirk needed no push into the center of the ring. Born May 24, 1924, in Cleveland, he graduated from Bowling Green State University in 1947. He cut his writing teeth as an Associated Press reporter covering the Sam Sheppard trial in Cleveland in the 1950s. Newkirk joined the Goodyear public relations staff, in 1959, and became vice president of corporate relations in 1980. No one doubted Newkirk's taste for the fight. Tough minded and outspoken, Newkirk could tell his bosses what they didn't want to hear—and still have a job the next day.

Mercer once called Newkirk into the chairman's office during a policy meeting. Mercer was not happy. He had just read a story in the *Beacon Journal* that he remembers "put my hair on end."

"Bill, why do you let guys print things like that," Mercer asked.

"Hey," Newkirk said, "if you don't want to read bad news, quit making it."

Mercer turned to his lieutenants. "I think you've just heard some words of wisdom," Mercer told the group. "When you guys have something going that's pretty hot, ask yourselves before you act: 'How would this play on the front page of the *Beacon*? Would you be proud to go home after people have read that in the paper?' If the answer is no, I don't care how much dough you think it's going to make for us—don't do it."

For the Goldsmith battle, though, Mercer wanted Goodyear's story plastered on the front page of every newspaper, played on every radio frequency, pictured on every television newscast. To Newkirk, filling that order would become the fight of his life, the one against the perfect opponent.

Newkirk began assembling his wordsmiths to turn the public and legislative tide against Goldsmith. He called Young Bob Mercer in from Houston, where he was Goodyear's regional public relations manager. He was asked to prepare two key statements: Tom Sawyer's introduction to the Goodyear Mayors' Teleconference, and the prepared part of the testimony Chairman Mercer would deliver to the congressional subcommittee.

"I think Bob's choice of words," Sawyer said of the senior Mercer, "was central to the success of the work of the war room during the takeover."

"Goldsmith made it easy for us," Young Bob said. "He seemed so damned evil."

James Michael Goldsmith was born in England, in 1933, to a Jewish German hotelier and a French Catholic mother. The second of two sons, he quit school at sixteen and supported himself for a while by gambling. A din of notoriety swirled around his unorthodox personal life. He was married three times and had eight children by four women. He amassed a fortune as a corporate raider who bought and broke up companies the way he divided his life among his families, convinced that he enhanced the value of all. A billionaire, Goldsmith held dual citizenship in Great Britain and France and was knighted in both countries. He came to the United States, in 1973, when the political environment in Britain turned hostile to the takeover strategy he refined there. Here, he found almost no one standing in his path.

By the end of the decade, America's primary business no longer was making tires and other commodities. It was making money. President Ronald Reagan championed a business world with few regulations and restrictions. Following a decade of rocketing inflation, the United States had tumbled into the worst recession since the Great Depression. Major corporation stocks were undervalued. A takeover artist such as Goldsmith could acquire companies and sell off their parts at a huge profit. The money flowed from the junk bond market. Financiers raised large sums by paying high interest rates on the junk bonds and making their profit once their takeover targets were broken up. Goldsmith took over with relative ease Diamond International, a diversified company with its roots in Diamond Match Company of Akron, Grand Union grocery stores, and Crown Zellerbach, a forestry products company.

His successes enhanced his notoriety and, in 1985, earned him an invitation to testify before a Senate subcommittee on corporate takeovers. In testimony, Goldsmith allowed that "raiders shouldn't put on a halo. They *are* doing it for personal gain." But the Anglo-French businessman didn't believe his gain should be perceived as hostile. He liked to ask: Hostile to whom? Management? Shareholders?

"The dead hand of the bureaucrat does not produce growth," he preached to the senators. "It does not produce innovation. It produces complacency, ossification, and decline."

Members of the committee heaped praise on Goldsmith. "You've done a great service to this country today," said Texas Senator Phil Gramm. "We hear arguments made on behalf of national interest for exports and job protection and investment and research and development, but it's obviously considered in this great capitalistic nation somehow a weak argument to say that we're trying to make money."

Basking in the afterglow, Goldsmith said: "It was one of the most remarkable days of my life. On the whole, they thought like me, and I've never had people so nice to me in my life. I'm not used to it."

A year later, Goldsmith set in motion the events that evoked a very different reception in Akron. In August 1986, a month after Goodyear's Camp Takeover, Goldsmith sat on the terrace of his new house in the south of Spain. From a Merrill Lynch list of takeover targets, he chose Goodyear over a southern railway and a group of major department stores. He already had been investing in all of them, buying Goodyear at about $33 a share. Merrill Lynch Capital Markets in New York had pledged $1.9 billion to back Goldsmith's bid. An old British ally, Hanson Trust, was ready with another $2.6 billion. Joining Goldsmith and his financial colleagues in the trenches of the Goodyear War were his own wordsmiths from Kekst and Company, a hired mouthpiece. A brilliant business strategist, Goldsmith saw the vulnerability of corporations such as Goodyear, which had attempted through diversification to offset the cyclical nature of an industry tied to auto sales.

"Some of the diversification was clearly not well thought out," said rubber industry analyst Harry Millis. Invariably, and with the benefit of hindsight, analysts specifically criticize Goodyear's friendly acquisition of Celeron Corporation, an oil company. Mercer's predecessor, Charles J. Pilliod, initiated the Celeron takeover, an $825 million stock exchange. Mercer completed the deal, then approved the construction of the All America Pipeline, the first to link offshore oil deposits on the West Coast with refineries in Texas. Celeron made Goodyear 44 percent nonautomotive, up from 18 percent. For years, Celeron was a drag on earnings and Goodyear's stock was undervalued, making the corporation an attractive takeover target.

"Goodyear was undervalued because it was undermanaged," said Saul Ludwig, managing director of McDonald and Company Securities in Cleveland and a respected rubber industry analyst. "I should say that in those years, with Pilliod and Mercer, that the company had more potential than it realized—profit levels pretakeover were rather average."

But Goodyear was still making money, a claim some of its competitors could not make. In 1985, Goodyear reported a profit of $412.4 million; Firestone, by comparison, reported a $103 million loss. The book value of Goodyear stock was $32.44 a share in 1985, indeed undervalued when compared with the approximate breakup value of more than $51. The dark side of breakup values, though, is that they can't be realized without literally killing a company—by breaking it up. Goodyear was so big and its brand name so generally revered in the industry that the idea of a takeover seemed preposterous, especially to many insiders.

"There was a complacency and probably a certain naivete," said Gaylon White, Mercer's former speech writer. "I've found the same thing in other companies: people feeling that it's not going to happen to us. A takeover attempt is like a car wreck. It happens to the other guy. It doesn't happen to you."

In September, Merrill Lynch representatives, at Goldsmith's behest, flew to Paris to complete one of the biggest hostile takeover plans in American corporate history. Late the following month, Mike Hudkins, Akron's deputy mayor for economic development, noticed the run-up in Goodyear stock. Hudkins told Tom Sawyer, the mayor: "Something strange is going on at Goodyear."

In fact, the company was in play. Merrill Lynch was buying Goodyear stock. Arbitrageurs also were buying on rumors of a takeover bid by a then-unknown raider. At the first hint of a possible raid, Mercer called into action the Goodyear SWAT team, which had been assembled months earlier as part of the general takeover defense. One of the first jobs was to identify the enemy. For that purpose, Goodyear brought on board the Carter Organization, which specializes in monitoring stock transactions and has extensive contacts in Wall Street's back offices. By Friday, October 24, Carter sleuths had fingered Goldsmith. That day, Goodyear hit $44 a share, a fifteen-year high, and the company publicly acknowledged it might be the target of a hostile takeover attempt. The next day, the *Beacon Journal* quoted sources identifying Goldsmith as the raider.

The Goodyear wordsmiths declared open season on Goldsmith. His phobias—ironically, he hated rubber, especially rubber bands and pencil erasers. His peccadilloes—he lived with his wife, an ex-wife who was his secretary, and a mistress, though not at the same time or place. His excesses—he had two more houses than he had women.

By all accounts, Mercer was the right man to take the raider on. "He had the balls to fight [Goldsmith] off," analyst Millis said. "Bob Mercer was the right guy . . . if you wanted to stay independent."

The contrast between Mercer and Goldsmith is dramatic. Mercer is educated. He holds a mechanical engineering degree from Yale University. He is a principled man. The father of five, he has been married to Mae Mercer for fifty years and was devoted to one company for more than forty years. He had been chairman of Goodyear, then the nation's thirty-fourth-largest corporation, since 1983. Considering his wealth—Mercer was paid about $1 million a year—he lived rather modestly in one home in west Akron. For a good time, he went to Cleveland Indians games. He had a reputation for remaining cool in a crisis, unlike the flamboyant, occasionally paranoid Goldsmith.

"He could deal with a volatile person," Gaylon White said of Mercer. "And if you read the history of Goldsmith, you knew he was an extremely volatile person with a huge ego."

Mind-numbing strategy sessions consumed the days and nights. Key executives shuttled between Akron and New York City to meet with the high-priced legal and financial talent the company had hired. One night, Mercer, company attorney Fredrick S. Myers and chief financial officer James R. Glass went to a restaurant in New York City to escape the cacophony of the advisers. Mercer took a paper place mat off the table, turned it over, and began listing the company's options: 1. Lie down and die. 2. Buy this guy out. 3. Find a white knight company to buy Goodyear. 4. Push the stock price out of reach by selling subsidiaries.

"The other option was to take gas," Mercer said.

Mercer and his lieutenants decided on a combination of options two and four. He told the bankers and lawyers this and announced: "I'm going to call on this guy."

"Oh, my God!" the advisers replied in unison. "You can't do that."

"Why not?" Mercer asked. "He happens to be our largest shareholder [11.5 percent of all Goodyear stock]. I ought to get to know him. This business of dealing with him through you is like trying to make love to your wife through her lawyer."

Hardly satisfying, but then Mercer's meeting with Goldsmith would not be, either. Mercer visited Goldsmith at his New York townhouse. The Goodyear chairman said he wasn't buying Goldsmith's line about improving the shareholders' value.

"Jimmy," Mercer asked, "our stock used to be twelve [dollars a share]. Where were you then?"

"Money wasn't available then," Goldsmith said. "Now, I can get all the money I want through junk bonds. That's the difference, Bob. Today, I can get the money. Then, I couldn't."

Ironically, Goldsmith never mentioned Celeron and the pipeline, the component of the diversification strategy that analysts say made Goodyear so vulnerable. "He didn't even know about Celeron," Mercer said. "He went through it with me, all these phrases—'unlock the value of the company'—and he never once mentioned Celeron. He was hitting me because we were in chemical products, and we had Goodyear Aerospace. His whole line was a bunch of baloney."

Mercer explained that the chemical products mostly went into tires and that

Steve Seigfried, shown with his wife Betty Lou, in November 1986, worked for Goodyear Aerospace at the time. When Loral Corporation bought the company the next year in the wake of the takeover attempt, it laid him off, two years before he planned to take early retirement. Seigfried had also lost his jobs when plants closed down at Sun Rubber, General Tire, and Bearfoot Company, a sole factory in Wadsworth. At the age of fifty-eight, he landed a job at Aerospace, hoping the company would outlast him and get him to retirement. (*Akron Beacon Journal*/Susan Kirkman)

Goodyear had been in aerospace since 1911. It built its first airplane tire even earlier, in 1909. "I was trying to explain to him what the real world was about," Mercer said. "I wouldn't say I was trying to be kind, but I was trying to be helpful. I told him: 'Jimmy, you know you're not wanted.'" All Goldsmith seemed to hear in Mercer's words was the hollow ring of another desperate CEO.

Among the many communications to employees, Mercer sent a letter warning that Goodyear would never be the same. Jobs would be lost. Debt would rise. Subsidiaries, such as Aerospace, would have to be sold. The Goodyear culture of long-term thinking would change. The message ran counter to all Mercer believed.

"I've never bought the idea that the shareholder is owner of the company," Mercer said. "They own a piece of paper with the company's name on it, and they'll get rid of that paper at the drop of an eighth of a point in the stock price. Our employees, whether union or otherwise, have a wife or husband and kids and years invested in the company, and they're looking at investing more years. First and foremost, you have an obligation to your customers. But you have to do the right thing by your employees. Then you have an obligation to your suppliers and to your community. . . . If you do all the other things right, the shareholder is going to make out like a bandit."

One Aerospace employee, Steve Seigfried, had never heard of Sir James Goldsmith. Seigfried wanted nothing more than to do such good work for a company that it would reward him on the job and later in retirement. "It just never worked out," he said. "I know I am not alone."

Seigfried had spent most of his career at rubber companies that relocated or went out of business before he landed a job as an electrician at Goodyear Aerospace in 1984. He went to work at Sun Rubber Company in Barberton, in 1945, when he was eighteen. Sun was shut down in the midst of a 1974 strike. Seigfried, after twenty-nine years, was left without a pension. He found work at General Tire for eight years. Then General's plant closed in 1982. Unemployed again at age fifty-five, Seigfried joined Bearfoot Corporation, a sole factory in Wadsworth. It went bankrupt and closed two years later. Still undaunted, Seigfried landed a $14.30-an-hour job at Aerospace. He was fifty-eight. Surely, he thought, profitable Goodyear Aerospace would outlast him and get him to retirement.

"I must be in that age group where I was affected by all the changes in industry," said Seigfried, who was seventy in 1997. "I was born in that era, along with others, where instead of getting a bite of The American Dream, you just get bit." He planned to take early retirement, in 1989, at age sixty-two. Instead, Seigfried found himself laid off by Loral Corporation when the New York company bought Goodyear Aerospace in 1987.

"When I finally was called back [a year or so later], I just didn't go," Seigfried said.

The prospect of Goldsmith taking over a company that had been one of Akron's premier employers for eighty-eight years stirred fear in the community as well. Writers of letters to the editor and callers to radio talk shows blasted Goldsmith, depicting him as an archvillain.

Letter writer C. E. Barker called Goldsmith "a money-hungry mongrel." Jack Reilly said Goldsmith's actions were those of a terrorist. Marshall Mickunas wrote: "I will not call him 'Sir' because I was taught that was a sign of respect. Goldsmith garners no respect in this city." The raider's allies got no respect, either. Merrill Lynch was nothing but "our present-day Benedict Arnold," wrote Mrs. Robert Woodliff. The forty-two brokers from the Akron office of Merrill Lynch Pierce Fenner and Smith weren't directly involved in targeting Goodyear, but they felt the heat, too. "The guys from Merrill Lynch would go down to the Portage Country Club, and nobody would speak to them," Bill Newkirk said. "They were pariahs."

The community began to show its disgust more forcefully. United Auto Workers Local 856 at Goodyear Aerospace withdrew about $70,000 from a Merrill Lynch account. Ohio Machine and Mold Company, a Goodyear supplier, withdrew $130,000. A total of 36,531 people signed an anti-Goldsmith petition in a drive organized by the University of Akron and two radio stations. John Seiberling delivered the petition to the congressional subcommittee.

Everyone, it seemed, cared—even students—about stopping Goldsmith. In Sandie Kreiner's Problems of Democracy class, Cuyahoga Falls High School seniors were intellectually and emotionally involved in The Goodyear War. Many of their parents and neighbors worked at Goodyear. Kreiner's father had worked there for thirty-six years. Her students began writing letters to senators, congressmen, and even to Merrill Lynch. They planned a Goodyear stock-buying drive at the school. They invented a game called Goldbuster. They put up a poster with a tire tread mark across Goldsmith's balding head.

"There is an emotional attachment to Goodyear," Kreiner said then.

Goodyear workers and re-
tirees confront Sir James
Goldsmith outside a
House subcommittee
hearing on November 18,
1986. More than 100
Goodyear supporters came
to Washington from
Akron to see Goldsmith
and others testify. (*Akron
Beacon Journal*/Ed Suba, Jr.)

Compared to the early days of the engagement, more and more skirmishes
now were being fought in public arenas. On November 13, armed with Young
Bob Mercer's words, Sawyer conducted the mayors' teleconference to collect financial data, including employment and taxes that might be lost if Goodyear plants
were to close. He was preparing for testimony before the commercial law subcommittee of the House Judiciary Committee, which John Seiberling had asked to
convene.

On Tuesday, November 18, Goldsmith appeared before the committee and
lectured a roomful of past and present Goodyear employees, as well as the law-
makers, on how the company should function. This time, he did cite Celeron as an
unsound diversification. Goldsmith said he would cut the corporate fat from

Goodyear and return it to its core business—tires. Then Congressman Seiberling used the words heard around the nation on the nightly national newscasts, words that resonated in Akron.

"You [have] stated: 'I certainly don't pretend to know the tire business,'" Seiberling said, pointing a finger at Goldsmith. "Now you are saying that you do know more about the tire business than those who have been in it for many years because you're deciding how Goodyear ought to operate. My question is: Who the hell are you?"

Seiberling said his blunt, memorable question came to him on the spur of the moment. Its incubation period, however, had taken a lifetime. "I was brought up with a family antipathy toward financial manipulators because of what happened to Goodyear and F. A. in 1921," said John Seiberling. "When I saw Goldsmith's maneuvers, I thought: I am going to do everything in my power to keep this from happening again."

Goldsmith was stunned by the vehemence of John Seiberling's assault. Mercer explained: "You have to understand—John Seiberling has his roots in the community and in Goodyear. This is not just an abstract issue to him." John Seiberling brought down the house with his acid question. Even Goldsmith applauded. "I

Then-US Rep. John Seiberling, shown at the November 18, 1986 hearing he requested of the House Judiciary subcommittee on mergers and competitiveness in U.S. industry. Seiberling, grandson of Goodyear's cofounder, berated Sir James Goldsmith for criticizing the company's operation while admitting he knew nothing about the tire industry. Seiberling concluded: "My question is: Who the hell are you?" (*Akron Beacon Journal*/Ed Suba, Jr.)

Goodyear Chairman Robert Mercer, left, talks with Sir James Goldsmith during a House Judiciary Subcommittee hearing on merger, policy, and competitiveness in U.S. Industry. During Goldsmith's attempted takeover of Goodyear, Mercer tried to tell him "that he was not just fooling with another company, another takeover target." Goodyear fought Goldsmith with words and money. The money— $94 million—bought Goldsmith off, but the words convinced him he should leave Goodyear to create its own future. (*Akron Beacon Journal*/Susan Kirkman)

think I managed to get across to him my contempt for him as an individual," Seiberling recalled.

Next, Mercer delivered remarks prepared by Young Bob. Chairman Mercer disputed Goldsmith's claims that Goodyear management had failed shareholders and that Goldsmith could do a better job: "In the last six years . . . our stock has appreciated 250 percent and we have maintained a yield of 5 percent. . . . I don't accept the claim that producing a spike in stock price through an implied promise to break up the company enhances anyone or anything other than the perpetrators."

There were more words from URW International President Milan Stone, from U.S. Senators John Glenn and Howard Metzenbaum, and from Sawyer, who carried the Goodyear mayors' message to Washington. John Nardella, former URW Local 2 president, sat among 120 workers and retirees wearing Goodyear blue caps in the gallery. He had fought the company on behalf of his union members. Now he fought for those members again and for Goodyear. On Goldsmith, he heaped disdain.

"I think this convinced people more than ever," Nardella said after the hearing, "what a goddarn screwball [Goldsmith] is. He's interested in one thing. If he says he is interested in investors, he is interested in a buck—and that's all."

Goldsmith got the message. He thought of the furor that had recently been created on Wall Street by admissions of insider trading by Ivan Boesky, who then squealed on others who had been using the system illegally. More than anything, though, Goldsmith looked around at all the angry faces beneath the bills of those Goodyear caps.

"Who are all these guys with the Goodyear hats?" Goldsmith asked Mercer.

"They're our employees," Mercer said.

"Did you bring them?"

"No," Mercer said, "they're here at their own expense, on their own time. I didn't orchestrate this."

The hostility in this takeover attempt flowed two ways. Before the hearing ended, Goldsmith whispered to Mercer: Let's work something out.

They met for lunch at the Hay Adams Hotel, where Goldsmith had a suite. Goldsmith had one day to act if he was to make a tender offer for controlling interest in Goodyear. The Ohio House and Senate were rushing through legislation that would make Goldsmith-style takeovers more difficult. Mercer and Goldsmith agreed tentatively on terms. Goodyear would buy back Goldsmith's shares at $49.50 and pay some of his expenses. To avoid accusations of "greenmail," Goodyear would make a tender offer for forty million other outstanding shares at $50 each.

Later, alone in his suite, Goldsmith reviewed a videotape of his performance at

Despite his attempt to take over Goodyear, Sir James Goldsmith is still a welcome guest as he attends the tenth anniversary of a conservative Washington think tank along with Jeanne Kirkpatrick and President Ronald Reagan. (*Akron Beacon Journal*/Ed Suba, Jr.)

Goodyear Chairman Robert E. Mercer greets well-wishers at a Goodyear victory rally held at the University of Akron's Rhodes Arena two days after Sir James Goldsmith ended his takeover attempt. (*Akron Beacon Journal*/Ed Suba, Jr.)

the congressional hearing. He saw a blustering, sweating, red-faced, demonic man.

"I can't believe how nasty I look on this thing," Goldsmith told a friend. "I look like a monster. It's incredible!"

Goldsmith finally had seen himself as Akron saw him.

Goodyear and Goldsmith changed each other forever. Goldsmith got out of America and then out of business, spending the final years of his life in politics. Goodyear sold off assets to begin paying off the debt for the stock buyback that got rid of Goldsmith. Goodyear's jewel, Goodyear Aerospace, went to Loral Corporation for $640 million and then to Lockheed Martin. Motor Wheel Corporation went to a group of its managers for an undisclosed amount.

"We sold off 19 percent of our business," Mercer said. "I think he would have sold off 40 percent, then I think he would have turned around and sold Goodyear Tire to the Japanese."

For years, Goodyear tried without success to unload its Celeron subsidiary. Goodyear finally sold Celeron, early in 1998, to Plains Resources, a Houston energy company, for $420 million. Goodyear faced other consequences as its long-term debt soared to $2.6 billion. At the time of the raid, Goodyear employed about thirteen thousand workers in Akron. In 1997, Akron employment was less than five thousand. Goodyear no longer claims Aerospace and Motor Wheel workers, but hundreds of layoffs account for the reduction in employment figures, too. Among the casualties was Young Bob Mercer, who became communications manager for DirecTV in California.

Analyst Saul Ludwig said Goodyear is stronger because Goldsmith focused its effort on tires. Analyst Harry Millis isn't as certain. "They are definitely a stronger tire company than they would have been with Goldsmith," Millis said, "but are they truly a better company long term? I don't know. The jury is out. We'll never know the answer to that because we don't know what would have happened to their aerospace business and so on. We don't know what they would have been able to build on."

The Goodyear War made history in Akron in 1986. The words that won the war are fond memories of old wordsmiths. The civic memory of the man who terrorized Akron without ever setting foot in the city belongs to the older generations. Goldsmith died, in 1997, at age sixty-four at his Spanish villa. His British spokesman, Patrick Robertson, spoke for Goldsmith's loved ones. He said this unorthodox extended family was "united in grief." There wasn't, however, a wet eye in Akron.

"Nobody's sorry he's dead," said Art Minson, retired Goodyear employee and longtime east Akron community activist. "Ain't that a shame?"

"He wasn't our kind of guy," Mercer said.

By the time Goldsmith died, Mercer had become chairman of the board of Roadway Express, spending winters in Florida and summers in Nantucket. Bill Newkirk was retired and living in Hudson. John Seiberling retired as congressman for the 14th District two months after his face-off with Goldsmith; Tom Sawyer now represents the Akron area in the House. Gaylon White, Mercer's speech writer, went on to become Eastman Chemical director of public relations for the Asia Pacific region. Rufus Johnson still worked at the Goodyear barbershop shining shoes.

"It's the same as before," said Johnson. "I'm just trying to hang on to something. This job beats having nothing, that's for sure."

Sandie Kreiner had become chairwoman of the social studies department at Cuyahoga Falls High School. The parents of her students work not for one company or in one industry but in the diverse economy that is Akron today. "The kids don't remember what happened," Kreiner said. "It just doesn't seem to bother them as much. They have a different philosophy of life."

Steve Seigfried officially retired, in 1992, at age sixty-five. He suffered a heart attack, in 1995. "I'm doing great now," he said. "I'm watching my diet. I'm getting around using a walker. I do things I should do. . . . If I can just keep going, that will be enough for me."

Two days after Goldsmith ended his takeover attempt and took Goodyear's money, Sawyer, the man whose first words had set the tone for Akron's response,

Ohio Governor Richard Celeste, left, holds up a T-shirt depicting Sir James Goldsmith getting the boot from Goodyear. He is joined by URW president Milan Stone, Goodyear Chairman Robert E. Mercer, and Akron Mayor Tom Sawyer. Celeste had just signed anti-takeover legislation. (*Akron Beacon Journal*)

addressed a victory rally at the University of Akron. He stood before the citizens of Akron and employees of Goodyear and praised the teamwork that had won the day. Then he had an admission.

"I have to make an apology," Sawyer told the audience. "I know I was quoted in the newspaper as saying: 'We sent the limey bastard home.' I don't use language like that, and I want to apologize to everybody here to whom that might have given offense. I did not say 'limey bastard.' I said 'slimy bastard.'"

Regardless, the final word on Goldsmith was the same.

2 1 Nevin Reengineers
Firestone

JOHN NEVIN, tall and lanky, with deep-set eyes and a shock of white hair combed back on his head, stepped into Akron on December 1, 1979. A cloud of cigarette smoke surrounded him, and he smiled as he shook hands with his new colleagues, a slight overbite giving the slightly manic but charming hint of a leprechaun's soul.

As the president of Firestone Tire and Rubber, Nevin was to be a new sort of leader in a Rubber City that had prided itself on homegrown talent. Nevin was an outsider; he had never worked in Akron or for a tire company before. And he was conspicuous. As a superstar marketing executive at Ford Motor Company and as chairman of Zenith Corporation, Nevin had sharpened his mind and his talent like a samurai's sword. He walked fast and he thought fast and he didn't suffer fools. In the president's office, with its dark wood paneling and marble columns, he hung a needlepoint of a tiger poised to pounce.

Firestone Tire and Rubber
Chairman and CEO John
Nevin, in 1984, as he does
his share for charity at the
United Way fund drive
kick-off. Nevin manned
the dunking machine,
with chances to dunk him
selling for $1. (*Akron
Beacon Journal*/Ted Walls)

In the coming decade at Firestone, Nevin would emerge as an excellent and durable target. His face, deeply lined and highly expressive, was carved for the editorial cartoonist's pen. His ever-present cigarette was the perfect villain's prop for the writers who chronicled his life. The whispered truth about his six-week-long hospitalization for a depressive illness while at Zenith provided fodder for pop psychologists. He was ego-driven, blunt, and colorful—when, in a national magazine, he called Firestone's upper managers "a culture of clones," the men showed up at their next meeting in matching blue suits and red Firestone ties. He was nervous and quick, with a craggy, high-pitched voice; he put his feet up on the desk, and he talked and laughed loudly in the once-regal hallways of Firestone's executive wing. He did it on purpose—because no one had done it before.

Under ideal conditions, Nevin would later say, he would have liked to have observed Firestone for a year before drawing his sword. But it is unlikely that John Nevin could wait a year for anything. And even if he could, Firestone could not. The company he took over was more than $1 billion in debt. It was weighted down by warehouse upon warehouse of unsold inventory and shackled, in the eyes of many observers, by inefficient upper managers. Plants were operating below capacity. The top financial officer, Robert Beasley, had been jailed for diverting money from the company's illegal slush fund into his own pockets. The ledger books were smeared with the red ink of the recall of the radial 500 tire. A proposed merger with Borg-Warner Corporation had just fallen through—the Chicago firm had been unwilling to pay more than $12 a share for Firestone's $25 stock. Analysts predicted bankruptcy could come in as little as six months.

Someone had to stop the bleeding.

"If you're sitting there and saying, 'We survived the Depression, therefore we'll survive this. We don't have to do anything,' then you're much more vulnerable than if you're making decisions," said Nevin. "I believe that the failure to make decisions is a much bigger problem than making bad decisions."

A week before Nevin arrived in the Rubber City, he met in Chicago with Leonard Firestone, the company founder's son. At the time, the Firestone family held seventeen million shares of company stock and still held tight control of the corporation founded in 1900. Firestone told Nevin he could expect to have freedom to act and that the family would support him. Nevin thanked him, they shook hands, and, a week later, he was in Akron. He rented an apartment in Tower Eighty, on North Portage Path. He drove his Dodge to the venerable tire headquarters on Firestone Parkway, and he began.

"I was never under more stress," he recalled later, "than when I was in Akron." Despite all the storms that followed Hurricane Nevin, one thing was clear as a June Akron sky: he made decisions. Three of them have become legend, both for Firestone and for Akron.

The first of those decisions came a scant three months after Nevin took the president's chair. On a Sunday evening, in early March 1980, Richard Riley returned to his home in west Akron after a month's vacation. The gentlemanly, round-faced chairman and CEO of Firestone had seen his share of trouble in his forty-one years with the company—in 1978, he was the man who declared to the world that Firestone was recalling 8.7 million of its performance-plagued radial 500s, the most difficult announcement to that point in the company's history.

Coworkers from Firestone's Barberton plant, formerly the Seiberling Tire and Rubber Company, greet each other outside the Grandview Grill after the plant's closing was announced. John Petti-ford of Barberton, left, planned to move out of the country with his wife and kids, while Walt Norman of Canal Fulton, right, planned to open his own business. The plant was one of six an-nounced for closure by Nevin in 1980. (*Akron Beacon Journal*/Bill Wade)

When Riley came through the door and turned on the light, he found a letter waiting for him. It was from John Nevin. Riley opened it and began to read. In two days, the letter said, Nevin was planning to recommend closing seven of the company's seventeen plants. Ten thousand people, from Pottstown, Pennsylvania, to Salinas, California, would be put out of work. Nevin had attached a note suggesting that the proposal be presented to the board of directors with a cover page signed by Riley.

After a sleepless night, Riley returned to the office the following morning and immediately summoned Nevin to his office.

"I read this damn paper of yours," Riley said. "I just found it shocking. I want to tell you first that now I understand better than I ever did why the board insisted on getting an outsider for this job."

Nevin, when he's not smiling, can appear as grim as an executioner. He nodded his head. Riley continued: "What you're recommending is clearly the right course of action. But none of us could have found our way to this conclusion the way you have. Don't bother with a different cover page," he said, "and don't bother with a different signature page. There isn't anybody on that board who is going to think I wrote this letter."

Nevin had made the decision alone. Now he would bear its weight alone. He had told almost nobody what he was considering—Akron is more small town than big city, and gossip, Nevin found, leaks out of its big companies "like a sieve." The new president had assembled a cadre of outside consultants as he began studying Firestone. One of them, Bill McGrath, had offered to act as a lightning rod, to take some of the heat for the decisions. Nevin told him no. And so, on the morning of March 19, 1980, John Nevin, alone, broke the news to the world.

Ted Sherman arrived for work that day, ready for another shift in the stock cutting room of Firestone's Seiberling Tire and Rubber Company plant in Barberton. Like many of his co-workers, Sherman had practically been raised at Seiberling. His father, Alexander, had recently retired after thirty-three years at the plant. Three of Sherman's uncles and many of his friends had worked there. Sherman had joined Seiberling in 1959, was laid off a year later, then had rejoined the company in 1967. The Seiberling plant was Barberton's largest employer, with more than a thousand workers on the payroll. But it was small enough that people referred to it as a family. Sherman believed the plant was doing well. And he knew he was doing well, making $14 an hour—a good, blue-collar living.

Then John Nevin's news sliced across the factory floor. Sherman and his co-workers looked at one another with shock, hurt, and anger. They had never met this Nevin, had never even seen him. And now, they felt, he had stripped them clean. The Seiberling workers would be laid off forever in a matter of months. The company offered severance packages—Sherman says he got "$8,400 for half my life." After the closing, Sherman watched Barberton slide into decline. Friends, their lives strained by the job loss, got divorced. Others left town. Two Seiberling men committed suicide. Sherman thanks God that his wife was working for the University of Akron at the time. Her income pulled the family through, and he considers himself one of the lucky ones. He enrolled in beauty school under the government-funded Trade Readjustment Allowance program, taught there for a while, then got a job cutting hair. But when he gets together with his Seiberling

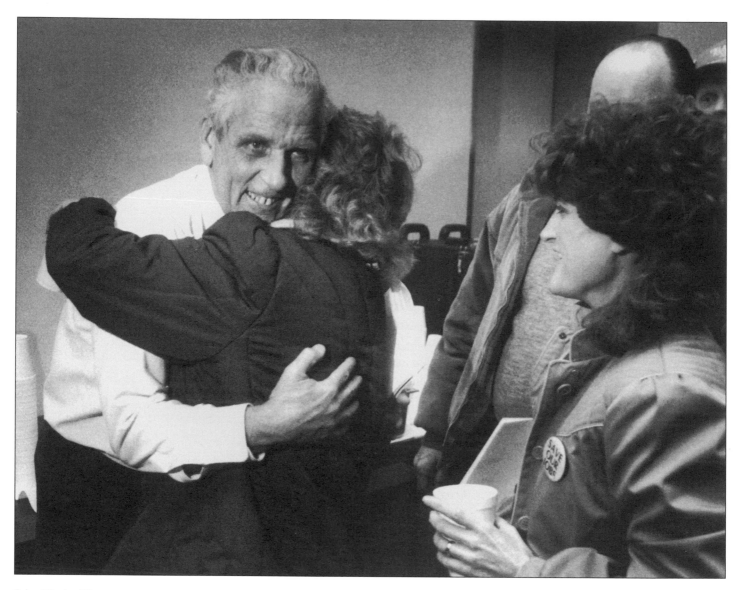

John Nevin, Firestone Tire and Rubber Company chairman and CEO, gets a hug from Doris Lowry, a bead wrapper at Firestone's Oklahoma City tire plant. Nevin announced, in 1987, that the plant would close, prompting a group of more than sixty workers to travel to Akron to make an appeal to keep it open. (*Akron Beacon Journal*/Don Roese)

cronies on the second Tuesday of every other month at Milich's Village Inn, the chicken restaurant rings with harsh words at the mere mention of Nevin's name. "He's a belly robber," Sherman said. "A hatchet man."

Sherman's hurt was multiplied by eighty-five hundred that March day in 1980. Another 1,345 were cut loose when Firestone announced, in October, that it was closing Akron's Plant 1, bringing the total layoffs to about ten thousand. Nevin had made the announcement from his Akron office, the prowling tiger watching from the wall. The Firestone president believed this was a battlefield amputation necessary to save a dying patient. Waiting even a couple of months would have put the company that much closer to bankruptcy.

"Part of the price is you know you're going to get criticized," Nevin said in 1997. "If you didn't want to take action, you never would have taken the job in the first place. I don't want to sound insensitive to this. I was sensitive to it. I had been sensitive at Zenith when I laid off in similar circumstances. Zenith was like Firestone in the sense that you had third-generation employees.

"When I was a young man, my dad lost his home in Maplewood, New Jersey. And I don't mean he sold it, I mean he lost it during the Depression. . . . I knew what it was to see a father impacted by that. There was no alternative here."

And there was no alternative to the reaction. From that day forward, when Nevin visited a Firestone plant, employees shrank in fear. They thought they were going to be next. The next cut, though, hit a very different target—not a worn factory building, but a well-manicured golf course: the Firestone Country Club, an Akron symbol nearly as treasured as Goodyear's blimp. The club was costing the company $750,000 a year in upkeep. Nevin sold it to the Dallas-based Club Corporation of America. The loss of the golf course hit the town just as hard as the loss of jobs. Like the helpless American sailors at Pearl Harbor who hurled potatoes at attacking Japanese planes, people in Akron began to unleash their anger on Nevin, writing letters to the editor and calling radio talk shows.

Those early cannon blasts faded as Nevin settled into his mission. He had closed the plants. He pared down the company's diversified products division and sold Firestone's money-losing plastics company for $200 million. He streamlined product lines, reducing the number of tire types from seventy-three hundred to twenty-six hundred. He cut inventory from 16.7 million to 9.7 million tires in the year following the plant closings. He also worked on upper management, pulling chess men from the board and replacing them with his own; by mid-1983, only five of twenty-five corporate officers remained from the time he became president. And the losses—Nevin called it a cash hemorrhage—came under control. By the fourth quarter of 1981, the company had turned an after-tax profit of $121 million. On paper, Firestone was growing stronger. And while local news stories focused on the pain of job losses, Nevin was getting favorable attention from the national press. "Firestone Tire and Rubber Company has finally turned around," began a November 1980 story in the *Wall Street Journal*.

Nevin continued to live at Tower Eighty. People encouraged him to buy a house; they even defined the five-block area where he should live, in the North Portage Path-Merriman Road area. This was the Rubber City. That's where the captains lived. But Nevin wasn't buying in. He spent many weekends at his home in Chicago, where one of his six children was still in school. He socialized little in Akron. If he dined out, it was likely with a group of his lieutenants at Lanning's or the Diamond Grille, where they discussed business. He was not the kind of company president Akron had grown accustomed to, the kind who lived among his colleagues and schmoozed at Portage Country Club and took the civic helm. Akron, for him, was defined by the walls of Firestone.

In 1981, he was named Firestone's chairman and CEO, furthering his almost complete control over the company. As long as those profit charts showed a line zagging upward, as long as the national business press portrayed him as a success, and as long as the Wall Street pencil-pushers nodded in approval, Nevin could do pretty much as he pleased. And so came the second of his legendary decisions.

The April 30, 1987, shareholders meeting at E. J. Thomas Performing Arts Hall was a routine one. When it was over, Nevin called the board of directors into a private meeting. When they emerged, the company put out a news release that covered barely half a page: "Following its Board of Directors meeting today, The

John Nevin, CEO and chairman of the Firestone Tire and Rubber Company, addresses the annual stockholder's meeting in March 1988. This was the last meeting before Firestone was sold to Bridgestone. (*Akron Beacon Journal*/Paul Tople.)

Firestone Tire and Rubber Company announced that it intends to relocate its headquarters to Chicago, Illinois."

In the Rubber Capital of the World, the announcement was akin to heresy. The town had lost most of its factories, but the residents still claimed ownership of four major tire headquarters. Coming, as it did, from Nevin, the decision blistered the hostility of the residents who took such pride in their city. It was his wife, people said. She's making him do it. Nevin's name, while it had never tasted like candy, turned to dirt. Letters poured in to the *Beacon Journal*.

"I have a name for Nevin, which you would not print, but which he probably would be proud to claim," Willard Fabing wrote in a letter to the editor. *Beacon Journal* columnist Stuart Warner went so far as to write a mock letter to Sir James Goldsmith, the Goodyear raider, asking him if he'd consider taking Firestone away from Nevin. Former Firestone President Mario Di Federico, an Akron native, filed a lawsuit against the board of directors, saying the move was a waste of company money. The company had, after all, recently completed a $40 million remodeling of its Akron offices. But Di Federico lost. In response to the runaway rumor that the move was forced by his wife, Nevin wrote his own letter to the editor, denying the claim and stating that Anne Nevin was registered to vote in Akron and had an Ohio driver's license.

Directly, at least, the move did not disrupt nearly as many lives as the earlier plant closings. About 150 people accompanied Nevin to a new headquarters that occupied five floors of a skyscraper on Michigan Avenue. The tire division, with about seventeen hundred employees, remained on Firestone Parkway. At the time, Firestone claimed the move to Chicago was made because that city is an important transportation, retail, and financial center. Kimball Firestone, the only family member on the board, said it would be easier to attract top-notch employees if the headquarters were in Chicago. "The main point," he added, "is that's what Mr. Nevin thinks."

For many who had to move, the decision was painful. Especially for those who felt they had no choice, and most especially for those who had deep roots in Akron. For John Nevin, though, the move was an easy one. His stormy image was safer in the Windy City. The insults would continue in Akron, but few could reach him on the upper floors of his Chicago high-rise. To the people in Akron, it seemed the move had been made for purely personal reasons. But there, in his posh new office overlooking Lake Michigan, John Nevin had a secret.

"I couldn't say it at the time, but this is a period of time where . . . I am negotiating for a joint venture. I'm seeking joint venture partners around the world," he said. Nevin was separating—physically and philosophically—Firestone's tire division from the rest of the company. From almost the day he joined the company, he had been making cloak-and-dagger overtures to merge the tire portion with another tire firm, and now the deal-making was heating up.

Hence the third decision.

In 1980, less than a year after taking the Firestone helm, Nevin telephoned Akio Morita, a Sony executive whom Nevin had gotten to know when he was the head of Zenith. At Zenith, in the 1970s, Nevin had often leveled acid criticism at Japanese electronics companies for their practice of underselling U.S. television makers. Zenith had gone so far as to sue several of the companies, a grave insult in Japan. Still, Nevin had maintained a friendly relationship with Morita. In the 1980 phone call, Nevin asked for some advice. He wanted to approach Bridgestone Corporation, Japan's largest tire maker, with an offer to sell Firestone's truck tire plant in LaVergne, Tennessee.

Nevin couldn't approach Bridgestone directly with the proposal—cold calling simply isn't done in Japan. But Morita, who was a friend of Bridgestone Chairman Kanichiro Ishibashi, could help open the discussion. Nevin wrote a letter to Ishibashi, stuck it in an envelope addressed to Morita, and mailed it off. A week later, Nevin got a phone call from Ishibashi. The two held a series of meetings, discussing the plant, which was less than ten years old but was operating at less than half its capacity—Firestone simply couldn't sell all the tires the factory was capable of producing. Bridgestone, which controlled more than half of Japan's tire market, was running out of room to grow there. It needed to crack the U.S. market, and the purchase of the LaVergne plant offered the opportunity. In 1983, Bridgestone bought the factory.

The sale was more significant to Firestone than just the $52 million profit it

Former Firestone Chairman Richard Riley shakes hand with Bridgestone Chairman Teiji Eguchi (left) as they are introduced by current Firestone Chairman and CEO John Nevin in May 1988. The two companies' merger agreement was nearly final, with Bridgestone having obtained 96 percent of Firestone's thirty-two million shares of stock with an $80-a-share tender offer. (*Akron Beacon Journal*/Lew Stamp)

represented. Nevin had been privately authorized by Firestone's board of directors to seek a joint venture with a foreign tire company. As early as 1983, Harvey Firestone's big, old, independent company was headed in a dramatic new direction. Nevin's objective was to spin off the tire company in a sale or merger, while keeping intact the rest of Firestone's businesses—most notably, the highly lucrative MasterCare retail and service stores. Over the next few years, amid all the other changes he was bringing to Firestone, Nevin was holding clandestine meetings with Bridgestone in Tokyo and San Francisco. Bridgestone slowly and deliberately studied the issue, weighed the options, considering and reconsidering. Nevin, the razor-sharp man of action, had to muster his patience on the long plane flights home.

Then, in 1986, things began to accelerate. Nevin traveled to Paris twice that year for meetings with François Michelin, discussing a partial joint venture with the French tire giant. The following February, he was in London to talk with Leopoldo Pirelli about a merger with Italy's largest tire maker. But in each case, there was a wrench in the works. The overlap of Firestone and Michelin's foreign business raised antitrust concerns, and the stock market crash, in October 1987, quelled the Pirelli talks. By November 1987, Nevin believed all his irons had gone cold.

Then, shortly before Christmas, the phone rang again. Akira Yeiri, Bridgstone's president, wanted to meet in Honolulu. The meeting took place December 18, 1987. Bridgestone was ready to deal. Yeiri offered two options: Bridgestone would buy all of Firestone's North American operations, or would go into a joint venture on the global tire operations, with Bridgestone as the majority partner. Nevin agreed to the latter proposal. But his phone kept ringing. Michelin and Pirelli were ready to talk again. In late January and early February, meetings were held with Michelin in Paris, with Pirelli in New York, and with Bridgestone in Los Angeles. Nevin was hopping from airplane to airplane; Firestone was the belle of the ball. On February 16, 1988, the Firestone board publicly announced plans to embark on a joint venture with Bridgestone: the Japanese company would pay $1.25 billion in cash for 75 percent of Firestone's world tire operations.

But Pirelli wasn't done. Three weeks later, Nevin received a late night phone call from Bob Troyer, Firestone's top public relations executive. Troyer had gotten a call from the *Wall Street Journal* informing him that Pirelli had placed an ad in the next day's edition offering $58 a share for all of Firestone's stock, which was then trading at $30. Pirelli was not happy that Nevin had accepted the Bridgestone offer without giving Pirelli the chance to continue negotiating. So it was going over Nevin's head—to the stockholders, the only body with more power than John Nevin. Nevin hung up the phone with Troyer and immediately dialed halfway across the world to Japan, where it was already Monday morning. He told Bridgestone's top brass what Pirelli was up to. Bridgestone finally acted quickly. The company offered $80 a share for stock that had been trading for less than $7 the day John Nevin had arrived in Akron. For that price, Bridgestone wanted all of Firestone, not just the tire division. Pirelli shook its head and walked away.

The old sign and the new are visible outside the Akron offices of Bridgstone/Firestone on the day it was announced the company was moving its headquarters to Nashville. Bridgestone/Firestone, which still maintains a nine-hundred-employee technical center in Akron, is the second-largest manufacturing company in Nashville. (*Akron Beacon Journal*/Ed Suba, Jr.)

On St. Patrick's Day 1988, in Chicago, stockholders approved the sale, and the old Firestone, the company that had defined so much of Akron, disappeared. It became known as Bridgestone/Firestone, the North American subsidiary of its new parent. Bridgestone had paid $2.6 billion to become, briefly, the world's largest tire company.

John Nevin, the man at the controls of the Firestone roller coaster, retired from the company on December 31, 1989. The leprechaun who wooed the world's tire companies found a pot of gold. He had made at least $20 million for himself in the sale to Bridgestone, plus a salary that reached as high as $6.4 million, including bonuses, in 1986. He had also carved his name into the tree of Akron history. Some remember him as a butcher, others as a savior, but virtually everyone who knew of him remembers him.

After retirement, Nevin remained in Chicago, using his Firestone earnings to buy a controlling interest in Budget Rent A Car Corporation, which is based in Chicago across the street from his old Firestone office. He served on various boards, but early in 1997, when he turned seventy, he eased into retirement. He had quit smoking—cold turkey, naturally—and he looked healthier, less drawn, less grim than he did eighteen years before when he walked into Akron that cold December day. In 1991, he received an honorary degree from the University of Akron, and he remained certain that he did good things in the city, offering generous and optimistic predictions about Akron's future.

Whatever he did for Akron—whatever people believe he did to Akron—one thing is certain: he was not the last one to do any of those things. In the wake of Nevin, General Tire and Uniroyal Goodrich were sold to foreign firms, and the headquarters of both companies pulled up their deep Akron stakes. Goodyear hired an outsider who had never worked in a tire company and who made millions while trimming away the company—and who, like Nevin, never bought a home in Akron. His name was Stanley Gault.

Nevin was the first wave of a tsunami that swept over Akron. The Rubber City had a lot of names for him, but there's one it never could have predicted: prophet.

22   Goodyear Rebounds

IT WAS A CHAT BETWEEN FRIENDS. Robert E. Mercer, Goodyear chairman and chief executive officer, thought he would do his successor, Tom H. Barrett, one last favor. So, during the waning days of Mercer's leadership, he pulled Barrett aside, and the men discussed how to fill an opening on The Goodyear Tire and Rubber Company's board of directors.

Mercer's retirement was creating two job openings: CEO and Goodyear board member. Mercer could have remained on the board, which has no sixty-five-years-old-and-out rule. He chose not to do so, believing that the best going-away present an old boss can give someone is a company without his shadow looming over it. "The whole team should function without the old guys sitting around trying to give them advice," Mercer said. "The world changes."

Goodyear had slipped into enough of a shadow. Two years earlier, in 1986, Anglo-French financier Sir James Goldsmith had raided Goodyear, and the company's world had changed. Goldsmith departed with $94 million of Goodyear's money, but that became only a part of the $2.6 billion indebtedness Goodyear took on. In all, Goodyear arranged a $4 billion restructuring loan, the largest ever put together for an American corporation. The company had become a cab stalled in competitive traffic, meter running. Mercer was getting out. Barrett had to pay the fare. Each day, Goodyear's interest payment cost it $1 million. Barrett didn't need more problems. He needed an ally on the board, someone with whom he felt comfortable.

"Before the nominating committee gets fully involved and you get a bunch of names you're not familiar with," Mercer said to Barrett, "is there anyone you'd like to have on the board?"

"Stan Gault," Barrett said instantly.

Barrett and Gault shared personal and professional history. "I was on the Rubbermaid board [since 1984], and he was a good friend of mine," Barrett said nearly a decade later. "He was a wonderful marketer. He had a record of success." Gault was sixty-three and in the final years of running Rubbermaid, the Wooster polymer products company that his father, Clyde, had helped to found. Stanley Gault, during his stewardship, had pushed Rubbermaid to near the top of *Fortune* magazine's most-respected company rankings.

"So I called Stan," Mercer said. "I told him that he and I would never sit on the same board because I was leaving in March and there is no meeting in March. But I invited him on as Tom's choice. There's a certain irony in that."

Perhaps the crushing competitive and economic pressures of the post-Goldsmith years would have undermined and doomed Barrett anyway. During his twenty-six troubled months at Goodyear's top post, the tire company slipped from number one to number three in the world. It recorded its first annual loss since the Depression. It slashed its dividend 77 percent. Its stock price plunged to a four-year low, even while the stock market was at record levels. As it turned out, Mercer's favor sealed Barrett's fate.

Gault joined the Goodyear board on Valentine's Day 1989. In early June 1991, under pressure from the Goodyear board, Barrett resigned as chairman and chief executive. Officially, he took early retirement. Barrett's replacement, announced in the same statement as his departure, was a man with no background in the tire business, an outsider to a company with a long and proud tradition of promoting from within. It was none other than Barrett's old friend from Rubbermaid, Stan Gault.

"Did I see it coming?" Barrett said. "Absolutely not."

Bob Mercer thought he had found the nearly perfect successor in Barrett, a Kansas farm boy who learned how to treat people, in part, from reading Dale Carnegie books. Mercer had put Tom Barrett to the test not only in production work worldwide but also in the boardroom, where contenders for the throne would present themselves and their ideas to the Goodyear directors. Twice a year, Mercer would review with Goodyear's board the company's succession plan. He wanted to familiarize the directors with the candidates. "Every time we had a board meeting," Mercer said, "we'd bring in some executives and require that they stand up and give us five minutes of *Horatius at the Bridge* and all the good stuff they were doing."

Though not as effervescent or loquacious as Mercer, Barrett passed these tests. He could explain production so that nonproduction types could understand that "good" and "comparatively cheap" deserve a place in the same sentence. He could explain a new tire in a way that infused it with instant credibility. Lights

Goodyear Chairman Tom Barrett speaks at a press conference following the company's annual meeting, in 1990, at Goodyear Hall. Barrett's tenure as chairman was production-oriented, rather than marketing-oriented. (*Akron Beacon Journal*/Ed Suba, Jr.)

didn't flash. Bells didn't ring. But Barrett's facts marched in long, straight lines.

Mercer, since 1983, had presided over the number one tire company in the world, with all the advantages that provides. When Mercer became chairman and CEO, Goodyear's long-term debt stood at $665.2 million, down from $1.17 billion the year before. Goodyear's Celeron subsidiary, which was building an oil pipeline from California to Texas, was a slight drag on earnings, but the company posted a $305.5 million profit and saw growth in domestic tire sales and its aerospace subsidiary.

But by 1989, when Barrett took the torch from Mercer, Goodyear was burdened with debt—nearly $3 billion. The post-Goldsmith sale of some top-performing subsidiaries, such as Goodyear Aerospace, made debt paydown more difficult because growth depended so heavily on tire sales. Mercer still thought the man for the job was Barrett, the production guru. So did analysts: "I don't mind seeing someone [as CEO] who has had a career in tires and wants to make them the best there is," John Pau, with Bear Stearns and Company in New York, said then. Even a decade later, analyst Harry Millis said Barrett was the right guy—for the immediate short term.

"Tom was a manufacturing guy," Millis said. "He understood what he had to do to get his costs down, and he did it."

Barrett did indeed get costs down, chiefly through layoffs and sales of assets. For most of his beleaguered tenure, Barrett labored to turn around a company with the superstructure of a battleship.

"During the big growth years [after World War II], we were trying to build factories as fast as we could because we could fill them with work and sell the products," Barrett said. "We built up a helluva structure. But that was back in the days of Russ DeYoung. We weren't growing at that rate anymore. We didn't need all those people." By the end of 1991, Goodyear's worldwide employment stood at 100,000. Barrett's corporate restructuring had cut twenty-seven thousand jobs, including eleven hundred in Akron. "I laid off twenty-six people who were directors or vice presidents," Barrett said. "They were people I knew. That was the hardest thing. But it had to be done for us to survive."

Analyst Millis agreed the layoffs were necessary but faulted Barrett's gradual completion. "He brought the consultants into one area at a time," Millis said. "The bloodletting just never stopped."

Barrett did more than cut costs. His dedication to research and development helped push through four new tire products. One tire, the best-selling Aquatred, along with the cost-cutting moves, yielded increased interest in a secondary stock offering that raised $582 million and retired more debt. Unfortunately for Barrett, he had to vacate the chairman's seat months before the debut of Aquatred and the success of the stock offering. Throughout his term, the company faced pressures in selling its products that he was not equipped to handle. At the end of 1989, Barrett's first year, Goodyear's earnings dropped to $189.4 million, from $350.1 million in 1988.

Other problems lapped at Barrett like waves at a beach. Shortly after he became CEO, in 1989, Goodyear became the largest U.S. company still doing business in South Africa. Facing political pressure from apartheid opponents and possible government sanctions, Barrett decided to sell the profitable subsidiary, which contributed about a third of Goodyear's more than $10 billion in annual sales abroad. The loss of South Africa weakened Goodyear's margin over competitors, which were buying their way to the top: in 1988, Bridgestone acquired Firestone; a year later, Michelin bought Uniroyal Goodrich. Both acquisitions shuffled the world rankings, but, ultimately, Michelin emerged as the leader followed by Bridgestone in second place and Goodyear in third.

"We looked at buying pieces of those companies," Barrett said, "but because of antitrust [laws], we couldn't do that. As an American company, you couldn't buy that much market share. But people offshore could. They came in here, into the world's largest market, and wreaked havoc with prices for years and years."

The 1990s ushered in no relief. An economic slowdown walloped the auto industry, which provides tire makers with about 25 percent of their revenue. By 1991, auto sales hit a trough, with the Big Three reporting losses for the first time in years. Chrysler, for example, lost $795 million on $28.1 billion in sales, less than half its sales only five years later. "If they weren't making money," Barrett said of Detroit, "we weren't making money."

In 1990, Goodyear reported a $38.3 million annual loss, its first in fifty-eight years. Much of it resulted from an $80 million charge for restructuring costs associated with the layoffs. The cost of building the All America Pipeline, $885 million, had to go on the books, too. Debt now stood at $3.28 billion. As a partial remedy to such depressing economics, Goodyear slashed its dividend by 77 percent early the next year. But the dividend cut, combined with a loss in the first quarter, sent the stock price down to a low of $12⅞ a share. In 1987, it had been at $71.

Stanley Gault, center, talks with board member and Goodyear Chairman Tom Barrett, left, at Gault's last annual meeting as the CEO of Rubbermaid in April, 1991. Gault, who had set a retirement date of May 1, would assume the head spot at Goodyear only thirty-five days later. (*Akron Beacon Journal*/Ted Walls)

"If you look at those losses," Barrett said, "they were caused by one-time charges—the restructuring costs and the pipeline. We were still making money. And we had that baby set up—the whole restructuring of the company—to make money in 1992." But Barrett wasn't destined to make it to 1992.

From inside the boardroom, Stan Gault watched as patience wore thin. Explanations fell on ears already being singed by shareholders whose investments were going south. Board members turned to Gault. Would he take over? Gault initially said no. He planned to retire from Rubbermaid in May 1991, at age sixty-five. Besides, accepting the Goodyear offer would mean unseating his old friend, his sponsor on the board.

Gault understood Barrett's concerns over layoffs and poor sales. When Gault was a General Electric executive running the appliance division in Louisville, Kentucky, he felt responsible for each of twenty-three thousand workers. "I used to be very concerned that if sales flagged and we had to lay off people, that we were going to affect hundreds of families, and they in turn would affect hundreds of other families," Gault said. He knew what financial adversity could do to a family. The Gaults weren't rich, despite the fact his father was one of Rubbermaid's founding investors. When Clyde Gault was fifty-six, he found himself broke, his son needing help to go to college.

Goodyear Chairman and CEO Stanley Gault poses, in December 1991, in his office at the Goodyear Headquarters building six months after taking the head position at the company. (*Akron Beacon Journal*/Kevin Casey)

"I went to the College of Wooster," Gault said, "because I had a small scholarship. I suspect if it weren't for the College of Wooster, I wouldn't have gone to college."

Sitting on the Goodyear board, though, Gault saw the growing frustration with Barrett's progress in stemming losses. When Barrett resigned, in early June 1991, Gault, who had retired from Rubbermaid thirty-five days earlier, had already agreed to take over. Ironically, Barrett's departure enhanced his personal stake in Goodyear. At the time, he owned about $1.98 million worth of Goodyear shares or options to buy shares. The day his resignation was announced, Goodyear stock rose $3\frac{1}{8}$ to $30\frac{1}{8}$.

Analyst Harry Millis explained why Barrett's time had come and gone so quickly. "If you had had a different person instead of [production-oriented] Tom Barrett, I think it would have been a disaster," Millis said of the early post-Mercer period. "But if you had not brought Stan in and picked up the market share, it also would have been a disaster. You had too much money tied up in modern, efficient capacity; it ain't efficient if it ain't running. The company needed to fill that [production] capacity. Tom was not the right guy to fill it. Stan Gault was."

For six years, Barrett didn't talk about that time. He went to work for American Industrial Partners, an investment group that turns around small companies. He continued to serve on the boards of four companies, including Rubbermaid. He broke his silence, in 1997, in an interview in his modest office at Cascade One in downtown Akron. "Any board is made up of personalities," he said. "One day a group got together and said we have someone who has a proven track record of successfully running a company—we should use him instead. Those things tend to snowball. He got a few members on his side—there were two or three people who were not my allies—and the party was over. I felt bad. I didn't want to sit around and complain and make it look like sour grapes. I just wish somebody would look at what I did someday and see that I played a role in the company's survival."

Stan Gault, the man who receives much of the credit for Goodyear's resurrection, places a share of that credit where Barrett had hoped. "I didn't come in and create anything new," Gault said. "I did what people should do: build on the foundation you find. I want to give credit to Tom Barrett, who had a lot of initiatives under way. We modified some of them, of course. We accelerated some. We emphasized some more than others."

Days after his arrival, Gault asked about four tires in the pipeline. He decided to launch all four at once, in October, rather than the customary practice of one at a time. The launch was not through the usual dealer channels and television ads. Instead, Gault opted for high-profile news conferences and an eighteen-city tour that began on the deck of the USS *Intrepid* aircraft carrier in New York. "They're too hot to handle, too hot to hold," he warned the New York press about Aquatred, one of the new tires.

Barrett had decided against launching the Aquatred because of the economy. "I could have done it," Barrett said. "I hadn't, because we were in a goddamn recession, and the first thing you pull back on is advertising. There is no point in advertising products that people don't have the money to buy." Gault, on the other hand, went after what money consumers had, introducing the tires personally in four cities.

"Everybody felt the change," said Chief Operating Officer Hoyt Wells, a Barrett ally who stayed on under Gault. "There was a tremendous energy. He was great with people. He was always selling our products. He pulled the trigger on a lot of the sales before we had scheduled them."

"The guy's a dynamo," analyst Millis said. "He has a helluva lot of charisma. Once the efficient capacity that Tom had built up was filled by Stan's marketing,

The Aquatred tire is introduced by Goodyear Chairman and CEO Stanley Gault during a high-profile news conference in New York City. Under Gault's leadership, Goodyear had begun to act like a consumer products company rather than a manufacturing company. (Goodyear Tire and Rubber Company)

you saw the results in earnings. It was dramatic." Actually, Goodyear posted a $658.6 million loss in 1992, due to a massive one-time charge of $1.07 billion to cover a change in accounting rules for retirement benefits. After that, profits rose like a rocket: $387.8 million in 1993; $567 million in 1994; $611 million in 1995.

The Aquatred got the attention of both consumers and the investment community, which Gault had learned to court from his Rubbermaid days. Goodyear began to think and behave like a consumer products company rather than a manufacturing company. Two days after Aquatred's New York splash, backed by two consecutive quarters of profit and a 130 percent increase in the value of Goodyear's stock since the beginning of the year, Gault announced a new share offering.

"We also were ready for that secondary offering," Barrett said, "but I admit that . . . Stan probably got a better price [$50] for it. He was, after all, a darling of Wall Street."

Early the next year, Gault announced Goodyear would sell some brand-name tires through Sears stores and other mass merchandisers. This time, Gault was not completing a Barrett initiative; Goodyear had a long-standing policy of selling tires in the replacement market only through its loyal network of dealers. "That was heresy—adding Sears, Discount Tire, Wal-Mart," Gault said. "I didn't think there was a choice. It was too much a potential for significant growth."

Marge DeLuca, former editor of the *Wingfoot Clan*, a Goodyear publication for employees, poses with her Doberman, Vito, in the office she now runs out of her home in Bath. DeLuca had twenty-four years with Goodyear when it discontinued the *Clan*, and consequently her job, in 1994. (*Akron Beacon Journal*/Ed Suba, Jr.)

Gault delivered on the promises he made when he took over. He paid down debt and built up the share price. Goodyear's stock split two-for-one and more than doubled in price—meaning shareholders' value more than quadrupled in just four years. In 1994, with regular increases in profits, Gault restored the dividend to its precut level. But the news wasn't always happy. In five years as chairman, Gault cut the work force another twelve thousand to eighty-eight thousand.

Marge DeLuca, the former editor of the *Wingfoot Clan*, a Goodyear publication for employees, considered herself a lifer. She had twenty-four years with the company, hiring in as a secretary after one year of college. As an editor, DeLuca knew them all: the guys building tires when the plants were humming, as well as the CEOs. Goodyear guards didn't need to see Marge DeLuca's identification badge to know she belonged. All they needed was to see her face. She'd been around awhile.

"We had lived in a time," DeLuca said, "when the CEO would come down the hall, slap you on the back, and jokingly call you a loafer. Chuck Pilliod was good for that."

The *Wingfoot Clan* had been around even longer—since June 1, 1912. But even institutions change. News can be delivered in a daily newsletter and by e-mail, computer to computer. The *Wingfoot Clan* ceased publication with the April 1994 issue, and with it went Marge DeLuca's job. Since her termination, she has continued to return to Goodyear's corporate headquarters as an outsider, doing a job on a contract basis. She stops at the desk in the grand lobby, fills out a visitor's badge, and clips it to her blouse. "There's not a lot of levity now," DeLuca said. "It's all serious stuff. Everybody has their guard up. I think getting rid of the *Wingfoot Clan* sent a message: There are no traditions anymore."

As the first outsider running Goodyear since E. G. Wilmer, in 1921, Gault probably found it easier to effect change in a company steeped in tradition. "I'd been at the company for forty years," Tom Barrett said. "I knew people. When I said to make changes, people may have chosen to say, 'I'm going to come in and argue with Tom first.' When someone comes in from the outside, you think differently. He has no emotional ties to the past. That scares the hell out of people."

Gault knew when to value ties to the past, however. That skill gave Goodyear the edge in a 1995 bidding war for controlling interest in Poland's leading tire company. For TC Debica, Goodyear and Gault went head-to-head with Michelin and Francois Michelin. Michelin, who runs the family tire business, would visit Debica. Then Gault would show up. This went on for ninety days, each man bringing his considerable personality to bear on the negotiations, meeting not only with Debica executives but also with the Polish prime minister, the news media, and financial analysts. "It got to be a personal matter between Francois Michelin and myself," Gault said.

Among Gault's commitments to Debica was retention of the company name and the Debica brand. "It was a strong brand in and of itself," he said, "and [keeping it] was very important to the people."

Debica was important to both Michelin and Goodyear. Since the collapse of Soviet bloc rule, Eastern Europe has been one of the world's fastest-growing economic regions, with a market of eight hundred million customers previously closed to Western companies. Michelin offered Debica the Michelin way of doing things—secretive and autocratic. Goodyear went out of its way not to be seen as arrogant, conceited, unilateral, or dogmatic. "I told them [at Debica]," Gault said, "that the ideas aren't all going to flow one way, that they had done some very smart things and that we wanted to use their smart ideas all around the Goodyear system. This isn't just a situation where all the good ideas flow from Akron."

Francois Michelin made one more visit to Debica than Gault—four to three—but Goodyear got more than 51 percent of Debica. The acquisition gave Goodyear operations in thirty-one foreign countries. As Gault pointed out, Goodyear had been an international company since 1910. But a strong international presence did not make Goodyear a global enterprise in ways that are important in today's competitive climate.

"A global enterprise is when you really are serving the world and serving it in the best possible way," Gault said. "That doesn't mean I serve India or I serve China because I ship exports into China. I'm talking about serving China the way *China* wants to be served."

One of Gault's first executive decisions at Goodyear emphasized his commit-

Goodyear Chairman and CEO Samir Gibara addresses stockholders and the Goodyear board of directors in April 1997. Gibara, Goodyear's first foreign-born chairman, sees globalization as the way for Goodyear to reclaim its title as largest tire maker in the world. (*Akron Beacon Journal*/Lew Stamp)

ment to that strategy, however symbolically. In the manner of Japanese companies, Gault upgraded Goodyear "employees" to "associates." Former chiefs Pilliod and Mercer praise Gault's leadership overall, but scoff at that change in the Goodyear lexicon.

"Stan came in and did what he was asked to do," Pilliod said with a chuckle. "Up until then, replacements came from employees, not associates."

"I really loved our employees," Mercer said. "I never called them associates. I gag at that. If the newest hire is an associate, then what the hell is your executive vice president?"

To Gault, the vice presidents and other top officers formed the ranks from which he could identify and cultivate his replacement. Those who no longer fit in at Goodyear found the exit door quickly, among them Chief Financial Officer Oren Shaffer and Executive Vice President John Fiedler, who headed Goodyear's North American tire division. Fiedler left, in 1994, and was replaced by Samir F. Gibara, who two years later succeeded Gault. "They have a global executive in Sam," Millis said. "I think Sam is the ideal guy—again."

Gibara, a native of Egypt who speaks Arabic, French, and English, is Goodyear's first foreign-born chairman. He has run Goodyear operations in France, Morocco, and Canada. Gault groomed Gibara by giving him unfamiliar assignments and heaping on the pressure. "I had five jobs in three years, and it was not easy," Gibara said. "But I learned a lot about the company."

Gibara's primary goal is to reclaim Goodyear's title as the largest tire maker in the world by 2000. Goodyear's new culture, he believes, makes the company more competitive. "That gives us the opportunity to respond much faster interstate or overseas. We're more cohesive."

The ascension of Gibara, because of his foreign roots and vast international experience, provoked community-wide speculation that Goodyear would follow Bridgestone/Firestone, Uniroyal Goodrich, and Continental General out of town. Gibara understands the genesis of the rumors: "With the trend toward globalization and regionalization, it is becoming less important to be based in any one city." But, he insisted, Goodyear values its corporate memory too highly to leave Akron.

"Akron has always been Mecca," he said. "For Goodyear, we have our roots here. If we went elsewhere, we would lose what makes the essence of The Goodyear Tire and Rubber Company. We would lose our contact with the polymer business [revolving around the University of Akron's College of Polymer Science and Polymer Engineering]. We would lose our people. We would lose our heritage. What other people call the memory of the company. I don't think any company can be successful if it loses its memory. Our memory is here."

23 Race on Sunday, Sell on Monday

WHEN THE INDY RACE CARS go home to Indiana for another May at the Brickyard, Hank Inman hears a radio no longer present. He can even see it, sitting on the workbench in his father's garage in the Oklahoma City suburb of Del City. Filled with tubes that glowed, this old, gold Sears radio lighted up the lives of Hank and his father, Henry.

On it, they listened as the St. Louis Cardinals beat the New York Mets to clinch the 1964 National League pennant and as the football Sooners of the University of Oklahoma ran roughshod over the plains. Those were glorious days of shared experience. But none were more glorious than the May days when the radio, tuned to station KTOK, transported Henry and Hank to the Indianapolis Speedway for the 500.

"Every Memorial Day my father would spend the entire day in the garage, futzing around with an old pickup," Hank Inman said. "He'd turn on that radio, tune to the Mutual Network, and the race would just engulf the garage."

Hank and his brother, John, would drift in and out of this racing cacophony,

Racers are ready for the 1913 Indianapolis 500. Jules Goux of France won on Firestone's nonskid tires, averaging under 76 mph. The racing rivalry between Goodyear and Firestone was and is at its fiercest at the Indy 500. (The University of Akron Archives)

receiving Indy 500 updates from their father. Hank and John weren't big race fans, but then neither was their father. They just liked the feel of the day together, the sound coming from the plastic radio with its oval speaker. "That workbench with its radio was like a tabernacle," Hank said.

In 1986, Henry Inman and his wife, Olga, came to Akron to visit their son. Hank Inman worked for Goodyear Tire and Rubber Company, which, along with Bridgestone/Firestone, maintains the only link to Akron's fabled past as tire-builder for the world. At Goodyear's Technical Center and at Firestone's Advanced Technology Workshop, workers build the race tires used in Indy-style competition. After his Akron visit, Henry Inman hoped to see the Indy 500 on television for the first time. "He was going to set up a TV in the garage when he went home," Hank said.

That year, rain forced postponement of the Indy 500, and Henry Inman never got to see the race. He died of a heart attack the day after the race was to have been run. Hank Inman and his family traveled to Oklahoma to bury Henry, and, after the funeral, they returned to the house. It was quiet in the garage. Much too quiet.

"I turned on the TV," Hank said, "and there was the Indy 500. I said to myself: 'I'm going to watch the whole thing.'"

After that, Hank would watch most of the race each year, drifting in and out of the room with the television, listening and remembering. Indy and that radio.

Indy and his father. "That's why Memorial Day and the race are so important to me," Hank said.

"It is *the* race," agreed Bob Johnson, Bridgestone/Firestone vice president of technology, "and the reason we got back into IndyCar racing."

Goodyear and Firestone's on-again, off-again racing rivalry goes back almost to the beginning of the auto tire industry itself. Both companies hold impressive records and, in fact, owned virtual monopolies for years. As one company would start to dominate the sport, the other one would drop out—not necessarily because of the competition. Goodyear, the most recent dominator, began racing around the turn of the century and was the first to quit the sport.

In 1902, P. W. Litchfield, then plant superintendent, talked Goodyear co-founder F. A. Seiberling into testing their new straight-side tires in English races. The Goodyear straight-sides were flops, but the company stuck with its racing program. Goodyear won its first Indy 500 in 1919. By then, its straight-side tires were on all but one of the top fourteen cars. With nothing left to prove, Goodyear abandoned racing for thirty-nine years.

Firestone tires were on the winning Indy racers for the next forty-seven years. Goodyear learned that wins at such high-profile races give a tire company's entire product line greater prestige. Tires that hold up under the heat and pounding of racing also score big with consumers.

"It shows how high-performance their product can be," said Sean Brenner, ed-

Hank Inman used to spend each Memorial Day of his youth in the garage with his dad, listening to the Indianapolis 500 on the radio. The 500 is "the race," the most important in the racing rivalry between Goodyear and Firestone, which goes back almost to the beginning of the tire industry itself. (*Akron Beacon Journal*/Matt Detrich)

itor of *Team Marketing Report*, a Chicago-based newsletter that tracks sports marketing. "It's the same reason Nike and Reebok get so involved in the NBA."

Opinion surveys revealed Goodyear tires had become the choice of the Geritol crowd, those pedal-off-the-metal, post-fifty speed conservationists. To heat up and age down its calcified image, Goodyear returned to stock-car racing in 1958. It added a division devoted entirely to racing, in 1959, and was back on the Indy track in 1965. Two years later, with A. J. Foyt riding the rubber, Goodyear bagged Indy again. A few years later, Firestone left the field.

"Race on Sunday, Sell on Monday" proved a winning strategy for Goodyear. And as long as Goodyear had a straightaway to the checkered flag, race-and-sell was a safe strategy. But in 1988, upstart Hoosier Tire, whose offerings had previously been limited to dirt-track racing, decided to challenge Goodyear's supremacy by rolling out a tire for the Winston Cup stock-car circuit. In its second outing, the little Lakeville, Indiana, company took home a victory, stopping Goodyear's win streak at 464.

The loss sent Goodyear's engineers back to the drawing board, and, within four days, a new tire was designed and shipped for testing. The results were so good that forty of the forty-two drivers at the next race were riding on the new Goodyear tires. Hoosier scored nine victories in twenty-nine races that season. From a numbers standpoint, Goodyear had won the skirmish. But drivers and crew chiefs complained that the competition between the companies had resulted in tires that were not as safe, a contention that both companies fought.

Goodyear's victory proved daunting. At the Daytona 500, the cathedral of stock-car racing, Goodyear introduced radials during the 1989 season that were faster and softer. Faster tires require softer, stickier compounds. Softer tires wear more quickly and become more dangerous. Initially, drivers couldn't keep their cars planted on the Florida track and crashed into walls. Then two inexplicable blowouts sent Bill Elliott to the hospital with a broken arm and Dale Earnhardt to the garage in search of a new side for his Chevrolet. The safety issues led even the legendary Richard Petty to complain.

"When it [Hoosier] came in '88," he said, "people were saying, 'Man, this is gonna be great. We've got competition with tires!' I said, 'Wait a minute. I lived through the competition between Firestone and Goodyear. I've been there. And it's not good for racing.'"

With no clear indication what was causing the problems at Daytona, Goodyear withdrew its tires, leaving Hoosier's bias-ply tires as the only ones available. Although company officials still couldn't explain the Daytona accidents, Goodyear was back on track with new radials within two months. Hoosier retreated to Indiana to work out its own version of the racing radial. Hoosier returned to Daytona in 1994, initiating Tire War II. In the second battle for brand superiority, Petty's remarks proved sadly prophetic. Drivers Neil Bonnett and Rodney Orr crashed on Hoosier radials during Daytona practice runs and died. None of the accidents could be pinned directly on the tire competition. Nor was it determined the tires were faulty.

"I don't think it's ever been established that there was anything wrong" with the tires, NASCAR President Bill France told *Car and Driver*, in 1995, "but the drivers got spooked."

9493

Barney Oldfield, with cigar, sits in a Mercer riding on some of the original Firestone nonskid racing tires, whose tread pattern is visible at right. The photograph is believed to have been taken in 1915 when Oldfield failed to qualify for the 1915 Indianapolis 500. The mechanic is unnamed. Oldfield became known as the man who never looked back during his seventeen-year racing career. (The University of Akron Archives)

Hoosier won three races that season, but by Daytona 1995, Hoosier had run up the white flag and left the stock-car circuit a tire monopoly for Goodyear. Hoosier's departure was just fine with Petty. "There are two areas where racing doesn't need competition," he said. "Tires because of the safety factor. And fuel because, the first thing you'd know, everybody would be running all-nitro or something."

Firestone's distinguished racing history began, in 1903, when racer Barney Oldfield set a mile-a-minute speed record in Indianapolis. Oldfield followed that feat, in 1909, by winning, again with Firestone tires, the first race on the Indy track. For the inaugural Indy 500 race, in 1911, company founder Harvey Firestone bought $50,000 in advertising. His reward was victory. After Goodyear's exit, in 1919, Firestone was virtually unchallenged and won every Indy 500 from 1920 through 1966.

By 1974, Goodyear was back in the sport and recording some victories. Consumers were choosing the more fuel-efficient and durable European radials, rather than American bias-ply tires. So Firestone put its motor sports program up on blocks to concentrate on converting its bread-and-butter passenger tire line to radial technology. "Racing was expensive for the company," said Al Speyer, Bridgestone/Firestone director of motor sports. "I could understand that. More important, coming from the engineering side, I could relate to the fact that racing tires weren't radial tires in 1974. They were bias and had little if any resemblance to where our street tires were going."

The cachet of racing the Indy 500, however, never quite surrendered its hold. Almost ten years before the final, tragic Tire War between Goodyear and Hoosier, Firestone took the first tentative steps toward a racing comeback.

In 1985, in the theater on the fifth floor of Firestone Plant 1 in Akron, Bill Genck gave the first and perhaps most important speech of his life. Genck had launched Firestone's Advanced Technology Workshop to build prototype tires and race tires. He started with three men. They transformed an empty building in hopes of starting production. Those hopes hinged, in part, on Genck's speech to members of United Rubber Workers Local 7. Genck asked that the rubber workers amend their contract to give those in the workshop the flexibility to do a variety of tasks.

"They voted overwhelmingly to do it," Genck said. "That was when things really started to change here."

Even more than Genck's workshop, it took a man whose name is infamous in Akron to rekindle Firestone's racing fires. Sir James Goldsmith struck the match. His financial fireworks failed to gain control of Goodyear but left it financially scarred and more vulnerable to competition on any front.

"Goodyear's problems did have an effect," Speyer acknowledged. "They did two things. Number one, it sent a message to critical racing management people around the United States, if not the world, that there was no guarantee of tire supply for any series by one manufacturer."

Jimmy Murphy's car sports Goodyear tires at the 1920 Indianapolis 500. Two years later, Murphy won the 500 on Firestone tires. (Goodyear Tire and Rubber Company)

Before Firestone could capitalize on Goodyear's difficulties, though, it had to adjust to a new owner, Bridgestone Corporation of Tokyo. Doubt over the new parent's commitment to the Firestone brand lingered like an oil slick on a racetrack. Among employees, dealers, and customers such as Ford Motor Company and General Motors Corporation, the caution flag was out.

"You could sit there in a meeting, and they'd say: 'Yeah, we're committed to the brand,'" Speyer said. "But as the people left the room, they weren't convinced. All the right words were said, but it's one of those axioms: Actions speak louder than words." So Bridgestone/Firestone management acted. They asked dealers what they wanted. The answer was nearly unanimous: Put Firestone back on the track at Indy, and we'll know you're serious about the brand.

A racing comeback required careful calculation. Speyer had watched the Hoosier-Goodyear War from the sidelines. He knew that Firestone must make durability and safety its priority. "If you have difficulty with your product, that can be terribly damaging," said Speyer. He also knew that Firestone should tread cautiously at first. "Nobody walks into the Final Four and just starts playing," he said, referring to college basketball. "The same is true in racing."

So Firestone, in the early 1990s, began sponsoring Indy Lights, the development series for IndyCar racing. The races are much shorter—about seventy-five

Bob Carey, who raced on Firestone tires, was awarded the National Championship of the A.A.A., based on ratings in the six major events for the past year, on both dirt and brick tracks. He finished first in three of the championship events—the Detroit race, the Syracuse race, and the Oakland race. *(Akron Beacon Journal)*

Wilbur Shaw hams it up as he shakes hands with Leonard Firestone after winning the Indianapolis 500 in 1947. (The University of Akron Archives)

miles—and in less powerful vehicles. Indy Lights offered Firestone racing on training wheels, a prelude to the big time. Bridgestone/Firestone Senior Vice President Trevor Hoskins took the next step. Hoskins took Yoichiro Kaizaki, Bridgestone/Firestone chairman, to the Indianapolis Speedway for the 1992 Indy 500.

"We wanted him to see what it looked like," Hoskins said.

Indy sold itself. Its throng of spectators. The high-pitched whine of its race cars. The fury in its pits, as crews raced to slap new tires onto the cars during stops. Every tire was a Goodyear. Kaizaki decided that should change.

Hoskins was back at the Speedway the following May to announce that Firestone was returning to the sport Goodyear had dominated for so long. He found himself an outsider. Firestone had been away from racing for so many years—almost two decades—that Indianapolis Speedway officials refused Hoskins permission to use track facilities for a news conference. He had to settle for the Speedway Motel near the track to make his announcement.

In the Advanced Technology Workshop, Genck's workers began to convert Indy Light racers from thirteen-inch rim diameter tires to fifteen-inch. It was the diameter Firestone would have to make for IndyCar racing and the hallowed Brickyard.

In September, Firestone had another announcement—that Pat Patrick Racing and driver Scott Pruett would test Firestone's Firehawk racing tires. Firestone's engineers followed Pruett from track to track and test to test—more than ten thousand miles in all. The battle intensified once Firestone actually got onto the track. Firestone won two races in 1995, which was two more than it expected to win in its first season.

During its second season, Firestone felt the sting of setback. At the 1996 Detroit Grand Prix, Firestone ran fast and well in dry qualifying, taking five of the top ten spots. Then, on race day, it rained. Firestone had not yet honed its wet-traction race tire, and it slipped back. Goodyear tires finished first, second, and third and were on six of the top seven finishers. That performance, as much as anything else, drove home the importance of the tire to the outcome of a race.

Christian Fittipaldi, a young star of the Championship Auto Racing Teams circuit and a Goodyear driver, broke down the components of racing success this way: "Seventy percent to tires, 20 percent to the car, and 10 percent to the guy behind the wheel." Whatever the winning combination, Firestone found it in three other prestige events in the 1996 season. It took the PPG IndyCar points championship and, on the same day, the inaugural U.S. 500 and the Indy 500. In 1997, Indy racers won nineteen of twenty-seven races on Firestone tires. Racing has so fired the soul of Firestone that its parent, Bridgestone, entered worldwide Formula One competition in 1997. At the end of that year, Goodyear announced it was withdrawing from Formula One after the 1998 racing season. The direct Goodyear-Firestone confrontation would continue on the Indy-car circuits.

Although most of the tires for Formula One events will be built in Japan, growth opportunities for Akron haven't been overlooked. Bridgestone/Firestone has invested $10 million in new equipment and personnel at the Advanced Technology Workshop. It increased Akron production of Firehawk IndyCar tires from 60 percent in 1996 to 90 percent in 1997.

During racing season—January to September—Genck and his tire builders go at their extruders, molds, curing presses, and other machines for ten to twelve hours each weekday and then return for Saturday work. Genck has added more than seventy people to work on the IndyCar and Indy Lights programs.

Goodyear has responded in cash and kind. Though the competing companies do not talk about the specifics of their spending, Stu Grant, Goodyear's manager of worldwide racing, acknowledged that Firestone's return has upped the ante. Goodyear spent twice as much on development in 1996 as it did in 1993.

At Goodyear's Technical Center in Akron, Ken Dunlap uses the most modern tire-building machines as well as constantly evolving equipment to make a better

Tony Owen does a final finishing inspection on Goodyear Racing Tires as they come off the line at the Goodyear Tech Center. (*Akron Beacon Journal*/Robin Witek)

radial race tire. "In the last ten years," he said in 1997, "there has been a lot of updating. Lasers. Computer panels. There are growing pains, but while the pressure is on, it's good. I like the competition."

At Goodyear, race tire builders apply their name as well as the company logo to every tire they produce. It is both signature and promise.

"For me, there's a pride," Dunlap said. "Race tires are just a little more important."

They need to withstand extreme conditions. Racers at the Indy track, with its corners banked only nine degrees, can top 235 mph. "You have to provide tires that enter the corner well, feel good to the drivers in the middle of the corner, and exit well," Grant said. "You don't have banking to assist the car around the corners. You have to rely on the tires."

In the days of Goodyear's IndyCar monopoly, Dunlap and his colleagues would have begun in February to build the six thousand tires needed for the month at Indy. Not in 1997, though. Because of Firestone, Goodyear devoted extra time to development. Dunlap and his fellow tire builders started building a month later than usual. That's not the only change Dunlap has witnessed since he joined the Tech Center, in 1986. Goodyear, he said, has easily tripled its Akron race-tire production and has become far more protective of its processes.

"In the '80s, we'd have two or three tours a week coming through our department," Dunlap said. "Goodyear was pretty open. We even had a Japanese tour. I have not seen that in [recent] years."

Racing has an impact beyond the hallways and work floors of Firestone and Goodyear. Both companies compete to score on the bottom line as well as at the finish line. At the bottom line, passenger tires, representing about two-thirds of the 254 million tires sold each year, count the most. And the high-performance segment of the passenger tire market has been one of the industry's hottest. According to *Tire Review* magazine, sales of high-performance tires grew an average of 63 percent between 1992 and 1995.

"You can't sell high-performance passenger tires if you don't have the credentials," said Bob Toth, a Goodyear marketing manager. "Racing gives us those credentials."

Tire makers consider racing a rolling laboratory, one in which they learn to build a better product. The very profile of the street tire, in fact, has changed because of racing technology: once as tall and lean as a supermodel, the street tire now looks more like a fat, squat sumo wrestler.

"We use it [racing] to help us design better Eagle high-performance tires, to prove our new mold chases [grooves] and constructions, to find new materials for truck tires and airplane tires," said Goodyear's Grant. The formula works for Firestone, too. Sales of the entire Firestone line increased 10 percent in both 1995 and 1996, which company executives willingly credit to racing victories. And sales of the high-performance Firestone Firehawk, in which racing technology is applied, have outpaced the company's ambitious projections.

At the dawn of every race day, though—especially every Indy 500—the finish line supersedes the bottom line. "It is still the best-known race in the world," said Firestone's Hoskins. "The coverage it gets throughout the world makes winning the Indy 500 our number one objective." No longer a stranger at the Brickyard, Trevor Hoskins now watches the Indy 500 from the pits along with various Firestone teams.

In Akron, Goodyear's Hank Inman still listens to each year's race with his ears but hears it in his heart, as he used to when the old tube radio glowed on his father's workbench. Hank's brother, John, who lives in Del City, inherited the old radio.

"If he's smart," Hank said, "he has it in the garage."

24 Rubber's Remains

THE REFLECTING POOL at the entrance of one of the world's most modern tire plants sparkles under the diamond of the rural Tennessee sun. An old barn adorned with a white cross watches from across a windblown field. A Jack Daniels distillery sits just up the road. This is Bridgestone/Firestone's Warren County plant, nestled among the region's cherry orchards and conspicuous as a ruby in a bowl of grits.

Opened in 1990 at a cost of $350 million, the factory blends a state-of-the-art Japanese interior with an American-designed exterior. It was the first American plant built in the post-Akron era of rubber dominance, a signpost to a new era of multinational tire companies headquartered far from Ohio. Like much of Bridgestone/Firestone, this facility mingles elements of the two cultures: a unionized Southern worker in a blue-and-white striped work shirt sits at a computer that commands Japanese robots—little remote-controlled carts with names on their sides: Lucky, Moe, Re-Run, and R2D2. The robots zip around, picking up uncured tire carcasses as the computer commands. The computer asks for two tires; the robot fetches them and moves into position next to a tire curing press—a big machine that clamps down over a tire like a giant clam shell. The

A Goodyear worker puts a green tire on a McNeil Co. Bag-O-Matic curing press in 1964. The Akron company's Leslie E. Soderquist designed the Bag-O-Matic, in the 1940s, to release tires mechanically from their molds. *(Akron Beacon Journal)*

press lifts the tires into position, and, when the hissing metal machine clamps down, the nameplate on its front cuts through all the changes with a reminder of where this began:

"McNeil Akron Bag-O-Matic."

In Akron, the Bag-O-Matic is a fabled beast, breathing fire onto a green tire, transforming it into the final product. Leslie E. Soderquist of McNeil Company designed the Bag-O-Matic, in the 1940s, to release tires mechanically from their molds. Soderquist, who died, in 1975, after thirty years with McNeil, held sixty-seven patents, fifty-six of them related to tire manufacturing. Most people in Akron never heard of him. But thousands used his machines every day. Now, with just a handful of tire-building jobs left in Akron, Soderquist's legacy takes on new significance. He is part of the Rubber Capital of the World that still exists.

We don't make tires in Akron anymore. But it would be pretty difficult for the rest of the world to make tires without Akron. This remains the place where

An employee at Smithers Scientific Services' Ravenna Division inspects the footprint of an earthmover's tire. He is testing tire-to-surface contact at various weights and inflation pressures. (Smithers Scientific Services)

the rubber industry comes when it needs to buy equipment, when it needs to buy special chemicals, when it needs custom mixing, when it needs machinery repaired, and when it needs to pick brains. Case in point: When you leaf through the geographical listing in *Rubbicana '97*, a directory of companies involved in the rubber industry, and you come to Akron, it looks like "Smith" in the phone book. The directory lists 134 companies in Akron. Surrounding towns and suburbs account for another 123. By comparison, New York City has twenty-two companies listed; Chicago has forty-one; Charlotte, North Carolina, the home of Continental-General Tire, has twenty-three; and Nashville, Tennessee, home to Bridgestone/Firestone, has seven. Barberton alone, with twenty-one companies, rivals most of these metropolises.

McNeil, now McNeil and NRM, still cranks out its Bag-O-Matics and other tire-building equipment at its Crosier Street facility. From big players such as ITW Akron Standard, Myers Industries, and Smithers Scientific Services to small, niche businesses such as Tech Pro and Polymer Valley Chemicals, the Akron area provides everything from big, expensive tire-making machines to the additives that make whitewalls white. A healthy number of rubber shops remain in the area, from Killian Latex, which makes condoms, to R.C.A. Rubber Company, which makes floor mats. In addition, the concentration of expertise has attracted a new cluster of Asian tire makers to the area; companies from Korea and China have opened research and development facilities in the Akron area in the 1990s.

In 1996, 16,700 people in the Akron area worked in the rubber and plastics industries, compared to 39,900 in 1970. Despite the drop—due chiefly to massive tire manufacturing job cuts—the area retains a high profile in the rubber and polymer industries. "Even though the tire companies aren't making tires in Akron, you've got your research and development, corporate offices—there's still a tremendous base of companies in this area that support the tire and rubber industry," said Jim Dowey, an executive with Illinois Tool Works, the parent company of Akron Standard. "If we're looking for an engineer who is familiar with the tire industry, we're not going to find him in San Jose. . . . The resources or access to the tire industry are still in northeast Ohio."

The story of the Rubber City can be found in the many roof peaks atop Akron Standard's facility on Englewood Avenue. Each peak represents an addition, and each of the more than thirty additions represents another period of growth for the

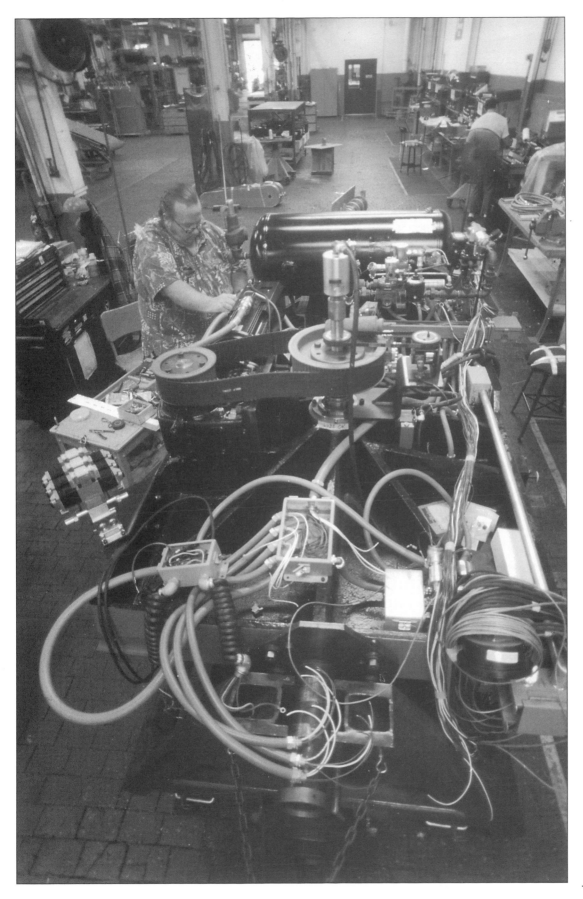

Robert Bauman works on an ITW Akron Standard machine that tests tire uniformity at the Englewood Avenue plant in Akron in 1992. (*Akron Beacon Journal*/Ted Walls)

company. Akron Standard Mold Company was born in 1918, a boom time in the area's rubber industry. General Tire founder William O'Neil was one of the original five incorporators. Like his competitors, he needed someone to make equipment to keep his factory running. The machine shop started in a small, utilitarian building, making tire molds, cores, and other equipment. Although some of the larger companies made their own equipment, outside suppliers were still needed. And Akron Standard thrived. The company grew from five employees, in 1918, to more than six hundred by the early 1950s. With each spurt of growth came a new roof peak.

Lowell Mulhollen arrived, in 1951, fresh out of Garfield High School, with a resume that consisted of a job packing groceries. Like so many in those days, he got hired because he knew somebody—surnames appeared multiple times on Akron Standard's employment roster. Mulhollen's wife, Gloria, was a secretary with the company. She had gotten her job a year earlier. Lowell started as an apprentice machinist. In 1951, Akron Standard was a big-shouldered cousin to the thriving rubber companies, pumping out equipment for rubber factories in the dimly lighted, clanging machine shop. It had expanded its Akron facilities considerably, had bought Lectromelt Casting Company in Barberton a decade earlier, and had just added another plant in Greenwich, Ohio, north of Mansfield. The company had just a couple of engineers: most of its machines were built from blueprints provided by the tire companies.

After a stint in the Korean War, Mulhollen returned to work at Akron Standard and began attending the University of Akron on the GI Bill. He earned a master's degree in industrial management in 1965. By then, Akron Standard had been sold to Cincinnati-based Eagle-Picher Industries. Akron's tire industry was cruising along, and, Mulhollen said, Akron Standard "was growing by leaps and bounds." The company was designing its own machines. Patents rolled in, and employment peaked at fifteen hundred in the 1960s.

Mulhollen's career was growing right along with the company. In 1971, he took over the tire mold division, and, in 1973, he became a vice president. Five years later, the one-time apprentice was named president of Akron Standard. The promotion was a blessing and a curse. Like the rest of the support companies in the region, Akron Standard had hitched its wagon to the rubber companies' horses. And those horses were tiring. In the recession of the early 1980s, Mulhollen had to lay off a lot of old friends. As someone who had raised two sons on an Akron Standard paycheck, he knew how difficult life would be for those he had to cut loose. He lost a lot of sleep.

But Akron Standard has survived. In 1990, Eagle-Picher sold the company to Illinois Tool Works of Chicago. Mulhollen was released a few years shy of retirement age, as the new owners brought in their own managers. The company, now called ITW Akron Standard, has narrowed its focus to machines that test tire and wheel uniformity. A job that used to consist of a worker running his hands along a sidewall to check for imperfections is now done by the highly technical equipment that is this company's bread and butter. The company controls 80 percent of the world market and ships 80 percent of its machines out of the United States. Akron Standard has shed some of its divisions and, in 1997, employed about 150 people at Englewood Avenue. Even in a global marketplace, where the location of

Don Moore of Oklahoma City cuts through steel belts on a tire he is repairing at Myers Industries on South Main St. in Akron in 1983. Myers was demonstrating how to use tire repair equipment. (*Akron Beacon Journal*/Don Roese)

a headquarters is relatively unimportant, Akron remains a logical choice, according to Akron Standard President Jim Chase. Why? The access to suppliers, machine shops, and the like remains the key.

Stalwarts such as Akron Standard, McNeil, and Myers Industries date to the early days of Akron's rubber industry. They have changed with the times and have managed to roll with the most recent punches. Others, though, formed or moved here as a result of the changes. People who lost their jobs during the foreign takeovers of the late 1980s, or who left when they saw their opportunities shrinking in Akron's tire companies, have managed to parlay their expertise into entrepreneurship, starting small niche businesses that serve the industry. And the foreign tire companies that came here have taken full advantage of the pool of displaced tire experts. Four Asian firms—Hankook Tire and Kumho Tire Company of Korea and Shanghai Tyre and Rubber Company and China Tire Holdings Company of China—opened research facilities in Akron in the early 1990s. China Tire faded from the picture and Shanghai's operation has remained small, but the two Korean companies have added considerable resources, both financial and human.

Two of those people tell an Akron story.

In the fall of 1971, Guy Edington, the ink barely dry on his diploma from Ohio State University, found himself settling behind a desk at General Tire, asking where the paper was stored so he could get to work. Edington, who grew up in Dayton, had come to General to work as a tire engineer, one of several brought in

Guy Edington heads the Montrose research center of South Korea's Kumho Tire Company. Edington worked as an engineer for General Tire for more than twenty years—nearly all that time in Akron—before accepting Kumho's offer to build the center from scratch. Kumho wants the center to engineer tires that meet requirements for the U.S. market. (*Akron Beacon Journal*/Jocelyn Williams)

during a flurry of hiring activity, in the early 1970s, that would prove to be the company's last in Akron.

In those years, General, Goodyear, Firestone, and Goodrich rippled with brainpower, even as the rolls of factory workers began to dwindle with an industrywide contraction. Their research and design departments, all housed in their Akron headquarters, remained the sources of some of the most significant advances in tire quality and sophistication. If a company wanted its tires to stop more quickly on a wet road, people like Edington were charged with figuring out a way. The young bachelor put in a year of training at General's plant in Waco, Texas, then settled into a new life in Akron.

A short time later, another young engineer, straight out of school, walked through the same front doors of General's East Market Street headquarters. His name was Ray Labuda, a native of Johnstown, Pennsylvania, east of Pittsburgh. Labuda had just completed his studies at the University of Pittsburgh and a training stint at General's Mayfield, Kentucky, plant. Labuda was assigned to the truck tire division, where Guy Edington worked. By that time, Edington was a relative sage. He introduced himself to Labuda. The two men were just a year apart in age, and they hit it off right away. Edington took Labuda on a tour of the office and introduced him around. The conversation drifted into idle chat, and Edington learned Labuda was renting the apartment next door to his.

The two men became fast friends. They began car-pooling. They moved out of the apartment building and, along with another General engineer, rented a house in Norton. They socialized together, and both excelled in their work. When, after a few years, Edington announced that he was engaged, he asked Labuda to be in his wedding.

Time passed. Labuda got married, too. The two men's wives became friends. The couples got together on holidays. They were sure it would go on forever. By the early 1990s, Edington and Labuda had established themselves as two of the best engineers at General Tire. But General was changing. The company had been bought by Continental AG, Germany's largest tire maker. Uneasiness floated like a bad spirit through the big east Akron complex. There were rumors of a headquarters move, of layoffs. Engineers who had been around twenty years or more, Edington and Labuda among them, were taking a hard look at their futures.

Half a world away, another relationship had matured. Two small tire companies had formed in South Korea: Hankook Tire, established in 1941, and Kumho Tire Company, formed in 1960. Each grew modestly, focusing primarily on the Korean market. Both were headquartered in Seoul, and they developed a sense of competition not unlike that between Goodyear and Firestone, which for years were the number one and number two tire makers in the world, respectively. As the Korean companies expanded globally, Hankook nipped constantly at Kumho's heels. By the early 1990s, Hankook was ranked number eleven worldwide and Kumho number ten. Both companies' names were becoming more recognized, not just in Korea, but around the world. To expand, other foreign companies had cracked North America by buying American firms.

The two Korean companies didn't have the resources or the opportunity to follow suit. So they chose a different tack. In the early 1990s, each decided to open a research and development center in the United States, to allow development of tires for the American market. And—not by accident—each decided to open its center in the Akron area. Even though the city's importance on the world's rubber stage had diminished with the foreign takeovers, the technology base remained here.

The idea behind these technical centers was to engineer products that would meet American specifications and expectations. So far, the ventures have shown very little effect on the coveted North American market. In 1997, Hankook and Kumho claimed a tiny fraction of the market, less than 1 percent.

Ray Labuda left General Tire in Akron to establish a research center in Montrose for South Korea's Hankook Tire in 1992. The company, which recently opened a new facility, in Green, had thirty-six employees in 1997. (*Akron Beacon Journal*/Jocelyn Williams)

"The potential is there," observed industry analyst Harry Millis. "But when you don't buy a major American company, it takes awhile to build distribution." Millis believed the most likely inroad for any smaller foreign company will be to hook a private label contract—an arrangement in which a company makes tires for a retailer such as Sam's Club or Sears. That guarantee of steady sales would justify building a factory in North America, which would in turn increase a company's chance of making other sales.

Hankook arrived first, in 1992. The Korean firm had been engaged in a trademark agreement with General; the two companies' technical people worked closely together in Akron. From that experience, Hankook knew that Akron was the entry point to America. It was the right place to open a technical center, and it was the right place to find good people.

The Korean managers had kept their eye on one sharp General engineer in particular—Ray Labuda. After a series of discussions, Hankook invited Labuda to be general manager of the new operation. There were plenty of unknowns at Hankook, but, facing a growing sense of instability at General, Labuda rolled the dice. In September of that year, he took a deep breath, accepted the job, and turned in his resignation at General.

"This seemed like an opportunity," Labuda said. "How often do you get that opportunity to open an R and D [research and development] center? It's once in a lifetime, actually. So I just kinda grabbed the ring, I guess."

In Hankook's office in Montrose, Labuda was teamed with a Korean manager, and the two set about establishing Hankook's American foothold. "We had nothing," Labuda said. "One of the guys had rented an office. But it really wasn't an R and D center. It was really just a place to hang your hat, and it had a phone there." They were starting a business from scratch, establishing everything from budgets to benefits plans.

The new office happened along at a time of change in Akron. In the early 1990s, Uniroyal Goodrich, owned by Michelin, was in the process of closing its Akron operations. Bridgestone/Firestone had just pulled its headquarters out of Akron, leaving its technical center here. Continental General was on the verge of moving its operations away. And Goodyear was trimming its staff under the leadership of Stanley Gault. There was a bounty of out-of-work and insecure tire experts, people with skill and experience looking for new opportunities. One of them was Guy Edington.

About a year after Labuda left, Edington's phone rang early one evening at the General Tire headquarters. He was the last one in the office, trying to catch up on some work. General, at the time, was being buffeted by the winds of Continental's ownership. A planned headquarters move had been announced, then delayed, then canceled. It was about to be on again, and everyone at General knew that the future would be rocky. And there, on the other end of Edington's phone, was a recruiter—a headhunter—calling about the position of general manager for Kumho Tire's new research and development center.

"I thought, 'Yeah, I do wanna talk about that,'" Edington recalled.

Kumho, literally translated, means a large, calm body of water; a golden lake. Edington's transition would not be calm, however. With Kumho, there was opportunity, but the future was uncharted. He accepted the job and found himself in a setting almost exactly like the one his old friend Ray had been in a year earlier. Edington was in charge of a very small staff—six people—in a rented office in Montrose, not far from Hankook's office. His mission was to build a research center from scratch. After twenty years on remarkably similar career paths, Edington and Labuda had each set out on a road less traveled, and it was the same road.

They are two of the lucky ones. Even with expansion, Hankook, Kumho, and Shanghai combined employed fewer than one hundred people in Greater Akron in the late 1990s. The pay and benefits are competitive with that offered by the larger tire companies, but the number of new jobs does not meet the number of people who were left out during the downsizing and headquarters relocations. Some engineers and chemists who wanted to remain in northeast Ohio have left the rubber industry altogether. Others have struck out on their own.

Mike Beck took a job as a chemist for Seiberling Tire and Rubber Company in 1967. He spent ten years working for the company, including a stint as the company's chief chemist in Kenya. But when Seiberling asked him to accept another foreign assignment, in the mid-1970s, he got out and joined a company that

Shanghai Tyre and Rubber Company, China's largest radial tire producer, opened a small research center in Fairlawn in 1993. Changzheng Dong, general manager of the facility, and Ken Immel, the center's chemical engineer, show a tire design called "Warrior" that they've worked on. (*Akron Beacon Journal*/Paul Tople)

supplied carbon black to the tire companies. In 1986, he left and formed Polymer Valley Chemicals, a small company that fills a small industry niche. Beck supplies clay, talc, and mica to rubber companies, elements used to put the "white" into whitewalls and white lettering on tires.

"Every major supplier to the rubber industry at one time or another had an office in Akron. And many of them still do," Beck said.

Even the plant closings, devastating as they were to northeast Ohio and other regions, turned up hidden opportunities. As factory officials undertook the bottom-line task of selling off equipment they no longer needed, plucky investors flocked to their doors. And so it came to be that John and Kay Putman, in the spring of 1982, wound up with eight filthy rheometers in the garage of their little split-level home in Wyoga Lake.

A rheometer is a quality control device that measures how rubber cures. John, then thirty-four, had worked for a cousin's company on rubber lab testing instruments since he was sixteen. He'd heard that a Firestone plant in Georgia was letting the things go for a song. Well, $40,000.

"We literally wiped out every savings account we had. We borrowed some from his father," Kay recalled. John and his father rented a truck, went down to Georgia and hauled the machines, each about four feet tall and weighing several hundred pounds, back home.

For weeks, the Putmans scrubbed, scraped, and scoured off the black gunk that had accumulated on the machines. Months passed before the Putmans made their first sale, for $10,000. At first, the business grew slowly; after a few years, the Putmans began to manufacture their own rheometers under the name Tech Pro, in Cuyahoga Falls. The Putmans now employ thirty workers, with half of their business coming from overseas.

"The rubber industry isn't that big. You have to be international now to expand," said Kay Putman. "Especially for our instruments. This isn't something that people buy truckloads of every month. You sell a machine, and they won't need another one for ten years or so. So you have to be constantly finding new markets, new customers."

Many of the small suppliers and service companies that dot the area's map believe the Akron metro area will continue as a stronghold for this second tier of rubber companies. "By redefining the know-how we had, we were able to adapt to changes in the marketplace," observed Richard Erickson, president and chief executive of the Akron Regional Development Board.

But others aren't so sure that Akron's niche in the industry is secure. John Cole is the president and CEO of Rogers Industrial Products, a company in Canal Place that makes tire-curing presses. Like Tech Pro, Rogers began as a small company that rebuilt old equipment before expanding into original designs and full-scale manufacturing. Cole feels the same pinch of foreign competition that transformed the tire industry over the past two decades. Companies in Asia and Eastern Europe are able to produce equipment more cheaply. Labor, he said, is still expensive in the Akron area, and it's becoming harder to compete. As his small factory, operating out of a former B. F. Goodrich plant, bustles with the noisy confusion of production, he keeps an eye to the future.

"You can't stay in Akron and compete with costs anymore. It's not going to be possible," Cole said. "We're going to have to have some relationship to have components made outside the United States. . . . Within five years, we won't be able to compete at all, with the wage levels and the cost of materials. We won't be able to do it."

There in the old rubber company plant, Cole ponders the question that has hung over Akron for a quarter century or more: Is this the Rubber Capital of the World? He doesn't have an answer. Few do. They simply go about their business, trying to avoid the mistakes of the past.

They know the history is in Akron. They know the knowledge is in Akron. But they also know the jobs are changing, evolving into a new but not-so-different field: polymers.

25   A Polymer Legacy

WHEN WILLIAM V. MUSE hit town in 1984 to run the University of Akron, he began snooping around its academic disciplines like a detective in search of a suspect. The only thing he lacked was a trench coat, though a lab coat might have been more appropriate. He kept his ear to the ground, his nose to the wind, and, although he discovered the scent of rubber was gone, Muse could hear the industry's ghosts. They were anything but dead and buried.

Where others heard laments of loss, of plants closed and jobs vanished, Muse heard the cry of a phoenix—and the phoenix was polymers. He moved calculatingly through department after department, in search of a means by which he could enhance the university and, with it, the city. Bill Muse was not afraid of rubber's ghosts.

Akron Mayor Don Plusquellic remembered Muse's pleasure in his discoveries and smiled. "He would say: 'Look at this beautiful university.' It is like the Hawaiian who walks along a path each day and sees this flower that the rest of us from the outside world recognize as beautiful, gorgeous, but that he doesn't even know is there. He sees it every day. Bill was telling us: You have this wonderful institution called the University of Akron, and you don't appreciate it. You see it as some little, hick college."

William Muse, then president of the University of Akron, stands with the Polymer Science Building in the background in 1989. The building, which opened in 1991, "became a symbol of the phoenix, a symbol not only of a university but of a city reaching for new heights, exerting itself as a player on the national scene," Muse says. (*Akron Beacon Journal*/Lew Stamp)

Muse, the outsider in Akron, detected more, something grand: "It was very clear to me that polymer science and polymer engineering was the University of Akron's niche in the national marketplace, an area in which we could gain and maintain international stature."

Akron, of course, had had such stature. It had been an international capital—the Rubber Capital of the World. Muse decided rubber, a polymer itself, could serve to regenerate a city. It had left behind a part of itself, dividing and multiplying like a living cell, those long necklace-like molecules that form everything from credit cards to dashboards.

Rubber chemistry and, subsequently, polymer science were nothing new to the university. Charles M. Knight had set up the first academic course and laboratory in rubber chemistry in 1910. During World War II, the University of Akron, with new laboratories for U.S. government-funded research, had become one of the many locations throughout the city where work was done to develop the synthetic rubber that kept the Allies on the road to victory. The university initiatives complemented the polymer research conducted by Akron's Big Four tire companies since the industry's infancy. Muse decided Akron, in 1984, needed to secure a new niche in the world marketplace. It could do so with a new, state-of-the-art Polymer Science Building in which a staff of stars would perform research and train the polymer scientists of tomorrow. The Polymer Science Building was completed in 1991. Muse called it "a symbol of the phoenix, a symbol not only of a university but of a city reaching for new heights, exerting itself as a player on the national scene."

Others, persons of all stripes and from all ranks, began to see and share Muse's vision. Norbert Bikales hadn't been to Akron for a while when he showed up in the early 1990s. The director of the National Science Foundation's Polymer Program knew that the former Rubber Capital of the World had endured one blow to the gut after another. Rubber shop closings followed by headquarters relocations had put the city's psyche on the ropes. Bikales was curious about the city that had emerged.

"What's going on in Akron these days?" he asked a cabbie at Akron-Canton Regional Airport.

"We've got a great polymer program at the university," the cabbie replied.

The answer surprised Bikales. Cabbies talking polymer programs? What's next? The answer soon loomed on the horizon in the form of the city's new skyline. From the back seat of the taxi, Bikales saw the two glass and steel towers, one shorter than the other, from miles away. With each exit, each turn, the forms grew larger.

Bikales directed the cabbie to take him to the University of Akron's Polymer Science Building. The cabbie turned off Broadway and onto University Avenue, finally dead-ending onto the circle in the shadow of these connected glass towers with their dramatic slanting overhead canopy.

"I suppose you're going to tell me that that's the Polymer Science Building," Bikales said.

"It is," the cabbie said proudly, yet matter-of-factly.

Frank N. Kelley, dean of the College of Polymer Science and Polymer Engineering, laughed in amazement and delight as he related this anecdote. In the cabbie's satisfaction, Kelley hears echoes of first Muse and then himself. At the groundbreaking in 1988, Kelley had rhapsodized that the new building would become "a beacon that would glow."

The University of Akron's Frank N. Kelley points to the future site of the Polymer Science Building in 1985. (*Akron Beacon Journal*/Ott Gangl)

The new Polymer Science Building rises in modern contrast to the steeples of St. Bernard's church as it takes shape in March 1989. (*Akron Beacon Journal*/Michael Good)

The 146,000-square-foot, $17 million Polymer Science Building has become the brightest symbol of both the city's rebirth and its future. More than a symbol, the science and engineering of polymers and the practical application of this knowledge make Akron different from such Rust Belt cities as Youngstown, where steel once was the heart of the community.

John J. Luthern grew up in Youngstown, earned his doctorate in polymer science at the University of Akron, and, in 1997, coordinated the polymer technology two-year associate degree program in the university's Community and Technical College.

"There was little or no steel research going on in Youngstown, whereas the legacy here in Akron is the research in polymers," Luthern said.

The men responsible for the university's early and continued attention to polymer science were not those with hoists and hammers. They were men of science, men of vision, men of leadership, men such as Charles M. Knight, G. Stafford Whitby, Maurice Morton, and Frank Kelley.

"This institution was very much interested in rubber right from the start," said Norman P. Auburn, who served as university president from 1951 to 1971.

In 1908, Charles M. Knight proved himself a practical man. He didn't just preach chemistry at Buchtel College, forerunner of the University of Akron—he practiced it. Akron's rubber industry was just emerging. Its captains and lieutenants took scientific questions to Knight, who, in turn, encouraged his students to get out of the university lab and apply their knowledge in the city's industrial setting. Knight helped to raise the money for a chemistry building, completed in 1909 and named for him. He made certain that it contained a rubber chemistry laboratory in which he could teach the world's first college course in this science. He stood before that first class on Tuesday, September 13, 1910.

For his assistant, Knight selected one of his early chemistry students, Hezzleton E. Simmons. When Knight retired as Buchtel professor of chemistry in 1913, Simmons succeeded him and went on to become university president. Simmons's emphasis on rubber chemistry until his retirement, in 1951, set the cornerstone for today's polymer science program. He hired G. Stafford Whitby during World War II and turned him loose on synthetic rubber research. In 1954, the year of his retirement, Whitby was awarded the prestigious Charles Goodyear Medal by the American Chemical Society's Rubber Division. In 1972, he was inducted into the International Rubber Science Hall of Fame.

Frank Kelley became director of the Institute of Polymer Science, in 1978, then went on to become dean of the College of Polymer Science and Polymer Engineering. He described Whitby as "the grand old man with all the corporate memory," who lured Maurice Morton from McGill University in Montreal to be the assistant director of UA's Rubber Research Laboratory.

Charles M. Knight helped to raise the money to build this chemistry building, which opened in 1909 and bore his name. It contained a rubber chemistry laboratory in which Knight taught the world's first college course in rubber science. (*Akron Beacon Journal*)

Morton arrived, in 1948, and did early on what had become commonplace by
the end of the twentieth century: he wrote research proposals that resulted in
grants, much of it from the military. Within a few years, Morton was ready to do
much more. "By 1952," he said, "I had already set my sights on having a Ph.D.
program. The challenge was that Akron was a tremendous technological center,
the Rubber Capital of the World, with a tremendous number of research staff
working in the rubber company laboratories." The industry was being under-
served by the very institution that decades earlier had committed itself to rubber.

Morton set out to convince Norman Auburn, the university president, of the
need for the doctoral program. "He was a good salesman," Auburn said. "He said
to me: 'If I am to continue my research, I have to have a body of students, graduate
students, to assist me.' . . . He was not an easy man to get along with, but I had a
great respect for him. He was determined. He was not easy to dismiss." Morton
succeeded: the university made its doctoral program in polymer science its first
Ph.D. program in any discipline. In 1956, the first five doctoral students in polymer science began their course of study.

Frank Kelley finished what Morton started. Kelley came from a long
Goodyear line. His grandfather worked in the rubber shop, as did his uncles. His
father was in sales accounting. His sister still works for the company. When Kel-

ley graduated from high school, he did what many young men in Akron did in the 1950s: he went to work for Goodyear.

After a year and a half of filing records, he said to himself: "There has to be more to life than throwing away old records and putting new files in a vault."

"Why don't you go to Akron and take rubber chemistry?" John Kelley asked his son.

"That conversation changed my life," Kelley said. "My father saw that the people who were at the core of rubber, other than manufacturing, were those who knew how to make synthetic rubber . . . and they wore those white lab coats."

When Kelley returned to the university after a career in the air force, $400,000 was trickling in annually from nonstate sources. Such money comes in the form of gifts, endowments for teaching chairs, and funded research. By 1996, the amount generated annually had grown to $9 million.

Kelley sells polymers with the fervor of a snake oil salesman. There is one difference: polymers aren't phony. They have become the salve on the Rubber City's economic wounds, the residue of rubber. "So much of polymer science grew from rubber science," Kelley says. "What's neat about Akron is that this is where our roots are." General Tire's former parent, GenCorp, and Goodrich are no longer in the rubber business, but they are in polymers. Bridgestone/Firestone and Goodyear both maintain research and development facilities in the city of their birth.

"In 1997," said Goodyear Chairman Samir Gibara, "the city is much better off with a Polymer Institute that is world class than it would have been with another two plants here. I mean, everybody has plants. You want a competitive advantage. To be distinctive. It is the intellectual legacy of the tire industry to the city."

"If there is any reason why we feel very comfortable here in Akron," said Nissim Calderon, Goodyear's vice president of corporate research, "it is because of the polymer program. It's like a window to the world of polymers."

∽

Graduate student Charles Chen, shown in 1986, sets up an experiment in a "dry box" that takes moisture out of polymers. The black hands protruding toward the camera are rubber gloves into which the scientist puts his hands and arms to work inside the box. (*Akron Beacon Journal*/Ron Kuner)

Steve Paolucci tests flame-retardant polyethylene material for tensile strength and elongation. The 1989 graduate of Stow-Munroe Falls High School's polymer program works for A. Schulman. (*Akron Beacon Journal*/Robin Witek)

Steve Paolucci and Laura Prexta are two members of the polymer generation who invested in the legacy and are reaping dividends. They share a bright-eyed intelligence and curiosity about their similar work worlds. Paolucci, though, never counted on becoming a part of the industry on which the Rubber City's image and future are being recast. Prexta never had a doubt that her future would be as bright and shiny as one of the plastic parts for which her company, Americhem, provides color. They grew up in Akron's suburbs—Paolucci in Stow, Prexta in Bath Township. Paolucci graduated from Stow-Munroe Falls High School in 1989, Prexta from Revere High School in 1988. Both excelled at science. The turning point for Paolucci occurred in his sophomore year in high school, when a biology teacher introduced him to the head of the school's new Polymer and Testing Program, Melanie Stewart.

"It was like a nuclear bomb in my life," Paolucci said.

Paolucci's parents were divorcing. There wouldn't be enough money for college. Paolucci wouldn't have had a problem back when Akron was the Rubber Capital of the World. He could have gone into the rubber shops with or without a high school diploma and earned enough to live comfortably. In fact, a high school diploma and college study were so nonessential to a decent lifestyle that Akron public schools did not keep track of that information for years. Officials estimated, though, that in 1950, when Akron's rubber industry was at its peak, the high school graduation rate was about 50 percent. By the mid-1990s, about 80 percent of students graduated from high school. A note in the margin of a mid-1960s Akron schools strategic planning study suggests that college may actually have been discouraged. At the time, approximately 45 percent of area high school graduates went on to higher education, about an eight percentage-point increase from the previous decade. "As an industrial city," the study asked, "should we be sending additional graduates to college? Are some now going who shouldn't?"

By 1986, when Melanie Stewart was addressing Steve Paolucci's class, most of Akron's rubber shops had closed. The job pool was drying up. Even a high school diploma was no guarantee of the high wages, generous benefits, and job security that had once been considered a birthright. Stewart and her teaching partner, Ed Borsuk, held up a mirror for the students and placed a diamond in front of it. Light bounced off the diamond, refracted and reflected into the mirror, emerging bright and shiny and sparkling.

"This," the teachers told their students, "is you."

Stewart regularly advised students that her polymer program could open many doors after high school—to advanced technical programs, to jobs, and to university study. Steve Paolucci wanted to try college but had to take a circuitous route. In Ohio, with more than 100,000 polymer jobs—more than thirty-five thousand in the Akron-Canton area alone—there is more than one way to get a polymer education and into the polymer business.

Harry J. Barth of The Hygenic Corporation, a rubber and synthetic products supplier to the health care industry, was eager to give Melanie Stewart's program a boost. In 1989, Barth was looking for a lab technician and encouraged Stewart to steer one of her students his way. When Steve Paolucci went to interview at Hygenic, he thought: "'This is it: lab technician. This is what I'd worked for.' I told Harry anything I could think of that would help me to get the job." By 1992, Paolucci was ready to move on. He got a job at A. Schulman as a research technician for a unit that makes flame-retardant polymers with electrical applications. And he enrolled at the University of Akron to earn a B.S. in chemistry.

Laura Prexta had advantages that Paolucci lacked. She was the daughter of scientists. Leslie and Roger Bain had met in graduate school. Roger became a professor of geology at the University of Akron. Leslie studied geology, did some additional work in chemistry at the University of Akron, and worked for the Bayer Corporation in Fairlawn. There was no question Laura Bain would go to college. She got hooked on lab work in her freshman year in high school and ended up choosing polymer science for her college study.

As the daughter of a UA faculty member, Laura did not face the financial constraints that gave Steve Paolucci pause. Her tuition was free, the equivalent of a scholarship. At the College of Polymer Science, Prexta won an assistantship and worked with Professor Frank Harris on synthesizing a new type of high-temperature polymer that can conduct light in a harsh environment, such as in the guts of a computer.

After earning her doctorate in the spring of 1997, Laura began to worry. It was time to join the work force, and she had heard horror stories from other graduates about the job market. Could she be too good and too expensive? A newly minted UA graduate with a doctorate in polymer science starts at an average salary of $63,000.

"There are jobs," she said, "but for Ph.D.s with little experience, it's tough."

Rejection letters piled up. Companies feared they couldn't satisfy Prexta's financial or intellectual needs. Americhem, headquartered in Cuyahoga Falls, was looking for a senior scientist for its Automotive Group, which puts the color into the hard plastic trim on autos. But Americhem usually recruits undergraduate science majors who need to work to pay for additional education. Searching for such candidates, Mike Fair, who is in charge of human resources at Americhem, talked with science department heads at the university, including Roger Bain, Prexta's father. Bain gave his daughter Fair's business card. She called. The job required someone who would be as comfortable with people in the Cuyahoga Falls plant as working alone in the lab.

Prexta grinned. "I wanted to have a job where I could be in the lab and then take what we'd learned there out to the customers. I'm not the best at the pure sci-

Laura Prexta earned a doctorate in polymer science at the University of Akron and now works for Americhem. She's holding color dispersion samples, which she evaluates for use in molded surfaces of plastic parts. She is framed by a polarizing light microscope that she uses in her work. (*Akron Beacon Journal*/Robin Witek)

ence, but I like interacting with people." The match seemed perfect. "I like working on something that, within my lifetime or in the next month or the next year, someone is going to be using," Prexta said. "That's what I like about Americhem."

~

At the University of Akron, Frank Kelley routinely gets mail from people he doesn't know. His usually is e-mail, carrying plaintive pleas from around the world from would-be graduate students in polymer science and polymer engineering. "Akron has an enormous reputation throughout the world relating to polymers," Kelley said.

The College of Polymer Science and Polymer Engineering is the largest, most comprehensive program in the country and, in 1997, was ranked second only to the University of Massachusetts, Amherst, by *U.S. News and World Report*. The College's Department of Polymer Science receives 150 applications for admission annually and accepts no more than twenty-five to thirty students; the Department of Polymer Engineering receives slightly fewer applicants but is just as selective in filling its master's and doctoral programs.

Even before the college popped up on the World Wide Web with its own page, foreign students were writing to Kelley. In 1996, 180 of three hundred graduate students came from twenty-five foreign countries. If those foreign students follow the pattern of their predecessors, 75 percent will remain in the United States to work. Of those remaining in the States, 40 percent find jobs in Ohio. This is the state where polymer-educated students long to be.

"I got an e-mail from one student who was absolutely eloquent in his explanation of how hard work makes up for a lack of this and that, in his case a 550 score on the test that indicates how well a student uses English as a second language," Kelley said. "We usually require a 600. . . . You realize here is a kid, sitting with his computer in this little hut in Nigeria or Latin America or China. He has gotten on the Internet and has seen our home page, and it says: Click here for letter to the Dean."

Melanie Stewart's high school program has not attracted the same attention. The junior program has twenty-five slots and the senior another twenty-five. During the 1997–98 school year, only eleven juniors and eight seniors were enrolled. "Students understand jobs like lawyer, doctor, salesman, even reporter," she said. "They have an idea what these things are. They have no idea what a lab technician does. We don't make an object. We make information. We monitor processes. We can't hand a student a bottle and say: We make bottles. We are abstract. They think they can do better."

Akron's East High had the same number of openings, with eighteen juniors and fifteen seniors enrolled and another twelve receiving exposure to polymers in Tech Prep Engineering. In the university's associate degree program, which was launched in 1994, twenty to forty students were enrolled in a program intended for fifty to 100.

"A parent wants to give their child a college education to get them out of manufacturing, not send them to college to go into manufacturing," UA's Luthern said. "People identify with the master's and Ph.D. programs, but we are sending our students out there as testing technicians, quality control technicians, research assistants, assistant design engineers. Our graduates will be responsible for the daily nuts-and-bolts operation of the plastics business or rubber business."

When Wayne DeCamp was with Landmark Plastic Corporation, he worried where he would find these nuts-and-bolts workers. He and officers of other small- to medium-sized plastics companies—Landmark has about two hundred employees—would seldom, if ever, have jobs for UA's newly minted polymer scientists and engineers with master's degrees and doctorates. A listing of continuing-education courses offered by the university reinforced DeCamp's concern. Among the listings were engineering courses, computer-design courses, other computer courses. There were no plastics courses. There was nothing for the people who run the machines of the polymer industry and check and control the quality of the materials produced. "What are you doing for technicians and operators?" DeCamp asked Kelley.

So, in 1994, under the direction of Nancy M. Clem, former course coordinator for continuing education, the university created the Akron Polymer Training Center in the former Ace Mitchell Bowling Supply building on East Mill Street. The center started with four courses in three classrooms and three laboratories. It has grown to dozens of courses, from mixing and processing rubber to injection molding of plastics. It is an education-business partnership, with companies such as Van Dorn in Strongsville consigning injection molders to the Polymer Training Center to show potential customers how they operate and with expert instructors such as Tom Hall, technical products engineer at GE Plastics in Independence.

The market for the training center's noncredit courses is primarily people already working in the industry, rather than those trying to break into it. In 1997, Charles Suran, project manager for Sajar Plastics, a custom injection molder in Geauga County, took a moldflow class designed to help the worker analyze an injected molded part before it is cut into its steel form. He worked in class with one of Sajar's molds.

"There's a real benefit," Suran said. "We need to raise the general level of training for everybody geared toward the polymer industry. There is always a shortage of plastic-knowledgeable people."

Landmark Plastic tries to send at least one employee to every applicable course at the training center. The training enables workers to improve their skills even as Landmark buys more automation for the machines that produce, primarily, horticultural packaging. With additional automation, Landmark expects to gain more business and to turn product handlers into "packaging technicians" who control computers.

Among the problems the polymer industry faces, according to Polymer Training Center director Clem, is the base pay of the entry-level machine operator, the person without the training from programs such as those at Stow or East High Schools or the university's two-year Polymer Technology offering. "They are not paying enough, and the industry doesn't want to come to grips with that," Clem said. "It's: 'Oh, my profit margin, my board of directors, my materials cost.' There are valid reasons, but $6 an hour is $12,000 a year. Could you live on that?"

A few companies, such as Steere Enterprises in Tallmadge, which makes specialty plastic components, start employees at about $8 an hour and still make a profit. "There are stellar companies in the industry," Clem said. "Steere pays excellently but is very, very particular about who it will hire. It hired seven people [in the fall of 1997] after interviewing three hundred."

Northeast Ohio has nearly four hundred polymer-related companies. Summit, Portage, and Medina counties, those served by the Akron Regional Development Board, have at least 220. They form a critical mass, a synergy. Although the Akron area possesses one of the greater concentrations of polymer activities in the world, very few people agree about what to call this place. Richard Knight, an economist and expert on the growth of cities, was often a guest lecturer at the University of Akron. He is credited with coining the term Polymer Valley. The ARDB sometimes uses the grandiose-sounding phrase Polymer Center of the Americas and other times the more humble Polymer Heights.

"I've never been comfortable using these glitzy terms like Polymer Valley," said UA Dean Kelley. "We resisted it for years, but everybody kept using it. What can you do?"

The breadth of polymer education opportunities in northeast Ohio keeps pace with the growth of polymer companies. The University of Akron added its two-year associate's degree program and also offers a bachelor of science degree in mechanical polymer engineering. In 1970, Case Western Reserve University in Cleveland offered the country's first B.S. program in polymer science. The Department of Macromolecular Science at Case Western is an outgrowth of World War II synthetic rubber research. Ranked fifth by *U.S. News and World Report*, the Case Western polymer program gives northeast Ohio two of the nation's top five.

In addition to their individual programs, the University of Akron and Case Western Reserve cooperate in EPIC (Edison Polymer Innovation Corporation), the consortium of the universities, polymer-related businesses, and economic development groups whose researchers seek solutions to practical problems. EPIC researchers, for instance, have contributed to development of such items as Joe Carter's Tack Tube, a foam rubber shell coated on the inside with a tacky polymer intended to replace pine tar as a grip enhancer on aluminum baseball bats.

Another stratum in northeast Ohio's polymer education-research base is the Advanced Liquid Crystalline Optical Materials Center at Kent State University. It includes UA and Case Western. Liquid crystals are used in laptop computers, high-resolution television screens, and switchable windows that become opaque, or frosted, with the flick of a switch and screen out heat and light. By attaching polymers to liquid crystals, researchers at the center are attempting to enhance the useful properties of each.

The rise of the phoenix has not gone unnoticed. Even people in unrelated industries have heard about it.

"If you show people in Tokyo a picture of the Polymer Science Building, I'm told they will know exactly where it is and what is done there," said Willard R. Holland, chairman of FirstEnergy Corporation, the Akron-based electric utility.

Polymer research, academic and industrial, has become the distinction carrying Akron into the next millennium. Many people, from the top of polymers' hierarchy to its rank and file, have contributed to assuring a future for Akron and its rubber legacy. "The recognition that Akron is now getting for successfully making that transition from an old-city rubber town to a bright, shining light in the world of high technology—I think the university played a major role in that," Bill Muse said.

In 1993, Andras Keller, professor emeritus of polymer science at Bristol University in England, came to Akron to serve as the Harold A. Morton Distinguished Visiting Professor of Polymer Science. He stayed at the Quaker Square Hilton and liked to explore the shops of Quaker Square. One day, a young store clerk asked Keller where he was from.

"England," he said.

"What do you do?"

"I'm a visiting professor at the University of Akron," Keller said.

"In what field?"

"In polymers."

"Oh!" the young woman said, "you must be a genius."

Keller told Frank Kelley that nowhere in the world—and he has been all over it—has he been made to feel as good about his profession as he has in Akron.

Keller's visiting professorship coincided with the University of Akron's adding Maurice Morton's name to the Institute of Polymer Science. Morton received many honors but this, he said, he would cherish most.

"It is a permanent reminder for people of where it all started," Morton said.

A reminder of what Akron was and is, of the men who put a glow on Akron's skyline as visible to a taxicab driver or store clerk as to an internationally famous polymer scientist.

"I believe one of the valuable things we've done," Kelley said, "is give this community back its pride."

26 The Changing of the Guard

ONCE, AKRON'S LEADERS came in extra-large, a size no longer available. These old Akron icons of action—the John S. Knights, Edwin J. Thomases, and Ben Maidenburgs—may have operated outside the public gaze, but their ways were no mystery. These men could be as subtle as a hammer lock. In the decades after World War II, when rubber was still king and its leaders were Akron royalty, decrees were as likely as broad-based decisions. The old leaders, Goodyear's Eddie Thomas and the other rubber company executives, and the *Beacon Journal*'s owner and editor Jack Knight and publisher Ben Maidenburg, wrapped the packages, tied them with ribbons, and handed them to the city they loved.

These were the power brokers to whom the community turned to settle strikes, rebuild downtown, attract business investment, and keep order in the city.

"We used to live in a kingdom," said Bill Jasso, former aide to Akron Mayor Don Plusquellic, "and it was easy to understand where the monarchs lived."

John S. Knight golfs at the Portage Country Club with Vice President Richard M. Nixon in 1959. (*Akron Beacon Journal*/Julius Greenfield)

They lived at Goodyear Tire and Rubber Company, at B. F. Goodrich Company, at Firestone Tire and Rubber Company, and at General Tire and Rubber. More than anywhere, however, the monarchs lived beneath the revolving *Beacon Journal* tower at Exchange and High streets.

Before his company went public on the New York Stock Exchange, in 1969, Jack Knight owned not only the *Beacon Journal* but also a growing group of Knight Newspapers. He had a kingdom and the power. When he wrote, Akron read and responded. When he spoke, often from a corner table at the Portage Country Club grillroom, men with political and corporate might hustled to carry out his grand schemes to improve Akron.

"No one would ever sit there except him," remembered John Ong, retired chairman of B. F. Goodrich. "He would get the chairmen of Goodyear, Goodrich, Firestone, and General and maybe one or two others, depending on the subject, and they'd sit down and say: 'Yes, this is something we need to do.' Then they'd decide: 'OK, you lead it, and the rest of us will support it.'"

"Their techniques might have been a little different in getting consensus," allowed Willard R. Holland, chief executive officer of FirstEnergy Corporation and chairman of Akron Tomorrow, a group of the city's current elite executives. It was a simpler time, but one fraught with potential abuse. But Ong, himself a civic leader of the first order, said leadership as practiced by Knight and Thomas isn't necessarily bad.

"They weren't arrogating power," Ong said. "A lot of good things came out of it. They were combining their influence to do good works and, generally, for reasons that they, at least, viewed as unselfish. They were acting in the interest of the community rather than the *Beacon Journal* or the Goodyear Tire and Rubber Company."

In the years since Knight held sway, Akron began to operate differently. Leaders emerged who recognized the need to build consensus, to be inclusive, and to be diverse, even though the process can be cumbersome and time-consuming. "Rather than three or four people making decisions—somebody from the *Beacon* and three or four people from the rubber industry—it is probably fifty to 100 people now," Mayor Plusquellic said.

Shortly before he died, in June, 1997, C. C. "Gibby" Gibson, a Goodyear vice president, the first executive director of the Akron Regional Development Board and president of the Knight Foundation, commented on the difference between leaders past and present. "In those days," Gibson said, "giants walked the earth. We will never replace Jack Knight, Eddie Thomas. . . . Today, giants no longer walk the earth."

Nothing illustrates the command of Jack Knight more convincingly than the story of how the Cascade One office tower came to be built. In 1966, the north end of South Main Street in downtown Akron had the look of a disappearing city. There, from a hole in the ground at the site of the former Quaker Oats factory, a parking garage took shape. One mayor, Ed Erickson, had started the project and another, John Ballard, would win the election because Erickson couldn't finish the job.

"We didn't have anything to put on top of it," Eddie Thomas said.

Knight approached his friend John Galbreath, the Columbus developer and

The Walgreens store at Howard and Bowery streets is being razed, in 1963, to make way for the Cascade parking garage. The view is looking north from the tenth floor of the Akron Savings and Loan Building. (*Akron Beacon Journal*/Ted Walls)

Beacon Journal president and editor John S. Knight clasps the hand of Columbus developer John Galbreath, seated beside Goodyear's Edwin J. Thomas at a Citizens for Progress event in 1966. Knight and Thomas were Akron's power brokers then, and the construction of the Cascade One office tower by Galbreath, Knight's friend, illustrated the newspaper owner's influence. (*Akron Beacon Journal*/Julius Greenfield)

fellow owner of thoroughbred racehorses, about topping off the parking garage with an office tower. Galbreath agreed with one condition: get the rubber companies to lease a floor each. So Knight invited civic and business leaders to the *Beacon Journal*. They met in a room used by the Knight Newspapers board of directors when it still met in Akron. Among those present was General Tire chairman Jerry O'Neil. He and the others were not strangers to this exercise of power.

"People put the arm on you," O'Neil said. "In this case, Jack Knight."

Knight urged these powerful men to support Cascade Plaza financially. O'Neil balked.

"Why should we rent space downtown?" O'Neil demanded.

"You're in Akron," Knight informed O'Neil angrily. "This is *your* town. It's where you made your money."

"Wait a minute," O'Neil retorted. "We do business all over the world at General Tire. We don't just do business in Akron. We don't owe our existence to Akron or anyone around here. Our shareholders are worldwide. It's our shareholders' money. I don't know why we should pay for a building that you people think it's smart to put up."

Knight huffed out of the room. O'Neil's argument rang hollow with a man who, since 1937, had been accumulating newspapers from the cusp of the Caribbean (*Miami Herald*) to the shores of the Great Lakes (*Detroit Free Press* and *Chicago Daily News*). Knight could have abandoned Akron as his empire expanded. He didn't, despite the fact that some in other communities nearly demanded it.

During an interview to determine whether Knight might be a worthy successor to the late *Chicago Daily News* publisher Frank Knox, attorney Laird Bell, an executor of the Knox estate, asked Knight: "Mr. Knight, don't you think the *Daily News* should be owned by Chicagoans?"

"I think it should," Knight replied, "provided they're qualified."

"Would you move to Chicago?" Bell asked.

"Akron is my home," Knight said. "I intend to keep it that way."

Jack Knight would own a house on Miami Beach and rent apartments in Detroit and Chicago, spending time in each city, with each newspaper. But Akron would always be home. O'Neil shared Knight's affection for their hometown and went along with propping up Cascade One. O'Neil's father had started General Tire, and his grandfather had built O'Neil's Department Stores. O'Neil believed his family had a responsibility to Akron to give back as well as take. No one was going to be able to lay failure of Cascade Plaza at the rubber companies' doorsteps.

Joining O'Neil to fill ten of Cascade One's twenty-four floors were Goodyear Chairman Russell DeYoung, who had replaced the retired Eddie Thomas, Firestone Chairman Raymond Firestone, Ohio Edison President D. Bruce Mansfield, First National Bank President Stanton Brightman, Akron-Dime Bank President Marion Richardson, and Knight. Some used their space. Some preferred to sublease it.

Goodrich was the only one of Akron's Big Four rubber companies that did not take a floor. Goodrich already occupied new space downtown. In 1964, the company had contributed nearly $4 million to the Opportunity Park project at the south end of Main. The project included the company's new world headquarters. Others, however, such as city officials, did not escape the pressure of Knight and Thomas.

"When I walked into the [meeting] room," former Mayor Ballard recalled, "Eddie Thomas was making a speech. He said: We want *everyone* to take a floor. Now, Mayor, the city will take a floor, won't it?'

Cascade One, the linchpin of Cascade Plaza in downtown Akron, was above ground and headed skyward in this December 1967 photo. Citizens for Progress, headed by *Beacon Journal* editor John S. Knight, persuaded rubber companies to lease floors in the project. (*Akron Beacon Journal*)

The face of downtown
Akron changes as the Cas-
cade One building, known
as the Akron Center building during the construc-
tion phase, takes shape in
1968. *(Akron Beacon Journal)*

"I said: 'Well, yes. The city will take a floor.'"

Ballard smiled at his naiveté. He was new on the job.

"I had no business saying that," he admitted. Only the City Council can make such a commitment. "I went back to the council and said: 'Now look, you turkeys, here was the situation. I couldn't say no.'"

Council members, in the end, went along. What choice did they have?

"When you look back on things community-wide that ran well, you get back to Cascade One," said John Frank, who retired at the end of 1997 as councilman for Akron's Ward 8. "You would never have had that building if not for Eddie Thomas, Jack Knight, the rubber companies, the banks. It basically got things moving . . . in Akron." The plaza filled up, with the Cascade Three office building and the Cascade Holiday Inn. Jack Knight had moved, and Akron shook—with a little help from Eddie Thomas.

Jack Knight and Eddie Thomas didn't begin their runs in Akron as chums. Thomas knew of Knight, who had played end on Central High's undefeated state championship football team of 1913. But Knight was four years older, so theirs was mostly a distant acquaintance until 1936 when, in troubled times, their paths converged.

Knight had come into his inheritance. With the death of his father, C. L., in 1933, Jack found himself the editor and owner of the *Beacon Journal* as well as a pile of debts. The Great Depression gripped Akron. Thomas, son of a postal worker, had begun his career at Goodyear after graduating, in 1916, from Central High. In 1936, Goodyear workers were organizing, striking, and demanding a larger share of the rubber pie. The city was about to explode with violence. Former Mayor C. Nelson Sparks went on the radio and denounced the "radicals and communists" behind the trouble and suggested that armed citizens might meet them in the streets.

In his corner office on the third floor of the *Beacon Journal*, Jack Knight began pounding out a front-page editorial on his typewriter. He scorched Sparks for his rabble-rousing and urged a cooler response. Then, with *Beacon Journal* business manager Jack Barry, Knight drove out East Market Street to Goodyear. They were met by President P. W. Litchfield and Thomas, then a vice president. "Let's get this thing settled," Knight said. "The town's a powder keg. Damn it, we're on the verge of a civil war."

"Jack," Thomas said, "nobody wants this strike settled more than we do. It's new to us. There are a lot of issues at stake. You can't settle them overnight."

"At least get started," Knight said.

"Don't pressure us!" Thomas retorted, according to Knight biographer Charles Whited. "You're sitting there comfortable as hell at your *Beacon Journal* and not helping very much. We can't give the company away, and we've got long-term relationships to think about. You go back and run your *Beacon Journal*, and we'll run Goodyear."

It was the beginning of a beautiful friendship. Knight would run the *Beacon Journal*. Thomas would run Goodyear until his retirement in 1964. And together, they would run Akron. They lunched together at the Mayflower Hotel in the Mayflower Club, which Jack Knight and three others founded, in 1931, when they had a falling out with the Akron City Club. They did community and professional business together, Thomas becoming, at Jack's invitation, the first non-newspaper industry person to serve on the Knight Newspapers board of directors. They played together, both of them golf champions at Portage Country Club.

"You'd hear all these stories about how Mr. Thomas and Mr. Knight would differ in opinion and still remain fast friends," said Dr. James Mercer, Thomas's son-in-law.

In 1956, someone mailed a death threat to Knight when he was in Miami for the winter. The writer believed Knight's *Miami Herald* was stealing the writer's ideas and using them in editorials. It didn't take police long to arrest—and hospitalize—the letter writer. A telegram arrived for Knight not long after. It read:

I HEAR SOMEONE HAS BEEN THREATENING YOUR LIFE. I'VE HAD THE SAME IDEA, WHEN YOU MISSED A TWO-FOOT PUTT. — EDDIE.

Knight experienced a series of devastating personal tragedies. His first wife, Katherine, died of a brain tumor in 1929. He suffered through that loss alone. But for the polio that crippled his son Landon, the war that killed his son John S. Jr., the brain tumor that ended the life of his son Frank, the deaths of his second wife, Beryl, and his last wife, Betty, both Thomas and Maidenburg were there for Knight as much as anyone can be in another person's time of loss.

The worst of the relentless bad times descended on Jack Knight on the morning of December 8, 1975. Eddie Thomas's telephone rang. The caller was *Philadelphia Inquirer* editor Gene Roberts, informing Thomas that Jack Knight's grandson, John S. Knight III, had been murdered. Johnny never knew his father, who died in battle two weeks before World War II ended in Europe and two weeks before Johnny was born in Columbus, Georgia. Jack Knight was devoted to the boy and showered him with affection. Knight gave Johnny the best schooling; Gibby Gibson pulled strings to get Johnny into Harvard University. Knight drew his grandson into the business. Johnny had just won a promotion to Page One editor of the *Philadelphia Daily News* at the time of his slaying.

Roberts wanted Thomas to tell Jack Knight the news.

"But Jack's not even here in Akron," Thomas told Roberts, according to Knight biographer Whited. "I think he's somewhere in Connecticut. . . . Besides, I'm not sure I'm the right person to tell him this. Shouldn't his brother [Jim] do it?"

"We've talked about it, Eddie, and you're the logical man," Roberts insisted. "Nobody's closer to Jack. Nobody can do it better."

When Thomas reached his friend by telephone, he told him the awful news straightaway.

"Jack," Eddie said, "I have a report from Philadelphia that Johnny was murdered last night. I don't have too many of the details yet. I'm sorry to have to call you and tell you."

Seconds of silence ticked away until they had turned into a minute. When he finally spoke, Jack Knight responded with a question that was no question: "Life is rough, isn't it?"

During Akron's tough times, Jack Knight was always on the spot. He lifted the city with his ideas, his money, and his example. But mostly, he influenced the community through his editorials. In 1954, rubber company strikes again rocked Akron. Goodyear workers, twenty-three thousand of them in the first nationwide action against the company, had been out for fifty-two days; twenty-two thousand Firestone workers for twenty-four days. Knight worried that the strikes were tarnishing Akron's image, which, without decisive action, might never recover sufficiently to make it attractive to other companies. Back at his typewriter, Knight produced one of his most famous Akron editorials—"Akron, Let's Go!"—which was published on the front page of the *Beacon Journal* on August 31, 1954.

Knight sought comment and action. Mayor Leo Berg responded with the notion of a group to promote Akron as a great place to do business. The group was known as the Area Development Committee, a forerunner of today's Akron Regional Development Board. Knight was the man who brought Berg's notion to fruition, however. In a conference room at the downtown O'Neil's store, Knight met with O'Neil's President Lincoln Gries, Polsky's President E. D. Warner, George Wilson of the Akron Chamber of Commerce, who would serve as the new committee's executive assistant, and others. "They were trying to decide how to

raise money to start this thing," recalled Wilson, "and they asked me." Wilson didn't know how; Knight did.

"There are five of us here [in addition to Wilson]," Knight said. "Let's each put in $5,000 to get this thing started." And each man, on behalf of his company, anted up. Through the offices of the ADC, Summit County landed the Chrysler Stamping Plant in Twinsburg and General Motors' Terex plant in Hudson.

Ben Maidenburg had no seat on the ADC at its formation. But over time, Maidenburg became Knight's voice on the committee. George Wilson traveled with Maidenburg as the ADC recruited businesses in the 1950s. "I think Ben and I traveled at least 100,000 miles a year calling on industries," Wilson said. "Ben would go anywhere if there was a sniff of a plant that had some jobs."

In the newsroom, Maidenburg, who was sandpaper on the outside and marshmallow underneath, scored his points with bluster. In the more civilized setting of business courtship, he could be smoothly persuasive. "He was one of the greatest boosters of Akron the city has ever had and one of my very closest friends," said Richard Buchholzer, developer of Chapel Hill and Rolling Acres malls and a former chairman of the Akron Regional Development Board. "The things they did

Ohio National Guard troops line Wooster Avenue, on July 18, 1968, in response to a weeklong civil disturbance in the Wooster Avenue area of Akron that had brought Ohio National Guard troops and Akron police into the area to keep the peace. (*Akron Beacon Journal*/Lewis Henderson)

[Knight and Maidenburg] were monumental, and they never sought credit for them."

Knight never thought he was doing anything unusual. The tradition of civic boosterism and industrial recruitment ran through Akron as surely as the Portage Path that Native Americans had used to traverse the terrain. "Way back in 1870," he was reminding people in a 1954 editorial, "a little folder put out by the then Board of Trade attracted Dr. B. F. Goodrich to the city and led to the establishment of a small rubber plant which was the forerunner of today's great industry."

In 1977, at age eighty-three, Jack Knight still was advocating strong leadership for the city: "I don't care who runs Akron. Just so somebody runs it. It's too important to be left alone."

Knight groomed his man, Maidenburg, in that tradition. As the *Beacon Journal*'s representative on the Area Development Committee, Maidenburg didn't merely go after new jobs for Akron. He sought to preserve old ones and to make them better, even serving as a mediator in labor negotiations. Of course, not everyone wanted Maidenburg's intervention, nor did everyone agree with his news policies. Superior Mold Company in Munroe Falls, for one, rejected his help during a five-month strike in 1961. And after the *Beacon Journal* ran a story about mixed-race children in 1970, a bomb exploded in Maidenburg's garage. The next year, the local organizer of the neo-Nazi White People's Socialist Party placed a bomb on Maidenburg's porch. This one, however, didn't go off.

In July 1968, Maidenburg thrust himself into the vortex of a weeklong civil disturbance that had brought Ohio National Guard troops and Akron police into the Wooster-Hawkins area to try to keep the peace and enforce a curfew.

Tensions came close to boiling over on Tuesday, July 23, 1968, a day of suffocating heat. Leaders of Wooster-Hawkins's predominantly African-American community gathered at Homell Calhoun's record shop on Wooster Avenue. They formed an eleven-man committee, led by John Roberts, a Boilermakers union official, and got word to Maidenburg, assistant news editor Al Fitzpatrick, and others at the *Beacon Journal* that they wanted to meet with Mayor Ballard before the situation worsened. Maidenburg arranged a meeting for seven that evening in the City-County Safety Building. Roberts and his committee sat down with Ballard, Police Chief Harry Whiddon, Summit County Sheriff Robert Campbell, Major General Sylvester DelCorso, head of the Ohio National Guard, and other city officials. George Hawthorne, a young Urban League representative, complained that the 10:00 PM curfew had not been enforced equally, that white citizens could move freely in areas outside Wooster-Hawkins.

"Do you know what it's like on the Avenue?" Hawthorne asked. He described families cooped up in "an airless cubicle where there is the smell of urine and those little animals we call roaches."

"Mayor," Hawthorne continued, "you tell 'em to go in on a ninety-degree night, and you've got hell on your hands. You haven't had a riot on your hands. You're pushing for it, but you haven't seen it yet."

Vernon Odom, the late executive director of the Urban League, reinforced Hawthorne's opinion. "We need a victory tonight," Odom said. "It might seem a little thing to you, but it's big to us in terms of our leadership. . . . We've got a power struggle on Wooster Avenue between the militants and the peace-loving people. If we fail and have to go back to our homes, we're going to have to lock our own doors."

Ballard wanted to send the leaders back into their community without a firm deal. Then came word, from Chief Whiddon, that violence had erupted in Cleveland. "I think we'd better go along as planned and effect the curfew," Ballard said.

What happened next was quintessential Maidenburg. He rose, an imposing figure—six-foot-four, he once tipped the scales at 280 pounds—and took center stage in the middle of the room. "I think these people are asking for a chance to prove they can end this thing," he argued. "If they can't do it, they'll be the first to admit it. The city has nothing to lose by giving them a chance. If it works, we've given them a victory. If they fail, they'll never again be able to come back here."

Maidenburg then addressed the African-American leaders directly. "If all you people who say you will do this will stand up and promise you will do it, by God, I say: Let's do it!" Every African-American leader rose to stand with Maidenburg. Ballard lifted the curfew. It was 9:10 PM. The Wooster-Hawkins leaders had fifty minutes to make themselves, their community, and Maidenburg look good. They did.

Ten years later, Bill Jasso did a retrospective on the disturbance as a reporter for WHLO radio. "I think that John Ballard has never forgotten that night I took over the city," Maidenburg told Jasso. "I thought the people should be given an opportunity to settle the problem in their neighborhood without having soldiers from the outside."

Leadership in Akron differs in 1997, in part because the large, powerful rubber companies closed their shops and, with the exception of Goodyear, moved their headquarters elsewhere. Leadership also differs because society has changed—more people demand to be heard. No one rules in Akron now. And everyone rules.

"We don't respond well to monarchy anymore," Jasso said. "Absent a monarchy, leadership is diverse, diffuse, scattered, inefficient—but more fair."

Among the first rank of 1997 leaders, there are those who swear that lawyer, industrialist, and developer David Brennan has claimed he runs Akron. Brennan indeed has been behind several 1990s downtown projects, such as the Canal Park baseball stadium and the Main Place office building. Former Councilman John Frank acknowledged that Brennan holds a position of prominence, but Frank does not believe Brennan has achieved—or deserves—the stature of Knight and Thomas.

"In the past, things were done quietly, behind the scenes," Frank said. "You didn't have a Dave Brennan making himself the self-appointed leader of the community. . . . He saw a vacuum, and he was smart. No one challenged him."

In 1993, when Brennan was one of nine founders of Akron Tomorrow, he lamented that times have changed. "This is nothing like the days when John S. Knight, E. J. Thomas, the rubber company chiefs, and a few others ran things," he said. "What they said went, and no one questioned them because they got things done."

Akron no longer operates that way, and the community is better for it, said *Beacon Journal* publisher John Dotson, who came to town in 1992. But long before Dotson arrived, *Beacon Journal* executives had stopped playing such audacious roles in public policy issues. In 1973, two years before Maidenburg retired as publisher, Mark Ethridge Jr. became the *Beacon Journal*'s editor. Ethridge sought to put an end to what he called the newspaper's civic "puffery."

"Ben, with the best of intentions, has run the paper as a shill for the community," Ethridge declared, pledging he would not do the same. Ethridge lasted three years. His replacement, the late Paul Poorman, found some middle ground so as not to exacerbate a growing void in leadership.

"Paul Poorman was always very enthusiastic," said former Goodyear Chairman Charles J. Pilliod, "but he didn't want it known too much that the *Beacon* was involved. He felt that was not his position—but he could come in with ideas." Poorman and Pilliod, for example, were prime movers behind the 1979 formation of the Akron Priority Group, an organization of high-powered business executives that would push important city projects, such as the rebuilding of downtown. "I tried to get Paul to serve on [Akron Priority Group]," Pilliod said, "but he thought that would be the wrong thing for him to do."

Dale Allen, who succeeded Poorman, lowered the *Beacon*'s profile even more. Interviewed in 1990 for a *Beacon* magazine article on Akron leadership, Allen said: "I don't know of any newspaper anywhere that can play the kind of role that Jack

Knight did. I don't know if they even want to. If journalists join in the running of the city, there's no way they can objectively report on the city. A city with an independent newspaper is better served than one where the paper is in bed with the leaders."

When Dotson became publisher, he met with groups and individuals to find out what they wanted from the newspaper. He learned that some community members still expected the *Beacon* to provide leadership. "As a result," Dotson said, "the paper is more thoroughly involved in the community now than I think it has been in the recent past. After those meetings with leaders and after talking with Dale Allen and [Associate Editor] David Cooper, I think we have pushed into the community in a rather strong way. . . . I know it was one of the reasons we undertook Coming Together."

Coming Together, a *Beacon Journal*-inspired but community-run effort to find common ground among the city's races, grew from a reporting project that examined ways in which the city had become divided over the years. Additionally, Dotson is a member of numerous community groups, including Akron Tomorrow. But Dotson would never return to the old-style leadership. He couldn't, even if he wanted to.

"Jack Knight was an owner," he said. "Ben Maidenburg was working for an owner. I am, essentially, a corporate executive. I work for Knight-Ridder. I don't have the resources of Jack Knight. I can't operate like an owner. Also, Ben Maidenburg was operating as Jack Knight's man—and that was very different. That's not to say I'm not involved. It's just a very different time."

In Akron's army of new leaders, there are many enlisted men and women, a few officers, but none of general rank. Instead of hometown boys Thomas, De-Young, or Pilliod running Goodyear, for example, the company is in the hands of a truly global CEO. Samir Gibara was born in Egypt and gained his business experience worldwide. His interest in his adopted home of Akron impresses such old-line leaders as Barbara Hiney, who helped to get passed Akron's first income tax, ran Goals for Greater Akron, and is a member of the Summa Health System board of trustees.

"I think he is a charming, interesting, brilliant man," Hiney said of Gibara. "I really do think it is amazing he has taken the interest he does in the community."

Still, Hiney recognizes the ever-shifting nature of Akron leadership. She is especially aware that few, if any, women are gaining prominence. She used to be able to tick off the most important women in the area: Mabel Riedinger on the Akron Board of Education, Frances McGovern in the state legislature, Frances Seiberling Buchholzer, the first woman to direct a state agency (Department of Natural Resources).

"I have breakfast every week with a group of women," Hiney said, "and I asked them who they thought were powerful women in Akron now. There was dead silence."

In some instances, it has been difficult to identify any leaders. In 1986, outside experts evaluating the University of Akron's Center for Urban Studies wanted to talk to the community leaders. "The problem was," said James Shanahan, the center's director, "they couldn't find it. . . . There was something like a vacuum at the top."

There are, however, plenty of foot soldiers, grass-roots leaders who serve on countless civic organizations and make things happen without ever winning a field commission. "Plain people" are running Akron, "and running it pretty well," Gibby Gibson said.

Akron Ward 3 Councilman Marco Sommerville is a graduate of Leadership Akron. Akron Regional Development Board Chairman Richard C. "Rick" Fedorovich, the current treasurer of the Leadership Akron board of trustees, also is a graduate. "I'm by far the youngest person who has been chairman of ARDB," said Fedorovich, forty-five, managing partner of Bober, Markey and Company, an accounting firm, "and I am one of the first service providers to be chairman. I think that is another witness for the transition. Clearly, my economic resources, what I can bring to bear, are not going to make a bit of difference in this community. My power is leveraged off of other people."

Sommerville feels the same way. "[What] I've tried to do is tie into people, like Vern Odom did," Sommerville said. "I try to tie into people who have the power in hopes that they will share some of their power with me. I think the mayor has done that."

Though extra-large leadership may be a stretch even for Don Plusquellic, Akron's mayor has demonstrated over the last decade throwback qualities that have reminded some observers of the outsized ghosts of Knight, Thomas, and Maidenburg. "Plusquellic owns the town, and I think he has earned the right to own it," said George Wilson, the state's first economic development director. "He's doing things, making this town look a lot better."

In a new day of more diffuse, diverse leadership, mayors such as Plusquellic use new vehicles, including public funding, to accomplish projects such as the Canal Park baseball stadium. "[Government] is the gorilla in the living room," said Justin Rogers, retired chief executive of Ohio Edison Company, "and in recent years Don Plusquellic has had a great deal to do with the community respect of the capability of municipal government."

Gary Gappert, the late director of the Institute of Futures Studies and Research at the University of Akron, said the com-

Akron City Councilman Marco Sommerville, shown here in his funeral home, is a modern-day leader who cannot use the methods employed by his predecessors. He tries to form links with others in hopes they'll share some of their power. (*Akron Beacon Journal*/Jocelyn Williams)

munity no longer anoints its more visible leaders from the ranks of the home-grown. "The city began to hire carpetbaggers. It started, I think, with John Nevin" at Firestone. But Tom Sawyer, former Akron mayor who now represents the area in Congress, said outsiders bring "a wonderful third dimension to leadership," particularly if they leverage their success in Akron into greater success elsewhere. For years, Sawyer said, Akron relied heavily on talent nurtured within its boundaries and on others who moved to the city and remained because in rubber, certainly, and in banking, to a lesser degree, Akron was considered the best a person could do.

Many people cite former University of Akron President William V. Muse, who now is president of Auburn University in Alabama, as the standard by which pass-through leaders should be judged. When Muse came to town, he realized quickly that Akron was floundering. "Akron was still waiting for Eddie Thomas and Jack Knight to come [back] and tell it what to do," he said. Yet he knew he should not assume the leadership mantle too boldly or hastily. "The last thing any community wants to hear is some guy coming from the outside who has all the answers."

Muse studied his new home—its people, its history, its social and civic structures—and concluded that "the university could and should play a role in the redevelopment and transformation of the city." One vehicle already was on the drawing board, a concept of former UA President Dominic Guzzetta and former Mayor Roy Ray: Span the Tracks. This would move the university physically deeper into the heart of downtown, with a new College of Business Administration Building at Broadway and University Avenue and the conversion of the former Polsky's department store building on South Main into university offices.

Muse helped not only to change a city but also to plant the seed of a new attitude toward newcomers who would lead if only they could overcome native mistrust. "One of the real problems of this town comes from its unwillingness to accept people from the outside," former *Beacon Journal* editor Dale Allen said in 1990. Allen came to Akron from Philadelphia in 1979.

But some nonnatives manage to break down the barriers to acceptance, whether real or imagined. Howard Flood, for example, spent much of his storied banking career in Akron and was recognized for his community service, in 1996, with the Bert A. Polsky Humanitarian Award, named for the former department store president. At the award ceremony, the *Beacon Journal*'s John Dotson described Flood as "a paradigm of an Akron community leader" who helped guide nearly every positive step for the city over the past thirteen years. Will Holland joined Ohio Edison (which changed its name, in 1997, to FirstEnergy) in 1991. He came from Detroit. In 1997, he was the company's chairman and chairman of Akron Tomorrow, Howard Flood's handpicked successor.

"From a personal standpoint," Holland said, "my wife and I have found this community to be very open and receptive. It's looking for leadership skills. One of the biggest things we have had to learn is how to say no."

At Leadership Akron retreats, participants often try to identify the up-and-coming movers and shakers. The late Paul Poorman, borrowing from Henry Ford, was fond of this pronouncement: "Asking who should be a leader is like asking who should sing tenor. Tenors sing tenor."

And leaders lead.

John Ong's impeccable credentials include leadership in such recent downtown projects as Inventure Place, home of the National Inventors Hall of Fame. When asked to talk about leaders and leadership, Ong philosophized: "Involvement is both conscious and evolutionary. The evolutionary aspect is that in a small city like Akron, senior executives of corporations are looked to to furnish leadership in a variety of civic and cultural and human welfare activities. That's just the way our society is organized, and I think it is a good way. When you are called upon, you want to do this, unless you are a really constipated sort of person."

"Ong is unique among Akron leaders," said attorney David Lieberth, who was instrumental in landing the National Inventors Hall of Fame for Akron. "Not only did he lead a traditional Akron company, but he also has been involved in so much of the community. He brought Inventure Place to fruition. Nobody else could have done it. Others started it, well-meaning volunteers. He finished the job."

To replace an Ong, much less the extra-large ghosts, requires a village of leaders and even institutions. Councilman John Frank suggests that area foundations are playing as great a leadership role in Akron as any individual. The GAR Foundation and the Knight Foundation, now headquartered in Miami, are throwing major support behind the Summit Education Initiative, which will function as a clearinghouse for private donations to schools. From Akron's foundations may emerge the next generation of women leaders, Linda Urda of the GAR Foundation and Jody Bacon of the Akron Community Foundation.

Houses of worship probably will always be important sources of guidance for the Akron community. But, again, the leadership will be shared rather than concentrated in the hands of one charismatic preacher. Once, for example, the Reverend Dallas Billington stood before thousands at the Akron Baptist Temple and directed his congregation how to vote on school levies.

John Ong, chairman of the B.F. Goodrich company in 1985. Ong is described as a leader of the first order, one who not only led his company, but was also involved in his community. *(Akron Beacon Journal)*

"He was a Billy Sunday-type preacher who made dramatic statements from the pulpit," said the Reverend Knute Larson, senior pastor at the Chapel, the largest church in Akron. "The pulpit was a place to speak for social issues. They were entrepreneurial guys who didn't ask anybody what they should say from the pulpit." Larsen practices a very different style of leadership. "Our founder, Carl Burnham, wouldn't have gathered a leadership team around him like I do," Larsen said.

In such sharing of leadership, futurist Gary Gappert found tomorrow's promise for Akron. Gappert envisioned the presence of a thousand persons, ordinary people populating ordinary neighborhoods but doing extraordinary things, large and small. "It takes not a thousand points of light but a thousand points of vision," Gappert said. "You have to get people to become visionaries in their own lives and activities."

Gappert spoke to visiting and local visionaries at the World Vinyl Forum in 1997, invoking poet Carl Sandburg: "The past is the sun gone down. The future is the sky, the sky of opportunities, the sky of tomorrow."

"We need leaders," Gappert said, "who talk about a sky of opportunities, a sky of tomorrow."

27 Life after Rubber

WHEN THE TIRE PLANTS fell silent and Akron lost its title as Rubber Capital of the World, the voices of the city did not die. Rubber workers, their sons and daughters, grandsons and granddaughters, have talked to one another, have shared their stories, as if the stories, by the telling and retelling of them, would preserve the way it was, cast light on the way it is, and give notice to the way it could be.

These storytellers wanted their stories to live on, pressed onto the pages of a newspaper or a book or between the leaves of the family Bible. Their stories became petals from a wedding bouquet, locks of a child's hair, the perfect report card, tucked away to be rediscovered and examined by another generation. They told not only what happened to rubber in Akron but also why. More important, they shared what happened to them, to their families, to their neighborhoods and city. One story triggered another. The story well was bottomless, its truths as clear as pure water. They had so much to remember, so much to share, so much that should not be forgotten.

Don Hicks, lawyer and amateur historian, had listened to the stories of his friend, Marie Douglas. She grew up in a family that lived in a small house on the grounds of Harbel Manor, where her father worked as an assistant to Harvey Firestone Sr., founder of Firestone Tire and Rubber Company. Her father sometimes drove Firestone on vacations. Marie went with him. She met Harvey Sr.'s famous camping companions: Thomas Edison, Henry Ford, and John Burroughs. She was like one of the Firestone children. Her many memories made her a human reservoir of personal and Akron history.

Hicks had thought many times of sitting with Marie, turning on a tape recorder, and asking her to talk once again about her Rubber City memories, because for every story that became a part of *Wheels of Fortune*, there are dozens more like Marie's that remain unrecorded. They could be lost if someone does not record and save them, even if it is a singular exercise, for one family only.

There are tens of thousands of stories in the Rubber City. And now people are talking to one another instead of at one another, as so often was the case when rubber management and labor stood hard nose to hard nose and refused to be the first to blink. Now both sides say they should have postured less and listened more, that they missed those moments when they could have changed Akron as the world was changing, growing smaller, more competitive.

Change, though inevitable, is frightening. Most of the rubber companies that drove Akron's economy for nearly a century are now under foreign ownership—and based somewhere else. Akron factories have crumbled before the wrecker's ball. Still other buildings stand virtually abandoned, awaiting an uncertain future. And, while struggling with the feeling that the apocalypse had come, Akron has had to ask itself important questions about its own future:

What has the city learned?

What building blocks does it have?

What does it build now, and are these the right blocks?

So much has happened since Akron received its city charter in 1836. It dug canals and built boats, produced farm machinery, manufactured clay products and sewer line products, and made flour and oats. Then, Benjamin Franklin Goodrich opened his rubber shop in 1870, followed by F. A. and Charlie Seiberling with Goodyear in 1898, Harvey Firestone Sr. in 1900, and Bill O'Neil with General Tire in 1915. And rubber was king in Akron for close to a century before radial technology, complacent management, restrictive union work rules, six-hour shifts, inefficient multistory plants, and triennial strikes made it easier, and more desirable, to shut down the plants here and send the work somewhere else.

Akron's first rubber company, Goodrich, was the first to get out of the business and the first to leave town, a victim of the marketing muscle of its larger competitors and of its own unwillingness to commit to tires. By the mid-1980s, Goodrich had shut down all Akron production and moved its headquarters first to Bath Township and then to Richfield. Its chairman, John Ong, sold off the tire unit to concentrate on Goodrich's specialty chemical and aerospace businesses.

"He made it the best at what it was best able to become," said an admiring U.S. Representative Tom Sawyer, Democrat from Akron. "He genuinely reinvented the company, and did so in the face of some pretty nasty criticism."

By this time, Akron's other rubber companies had halted most local production as well, yet Akron kept trading off its reputation as the Rubber Capital of the World. After all, Akron was still the headquarters of Firestone, Goodyear, General

Tire, and Uniroyal Goodrich. And in some ways, the city was better off. Labor relations were relatively peaceful, if for no other reason than all the plant closings had reduced the ranks of the United Rubber Workers union. The air was clean, the professional base solid and prosperous.

Akron's white-collar jobs, however, soon became a rare commodity in a wrenching, industrywide consolidation and a flurry of foreign takeovers. Bridgestone of Japan took over Firestone. Michelin of France bought Uniroyal Goodrich, and Continental of Germany bought General Tire. The foreign companies had reason to leave Akron and all its baggage far behind. Akron did not exactly embrace its newcomers. The United Rubber Workers kept xenophobic signs posted, warning visitors not to park their foreign cars in union lots. Facing pettiness and, occasionally, downright hostility, the new parents moved most Akron operations to the more cooperative, labor-friendly climate of the South, beginning with Bridgestone/Firestone's move to Nashville, Tennessee.

But the rubber companies could not take away the city's core competency or the surviving symbols of its heritage. Akron's polymer knowledge is more than tread-deep—indeed, rubber was the first polymer. The departures would not prevent the city from determining its future by building on its past strengths. "Our intellectual legacy," Goodyear Chairman Samir Gibara called it.

Even as Bridgestone/Firestone removed its headquarters, the company acknowledged Akron's place as a center of polymer knowledge by maintaining and later expanding research and racing operations here. The machinists at McNeil and NRM make the tire-building machines being exported to Debica, Goodyear's Polish acquisition. The workers at Akromold, Superior Mold and Die Company, and many other shops make the molds that form all manner of objects found in our houses, our cars, our businesses. The color concentrate producers at Americhem put the color into the thermoplastics that end up on the dashboards and elsewhere in autos.

At the same time, Akron has changed dramatically. Its economy is more diversified, its employment base is shifting. Goodyear, with forty-seven hundred workers, is still Akron's leading employer. But today, it is followed by Summa Health System, with 3,850 employees, and Summit County government, with 3,470, rather than by other rubber companies. Goodyear will probably never build another full-scale plant in Akron, but it is expanding its technical center by eighty jobs for engineers and scientists. Those professional positions, Gibara said, more than make up for the elimination of 150 bias-ply race tire jobs that have gone to Chile.

Still, the Chile decision revived suspicion in a community all too familiar with, and lacerated by, plant closings, downsizings, outsourcing, and every other soft euphemism for the harsh reality of job loss. Would radial race tire jobs be the next to go? How about Goodyear's headquarters? Gibara, a native of Egypt who received his education and much of his business experience abroad, learned to field such questions adroitly. "The community and our industry have gone through a major trauma," he said. "So we are reacting like anyone would react who has been traumatized."

In 1996, Gibara spoke at Wingfoot Lake Park to kick off the company's United Way drive. The first question was about the possible sale of the park, which

Goodyear opened as a recreational facility for employees and their families in 1970. The sale of the park has been rumored ever since Sir James Goldsmith raided Goodyear, in 1986, and the company sold off several assets, including its jewel, Goodyear Aerospace, to pay off debt. Gibara obligingly quelled the Wingfoot Lake rumor. The employee park survived the tough years, a testament to Goodyear's benign paternalism and community commitment. To date, it has attracted three million visitors. When Stanley Gault brought the *Spirit of Akron* blimp back to Wingfoot Lake shortly after he took the helm of Goodyear, in 1991, the wounded community swelled with approval.

Gault arrived in a city that no longer was the capital of anything to guide a company that had fallen from number one to number three in the world. From his experiences at Goodyear and, before that, Rubbermaid, another of the region's major polymer companies, Gault had a dual appreciation of the industry's grip on the community and its citizens. Now retired, he believes Akron will emerge as "the center of excellence in polymers," with Goodyear's research and development operations its underpinning and the University of Akron's College of Polymer Science and Polymer Engineering its crown. In 1997, the university's polymer science program was ranked second in the nation; students from all over the world begged for admission. Dean Frank Kelley elevated the college's reputation by recruiting the best and brightest faculty members and by soliciting funds for their salaries and for top-echelon research. University President William Muse saw that

Landmark Plastic Corporation employee Carmelita Stivers works at the thermoforming inspection end of a machine that produces horticultural plant containers. For years, Akron city officials had tried to get the big rubber companies interested in a site near the Akron Fulton International Airport. Landmark chose the site and built the largest industrial plant in Akron in the last twenty-five years. (*Akron Beacon Journal*/Paul Tople)

Kelley's faculty had a new, state-of-the-art facility to practice and teach polymer science and engineering. And when the glassy twin towers of the university's new Polymer Science Building pierced the sky, in 1991, the greater community shared in Kelley and Muse's pride. The structure was downtown's first new building in nearly a decade, as well as the embodiment of Akron's primary hope for the future.

During its rubber days, Akron was sometimes accused of failing to put a premium on education. Gary Gappert, the late director of the Institute of Futures Studies and Research at the University of Akron, said Akron had "a small corporate elite, a large blue-collar labor force, and a thin middle class."

In "It's the Polymers! Stupid," a 1996 academic paper, Gappert wrote: "For almost two generations, there was a substantial brain drain because of the lack of a substantial number of professional job opportunities. It was easier for a high school dropout to get a job punching out tires at a factory than for college graduates to return to Akron and obtain an appropriate professional opportunity."

Jim Walker once worked at Goodyear as a pipe fitter. He went on to earn a master's degree and teach at Jackson High School. Walker reengineered himself before the paradigm shift in the rubber industry. This battle-scarred veteran of change tells his students and other young people this: "Become one of Montaigne's capable persons." Michel de Montaigne, the sixteenth-century essayist, believed that in a world of change, the only thing a person could know fully was himself. If people knew themselves and became "capable," they could learn new things—in other words, change with the world.

"You have to have enough fundamental skills that you can be retrained every five to seven years," Walker suggested.

If Akron's future is polymers, however, a variety of skill sets may never be necessary. Akron and northeast Ohio now have more polymer-related jobs than any state: 17,300. In 1994, one of the flowers of the polymer industry, Landmark Plastic Corporation, sprang up in a swale off Kelly Avenue in southeast Akron. Founded in 1984 by Leo Merzweiler and his son, Robert, Landmark had grown fast and strong. The company, a maker of products used by the horticultural industry, needed a new headquarters and plant for its two hundred employees. In a deliciously ironic move, Landmark selected the Akron Fulton International Airport area—one rubber company after another had rejected that location for a new, modern, single-story tire plant.

"We'd have torn the airport down," former Akron mayor and current state senator Roy Ray said. "We were always offering the airport. . . . We kept telling Goodyear, Firestone, Goodrich, General, Uniroyal, anyone who wanted to come in: We'll put in sewer and water. Throw in a rail spur. We'll de-annex. Give it to Green. We'll do anything. Just build a plant out there."

No rubber company did. It took a new polymer company, Landmark, to build the largest industrial plant in Akron in the last twenty-five years: two hundred thousand square feet on fifty-five acres.

The abandoned interior of what would become the Advanced Elastomer Systems headquarters stands in silent neglect prior to its renovation. In this building, once owned by B.F. Goodrich, workers had made products ranging from rubber bands to America's first space suits. (*Akron Beacon Journal*/Ed Suba, Jr.)

"Some people say: 'Yeah, but those jobs don't pay that much,'" Akron Mayor Don Plusquellic said. "Maybe they don't—now. But I'm sure when Benjamin Franklin Goodrich opened his shop, he didn't start with a 328-page union contract that said: 'We're going to pay this, that, and the other thing.' Companies start small. Industries start small."

Even comparative strangers to Akron have heard rubber's ghosts, their messages, their lessons. From a willingness to listen came the preservation and transition of one of the city's most enduring symbols—the rubber shop. Once, the B. F. Goodrich complex on South Main Street encompassed sixty buildings with seventy-five acres of space, a city within the city. Some of the complex suffered the wrecking ball. Some buildings stand empty. But much of the complex has been turned into Canal Place. Law offices occupy former Goodrich executive suites. Embryonic businesses gain strength in the city's incubator. Alan Robbins's Plastic Lumber Company puts rubber's intellectual legacy—polymer technology—to use in building outdoor furniture. The Spaghetti Warehouse pulls in diners without lunch pails.

Most visible, though, has been the regeneration of Goodrich Building 41 for the headquarters, labs, and production facilities of Advanced Elastomer Systems, a use that is historically appropriate as well as broadly satisfying. For years,

The renovated atrium of the Advanced Elastomer Systems building is a dramatic change from the graffiti and pools of water that greeted company president Roger Sellew when he visited old Building 41 of the former B.F. Goodrich complex in late 1993. "It looked like Bosnia," he said. "It looked bombed out." (*Akron Beacon Journal*/Ed Suba, Jr.)

Goodrich was arguably the technological innovator in the rubber industry. In Building 41, workers made products as mundane as rubber bands and as exciting as America's first spacesuits. AES, a creation of Monsanto Company and Exxon Corporation, makes thermoplastic elastomers—pellets of rubbery plastic that other companies turn into everything from auto parts to the soft inserts on the grips of toothbrushes. It is new technology that emerged, like so much in the polymer industry, from an Akron laboratory—in this case, the Monsanto Company lab in Bath Township.

AES President Roger Sellew first toured Building 41 late in 1993. It had been abandoned and neglected for years. Most of its windows had been broken. Pools of water collected everywhere. It contained one of Akron's more extensive collections of urban graffiti. On one old door was scrawled a grim reminder: "All gone. No work."

"It looked like Bosnia," Sellew said. "It looked bombed out."

Sellew did not have to move to Building 41 from St. Louis; he had many other choices. "It is something that neither of our parents would have done," he said. But Sellew heard rubber's echoes. He felt the pull of rubber's rich heritage. And, in the risk-taking spirit of the city's rubber barons, B. F. Goodrich, the Seiberling brothers, Harvey Firestone, and Bill O'Neil, AES offers evidence that Akron is not spinning its tires, nor is it stuck in the ruts of its past.

"The symbolism was so rich," said Margaret M. Mattix, AES vice president for the Americas. "To move in downtown and breathe life back into an old factory that has lost its jobs to changes in the industry . . . and your company is based on replacing traditional rubber with the next wave of technology."

AES doesn't sell pellets of rubbery plastic as much as it sells knowledge about how to use the pellets. AES creates prototypes for customers who visit the lab to see how they can use thermoplastic elastomers to make a better item than they are making with other plastics or rubber. Akron also attracted AES because of the city's large pool of professional talent. Many engineers, scientists, and others chose not to relocate, or weren't invited, when Michelin took Uniroyal Goodrich to Greenville, South Carolina, and Continental General left for Charlotte, North Carolina.

"The skills we gained, the people we gained are truly great additions to AES," Sellew said.

And a building and a city, and the people who inhabit both, live on to create new memories for future storytellers.

Akron cannot fully realize its future, however, without squarely confronting the residue of its rubber past. Some of the remains are grim reminders of loss and failure; others are icons of glory and achievement. The U.S. Environmental Protection Agency had the job of eliminating one lingering rubber mess, with the

The newly-completed USS *Akron* peeks out from the Goodyear Zeppelin airdock in August 1931. The ship was christened by first lady Lou Henry Hoover and was based in Lakehurst, NJ. The vacated airdock was then used to build the *Akron's* sister ship, the *Macon*. (Goodyear Tire and Rubber Company)

$32 million Superfund cleanup of the Industrial Excess Landfill in Uniontown. Goodyear, Firestone, B. F. Goodrich, and General Tire dumped 1.7 million gallons of waste chemicals in the landfill before it closed in 1978. The Ohio Environmental Protection Agency handled another mess—but one not unique to Akron. The former Regenesis tire dump—once known euphemistically as Sid's Tire Service in Norton—contained four million used tires. Although only a fraction of Ohio's 130 million used tires, the Norton pile was an unsightly nuisance as well as a hazard: in dry conditions, it attracted fire starters; in wet conditions, it bred mosquitoes. Its $2.8 million cleanup was to be completed by the end of 1998.

Rubber, however, has left Akron more than carcasses. The most obvious, and probably the most magnificent, reminder of the city's former greatness squats on 8.5 acres off U.S. 224 in south Akron. No one knows what will happen to the spectacular Akron Airdock, which is listed on the National Register of Historic Places and is designated a National Historic Civil Engineering landmark. But it would be heresy to suggest this monument to engineering genius should be erased from the landscape like the toxic dump or Sid's tires. The Airdock deserves a future worthy of its exalted past.

Built by Goodyear during the Depression, the Airdock gave birth to the fabled USS *Macon* and *Akron* rigid airships in the 1930s. Men and women worked shoulder to shoulder at the Airdock during World War II, building Corsair FG-1 fighter planes, blimps, gas masks, and other combat equipment. The last navy defense blimp rolled out of the Airdock in 1961. In recent years, it has housed little activity. Although the Houston Astrodome has surpassed it, the Airdock, with 364,000 square feet, was once the largest building without interior supports. It is large enough for seven football fields or thirty-five tennis courts, with no obstructed views.

"It's a phenomenal building," said Joe Johnson, an engineer with Lockheed Martin Tactical Defense Systems, which bought the Airdock in 1996. "The person who did the calculations for this building had to spend years."

The Airdock rose, from excavation to completion, in fourteen months.

"This was 1929," said Charles J. Carlise, assistant to the president of the Lockheed Martin unit. "Before computers. This was all slide rules. Hand done. This building doesn't get the press it ought to have. It's at least as impressive as the Eiffel Tower, the Golden Gate Bridge."

Even with nothing going on inside, the giant, half a black egg holds the community awestruck. In the mid-1970s, the Airdock was opened to the families of

The Airdock, an engineering marvel, is shown in a rare opening to the public that drew three hundred thousand people to a United Way campaign event in 1986. No blimp had been in the Airdock for twenty-five years. (*Akron Beacon Journal*/Paul Tople)

Goodyear Aerospace workers for the first time in more than forty years. No one kept count or checked IDs, but thousands who weren't among the Aerospace family, more than anyone anticipated, flocked through the Airdock's two 609-ton doors. The 1986 United Way Fund campaign kickoff drew three hundred thousand people. Since then, the Airdock has been opened for an occasional special event, such as a presidential campaign rally for Bill Clinton, in 1992, and a black-tie dinner for the National Inventors Hall of Fame.

"I don't know if it is curiosity or pride, but it certainly is an enduring symbol of the community," Carlise said.

The Airdock went with the sale of Goodyear Aerospace, first to Loral Corporation, then to Lockheed Martin, in the wake of Goldsmith's raid on Goodyear. With each new owner, the Airdock's first name changed—if only legally. In inside circles, it is still Plant A, a carry-over from the Goodyear Aircraft days. But most people refer to it, still, as the "Goodyear Airdock" or simply "the Airdock." Nothing else sounds right.

Although no one has fixed on a new, definitive role for the Airdock, Lockheed Martin continues to seek blimp or balloon business, to search for a breakthrough that could reinflate the lighter-than-air industry. "A lot of countries are interested in monitoring their borders because they don't trust their neighbors or have problems of one sort or another," Carlise said. "It's very expensive to have aircraft patrolling and, also, provocative at times."

In the event some purpose is decided, the Airdock can swing into production with dispatch. "No one," said facilities engineer Joe Johnson, "has dropped the ball in maintaining the building. Everyone wants to keep it up."

In the meantime, the world's largest garage is leased to Aircraft Braking Systems, Lockheed Martin's on-site neighbor. ABS uses the Airdock mostly for storage. Its parts are tiny when compared with the great airships into which Akron

A worker moves up a side of the Goodyear Airdock in October 1997. Before the winter set in, workers continued the ten-year project of rubberizing the Airdock's roof, including its sides. (*Akron Beacon Journal*/Karen Schiely)

Joe Johnson, an engineer with Lockheed Martin, describes the Airdock as "a phenomenal building," one with 364,000 square feet of space, large enough for seven football fields or thirty-five tennis courts. The building was built in fourteen months without computers to do the calculations—-all the engineers had were slide rules. (*Akron Beacon Journal*/Karen Schiely)

workers once breathed life. From the catwalks of steel and wood twenty-two stories above, the piles of braking parts look like Kansas wheat fields from an airplane, fields oddly harvested in circular cuts. People have suggested various uses for the building, some serious, some frivolous: an airship museum to augment the Hall of Fame corridor from Cleveland (Rock and Roll) to Akron (Inventors) to Canton (Pro Football); a year-round amusement park; an American Wimbledon complex, with thirty-five tennis courts and grandstand seating.

"Maybe the Aeros could practice there," joked Bob Mercer, former Goodyear chairman, referring to Akron's AA baseball team.

On a fall day in 1997, Charles Carlise and others walked the roof of the Airdock. From this vantage point, they could see Akron's past, present, and future. The immediate landscape is one of a city whose past is slowly fading onto the pages of history books, a past that the latest crop of young professionals knows only from family folklore.

Not so long ago, sulfur, ash, and the essence of reclaimed rubber blasted into Akron's skies. Not so long ago, huge, multistory plants strained to operate around the clock on four production shifts. Not so long ago, thirty thousand workers streamed into the so-called gum mines to punch out tires, hoses, and belts, then spilled into the gin mills to pound down shots and beers. Not so long ago, eleven thousand URW pickets formed rings around the gates of Akron's rubber factories in the celebrated Strike of '76. Not so long ago, Akron staked its prosperity, its very identity, on the inexorable rotation of factory time clocks.

Easier to see than the ghosts of rubber factories is the hope. Almost in the shadow of the Airdock, Landmark Plastic Corporation's two hundred polymer employees work with rubber's legacy. At its East Market Street headquarters, at its nearby research and development offices and Technical Center, and just into Portage County at Wingfoot Lake Park and the Airship Hangar, is the reassuring presence of Goodyear, and nearly five thousand workers. At Firestone Parkway, Bridgestone/Firestone maintains a steady employment base of nearly one thousand. To the northwest, in downtown Akron, the Advanced Elastomer Systems Building, with its two hundred workers, stands as a symbol of answers found to questions rubber left. A few blocks from AES, the University of Akron may be nurturing, among its twenty-three thousand students, the next entrepreneurs to hear the echoes of Frank Seiberling, B. F. Goodrich, Harvey Firestone, and Bill O'Neil.

Akron's image is different now. It is becoming one of a city without disruptive factions, a city where people talk to one another, where they listen and cooperate. The George Gund Foundation was so impressed with what has been going on in Akron that, in 1994, it gave a $500,000 grant to Inventure Place, believed to be the largest gift ever given to an Akron project by a Cleveland organization.

In pockets all over the city are former working-class neighborhoods on a comeback—neighborhoods such as the one around Highland Square. Twenty years ago, North Highland Avenue, like rubber, was dying. The late Gary Gappert, who lived in the neighborhood, watched it happening. Older couples and widows owned many of the homes. Families abandoned this and nearby blocks for the suburbs. The future looked bleak. Then things began to change. Professionals with young families, such as Wayne Baker, a member of the University of Akron history faculty, began moving in. One of the young mothers told Gappert that living on North Highland Avenue was like living in a dream—rambling old homes, sidewalks in front of them, stores within walking distance.

In Germany, said urban expert Richard Knight, the people are fond of the expression: "Houses make the town. People make the city." North Highland Avenue again has the best of both. It has changed, evolved, found its answer. In Building G at Lockheed Martin Tactical Defense Systems headquarters, executives haven't given up on finding a way to use Plant A, the Airdock. This new incarnation of an old company questions itself, admits it does not have all the answers, listens to others, keeps searching. It is like its city.

Akron doesn't have all the answers, either. But it no longer resents the questions that would inform its strange, sometimes frightening, future. Akron is changing. Its storytellers prove it. Their stories have become fond memories rather than laments. No longer is Akron a city afraid of its own great shadow—the shadow of rubber.

Sources

All original research is in the Wheels of Fortune collection at the University of Akron Archives. The sources cited for each chapter have been alphabetized by last name of author or interviewee, by name of archival collection, or by title of publication.

Chapter One

Beacon Journal files; Ed Kalail, interview by David Giffels, Akron, OH, 18 September 1996; Kenneth Moorer, interview by Katie Byard, Akron, OH, 16 September 1996; M. G. "Jerry" O'Neil, interview by David Giffels, Akron, OH, August 1996; Roy Ray, interview by David Giffels, Akron, OH, September 1996; Nate Trachsel, interview by Steve Love, Green, OH, 23 August 1996.

Chapter Two

Hugh Allen, *The House of Goodyear* (Cleveland: The Corday & Gross Co., 1949); Hugh Allen, *Rubber's Home Town* (New York: Stratford House, 1949); *Beacon Journal* files; Mansel G. Blackford and K. Austin Kerr, *BFGoodrich: Tradition and Transformation, 1870–1995* (Columbus: Ohio State University Press, 1996); Norman Brauer, *There to Breathe the Beauty* (Dalton, PA: Norman Brauer Publications, 1995); Rita Dunlevy, interview by David Giffels, Akron, OH, October 1996; Richard Erickson, interview by Steve Love, Akron, OH, 7 August 1996; Colonel David M. Goodrich's reminiscences, letters, and papers, Goodrich Collection, UA Archives; The Goodyear Collection, UA Archives; Karl H. Grismer, *Akron and Summit County* (Akron: Summit County Historical Society, 1952); Elbert Hubbard, "Little Journey to the Home of BFGoodrich," B. F. Goodrich Collection, University of Akron Archives; Charles E. Kittieger, interview by Arthur Blower, 1943, Goodrich Collection, University of Akron Archives; George V. Knepper, *Akron: City at the Summit* (Virginia Beach, VA: The Donning Co., 1994); George Knepper, interview by Steve Love and David Giffels, Akron, OH, 5 June 1996; Robert Koch, interview by David Giffels, Fairlawn, OH, 4 October 1996; Percy S. Leavitt, "History and Statistics Appertaining to the BFGoodrich Co. for Forty Years from 1870 to 1910," Goodrich Collection, UA Archives; David Lieberth, interview by Steve Love, Akron, OH, 22 August 1996; Alfred Lief, *The Firestone Story* (New York: McGraw-Hill Book Co., 1951); Alfred Lief, *Harvey Firestone* (New York: McGraw-Hill Book Co., 1951); Daniel Nelson, *American Rubber Workers and Organized Labor, 1900–1941* (Princeton, NJ: Princeton University Press, 1988); Dennis J. O'Neill, *A Whale of a Territory: The Story of Bill O'Neil* (New York: McGraw-Hill Book Co., 1966); M. G. "Jerry" O'Neil, interviews by David Giffels, Akron, OH, August 1996 and by Steve Love, Akron, OH, May 1997; Don Plusquellic, interviews by

Steve Love, Akron, OH, 8 and 12 August 1996; William Prather, interview by Katie Byard, Akron, OH, 18 June 1996; The F. A. Seiberling Collection, Ohio Historical Society Archives, Columbus, OH; John F. Seiberling, interviews by Steve Love, Akron, OH, 2 July 1996 and 30 April 1997; Seiberling family tapes and papers, Stan Hywet Hall and Gardens.

Chapter Three

Akron Baptist Temple fiftieth anniversary book (Josten Yearbook Co., 1985); *Beacon Journal* files; Charles Billington, interview by Ron Kirksey, Akron, OH, 18 July 1996; Dallas F. Billington, *God is Real* (Milford, OH: John the Baptist Printing Ministry, 1962); John Buck, interview by David Giffels, Spencer, WV, 12 September 1996; Sheila Buck, interview by David Giffels, Spencer, WV, 12 September 1996; Walter Buck, interview by David Giffels, Spencer, WV, 12 September 1996; T. R. Cummings, interview by David Giffels, Spencer, WV, 12 September 1996; Betty Dunlevy, interview by David Giffels, Akron, OH, September 1996; Gene Elmore, interviews by Katie Byard, Spencer, WV, 28 August 1996, and David Giffels, Spencer, WV, 12 September 1996; Grismer, *Akron and Summit County;* David Hedges, interview by David Giffels, Spencer, WV, 13 September 1996; Tressie McGee, interviews by Katie Byard, Akron, OH, July 1996, and by David Giffels, Akron, OH, September 1996; James P. Mylott, *A Measure of Prosperity: A Roane County History* (Charleston, WV: Mountain State Press, 1984); Phillip Obermiller, interview by Ron Kirksey, Cincinnati, OH, 26 July 1996; (Roane County) *Weekly Bulletin*; Roane County Historical Society; Terry Williams, interview by David Giffels, Spencer, WV, 12 September 1996.

Chapter Four

Allen, *Rubber's Home Town*; Paul E. Appleby, interviews by Steve Love, Akron, OH, 5 August 1996 and 5 May 1997; *Beacon Journal* files; Mary Seiberling Chapman, interview by Steve Love, Akron, OH, 19 September 1996; Sally Harrison Cochran, interview by Steve Love, Akron, OH, 25 July 1996; Grismer, *Akron and Summit County*; Knepper, *Akron*; Irene Seiberling Harrison, interview by Trevor Hoskins, 1988, Goodyear Collection, UA Archives; Maurice O'Reilly, *The Goodyear Story* (Elmsford, NY: The Benjamin Co., 1983); Mary Popiel, interview by Steve Love, Akron, OH, 21 June 1996; The F. A Seiberling Collection, Ohio Historical Society Archives; interviews with Seiberling family members, Stan Hywet Hall and Gardens; John F. Seiberling, interviews by Steve Love, Akron, OH, 2 July 1996 and 30 April 1997; U.S. Census Bureau reports.

Chapter Five

Paul E. Appleby, interviews by Steve Love, Akron, OH, 5 August 1996 and 5 May 1997; *Beacon Journal* files; Eileen Beck, interview by Maura McEnaney, Akron, OH, 17 September 1996; Norma Charlton, interview by Katie Byard, Akron, OH, 16 September 1996; C. P. Chima, interview by Ron Kirksey, Akron, OH, June 1996; Harvey S. Firestone with Samuel Crowther, *Men and Rubber* (Garden City, NY: Doubleday, Page & Co., 1926); John Frank, interview by Jim Quinn, Akron, OH, 5 January 1997; Kevan Delany Frazier, "Model Industrial Subdivisions: Goodyear Heights and Firestone Park And The Town Planning Movement In Akron" (master's thesis, Kent State University, 1994); Goodyear Collection, UA Archives; Jack Heslop, interview by Steve Love, Munroe Falls, OH, 6 January 1997; Archives of Stan Hywet Hall and Gardens; Jane Kaneas, "The Corner Grocery Store," family collection, Akron, OH; Susan Judge, interview by Maura McEnaney, Akron, OH, October 1996; Clarice Finley Lewis, interview by Steve Love, Akron, OH, 25 June 1996; Clarice Finley Lewis, *A History of Firestone Park* (Akron: Firestone Park Citizens Council, 1986; F.A. Seiberling Collection, Ohio Historical Society Archives); John F. Seiberling, interviews by Steve Love, Akron, OH, 2 July 1996 and 30 April 1997; Don Welker, interview by Katie Byard, Akron, OH, 16 September 1996; Mary Welker, interview by Katie Byard, Akron, OH, 16 September 1996.

Chapter Six

James Gilger, interview by Steve Love, Mesquite, TX, 6 January 1997; Ben Kastein, interviews by Jim Quinn, Akron, OH, 17 July 1996 and 10 October 1996, and interviews by Steve Love, Akron, OH, November 1996 and March 1997; Carl "Bud" Lawley, interview by David Giffels, North Canton, OH, 10 January 1997; Edgar Lyle, interview by Steve Love, Akron, OH, 20 May 1996; Susan McGrath, interview by Jim Quinn, Akron, OH, 4 December 1996; Daniel Mainzer, interview by David Giffels, Cuyahoga Falls, OH, 7 January 1997; John Nardella, interview by Katie Byard, Akron, OH, 22 January 1997; Daniel Nelson, interview by David Giffels, Akron, OH, 7 January 1997; Walter Reed, interview by David Giffels, Mogadore, OH, 3 January 1997; John F. Seiberling, interviews by Steve Love, Akron, OH, 2 July 1996 and 30 April 1997; Waldo Semon, interviews by Steve Love, Hudson, OH, 28 May 1996, 12 June 1996, 25 June 1996, 24 July 1996, 31 July 1996; Richard Simmons, interview by Steve Love, Springfield Township, OH, 11 June 1996; Judge William Victor, interview by Jim Quinn, Akron, OH, 11 December 1996; Jean Vondekamp, interview by Jim Quinn, Akron, OH, 4 December 1996; Bob Walker, interview by David Giffels, Akron, OH, June 1996; Rebecca Heisler Weissfeld, interview by Steve Love, Akron, OH, June 1996.

Chapter Seven

Hugh Allen, *The Story of the Airship (Non-Rigid)* (Chicago: The Lakeside Press, R. R. Donnelly & Sons Co., 1942); Bertl Arnstein, interview by David Giffels, Akron, OH, 26 November 1996; Dr. Gerald Austen, interview by David Giffels, Akron, OH, November 1996; Emil "Fred" Bauch, interview by Glenn Gamboa, Cuyahoga Falls, OH, 14 October 1996; *Beacon Journal* files; Goodyear Collection, UA Archives; tributes to Karl Arnstein and Walter Mosebach, compiled by Goodyear upon their retirement; Katharine Litchfield Hyde, interview by Steve Love, Shaker Heights, OH, 9 December 1996; Ernst Lehmann and Harold Mingoes, *The Zeppelins* (London & New York, Putnam, 1927); P. W. Litchfield, *Autumn Leaves* (Cleveland: The Corday & Gross Co., 1945); Paul W. Litchfield, "The Case for the Super-Dirigible," *World's Work*, January 1926; P. W. Litchfield, *The Industrial Republic* (Cleveland: The Corday & Gross Co., 1946); P. W. Litchfield, *Industrial Voyage* (Garden City, NY: Doubleday & Co., 1954); Ruth McKenney, *Industrial Valley* (Ithaca, NY: ILR Press, 1992); Nelson, *American Rubber Workers*; Daniel Nelson, interview by Katie Byard, Akron, OH, August 1996; O'Reilly, *The Goodyear Story*; Edwin J. Thomas, memoir, courtesy of Dr. James and Jean (Thomas) Mercer; *Present Status of Zeppelin Airships in the United States* (Akron: Goodyear-Zeppelin Corp., 1930); Tom Schubert, interview by David Giffels, Akron, OH, 27 November 1996; Edwin J. Thomas, interview by Benjamin Kastein, The Rubber Division Library, University of Akron.

Chapter Eight

Beacon Journal files; C. C. "Gibby" Gibson, interview by Steve Love, Fairlawn, OH, 1 October 1996; Jack Gieck, interview by Steve Love and David Giffels, Akron, OH, 30 July 1996; Goodyear Collection, UA Archives; Litchfield, *Industrial Voyage*; James Mercer, interview by Steve Love, Akron, OH, 23 October 1996; Jean Thomas Mercer, interview by Steve Love, Akron, OH, 23 October 1996; John Moore, interview by David Giffels, Bath, OH, 26 July 1996; Charles J. Pilliod, interview by Steve Love, Akron, OH, 9 October 1996; Edwin J. Thomas, interview by Ben Kastein, The Rubber Division Library, University of Akron; Edwin J. Thomas, memoir, courtesy of Dr. James and Jean (Thomas) Mercer.

Chapter Nine

Akron Times-Press files; Allen, *The House of Goodyear*; *Beacon Journal* files; Blackford and Kerr, *BFGoodrich*; Kenneth Coss, interview by Glenn Gamboa, Coventry Township, OH, 16 September 1997; Michael J. French, *The U.S. Tire Industry: A History* (Boston: Twayne Publishers, 1990); Grismer, *Akron and Summit County*; John D. House, *Birth of a Union*, autobiography, courtesy of the House family; John D. House II, interview by Katie Byard, Astor, FL, 5 June 1996; Gene L. Howard, *The History of the Rubber Workers in Gadsden, Alabama, 1933–1983* (Gadsden, AL: URW Local 12, 1983); Litchfield, *The Industrial Republic*; McKenney, *Industrial Valley*; Albert J. Lucas, interview by Katie Byard, Akron, OH, 20 June 1996; *A Mighty Fine Union: A URW Golden Anniversary History* (Akron: United Rubber, Cork, Linoleum and Plastic Workers of America, AFL-CIO, CLC, 1985); *Modern Tire Dealer,* January 1997; Nelson, *American Rubber Workers*; Daniel Nelson, interview by David Giffels, Akron, OH, 29 October 1996; *Rubber and Plastics News,* 25th anniversary edition, 12 August 1996; John Sellers, interview by Glenn Gamboa, Pittsburgh, PA, 15 September 1997; Kenji Shibata, interview by David Giffels, Nashville, TN, 4 April 1997; *URW: A Quarter-Century Panorama of Democratic Unionism* (Akron, OH: United Rubber, Cork, Linoleum and Plastic Workers of America, AFL-CIO, 1960); Howard Wolf and Ralph Wolf, *Rubber: A Story of Glory and Greed* (New York: Covici, Friede Publishers, 1936).

Chapter Ten

Blackford and Kerr, *BFGoodrich*; Dr. Michael J. Deutch, "History, Magnitude and Lessons of the Synthetic Rubber Program of World War II," speech to Washington Rubber Group, 1978; Stephen Fenichell,

Plastic: The Making of a Synthetic Century (New York: HarperBusiness, 1996); Vernon Herbert and Attilio Bisio, *Synthetic Rubber: A Project That Had to Succeed* (Westport, CT: Greenwood Press, 1985); Frank A. Howard, *Buna Rubber: The Birth of An Industry* (New York: D. Van Nostrand Co., 1949); Ben Kastein, interviews by Steve Love, Akron, OH, November 1996 and March 1997; J. A. Krug, "Wartime Production Achievements and the Reconversion Outlook," report to the War Production Board Report, Washington, D.C., 9 October 1945; Litchfield, *Industrial Voyage*; O'Neill, *Whale of a Territory*; "The Man Who Made Wartime Rubber," *Reader's Digest,* April 1945; Waldo Semon, interviews by Steve Love, Hudson, OH, 28 May 1996, 12 June 1996, 25 June 1996, 24 July 1996, 31 July 1996; Waldo Semon and Benjamin S. Garvey, interviews by Herbert A. Endres, The Rubber Division Library, University of Akron; Elizabeth M. Smith, ed., *Waldo Lonsbury Semon: A Man of Ideas* (Brecksville, OH: Geon Co., 1993); *Time,* 12 April 1943; Alvin W. Warren, interview by Steve Love, North Canton, OH, 3 March 1997; Edward R. Weidlein, Colonel Bradley Dewey, Ernest T. Handley, James D. D'Ianni, G. Stafford Whitby, interviews by Ben Kastein, The Rubber Division Library, University of Akron; Tony Weitzels and Philip Handerson of Florez Inc., manuscripts, B. F. Goodrich Collection, UA Archives.

Chapter Eleven

Akron city directories, 1913–1963; Allen, *The House of Goodyear*; Allen; *Rubber's Home Town*; *Beacon Journal* files; Blackford and Kerr, *BFGoodrich*; Mary Wagner Carr, interview by Thrity Umrigar, Akron, OH, 13 November 1996; Luella Cordier, history of the Heupel family, family collection, Kent, OH; Luella Cordier, interview by David Giffels, Kent, OH, 18 April 1997; John Dalton, interview by David Giffels, Akron, OH, 16 April 1997; Philip J. Dietrich, *The Silent Men* (Akron, OH: The Goodyear Tire & Rubber Company, undated); Ray Dove, interview by David Giffels, Akron, OH, 13 December 1996; Betty Dunlevy, interview by Thrity Umrigar, Akron, OH, 15 November 1996; Rita Dunlevy, interview by Thrity Umrigar, Akron, OH, 15 November 1996; Dr. Kathleen Endres, interview by Thrity Umrigar, Akron, OH, 11 November 1996; 1941 contract between Goodyear Tire and Rubber Co. and United Rubber Workers Local 2; Hugh Davis Graham, *The Civil Rights Era: Origins and Development of National Policy, 1960–1972,* (New York: Oxford University Press, 1990); Grismer, *Akron and Summit County*; Patricia Gritton, interview by Thrity Umrigar, Akron, OH, 5 November 1996; Henry Haas, interview by Thrity Umrigar, Akron, OH, 5 November 1996; Hazel Humphrey, interview by Thrity Umrigar, Akron, OH, 14 November 1996; Knepper, *Akron*; Lief, *The Firestone Story*; Shirla McClain, "The Contributions of Blacks in Akron: 1825 to 1975" (Ph.D. diss., University of Akron, 1975); Tressie McGee, interview by Katie Byard, Akron, OH, July 1996, and David Giffels, Akron, OH, April, 1997; Marcus S. Miller, "The Deaf and the Hard of Hearing in Akron Industry" (master's thesis, University of Akron, 1943); William R. Miller, interview by David Giffels, Akron, OH, December 1996; Art Minson, interview by Steve Love, Akron, OH, 1 August 1996; Nelson, *American Rubber Workers*; Kenneth Nichols, *Yesterday's Akron: The First 150 Years* (Miami, FL: E.A. Seeman Publishing, Inc., 1975); Rosemary Olenick, interview by Thrity Umrigar, Akron, OH, 13 November 1996; John Ong, interview by Steve Love and David Giffels, Richfield, OH, 16 December 1996; O'Reilly, *The Goodyear Story*; Clark Smith, interview by Thrity Umrigar, Akron, OH, 11 November 1996, and David Giffels, Akron, OH, 11 July 1996; Richard Snader, interview by Steve Love, Fairlawn, OH, 3 June 1996; Otis Spurling, interview by Thrity Umrigar, Akron, OH, 22 November 1996; Jewel Vanke, interview by David Giffels, Spencer, W. Va., 12 September 1996; Violet McIntyre White, interview by Ron Kirksey, Akron, OH, 6 August 1996; Clyde D. Wilson, *Akron History of the Deaf: 1913–1993* (self-published, 1993); Clyde D. Wilson, interview by David Giffels, Akron, OH, 17 April 1997; Warren Louis Woolford, "A Geographic Appraisal of Major Distributional Changes in the Akron, Ohio Black Population 1930–1970" (master's thesis, University of Akron, 1974).

Chapter Twelve

Allen, *The House of Goodyear*; Allen, *The Story of the Airship*; *Beacon Journal* files; Blackford and Kerr, *BFGoodrich*; Stanley Gault, interviews by David Giffels, Akron, OH, 21 February 1997, and by Steve Love, Akron, OH, 13 March 1997; Jack LaFontaine, interview by David Giffels, Akron, OH, 3 March 1997; Lief, *The Firestone Story*; O'Neill, *Whale of a Territory*; O'Reilly, *The Goodyear Story*; John Perduyn, interview by David Giffels, Akron, OH, 4 March 1997; Tom Riley, interview by David Giffels, Akron, OH, 4 March 1997; Vincent J. Rubino, "LTA Memories of a Non-Com," Moffett Field Historical Society Museum, Sunnyvale, CA; Vince Rubino, interview by David Giffels, Cuyahoga Falls, OH, 28 February 1997.

Chapter Thirteen

Paul E. Appleby, interviews by Steve Love, Akron, OH, 5 August 1996 and 5 May 1997; Richard Bauman, interview by Steve Love, Akron, OH, January 1997; *Beacon Journal* files; Blackford and Kerr, *BFGoodrich*; Charles Brady, interview by David Adams, Akron, OH, April 1997; *Consumer Reports*, October 1973; *Firestone Non-Skid*, Firestone company newspaper, 1972 through 1979; French, *The U.S. Tire Industry*; Robert Koch, interview by David Giffels, Fairlawn, OH, 4 October 1996; Robert E. Mercer, interviews by Steve Love, Daytona Beach, FL, 22 April 1997 and Akron, OH, 17 June 1997 and 19 June 1997; "Michelin Goes American," *Business Week*, 26 July 1976; "The Michelin Man Rolls into Akron's Backyard," *Fortune*, December 1974; Daniel Nelson, interviews by Katie Byard, Akron, OH, August 1996, and by Steve Love, Akron, OH, March 1997; Alan Ockene, interview by David Giffels, Akron, OH, 15 August 1996; M. G. "Jerry" O'Neil, interview by David Giffels, Akron, OH, August 1996; John Ong, interview by Steve Love and David Giffels, Richfield, OH, 16 December 1996; O'Reilly, *The Goodyear Story*; Charles J. Pilliod, Jr., interview by Steve Love, Akron, OH, 9 October 1996; "Riding with Radials," *Dun's Review*, October 1971; *Rubber and Plastics News*, 12 August 1996; John F. Seiberling, interviews by Steve Love, Akron, OH, 2 July 1996 and 30 April 1997; Donald N. Sull, Richard S. Tedlow, and Richard S. Rosenbloom, "Managerial Commitments and Technological Change in the U.S. Tire Industry," (Boston: Harvard Business School, Division of Research, undated); Richard S. Tedlow, "Hitting the Skids: Tire and Time Horizons" (Boston: Harvard Business School, Division of Research, 1991); Bill Terrall, interview by David Giffels, Akron, OH, 11 June 1997; Bob Troyer, interview by David Giffels, Akron, OH, 12 June 1997; Alvin W. Warren, interview by Steve Love, North Canton, OH, 3 March 1997.

Chapter Fourteen

John Ballard, interview by Steve Love and Jim Carney, Bath, OH, 31 January 1997; *Beacon Journal* files; Judge Sam Bell, interview by Charlene Nevada, Akron, OH, 28 January 1997; Blackford and Kerr, *BFGoodrich*; Bill Breslin, interview by Charlene Nevada, Canton, OH, 8 January 1997; Jim Burdon, interview by Charlene Nevada, Akron, OH, February 1997; Bill Carpenter, interview by David Giffels, Akron, OH, April 1997; Matt Contessa, interview by David Giffels, Akron, OH, 24 March 1997; Department of Labor, *Collective Bargaining in the Rubber Industry* (Washington, DC: GPO, 1976); *Detroit Free Press* files; John DiGuiseppe, interview by Charlene Nevada, Jeddo, MI, January 1997; Stu Feldstein, interviews by Charlene Nevada, Akron, OH, January 1997, and by David Giffels, Akron, OH, April 1997; Gerald R. Ford, interview by David Giffels, Rancho Mirage, CA, 12 March 1997; "How a Union Leader Keeps Busy Keeping Strikers' Spirits High," *Wall Street Journal*, 8 July 1976; Tom Jenkins, interview by Charlene Nevada, Akron, OH, February 1997; Phil Kaster, interview by David Giffels, Akron, OH, March 1997; Jefferson Keener, interview by David Giffels, Akron, OH, March 1997; Robert Keener, interview by David Giffels, Akron, OH, March 1997; John McAlarney, interview by Jim Carney, Tallmadge, OH, January 1997; John Nardella, interview by Charlene Nevada and Jim Carney, Akron, OH, 22 January 1997; John Ong, interview by Steve Love and David Giffels, Richfield, OH, 16 December 1996; Conrad Ott, interview by Jim Carney, Akron, OH, January 1997; Peter J. Pestillo, interview by Glenn Gamboa, Detroit, MI, 23 April 1997; Kenny Rinesmith, interview by Charlene Nevada, Lady Lake, FL, February 1997; "Rubber Is the Next Big Problem," *Business Week*, 23 April 1979; Glen Sengpiel, interviews by Jim Carney, Akron, OH, January 1997, and by David Giffels, Akron, OH, March 1997; "The Textbook Nixon," *Los Angeles Times*, 27 April 1994; Nate Trachsel, interviews by David Giffels, Akron, OH, 30 May 1997, and by Steve Love, Green, OH, 23 August 1996; *The United Rubber Worker*, September 1965, January-February 1976, September 1976; William J. Usery, interview by Charlene Nevada, Washington, DC, February 1997.

Chapter Fifteen

Allen, *The House of Goodyear*; "Automobiles' Happy 100th: The Defining Element of American Life Celebrates Its Centennial," *Popular Mechanics*, May 1996; John Ballard, interview by Steve Love and Jim Carney, Bath, OH, 31 January 1997; *Beacon Journal* files; Blackford and Kerr, *BFGoodrich*; Bill Breslin, interview by Charlene Nevada, Canton, OH, 8 January 1997; David Cole, interview by David Adams, Ann Arbor, MI, 18 March 1997; Matt Contessa, interviews by Charlene Nevada, Akron, OH, 15 January 1997 and 27 February 1997; William Dannemiller, interview by Katie Byard, Akron, OH, 31 May 1996; Wilmer Davis, interview by Charlene Nevada, Akron, OH, January 1997; Department of Labor, *Collective Bargaining in the Rubber Industry* (Washington, D.C: GPO, 1976); Richard Erickson, interview by Steve Love, Akron, OH, 7 August

1996; Douglas Fraser, interview by David Adams, Detroit, MI, April 1997; French, *The U.S. Tire Industry*; Grismer, *Akron and Summit County*; Gerald Gelvin, interview by Jim Carney, Akron, OH, February 1997; Howard, *The History of the Rubber Workers;* "Joining to Save Jobs in Akron," *Business Week,* 12 February 1972; Robert Kidney, interview by Steve Love, Silver Lake, OH, 1 May 1997; "The Max Factory," *Automobile,* December 1996; *Modern Tire Dealer,* January 1997; Jack Moye, interviews by Charlene Nevada, Jackson Township, OH, February 1997, and by Katie Byard, Jackson Township, OH, 7 June 1996; John Nardella, interviews by Charlene Nevada and Jim Carney, Akron, OH, 22 January 1997, and by Katie Byard, Akron, OH, 1 July 1996; Nelson, *American Rubber Workers*; Peter J. Pestillo, interview by Glenn Gamboa, Detroit, MI, 11 February 1997; Jim Phelps, interview by Charlene Nevada, Akron, OH, January 1997; Charles J. Pilliod Jr., interview by Steve Love, Akron, OH, 9 October 1996; Don Plusquellic, interview by Steve Love, Akron, OH, 12 August 1996; "Quiet Akron Factories Are Sign of Multinationals' Spread," *Washington Post,* 4 March 1979; "Rubber: Short-run Prosperity Ahead," *Business Week,* 4 October 1976; Edwin H. Sonnecken, interview by Jim Carney, Akron, OH, February 1997; Don Stephens, interview by Charlene Nevada, Akron, OH, February 1997; Milan "Mike" Stone, interviews by Charlene Nevada, Springfield Township, OH, 11 February 1997, and by Steve Love, Springfield Township, OH, March 1997; Robert Strauber, interview by Jim Carney, Myrtle Beach, SC, February 1997; Arthur Stuart, interview by David Adams, Southfield, MI, April 1997; Sull, Tedlow, and Rosenbloom, "Managerial Commitments"; Tedlow, "Hitting the Skids"; Edwin J. Thomas, interview by Ben Kastein; Edwin J. Thomas, interview by C. E. Schetter, Goodyear Collection, UA Archives; *The United Rubber Workers* (January–February 1976); George Vasko, interview by Charlene Nevada, Akron, OH, January 1997; Jim Walker, interview by Steve Love, Jackson Township, OH, 15 May 1996; H. Wolf and R. Wolf, *Rubber;* Richard A. Wright, *Detroit, Inc.: A Brief History of the First 100 Years of the Automobile in the U.S.* (Dayton: On-line book, Wright State University Dept. of Communications, 1996); Bob Young, interview by Charlene Nevada, Akron, OH, February 1997.

Chapter Sixteen

Beacon Journal files; Andrew Dakoski, interview by David Giffels, Stow, OH, June 1997; Tony Fanizzi, interview by David Giffels, Akron, OH, June 1997; Beech Fannin, interviews by Steve Love, Akron, OH, 28 May 1997, and by Mary Ethridge, Akron, OH, 13 May 1997; Henry "Hank" Fawcett, interview by Mary Ethridge, Akron, OH, 21 May 1997; Catherine "Kitty" Garlock, interview by Jim Carney, Akron, OH, January 1997; Wesley Lake, interview by Mary Ethridge, Akron, OH, 13 May 1997; Lief, *The Firestone Story;* Joe Seymour, interview by David Giffels, Akron, OH, July 1996; Richey Smith, interviews by Steve Love, Akron, OH, 7 January 1997 and Medina, OH, 27 May 1997; Ed Wilson, interview by Mary Ethridge, Akron, OH, 28 May 1997.

Chapter Seventeen

Doug Alge, interview by Steve Love, Akron, OH, 20 June 1997; *Annual Report* (Cooper Tire & Rubber Co., 1996); *Beacon Journal* files; Patricia J. Brown, interview by Steve Love, Findlay, OH, 20 June 1997; *Buyside,* (Sonoma, CA: Buyside Ltd); *Cooper Tire and Rubber Company* (Findlay, Ohio: Cooper Tire & Rubber Public Relations Department, 1997); James S. Kovac, interview by Steve Love, Findlay, OH, 24 June 1997; Harry Millis, interview by Steve Love, Willoughby, OH, 25 June 1997; *Modern Tire Dealer,* March 1997; M. G. "Jerry" O'Neil, interview by Steve Love, Akron, OH, May 1997; Floyd Rader, interview by Steve Love, Findlay, OH, 20 June 1997; J. Alec Reinhardt, interview by Steve Love, Findlay, OH, 20 June 1997; Patrick W. Rooney, interview by Steve Love, Findlay, OH, 20 June 1997; *Rubber and Plastics News,* 10 February 1997; Mike Saum, interview by Steve Love, Findlay, OH, 20 June 1997; John Stozich, interview by Steve Love, Findlay, OH, 20 June 1997; *The World Tyre Industry: Emerging Tyre Manufacturers* (the Economist Intelligence United Limited, 1977).

Chapter Eighteen

Jody Bacon, interview by Thrity Umrigar, Akron, OH, 16 April 1997; *Beacon Journal* files; Blackford and Kerr, *BFGoodrich*; Jim Bower, interview by David Giffels, August 1997; Jerry Casale, interview by David Giffels, Cuyahoga Falls, OH, 18 July 1997; *Charitable Foundations Directory of Ohio* (Columbus, OH: Attorney General Betty D. Montgomery, 1997); Rita Dove, interview by David Giffels, Charlottesville, VA, 31 August 1997; C. C. "Gibby" Gibson, interviews by Thrity Umrigar, Akron, OH, 18 April 1997, and by Steve Love, Fairlawn, OH, 1 October 1996; Grismer, *Akron and Summit County*; Chrissie Hynde, interview by

David Giffels, London, 20 August 1997; George Knepper, interviews by Thrity Umrigar, Akron, OH, 22 April 1997, and by Steve Love and David Giffels, Akron, OH, 5 June 1996; Robert Koch, interview by David Giffels, Fairlawn, OH, 4 October 1996; David Lieberth, interview by Steve Love, Akron, OH, 22 August 1996; Lief, *The Firestone Story*; Mark Mothersbaugh, interview by David Giffels, Cuyahoga Falls, OH, 18 July 1997; *Newsweek,* 30 December, 1996; M. G. "Jerry" O'Neil, interview by David Giffels, 4 August 1997; O'Neill, *Whale of a Territory*; Brad Pringle, interview by David Giffels, August 1997; *Service For All: The Story of Akron General Medical Center 1914–1986* (Akron, OH: Akron General Medical Center, 1986); Barbara Tannenbaum, interview by David Giffels, Akron, OH, August 1997; Nita Lee Terzic, interview by David Giffels, August 1997; Bob Troyer, interview by Thrity Umrigar, Chicago, IL, 24 April 1997; Bernice Vigar, interview by Thrity Umrigar, Akron, OH, 28 April 1997; Joseph Frazier Wall, *Andrew Carnegie* (New York: Oxford University Press, 1970).

Chapter Nineteen

James Alkire, interview by Steve Love and Ron Kirksey, Akron, OH, 19 August 1996; *Beacon Journal* files; Anne Berrodin, interview by Diane Lore, Akron, OH, July 1997; Louie Berrodin, interview by Diane Lore, Akron, OH, July 1997; Blackford and Kerr, *BFGoodrich*; Mike Connor, interview by Steve Love, Akron, OH, 5 August 1997; Matt Contessa, interviews by Charlene Nevada, Akron, OH, 15 January 1997 and 27 February 1997, and by Diane Lore, Akron, OH, June 1997; Charles Deitle, interview by Diane Lore, Akron, OH, July 1997; Rocky Galloway, interview by Diane Lore, Akron, OH, June 1997; and Gary Gappert, interviews by Steve Love, Akron, OH, 10 September 1997, and by Diane Lore, Akron, OH, July 1997; Albert Gilbert, interview by Diane Lore, Akron, OH, June 1997; Earl Givens, interviews by Steve Love, Akron, OH, July 1997, and by Diane Lore, Akron, OH, July 1997; Marie Givens, interviews by Steve Love, Akron, OH, July 1997, and by Diane Lore, Akron, OH, July 1997; Ken Mayland, interview by Diane Lore, Akron, OH, July 1997; Art Minson, interviews by Steve Love, Akron, OH, 1 August 1996, and by Diane Lore, Akron, OH, July 1997; M. G. "Jerry" O'Neil, interview by Steve Love, Akron, OH, May 1997; Roy Ray, interview by Steve Love, Akron, OH, 12 August 1997; Isabelle Reymann, interview by Diane Lore, Akron, OH, June 1997; Nancy C. Rosche, interview by Diane Lore, Akron, OH, July 1997; Herb Stottler, interview by Diane Lore, Akron, OH, July 1997; Howard Walton, interview by Diane Lore, Akron, OH, July 1997; Harold White, interview by Diane Lore, Akron, OH, July 1997.

Chapter Twenty

Allen, *House of Goodyear*; *Beacon Journal* files; Tom Binns, interview by Glenn Gamboa, Barberton, OH, 3 April 1997; Blackford and Kerr, *BFGoodrich*; Mary Seiberling Chapman, interview by Steve Love, Akron, OH, 19 September 1996; Ivan Fallon, *Billionaire* (New York: Little Brown & Company, 1992); Michael French, "Structure, Personality, and Business Strategy in the U.S. Tire Industry: The Seiberling Rubber Company, 1922–1964," *Business History Review* (1993); Rufus Johnson, interview by Glenn Gamboa, Akron, OH, March 1997; Sandie Kreiner, interview by Glenn Gamboa, Cuyahoga Falls, OH, February 1997; Edward Lamb, *No Lamb for Slaughter* (New York: Harcourt, Brace & World Inc., 1963); Robert E. Mercer, interviews by Steve Love, Daytona Beach, FL, 22 April 1997 and Akron, OH, 17 June 1997, and 19 June 1997; Robert G. Mercer, interview by Steve Love, El Segundo, CA, June 1997; William Newkirk, interview by Steve Love, Hudson, OH, 13 June 1997; Tom Sawyer, interview by Steve Love, Akron, OH, 27 June 1997; F. A. Seiberling Collection, Ohio Historical Society; Steve Seigfried, interview by Glenn Gamboa, Barberton, OH, February 1997; Sally Bedell Smith, "Billionaire with a Cause," *Vanity Fair,* May 1997; Geoffrey Wansell, *Tycoon: The Life of James Goldsmith* (New York: Atheneum Macmillan Publishing Co., 1987); Gaylon White, interview by Steve Love, Singapore, 20 April 1997.

Chapter Twenty-One

Beacon Journal files; "Firestone, Inc.," case study prepared as a class supplement, Harvard Business School (June 1988); "Firestone: It Worked!" *Forbes,* 17 August 1981; Roy Gilbert, interview by David Giffels, Akron, OH, September 1997; Bill McGrath, interview by David Giffels, Akron, OH, 5 September 1997; John J. Nevin, "The Bridgestone/Firestone Story," *California Management Review* (summer 1990); John Nevin, interview by David Giffels, Chicago, 12 September 1997; John J. Nevin, "Product Quality, Corporate Competitivity and Consumerism," *Advances in Applied Business Strategy* 1 (1984); *Rubber and Plastics News,* 12 August 1996; Alexander Sherman, interview by David Giffels, Akron, OH, 23 September 1997;

Ted Sherman, interview by David Giffels, Akron, OH, 23 September 1997; Richey Smith, interview by David Giffels, Medina, OH, 9 September 1997; Bob Troyer, interview by David Giffels, Chicago, IL, September 1997.

Chapter Twenty-Two

Paul E. Appleby, interviews by Steve Love, Akron, OH, 5 August 1996 and 5 May 1997; Tom H. Barrett, interview by Glenn Gamboa, Akron, OH, 28 July 1997; *Beacon Journal* files; Marge DeLuca, interview by Steve Love, Akron, OH, 13 May 1996; Stanley Gault, interview by Steve Love, Akron, OH, 13 March 1997; Samir F. Gibara, interview by Steve Love and David Giffels, Akron, OH, 28 March 1997; Trevor Hoskins, interview by Steve Love, Nashville, TN, 17 February 1997; Robert E. Mercer, interviews by Steve Love, Daytona Beach, FL, 22 April 1997 and Akron, OH, 17 June 1997 and 19 June 1997; Harry Millis, interview by Steve Love, Willoughby, OH, 25 June 1997; Charles J. Pilliod Jr., interview by Steve Love, Akron, OH, 9 October 1996; Hoyt Wells, interview by Glenn Gamboa, Akron, OH, 24 July 1997.

Chapter Twenty-Three

Beacon Journal files; Sean Brenner, interview by Glenn Gamboa, Chicago, IL, 4 February 1997; Ken Dunlap, interview by Steve Love, Mogadore, OH, 15 February 1997; Christian Fittipaldi, interview by Glenn Gamboa, Orlando, FL, 11 February 1997; Bill Genck, interview by Steve Love, Akron, OH, 19 February 1997; Samir F. Gibara, interview by Steve Love and David Giffels, Akron, OH, 28 March 1997; Stu Grant, interview by Steve Love, Akron, OH, 14 February 1997; Goodyear Collection, UA Archives; Ed Hinton, "A Dangerous Competition," *Car and Driver,* April 1995; Trevor Hoskins, interview by Steve Love, Nashville, TN, 17 February 1997; Hank Inman, interview by Steve Love, Akron, OH, 13 February 1997; Bob Johnson, interview by Steve Love, Akron, OH, 19 February 1997; Lief, *The Firestone Story*; Lief, *Harvey Firestone*; O'Reilly, *The Goodyear Story*; Al Speyer, interview by Steve Love, Nashville, TN, 18 February 1997; Bob Toth, interview by Glenn Gamboa, Orlando, FL, 11 February 1997.

Chapter Twenty-Four

Doug Allen, interviews by David Giffels, Akron, OH, 28 June 1996 and 20 October 1997; Mike Beck, interview by David Giffels, Akron, OH, 12 June 1996; Jim Chase, interview by Mary Vanac, Akron, OH, September 1997; John Cole, interview by David Giffels, Akron, OH, 16 July 1996; Changzheng Dong, interview by David Giffels, Fairlawn, OH, 20 October 1997; Jim Dowey, interview by Mary Vanac, Akron, OH, September 1997; Christopher Eck, interview by David Giffels, Peoli, OH, 3 October 1997; Guy Edington, interview by David Giffels, Bath, OH, 21 October 1997; Richard Erickson, interview by Mary Vanac, Akron, OH, September 1997; Kenneth Immel, interview by David Giffels, Fairlawn, OH, 20 October 1997; Ray Labuda, interview by David Giffels, Green Township, OH, 22 October 1997; Harry Millis, interview by David Giffels, Willoughby, OH, October 1997; Lowell Mulhollen, interview by David Giffels, Akron, OH, 14 October 1997; John Putman, interviews by Mary Vanac, Cuyahoga Falls, OH, September 1997, and by David Giffels, Cuyahoga Falls, OH, 14 October 1997; Kay Putman, interviews by Mary Vanac, Cuyahoga Falls, OH, September 1997, and by David Giffels, Cuyahoga Falls, OH, 14 October 1997.

Chapter Twenty-Five

Norman P. Auburn, interview by Jim Carney, Akron, OH, August 1997; Blackford and Kerr, *BFGoodrich*; Nissim Calderon, interview by Steve Love, Akron, OH, 18 June 1996; Nancy M. Clem, interview by Steve Love, Akron, OH, 26 September 1997; Pete Cookro, interview by David Giffels, Akron, OH, 14 June 1996; Wayne DeCamp, interview by Steve Love, Akron, OH, 8 October 1997; Sandra B. Erlanger, "A Pride of Polymers," *CWRU: The Magazine of Case Western Reserve University* (August 1991); Samir F. Gibara, interview by Steve Love and David Giffels, Akron, OH, 28 March 1997; "Hands On Plastics," a joint project of the American Plastics Council and National Middle Level Science Teachers Association 1995 (Washington, DC: The American Plastics Council Inc., 1997); Anne L. Heald, interview by Steve Love, Stow, OH, 26 September 1997; Richard Hoover, interview by David Giffels, Akron, OH, 11 August 1997; Frank N. Kelley, interviews by Steve Love, Akron, OH, 24 June 1996, 3 July 1996, and 27 January 1997; George W. Knepper, *New Lamps for Old: One Hundred Years of Urban Higher Education at the University of Akron* (Akron, OH: The University of Akron, 1970); Richard Knight, interview by Steve Love, Akron, OH, 13 August 1997; Howard Lawson, interviews by David Giffels, Akron, OH, 11 August 1997, and by Steve Love,

Akron, OH, 3 October 1997; John J. Luthern, interview by Steve Love, Akron, OH, 2 October 1997; Robert Merzweiler, interview by Steve Love, Akron, OH, November 1997; Maurice Morton, "From Rubber Chemistry to Polymers: A History of Polymer Science at The University of Akron," *Rubber Chemistry and Technology* 62, no. 1 (March–April 1989); William V. Muse, interview by Steve Love, Akron, OH, 17 October 1996; O'Reilly, *The Goodyear Story*; Steve Paolucci, interview by Steve Love, Akron, OH, 1 October 1997; Laura Prexta, interview by Steve Love, Cuyahoga Falls, OH, 2 October 1997; Melanie Stewart, interview by Steve Love, Stow, OH, 26 September 1997; Charles Suran, interview by Steve Love, Middlefield, OH, 3 October 1997; John West, interview by Katie Byard, Kent, OH, September 1997; G. Stafford Whitby, Maurice Morton, and Paul J. Flory, interviews by Herbert Endres and Ben Kastein, The Rubber Division Library, University of Akron.

Chapter Twenty-Six

Bruce Adams, *Building Healthy Communities* (Charlottesville, VA: Pew Partnership for Civic Change, Leadership Collaboration Series, 1995); John Ballard, interview by Steve Love and Jim Carney, Bath, OH, 31 January 1997; *Beacon Journal* files; John Bickle, interview by Katie Byard, Akron, OH, 9 September 1997; Richard Buchholzer, interview by Katie Byard, Akron, OH, 12 September 1997; John Dotson, interview by Steve Love, Akron, OH, 19 September 1997; John Frank, interview by Katie Byard, Akron, OH, 10 September 1997; Gary Gappert, interview by Steve Love, Akron, OH, 10 September 1997; Barbara Hiney, interview by Katie Byard, Akron, OH, 20 August 1997; Willard R. Holland, interview by Steve Love, Akron, OH, 9 September 1997; Bill Jasso, interview by Katie Byard, Akron, OH, 29 August 1997; the Reverend Knute Larson, interview by Katie Byard, Akron, OH, 11 September 1997; David Lieberth, interview by Steve Love, Akron, OH, 22 August 1996; James Mercer, interview by Steve Love, Akron, OH, 23 October 1996; William V. Muse, interview by Steve Love, Akron, OH, 17 October 1996; M. G. "Jerry" O'Neil, interview by David Giffels, Akron, OH, August 1996; John Ong, interview by Steve Love and David Giffels, Richfield, OH, 16 December 1996; Charles J. Pilliod Jr., interview by Steve Love, Akron, OH, 9 October 1996; Don Plusquellic, interview by Steve Love, Akron, OH, 12 August 1996; Justin Rogers, interview by Katie Byard, Akron, OH, 25 August 1997; Marco Sommerville, interview by Katie Byard, Akron, OH, 21 August 1997; Charles Whited, *Knight: A Publisher in the Tumultuous Century* (New York: E. P. Dutton, 1988); George Wilson, interview by Katie Byard, Akron, OH, 9 September 1997.

Chapter Twenty-Seven

Beacon Journal files; Charles J. Carlise, interview by Steve Love, Akron, OH, 14 October 1997; Gary Gappert, interview by Steve Love, Akron, OH, 10 September 1997; Stanley Gault, interview by Steve Love, Akron, OH, 13 March 1997; Samir F. Gibara, interview by Steve Love and David Giffels, 28 March 1997; Joe Johnson, interview by Steve Love, Akron, OH, 14 October 1997; Richard Knight, interview by Steve Love, Akron, OH, 13 August 1997; Litchfield, *Industrial Voyage*; Margaret M. Mattix, interview by Steve Love, Akron, OH, 30 June 1996; Robert E. Mercer, interview by Steve Love, Daytona Beach, FL, 22 April 1997, and Akron, OH, 17 June 1997 and 19 June 1997; Don Plusquellic, interview by Steve Love, Akron, OH, 12 August 1996; Roy Ray, interview by Steve Love, Akron, OH, 12 August 1997; Tom Sawyer, interview by Steve Love, Akron, OH, 27 June 1997; Roger Sellew, interview by Steve Love, Akron, OH, 30 June 1996; Al Shuluga, interview by Steve Love, Akron, OH, 14 October 1997; Jim Walker, interview by Steve Love, Jackson Township, OH, 15 May 1996.

Index

ABOUT THE AUTHORS

Steve Love, staff writer for the *Akron Beacon Journal,* has a BA in journalism from California State University at Chico. He is coauthor, with Gerry Faust, of *The Golden Dream.*

David Giffels, staff writer for the *Akron Beacon Journal,* has BAs in English and mass media and an MA in English from The University of Akron.

ABOUT THE EDITORS

Debbie Van Tassel, an editor at the *Akron Beacon Journal,* has a BA in communication from Seton Hall University. She is a member of the Sunday Magazine Editors Association.

Susan Kirkman, picture editor at the *Akron Beacon Journal,* has a BSJ from Ohio University. She was picture editor for *Eye of the Storm,* a book on the Gulf War.

ABOUT THE BOOK

Wheels of Fortune: The Story of Rubber in Akron was designed and typeset on a Macintosh in QuarkXPress by Kachergis Book Design of Pittsboro, North Carolina. This book was typeset in Garamond 3, a typeface originally designed for linotype in 1936 by Morris Fuller Benton and Thomas Maitland Cleland for American Type Founders. This linotype version was based on seventeenth-century copies of Claude Garamond's typefaces that were designed by Jean Jannon.

Wheels of Fortune: The Story of Rubber in Akron was printed on 70-pound Mohawk Vellum and bound by McNaughton & Gunn Lithographers, Inc. of Saline, Michigan.